TED WILLIAMS AT WAR

Published by Rounder Books, an imprint of

Rounder Records Corp.
One Rounder Way
Burlington, MA 01803

ISBN: 1-57940-125-2

Book design by the Ted Williams Design Group

Nowlin, Bill, 1945-
Ted Williams at War

1. Williams, Ted, 1918 - 2002. I T.
2. Williams, Ted, 1918 - 2002.
   Career in the military.

First edition
2005910889
796.357
(B)

ISBN: 1-57940-125-2

9 8 7 6 5 4 3 2

Printed in the United States of America

THANKS TO:

Eric Abel

Todd Anton

Lee Ballenger

Brian Barasch

Jim Belshaw
Albuquerque Journal

Connie Brown

Ed Buchser

Carrol Burch

Jack Campbell

Bill Churchman

Jerry Coleman

Frank Cushing

Susan Debow

Dan Fierman

Kent Fischer
St. Petersburg Times

Walt Ford

Frank Gages

Jim Galchick

Geography and
Map Division,
Library of Congress

Lee Ann Ghajar
*Curator of Exhibits
The Women's Memorial*

Brian Gleason

John Glenn

Richard Gross

John Gunn

Lynn Hagen

Ned Harrison

Chad Hassett

Jimi Lee Haswell

Larry Hawkins

Jan K. Herman

Dick Johnson

Terry Kitchen

Howard C. Ligon

Eduardo "Wayo" Martinez

Dave McCarthy
Ted Williams Museum

Roger McCully

Dan Meador,
Marine Corps Aviation Association

Jon Mendes

Steve Milman

Steve Netsky

Tom O'Hara,
Marine Corps Aviation Museum

Jack Polidoro

Tommy Prater

Charles "Skip" Rothrock

Brad San Martin

Tim Savage

Virginia Stickney

Gen. Larry S. Taylor

Omer Tipton

John Toler

Earl Traut

John Virant

Cherie Ward

George Warnken

Earl E. Weller

Claudia Williams

*And all the service people who
agreed to interviews and loaned
photographs for use in this book.*

Color Insert Credits

Page 1: *Photograph by Howard C. Ligon,
log book courtesy of Claudia Williams,
yellow sheet courtesy of Earl E. Weller,
photograph at El Toro by Bill Nowlin*

Page 2: *Photos in Flight Ops courtesy
of Charles "Skip" Rothrock; darkroom
photos by Lee Scott, courtesy of
Virginia Stickney*

Page 3: *Shipboard photos: Ted on hospital
ship, with baseball glove, courtesy of
Commander Nancy Crosby. Ted with
Navy Nurse Margie L. Carter, courtesy
of Margie Carter. The ship in the background is another hospital ship, the
Jutlandia, from Denmark. Countryside
photos by Ed Buchser.*

Page 4: *Photo in center at K-3, by Ed
Buchser. Four other photos courtesy of
Charles "Skip" Rothrock. Note John
Glenn in lower two photographs.*

Page 5: *From upper left: Ted's jet at Suwon,
Korea, with nose off, photograph by John
Dager. Aerial view of K-3, by E. Buchser.
Two photos of Williams' jet after crash
at K-13, Suwon, by Larry Niswenden.
Bottom photo courtesy of Claudia Williams.*

Page 6: *Group photo and baseball glove
photo courtesy of Charles "Skip" Rothrock.
Base scene photo at bottom and one of
Ted peeking into Korean "restaurant"
(understood to be a brothel) by E. Buchser.
Photograph with Capt. Harvey Jensen,
VMF-115, courtesy of Harvey Jensen.*

Page 7: *Photographs in Korean countryside
by Ed Buchser except one at lower right by
Lee Scott, courtesy of Virginia Stickney.*

Page 8: *Photograph of Ted Williams courtesy
of Claudia Williams. All other items from
collection of Bill Nowlin. Topps Heritage
Time Capsule card (2001) with Ted Williams
and Korean War-worn uniform, courtesy of
the Topps Company.*

**For additional photography, see the photo gallery
for this book at www.rounderbooks.com**

TED WILLIAMS AT WAR

BY BILL NOWLIN

ROUNDER BOOKS

TED WILLIAMS AT WAR

Ted Williams on board hospital ship off Korea, 1953.
Courtesy of the May Williams Collection.

INTRODUCTION

Ted Williams at war. Ted Williams was one of the very few major league ballplayers to serve in more than one war, and the only Hall of Fame player to serve in two wars.[1] Of those ballplayers who did serve, rather few saw actual combat. Ted Williams flew dive-bombing missions over enemy lines during the Korean War, his Panther jet slashing down from the skies while the enemy threw everything they could against him – anti-aircraft and small arms fire alike. These were harrowing missions; his Panther jet took hits on more than one mission.

Alex Rodriguez, like Ted, is the highest-paid player of his era. Imagine A-Rod, strapped into a single-seat jet aircraft, prepared to drop 250-pound and 500-pound bombs, sometimes pulling out of his dive at an altitude as low as 300 to 500 feet. Imagine Roger Clemens bringing his plane into a dive while enemy ground forces and anti-aircraft gunners – perhaps in Iraq or Afghanistan – fired hundreds of rounds at his plane. Imagine Barry Bonds, or one of today's premier players crash-landing his severely shot-up jet, watching it burn to a crisp – and then piloting a replacement plane on another mission less than 24 hours later. Ted Williams is truly one of a kind – an American hero.

There aren't too many athletes like a Ted Williams, a Jerry Coleman, or a Pat Tillman.

Ted Williams flew 39 combat missions in Korea. Every time his F9F jet streaked into a steep dive to attack the target of the day, Williams inhaled the fumes from his 20MM machine guns as he let loose with suppression fire to disperse Communist ground troops. Captain Theodore S. Williams USMC flew as John Glenn's wingman on a number of missions in Korea and, on more than one occasion, Williams felt the impact of bullets and secondary explosions on the fuselage of the plane he piloted. The day he was hit hardest, he had to wrestle with the control stick to keep the aircraft on course, after its hydraulics had been blasted out of commission. His radio was shot out, too, so he couldn't communicate. He couldn't get the wheels down, and so he brought in the plane on its belly, scraping down the runway at maybe 200 knots an hour.

That was Ted Williams at war.

In all, Williams lost most of five baseball seasons as a hitter – prime years – while serving as a Naval Aviation Cadet and in the United States Marine Corps.

The Korean War wasn't the only kind of war Ted Williams fought.

It seemed like Ted Williams was often at war – with Boston sportswriters, with (some of) the fans, with his draft board, with his wives, with "gutless politicians" – even with the pigeons he blasted at Boston's Fenway Park. He would agree he was even at war with himself a good portion of the time. Ted Williams was a dynamic, restless, goal-oriented individual, a "triple type A" personality with a relentless drive in pursuit of perfection at whatever field he chose to master. He did not suffer fools and had little tolerance for mediocrity.

David Halberstam, in *The Teammates*, wrote that Ted "won 33,277 arguments in a row... the undisputed master of contentiousness." He was opinionated, argumentative, combustible, and controversial – though when he wasn't busy explaining why he was right about this thing or that matter, he displayed an overpowering curiosity and a will to learn about that which he did not know.

People who really knew Ted often say that when he took up a new line of inquiry one day, by the time you saw him the next time – maybe even just the following day – he'd have become somewhat of an expert on the subject. One of his Marine Corps flight instructors, Bill Churchman, couldn't have been more impressed with Ted's native intelligence and single-minded determination to learn. "If you were to say to Ted, 'We're going to give you two years off from your present duties, and we want you to become a Shakespearean scholar,' he'd be the best in the world. You could use that same theory in any field – computers, law, whatever. He'd master it."[2] Ted would attack a subject that interested him. Former New York Yankee Tommy Henrich said that Williams could have been "the world's leading brain surgeon or nuclear scientist."[3]

Dr. Sidney Farber, the "father of chemotherapy" with whom Williams worked closely for decades as Ted lent his name to the Jimmy Fund fight against cancer in children, said that Ted "didn't just lend his name to the Jimmy Fund. He gave his heart." Dr. Farber also noted Ted's "keen understanding of the problems of research and the care of patients in a field regarded as hopeless. If he had gone to college or medical school, he'd have been outstanding there. Anything he entered, he'd have been a leader in that field. He has followed our research. He has asked questions about our work which amazed me, demonstrating as they did his instinctive understanding of the methods of research. He couldn't ask the questions because of anything he had read because there had been nothing printed about some of the things he asked about. This is pioneering. Yet, he follows the principles."[4]

Williams never lost an argument, Halberstam wrote, "because he was bright and he marshaled his facts and argued well, but also because he shouted all the time and appointed himself judge and jury at the end of each argument to decide who won."[5]

Of course, that approach wouldn't work in dealings with superiors in the United States Marine Corps. And Williams generally did respect authority. He never warred with umpires; this man who was so volcanic in some areas was never once tossed from a major league ballgame and indeed earned the respect of umpires by his refusal to show them up on, say, a called strike when they had erred and he knew he was right. Fellow ballplayers got along fine with Ted Williams. He never feuded or fought with players, either on his own team or those on opposing teams. To the contrary, he was always willing to help another hitter, often to the displeasure of Boston owner Tom Yawkey.

His ongoing war with the "knights of the keyboard" – particularly the Boston writers – and with the loudmouth fans who tried to ride him from the safety of the grandstand, may have served a purpose. Ed Linn argues that Ted thrived on being combative. "Despite his protestations," Linn wrote, "Ted was always unhappy when he was being ignored by his blood enemies, the sportswriters. 'When things got too quiet,' one of them says, 'you could always count on Teddy boy to do something to get himself back in the headlines.'"[6] Many of his public explosions came while Williams was mired in a slump, or frustrated with his play. The blowups may have served a purpose; he seemed to hit better after he stirred things up and got the juices flowing.

Though he never wanted to enter the military, in many ways his military service defines the Ted Williams legend.

And, though Ted Williams fought in all these many wars, this book focuses not on the battles of baseball, nor those of his personal life, nor the battles against salmon harvesters in Eastern Canada, but on that military service.

Ted Williams biographies always touch on his two stints in the service, devoting a chapter or two to covering these years of his life. Neither author nor fan would fail to wonder what career statistics Williams might have posted had he played uninterruptedly during the prime seasons when he was 24, 25 and 26 years old, and had he played for the full 1952 and 1953 seasons. But any full biography has a lot to cover, when dealing with a life as full as that of Ted Williams. *Ted Williams At War* will look at his five years devoted to serving his country in the military, to accord this extremely important part of his life the full attention it merits.

Many have said that "Ted Williams was the real John Wayne." Ted himself understood the drama of the day he crash-landed his plane, and saw it as the way any movie on his life should open.

Capt. T. S. Williams, USMCR.
Courtesy of Claudia Williams.

NOTES

1) *There are 24 Hall of Fame players who devoted at least a full season due to military service, according to Jim Hamilton of the* Oneonta Star *– three from World War I (George Kelly, Herb Pennock, and Eppa Rixey), nineteen from World War II (Luke Appling, Bill Dickey, Joe DiMaggio, Bobby Doerr, Bob Feller, Charlie Gehringer, Hank Greenberg, Billy Herman, Bob Lemon, Ted Lyons, Johnny Mize, Stan Musial, Pee Wee Reese, Phil Rizzuto, Red Ruffing, Enos Slaughter, Warren Spahn, Ted Williams, and Early Wynn), and two from the Korean War (Whitey Ford, Willie Mays, and Ted Williams). Non-player Lee MacPhail served in both World War I and II. Many others served, but either after their career (e.g., Mickey Cochrane and Christy Mathewson) or before their career in the majors began (e.g., Yogi Berra, Jackie Robinson, and Hoyt Wilhelm).*

2) *Interview with Bill Churchman, April 27, 1997.*

3) *Jim Prime and Bill Nowlin,* Ted Williams: The Pursuit of Perfection *(Champaign, IL: Sports Publishing, 2002), p. xi.*

4) *Mike Gillooly, "Dr. Farber Tells How Slugger Inspires Kids," Boston Evening American, January 10, 1958.*

5) *David Halberstam,* The Teammates *(New York: Hyperion, 2003), pp. 14, 15.*

6) *Ed Linn,* Hitter *(NY: Harcourt Brace, 1993), p. 135.*

Major John Glenn listens to squadronmate Captain Ted Williams describe a maneuver, airbase K-3, Korea, 1953.
Collection of Bill Nowlin.

HOW THE MOVIE STARTS

"Now I'll tell you how it's supposed to start... It's in a fighter plane, see, flying, from the pilot's eye, over KOREA. Seoul. And it's flying, slow and sunny and then bang WHAM BOOOOMMM the biggest goddamn explosion ever on the screen, I mean BOOOOOMMM. And the screen goes dark. DARK. For maybe ten seconds there's NOTHING. NOTHING. And then when it comes back there's the ballpark and the crowd ROARING... and that's the beginning."

Ted Williams[1]

If there were ever a film made of Ted Williams' life, that's how he envisioned it opening. It starts with a dive-bombing mission during the Korean War, Captain Theodore S. Williams (service number 037773) in his F9F-5 Panther jet. From 26,000 feet, sometimes their progress seemed slow, though the jets were streaking north at over 500 miles per hour. It was sunny, but the temperature outside the cockpit was minus 65 degrees Fahrenheit, and any pilot who plunged into Sea of Japan waters off the Haeju Peninsula had to be rescued quickly. Splashing down into the near-freezing salt water, you would lose consciousness within 30 to 60 minutes even if you were wearing the rubber survival suit. At two hours, there was about a 50% survival rate. Without the suit, you might have as few as two or three minutes.[2] There were scores of pilots on this mission – a "max effort" combining the Marines, Air Force, and Navy – but every one of those pilots was very much alone in his aircraft. Ted's eyes scanned the ground below through his flight goggles – the famous eyes that had already helped win him four American League batting titles. It was relatively silent, except for the occasional crackle of static and the minimum amount of chatter over the radio.

The hilltops below looked peaceful from five miles high. So did the clouds below and the clear blue late morning sky. It was 10:52 a.m. on 16 February in the year 1953.

Then Major Tom Sellers of VMF-115 called for the strike, and Captain Williams' division leader, Major Marvin K. Hollenbeck, gave the word and the four jets from VMF-311 bore to the right and dipped down, heading into their dive. As the jets streaked earthward, the ground rushing closer, Williams and the others could see enemy troops scattering from their personnel shelters below, running from one building to another, as the Marine pilots opened up suppression fire with their 20MM cannon and began to fire bursts of rounds. There was some scattered ground fire, some bullets heading up toward the jets as they came in low – 1,000 feet or less, to drop their 250-pound bombs.

Man's Magazine cover, April 1961.
Courtesy of Bill Nowlin.

Then suddenly, there is silence again as the Panther pulls out of its dive, having delivered its payload, climbing, heading downriver and following the preplanned route out toward the ocean. For three or four seconds, the hills looked peaceful again, and the blue sky looked serene. But Williams had a problem. It wasn't a noise, not a WHAM BOOOOMMM! It was a whole lot of bright red lights on the instrument panel. That was not something any pilot ever wanted to see. "When I pulled up out of my run, all the red lights were on in the plane and the damn thing started to shake. The stick stiffened up and was shaking. I knew I had a hydraulic leak. Fuel warning light, fire warning light, there are so many lights on a jet that when anything serious goes wrong the lights almost blind you. I was in serious trouble."[3]

Ted Williams' jet after crash at K-13, Suwon, Korea.
Photos courtesy of Frank Cushing (top) and Larry Niswenden (bottom).

Ted barely made it back alive. He crash-landed his plane at an Air Force base. Unable to lower his wheels, or effectively work the flaps to brake the plane's speed, his jet scraped down a few thousand feet of tarmac before grinding to a halt. The noise was terrific, raw metal screeching on the concrete runway as the plane tore along at 200 knots an hour. Sparks flared out behind the skidding craft, with a cloud of smoke billowing out behind. The moment it cut off hard to the right and ground to a stop, out Ted jumped, running for cover before his plane was engulfed in flame.

He had to get transport back to his own base on another aircraft. The one he'd been flying was toast.

The next morning, he was up again on another mission for Marine Air over Korea.

Ted Williams was at war. Ted Williams was at war with the Communists in Korea, and with the "gutless politicians" who sent him there. He battled on the home front as well: he battled on the ball field and he battled in his personal life.

Sometimes he enjoyed the combat. Sometimes he went too far. Anger could energize him; it could also get him in hot water. He loved to dish it out, and he respected most those who could dish it right back. He enjoyed a good battle of words, and he enjoyed battling the bonefish and tangling with the tarpon. He enjoyed trying to outwit both the man on the mound and the Atlantic salmon on the Miramichi River in New Brunswick.

This is the story of Ted Williams at war, the nearly five years carved out of his career as a major league ballplayer. It is a story of the training, those 39 combat missions, and how Ted Williams became regarded as a military hero for the service he rendered his country. Shot down once, and his plane badly damaged another time, he survived and came back to baseball.

As the BOOOOOMMM renders the screen black, we hear the crowd ROARING. It's August 9, 1953. Fenway Park in Boston, and the crowd is 27,000 strong. The score is 5-2, Boston's down, and it's the bottom of the seventh inning. Suddenly, the volume rises in crescendo and becomes overwhelming. The Kid is coming out to hit. The picture clarifies again and we see the wrists of the hitter grinding his hands on the handle of the bat. Grinding so hard, you'd swear sawdust was going to fall to the field. The count ran to 3 and 1. A Mike Garcia fastball heads straight in. Then another BOOM – but this time it's the sound of a wooden baseball bat hitting the pitch, hard. They say the ball sounded different, louder, when Ted hit one just right. A long home run sails up into the seats in right field, and we see Ted Williams – head down – cross the plate, having rounded the bases. The hero is back from the war. The prodigal son has returned.

Ted on beach near Pohang.
Photo by Ed Buchser.

Next we cut to a much quieter (but a little shrill) WHIRRRRRRRRRR sound – a fishing line sailing out on a cast, and then, almost imperceptible, the sound of the fly hitting the water. All of a sudden it's the quiet and solitude of fishing the boneflats in the Florida Keys.

That's where he was when he got the news he was being recalled to the Marines.

Fishing.

NOTES

1) *Richard Ben Cramer,* What Do You Think of Ted Williams Now? *(NY: Simon & Schuster, 2002), p. 36.*

2) *Information from a U.S. Navy flight surgeon, via communication from Jon D. Mendes, June 4, 2004.*

3) *Ted Williams,* My Turn At Bat *(NY: Fireside: 1969, 1988), p. 179.*

Ted takes the oath of office, enlisting in the Navy's V-5 program, May 22, 1952.
Photograph courtesy of the Cleveland Public Library.

CHAPTER 1 – TED WILLIAMS AGAINST THE DRAFT

Here was a kid, The Kid. It was Sunday, October 5, 1941 and he was back in San Diego playing in a ballgame in his hometown for the first time in four years. The game was at Lane Field, home of the Pacific Coast League Padres, for whom Ted had played in 1936 while still in high school and in 1937, fresh out of school. It was an exhibition game between Pirrone's All-Stars and the San Diego All-Stars, and Ted was there with his Red Sox teammate Jimmie Foxx. Ted had three years of major league ball under his belt, and just one week before to the day, on September 28, Ted Williams had gone 6-for-8 in a doubleheader in Philadelphia to boost his .39955 average to .406 in one day's work. It was the last day of the major league season. Williams became the first .400 hitter in over a decade – and the last one of the twentieth century, as it happens.

He couldn't have known that then. For all he knew, he was going to do it again in 1942. He didn't lack for self-confidence. Across the Pacific, though, plans were being laid for a major, unexpected air assault on the United States Navy based at Pearl Harbor in the Territory of Hawaii. Japanese pilots were being trained to hit Pearl, and hit hard – to devastate American Naval forces with a knockout blow that would free Japan to expand its sphere of influence throughout the Pacific region. Fans at Lane Field could see the Pacific from their seats, some of them. The devastating raid two months later, on December 7, caught the entire nation by surprise. The 23-year-old Kid hadn't even had time to truly digest and savor his accomplishment in 1941, when suddenly hundreds upon hundreds of other young men had been killed in the air attack.

It wasn't as though war was unexpected, but the country had largely been looking across the Atlantic. Events in Europe had been unfolding for some time, and the ballplayers were well aware that they could be called to duty, as many had been just a quarter century beforehand. Lend Lease was underway, having been enacted March 11, 1941, and American military equipment and supplies were being sent to the European theater. Although the United States wouldn't commit ground troops until 1943, in North Africa and Italy, the country was developing its capacity for war and sending aid to America's allies abroad. As far as the general public viewed matters, though, the brazen Japanese attack on American soil came out of the blue and dealt a terrible blow to American armed forces in the Pacific and to American pride, dealing death to around 2,400 and crippling the fleet, destroying five of the eight battleships stationed there and damaging many other ships and aircraft. Two days later, on December 9, Cleveland Indians star pitcher Bob Feller volunteered to join the Navy. He would miss nearly four years of baseball, but earn eight battle stars during his military service.

Taking a cut at Lane Field, San Diego, October 1941.
Courtesy of Autumn Keltner.

A year beforehand, Ted had registered for the military draft and knew he was subject to call. With the enactment of the Selective Training and Service Act of 1940, the United States had for the first time established a system of conscription in peacetime. The system worked through local boards and Ted Williams had dutifully registered for the draft in Hennepin County, Minnesota. Ted's board

Young recruit Williams before G.I haircut.
Courtesy of the May Williams Collection.

was based in Minnesota, because he'd played a year for the Red Sox affiliate Minneapolis Millers in 1938 and liked the fishing and the hunting and local girl Doris Soule so much that he returned there after the baseball season in 1939 and 1940. Because it really was still peacetime, it was possible for many people to remain unaware of what in retrospect were the building pressures toward U.S. entry into war. Royal Canadian Air Force tail gunner, and ace pilot, Phil Marchildon was a major league pitcher for the Philadelphia Athletics, present at Shibe Park when Ted went 6-for-8 to post his season-ending .406 mark. Marchildon, in his autobiography, wrote that Ted "later claimed that until the Japanese bombed Pearl Harbor he was hardly aware there was a war going on."[1]

Fortunately, Williams was granted a deferment. In fact, Ted Williams might never have hit the legendary .406 batting mark in 1941 had he not been deferred. An Associated Press story datelined Minneapolis on January 27, 1941, reported that Williams had been informed by his local draft board that he was subject to call in the summer of 1941 unless he was deferred. When completing the Selective Service forms, Williams stated that he was the sole support of his mother May Williams of San Diego. The draft board granted Williams deferment and classified him III-A. He was therefore able to report to spring training and enjoy a spectacular 1941 season with the Red Sox.

Some ballplayers had already been called up even before Pearl Harbor, though Detroit Tigers slugger Hank Greenberg was the only major leaguer. Greenberg, although 30 years old, was inducted into the Army on May 7, 1941, nineteen games into the season. He only served a short stint and was discharged on December 5, 1941, two days before Pearl Harbor. About face. "Hammerin' Hank" signed right back up and joined the Air Corps, serving until mid-1945. His first day back in baseball, Greenberg homered, and he led the Tigers to the 1945 pennant and World Series. Baseball history would be very different had Ted Williams been called up in mid-'41, too.

Ted's mother, May Venzor Williams.
Photograph courtesy of the May Williams Collection.

The news from Pearl Harbor galvanized the nation. Newspaper readers perusing the paper that very day of infamy may have noticed an AP dispatch dated December 6. "Williams Still III-A, Draft Official Says," reported the *New York Times* of December 7, 1941. There had been a report out of San Diego that May Williams, Ted's mother, claimed her son had been reclassified to I-A. Not so, replied George W. Price, chairman of the Minneapolis draft board. Perhaps May Williams had been confused, Price suggested, by his board's November request for "certain affidavits" related to Ted's draft status. Williams was still classified III-A. The timing may not have been ideal, when Price and his board learned just the next day of the attack on Pearl Harbor. The board may soon have felt under pressure to reclassify the young and fit Mr. Williams. Any deferment would now attract more scrutiny.

Ted himself was in Princeton at the time, about forty miles north of Minneapolis, duck hunting. He'd just gotten back to his hotel when he heard the radio bulletin about the air attack. "Frankly, none of this war talk had meant a damn

Ted Williams and Doris Soule in Minnesota.
Photographs courtesy of the May Williams Collection.

thing to me up to then," Ted later wrote. "I had read where some admiral had said if the Japanese got too frisky we could take them in six months, so I'd pretty much dismissed them as a threat. Hitler had been giving Europe fits, and things were looking bad all over, but it hadn't sunk in on me yet. All I was interested in was playing ball, hitting the baseball, being able to hunt, making some money."[2]

A few weeks later, having presumably studied Mrs. Williams' affidavits (and considered the new circumstances posed by Pearl Harbor), Ted Williams was reclassified I-A.

There were bigger questions for organized baseball. After Pearl Harbor, with the nation reeling in shock, the question was raised: would there even be a major league season scheduled in 1942? It was a time of great uncertainty. What was the right thing to do? Commissioner of Baseball Kenesaw Mountain Landis posed the question to President Roosevelt: should we prepare for baseball, or should major league ball disband for the duration and join the war effort? Roosevelt didn't hesitate; on January 15, he gave baseball the green light and declared that baseball was important to the nation's morale. It would stand as one of the symbols of what American men were fighting for, and why American women were entering the factories and the work force in such large numbers.

FDR's "green light" letter.

My dear Judge:

Thank you for yours of January fourteenth. As you will, of course, realize the final decision about the baseball season must rest with you and the Baseball club owners – so what I am going to say is solely a personal and not an official point of view.

I honestly feel that it would be best for the country to keep baseball going. There will be fewer people unemployed and everybody will work longer hours and harder than ever before.

And that means that they ought to have a chance for recreation and for taking their minds off their work even more than before.

Baseball provides a recreation which does not last over two hours or two hours and a half, and which can be got for very little cost. And, incidentally, I hope that night games can be extended because it gives an opportunity to the day shift to see a game occasionally.

As to the players themselves, I know you agree with me that the individual players who are active military or naval age should go, without question, into the services. Even if the actual quality to the teams is lowered by the greater use of older players, this will not dampen the popularity of the sport. Of course, if an individual has some particular aptitude in a trade or profession, he ought to serve the Government. That, however, is a matter which I know you can handle with complete justice.

Here is another way of looking at it – if 300 teams use 5,000 or 6,000 players, these players are a definite recreational asset to at least 20,000,000 of their fellow citizens – and that in my judgment is thoroughly worthwhile.

With every best wish,
Very sincerely yours,

Franklin D. Roosevelt
Hon. Kenesaw M. Landis
333 North Michigan Avenue
Chicago, Illinois

Baseball was to be played. Individual players, though, each had their own draft status, and Ted Williams had been assigned his classification during the 1941 season. Most able-bodied single young men were I-A, and the first to be called. Ted had been ruled III-A, however, as the sole support of his mother. Ted's parents had divorced a few years earlier. Ted's younger brother Danny had joined the Army on February 16, 1942. As it turned out, Army life didn't agree with Danny. He was discharged on August 18, 1943, with an other-than-honorable discharge. Word was that he kept leaving to visit his wife and young son Dan, Jr. None of this ever became public knowledge at the time. It might have made life much harder for Ted if it had. In any event, Danny Williams was in no position to support his mother, who was eking out a living doing good works with the Salvation Army. Ted was earning good money, and sending much of it home. There was never any doubt that he was indeed the sole support of his mom.

That didn't prevent the draft board in Minnesota from reversing themselves and re-classifying Williams I-A in early January 1942. The year began with a headline in the *Boston Sunday Advertiser*: "Sox to Lose Williams in Draft; Ted I-A, to be Examined Thursday."[3] "This is not a false alarm," Joe Cashman's story informed readers. For his part, Williams "cut loose with a burst of boyish enthusiasm today when he learned that he had been ordered by his draft board to report for preliminary physical examination in Minneapolis, Jan. 8. 'Say,' he shouted, 'I just hope I get in Hank Greenberg's company! Boy, would we have a heluva hitting club!... Maybe they'll put me on Company B. That would be swell you know – B there when they go and B there when they come back.'" It didn't sound as though the gravity of war had yet sunk in.[4]

Ted passed his physical on January 8. Dr. F. J. Pratt termed Ted a "healthy specimen." "I guess they need more men," Ted said, in a bit of understatement. He said that he anticipated being called to report for induction at nearby Fort Snelling.[5] The *Boston Record* reported on January 14 that Williams had written the Red Sox explaining he was likely to be examined at Snelling on the 25th of the month.

The very day before he was to report, though, the draft board took an appeal to the ruling and ordered Williams to stand by for further instructions. For the next four to five weeks, there were occasional bits in the Boston press, saying that the Red Sox had tried repeatedly but been unable to locate the batting champ. As late as February 20, Joe Cashman wrote in the *Record*, that Ted Williams "remains a mystery man. He's been sent a contract, even though he [is] classified I-A in the draft. Naturally, he won't pay any attention to the baseball document unless he should be put back into class III-A."[6] That same day, his draft board stated that Ted remained I-A. He was reportedly hunting and fishing in Minnesota.

Cashman's comment was so matter of fact that one might not have predicted the storm that was about to burst. He's I-A unless he's put back in III-A. If that happens, that happens. That was the tenor, in context, of Cashman's remark.

Columnist Dave Egan, already a Williams antagonist, showed sympathy for the 23-year-old. He admitted to past battles with The Kid, but now argued that Ted's draft board was placing Williams' reputation in peril by taking so long to study the matter of his proper classification. "This should not be a tremendous problem to solve," he wrote. "Either Williams' mother is dependent upon him, or she is not. If she is, he should be deferred, as everybody else under the same set of circumstances has been. If she is not, he should be inducted into the Army, as everybody else under the same set of circumstances has been." The logic was as simple as could be. The problem, as Egan saw it, was that it was taking so long. "His draft board has issued a number of conflicting statements. It has conducted a lengthy investigation to determine a simple fact. The press has begun to take note of his case. The public has begun to murmur. And the Kid is in deadly peril."[7]

After Ted had been reclassified from III-A to I-A, Ted later explained, a friend urged him to explain his situation to an attorney who worked with the Selective Service Appeals Agent for the governor of Minnesota. "He took it to the Appeals Board, but they voted me down. This really got the attorney mad, and he said he was going to go to the Presidential Board, to General Hershey."[8] The Hennepin County Draft Board No. 6 voted down the appeal unanimously, 5-0.

Williams was on his own here. He had no father to rely on, no agent, no other counsel to turn to. He had borrowed money from the Red Sox to remodel his mother's house on Utah Street in San Diego. He had purchased three annuities totaling $6,000 on his mother's behalf, and if the payments were not kept up through 1942, he would forfeit them. Friends helped him locate an attorney named John Fagre, and Fagre brought in his boss, Wendell Rogers. They were attorneys, but not his attorneys per se. "I hired nobody at any time. And I never spent a single cent on the case," he ultimately told sportswriters in mid-May. Fagre and Rogers were state advisors to draftees and they helped Williams in that capacity.[9] When Rogers in particular offered to help, Ted tells us, "I just let him take charge."[10]

Rogers had struck out the first time, and he struck out again going to Colonel J. E. Nelson, the head of Selective Service in the State of Minnesota – even though Nelson admitted that Williams likely qualified for deferment. However, he told Rogers and a man from another draft board, when they both approached him on Williams' behalf, "this case is an exception." Ted's celebrity fixed him under a spotlight. The appeals bought a bit more time. On February 1, appeals agent Herbert W. Estrem appealed to the national board. (By this time, Rogers himself had been drafted and chose to enlist in the Navy.) "But Col. Nelson was most fair," Ted told Joe Cashman, "He promised to study my files. When he did so he offered to appeal to a higher board." Rogers notified Estrem, and Estrem got in touch with Williams.

On February 27, news stories revealed that word had come back over the signature of President Roosevelt (most likely a formality, not reflecting the President's personal involvement) re-classifying Ted Williams to III-A. The *Record*'s February 28 headline read, "Roosevelt Defers Ted Williams; Re-Classified III-A in Army Draft." Ted promptly signed and returned his Red Sox contract. The story said that Williams had not asked for re-classification but the appeals agent had processed an appeal on his behalf. An extremely rare editorial by Sam Cohen, the sports editor of the *Record* said, in capital letters, THE KID MADE NO APPEAL. The editorial saw the President's decision as consistent with his support of athletics and a further green light to American sports. "Williams, like all other American youths, was willing to don khaki and take up a gun and join in the drive on the Axis but the appeal board found after investigation that Williams' induction would 'put undue hardship on his mother' who is dependent on the Sox slugger." The editorial noted that Ted had "talked gleefully about dropping his bat and taking up a gun and knocking some Japs out of the park."[11]

The news of the re-classification set off a firestorm of comment and criticism. Some columnists erupted when they heard that the reigning batting champ had been excused from military service. There developed quite a prolonged and public brouhaha over Williams' draft status. From III-A to I-A and then back again to III-A. Ted Williams was a national figure by now and people wanted to know: Had Ted really appealed the re-classification to I-A? Was he trying to avoid military duty, this strong and healthy young man? Editorials railed against the decision. Public pressure was intense. The *Boston Herald*'s Bill Cunningham wrote, "It looks as if the sports world may see another crucifixion."

Harold Kaese of the *Boston Globe* seemed inclined to incite and inflame: "The first reaction from all sides yesterday seemed to be 'Wait'll he comes to bat – wow! Boy, they'll just ride him out of the league.' Those with sensitive ears hear strings being pulled... There is suspicion. There is contempt. There is hatred."[12]

The papers, particularly in Boston, were chock full of advice from this person or that – even the "man in the street," many of whom were asked what Williams should do. Everyone had an opinion, and almost no one with a typewriter and a platform hesitated to offer their own. Ed Linn says that one Boston paper even hired a private investigator to check up on May Williams' situation in San Diego, to see if she was indeed receiving support from her son.[13]

The Red Sox brass had expected Williams to be deferred. In the same story that ran the morning of December 7, it was reported that ever since he'd joined the Red Sox, "Ted had sent the majority of pay checks to his mother. As a matter of fact, he wouldn't even personally collect them. He'd leave it to one of the front office secretaries to mail the checks to the Coast."[14]

How active had Williams been in appealing – did he request it, or did he consent to it? Was he passive, or had he taken a more active role? Shirley Povich wrote in the *Washington Post* that Ted "had no part in his deferment" and reported that Williams had not previously signed his Red Sox contract for 1942 because he assumed he would be in a military training camp before the Red Sox spring training camp had opened.[15]

Estrem stated forthrightly that he had investigated the case on his own initiative, explaining "I was personally interested in this case because of the unusual circumstances." Between the obligations to the annuities, the operations his mother required, and remodeling her house, Estrem believed Ted Williams to be nearly broke. Colonel Nelson countered, saying that Williams had sought the deferment. Estrem replied that "technically he did request it" but that "it should be stressed that he consented to the appeal... Williams' attitude was never persuasive; it was rather informative." In effect, Estrem told the papers that he, Estrem, had pressed the matter because he worried that Ted's mother might be unfavorably impacted by the loss of her son's support.[16]

It was a semantic distinction. Clearly, Ted wanted deferment, if for no other reason than so he could meet the financial obligations he'd incurred. In 1942, he was due to receive a big boost in salary, to an estimated $30,000 a year. At the time, Naval cadets were being paid $105 per month, or $1,260 annually. When a cadet won his wings and became an ensign, the salary jumped to $2,940.

Dave Egan devoted a column to the matter for several days running, every one of them calling for simple justice. He acknowledged having termed Ted a "spoiled brat" a couple of years earlier. Now, though, he backed Ted to the hilt. John Quincy Public, he wrote, wanted Williams to become a demi-god, to live up to a myth. That demi-god would drop the bat, grab a duffel-bag and a gun and march off to war. It would be unfair to impose myth on The Kid, he wrote. There was almost a "lynch law" mentality at play in the haste of some writers to condemn Williams. Egan urged restraint, fair treatment and a little less hypocrisy, noting that "the very reporters who interviewed the sidewalk solons, and the very desk men who write the bitter headlines, are also in III-A, for the reason that Ted Williams is in III-A."[17]

The Boston press was waging a war of its own on Williams, while the *Record* stood up for the beleaguered ballplayer. "We are lynch-law journalists... More than one Boston newspaper has suggested that Williams should enlist. He should enlist," Egan continued, "provided that all the reporters and all the desk-men and all the editors similarly in III-A enlist in a body with him."

Egan elaborated. After the deferment, Ted would be playing baseball "because this is a democracy... Teddy Williams will be a symbol of the kind of democracy which this nation is fighting to preserve. There is room in it for ball players and brick layers, and merchants and mechanics, and clerks and clerics, and newspapermen and nobodies. And all of them (Teddy Williams with the rest) live under the same just code of laws." Everybody is judged alike under the draft, and the specific "court of appeals" set up to hear such cases ruled in his favor. That should not be taken to prove favoritism, but to prove that the system works, judging each case on its merits. Egan's faith in the system was perhaps naive, but his support of Williams was steadfast.

George Leary, chairman of Board 15 in Boston's North End added, "Hundreds of boys have been deferred by our board because they are the sole support of their mothers, and I haven't heard any criticism about such decisions."[18]

A week later, Egan even ran a column decrying those "waving their false flags of patriotism" who he likened to the Ku Klux Klan, and warning that this could presage a return of Prohibition and endanger everything America stood for.[19]

A couple of Red Sox players spoke up, too. Charlie Wagner said, "His case is like mine and I haven't run into any difficulty. I have parents who are dependent upon me. So I was placed in III-A right after registering and my classification hasn't been changed." Jimmie Foxx concurred: "Ted's circumstances are similar to those of Charlie Wagner and Eddie Pellagrini, both of whom are in III-A. The Kid need make no apologies."[20]

Ted was torn in two directions. His mother had been operated on in the fall of 1941, and needed another operation. Ted asked his mother to have her doctor write the board so they could decide. The doctor wrote that she was unable to work. Hotel keeper A. M. Gagen of the Gagen Hotel in Princeton said, however, that Ted had told him he would probably enlist.[21]

When Williams decided to appeal, and seek to have his deferment reinstated, he told reporters during spring training that the decision had been his and his alone. Williams took the heat, and took the Sox off the hook. "Without saying so, they really advised against it. So don't blame anybody except me. It was my own decision and nobody else's."[22]

Those in the Red Sox organization had seemed to distance themselves from Ted, and did not appear supportive of his stance, though it was but to stick up for his rights. Even before the appeals, both Red Sox GM Eddie Collins and manager Joe Cronin assumed Williams' induction was a foregone conclusion and made statements reflecting that belief. They warned him that he would bear the brunt of public disfavor should he fight for the deferment.

At Cronin's suggestion, Williams visited the Great Lakes Naval Training Center on March 4 and was shown around by former Tigers catcher Mickey Cochrane, then running the Center's athletic program. Cochrane impressed and even charmed him, and Ted said, "I'm weakening. I'm about to enlist right now." But then Cochrane committed a tactical error. He told Ted, "It's going to be awful tough to play ball. You try to play ball this summer, they'll boo you out of every park in the big leagues." That was not the right approach. Ted recalled the moment years later: "Boy, I saw fire. I said to myself, I don't give a damn who they boo or what they do. I've heard plenty of boos. I'm going to play ball if I can."[23]

Williams remembered that Boston's owner Tom Yawkey "said he didn't think it would be smart for me to come to spring training." Another front office gaffe. Even Quaker Oats got in the act. Ted had signed an endorsement deal with them,

Ted calls his mother in San Diego to tell her of his enlistment in the Navy.
Courtesy of the Boston Public Library.

gladly. He really liked the cereal ("I used to eat them all the time.") The company canceled its contract "and I haven't eaten a Quaker Oat since."[24] Ted's business manager James A. Silin recommended he enlist: "Be sure you do the right thing. Your baseball career as well as your patriotism and your future happiness for many years to come are at stake. If you enlist, you will gladden the hearts and stir the Americanism of thousands of kids to whom you have been and should always remain an idol. Don't let those kids down, Teddy. If you accept deferment from the army, you will ruin the greatest baseball career of all time."[25]

Ted Williams found himself at war – at war with the draft and at war with a characterization of public opinion that wanted to tell him what to do. He was more determined than ever to stay the course. "I've just made the most important decision of my life," he told reporters at spring training in Sarasota. "I know that. If I didn't think I was justified in asking for reclassification, I wouldn't have done it. If I hadn't done it, I wouldn't have been doing right by my mother. If I wasn't sure of that, I couldn't steel myself to face all the abuse I'm encouraging." Williams added that he had never hired anyone to represent him, and that he never spent a single cent on the case.

He did wonder why he'd been singled out. Other ballplayers were III-A, too, notable among them one Joe DiMaggio and one Stan Musial. Williams was always somewhat of a lightning rod, though; something about him attracted scrutiny. Late in life, Ted offered perspective to David Pietrusza, "III-A was pretty normal, standard procedure. But not for athletes. When you're an athlete you become a target. Got a physical ailment that would ordinarily get you out? It won't. Not if you can throw a baseball or a left hook. Over 30 and got six or seven kids? That won't get you out if you're an athlete, and the press starts analyzing your case. It'll get anyone else out – but not the athlete."[26]

Only a few spoke in Ted's defense. John Kieran of the *New York Times* noted in a March 3 column that the decision had been made by the Presidential board that was constituted for just these sorts of appeals. "Who is to make these decisions," Kieran asked, "the legally appointed officials with all the evidence at hand or the sideline critics who can know little about it? They aren't picking this army by popular vote – or even unpopular vote. If the Army wants Ted Williams he won't be asked, he'll be told. Until then he should be free to go about his business, which is baseball."

Ted on day of enlistment.
Courtesy of the Boston Public Library.

At least one baseball man backed Ted up privately. Will Harridge, president of the American League, "told me to keep my chin up, that I wouldn't have been deferred in the first place if I wasn't in the right."[27] And Joe Cronin finally came around, too. "I'm certain that his is a most worthy case and that Ted wouldn't hesitate an instant about jumping into the Army when and if he is called. If Uncle Sam says fight, he'll fight. Since he has said play ball, Ted has the right to play."

Newspapers all over the country expressed themselves, almost uniformly negatively. So did individuals, many of them anonymously. One self-appointed patriot mailed Williams a single yellow sheet of paper every day, clearly suggesting that Williams was yellow, afraid to put himself in harm's way.

Ted said, "You would have thought Teddy Ballgame bombed Pearl Harbor himself. Unpatriotic. Yellow. Those were the milder epithets. One Boston paper hired a private detective and sent him to San Diego to see if I was really supporting my mother."[28] Never one to back down in the face of controversy, Ted stubbornly stood fast – and found support from the fans in the stands, many of whom were military personnel out to enjoy a ballgame. There was no shortage of servicemen; almost every ballpark admitted them without charge. There was no public outcry at the park. Most fans were supportive, but not aggressively so. It simply wasn't the political issue that the newspapers had posed. Fans just weren't agitated about the matter. They saw a great ballplayer and applauded him and his play. Not even the servicemen were upset. To the contrary, some 2,000 service personnel turned out in Tampa for a Red Sox exhibition game, and they were demonstrative in cheering for Williams.

On March 15, for instance, before an exhibition game against the Senators, several members of the Red Sox team went up into the stands to make a recording that would be broadcast to soldiers in overseas bases. So many fans pressed in to try for a Ted Williams autograph that it became uncomfortable for the Sox slugger.

The cheers overwhelmed the jeers. It wasn't even close. Even in the towns the Red Sox barnstormed through on their way north, towns with sometimes a significant quota of servicemen in the stands, Ted was warmly welcomed. Ted made his way through spring training, and into the regular season, not having to cringe or take abuse from the crowds. The controversy was resolved by cheers of the crowds. Williams had worried, though, as he headed back to Boston. He reported that his mail was running 60-40 in his favor, but that 40 percent could produce a lot of boos. "If a middle-aged man boos me, I just feel sorry for him because I think he ought to know better. But if the kids, even though I realize they may be ignorant of the facts, start to get on me, I'm afraid that may prove a little tough to take."

There was anticipation as the annual pre-season City Series against the Boston Braves approached. But Boston fans cheered, too. The United Press noted that there were about four "deadend kids" who booed Ted from the Fenway Park bleachers, while the rest of the 8,186 fans and 600 servicemen at the ballpark offered "hearty rounds of cheers and handclaps" on each of his four trips to the plate.[29] Ted even tipped his cap to the bleachers as the game started. Joe Cashman wrote that "you could hear the cheers downtown... the count was a conservative 100 to 1 in Ted's favor."[30]

Williams wavered more than once, though. Some of the abuse got to him. Ed Linn reports that Ted failed to join the team at the train station before an early season road trip, and GM Eddie Collins found The Kid alone in his room, despondent and discouraged. He hadn't even packed for the trip.

He told Collins, the man who'd first signed him to the Red Sox, "I'm through with baseball. To hell with everything. I'm going to enlist. I can't take any more of it. If I could have just paid three more installments on my mother's trust fund, she'd have been all set."

Collins told him to get packed and get to the train station, reassuring Williams that if he were called up, the Red Sox would make those payments on his behalf. Then he added further encouragement, saying "If you let them ride you into the service, they'll be riding every other ballplayer in, too. When the government wants you, they'll let you know, don't worry about that."[31]

Ted finally decided, and told Collins, "My mind is made up. I am going to play ball this season. My conscience is clear. I have as much right to be exempted as anybody else. I have my mother to support. Before my status was changed to I-A, I made commitments which I must go through with. I can do so by playing ball this year. When the season is over, I'll get into the Navy as fast as I can."[32]

He won Jack Malaney's support. Malaney was sports editor of the *Boston Post*, and a columnist for *The Sporting News*. Malaney wrote, "The more thoughtful will appreciate that Williams knows is own situation better than anybody else. If he were Joe Zilch, nothing would be thought of his being taken out of I-A and put into III-A. But he happens to be Ted Williams, the great batsman…"[33] Malaney anticipated some people asking whether Ted didn't really already have enough money put aside to adequately set up his mother. No, he said, the pay was mediocre at first, and though Ted had no bad habits, he enjoyed expensive autos, guns, and movie cameras. "He is generous to a fault. If he got $18,000 last season, he probably wound up with little more than $4,000 of it."

Williams had Collins' support. He won favor on the road, too. He was given an ovation on March 11 at the first exhibition game. Likewise, he won tremendous support from the 2,000 soldiers and 48,000 fans who packed Yankee Stadium in mid-April on the first road trip. "It turned out," Michael Seidel wrote, "that writers such as Grantland Rice were absolutely right about baseball in wartime America. The nation, even its trainees and fighting forces, delighted in the image of normalcy and energy displayed on the ball field. It was a tonic, not an outrage, that the season continued and that the finer players were still on the field."[34] The fans who did get on Ted's back did so because they felt they could have played that ball better, or hit that other one safely.

"Now Batting for Uncle Sam" - Pictorial News of the Day feature showing Ted Williams and Johnny Pesky.
Collection of Bill Nowlin.

Tom Yawkey mentioned that there had been 2,000 cases referred to the President's appeals board, the way Ted's case had been, and only 87 of the appeals had been rejected. The only one which occasioned significant criticism was that of Ted Williams. Much of the press gave him support. A lengthy editorial in the *Boston Globe* expressed sympathy for the young man whose personal affairs were being discussed by "what seems like 130,000,000 fellow citizens." The editorial asked for good sportsmanship from the fans, decrying the pack instinct that could infect a crowd.[35]

In mid-May, on the 13th, another brief flap occurred when a Selective Service public relations officer in Cleveland said Williams "probably" would be taken in the next round of callups, but George Price back in Minnesota said that Williams remained III-A and there were no plans to reopen the matter yet again. Minnesota draft headquarters agreed that the case was closed.

Having made his point, on May 22 Williams left his hotel and went to a government office at 150 Causeway Street in Boston and enlisted in the Navy. Columnist Bob Considine called Ted's enlistment "a study in nonchalance," writing that Williams hadn't even told Cronin or Yawkey of his plans.[36] He'd been recruited, quietly, outside the limelight. He'd won the battle of public opinion, and now he signed up to do his duty. The timing was such that he could take classes throughout the 1942 season and then enter the Navy's V-5 program late in the fall. The annuities he had purchased could now be paid in full, and his mother set up reasonably well for the leaner years to come. Ted Williams was heading off to war in the service of his country.

Lt. Ted Williams.
Courtesy of the May Williams Collection.

NOTES

1) *Phil Marchildon, with Brian Kendall,* Ace *(Toronto: Penguin Books, 1994), p. 104.*

2) *Williams,* My Turn At Bat, *op. cit., p. 97.*

3) Boston Sunday Advertiser, *January 4, 1942. Ted informed GM Eddie Collins by telephone on January 3. The news, according to the January 8 issue of* The Sporting News, *was "like a bombshell" to the Red Sox.*

4) *Associated Press dispatch, January 3, 1942.*

5) *AP dispatch, January 8, 1942.*

6) Boston Record, *February 20, 1942.*

7) Boston Record, *February 23, 1942.*

8) *Williams,* My Turn At Bat, *op. cit., p. 98. Knowing Ted Williams' personality, one might hazard a guess that the attorney was not the only one riled by the decision.*

9) Boston Record, *May 10, 1942.*

10) *Williams,* My Turn At Bat, *op. cit., p. 98.*

11) Boston Record, *February 28, 1942.*

12) Boston Globe, *February 27 & 28, 1942.*

13) *Linn,* Hitter, *op. cit., p. 124.*

14) *"Mother Bares Teddy's Status," Associated Press story datelined San Diego, December 7, 1941.*

15) Washington Post, *March 2, 1942.*

16) Boston Record, *February 28, 1942.*

17) Boston Record, *March 2 & 3, 1942.*

18) Boston Record, *March 1, 1942.*

19) Boston Record, *March 8, 1942.*

20) Boston Record, *March 2, 1942.*

21) Washington Post, *March 4, 1942.*

22) *Linn,* Hitter, *op. cit., pp. 127, 128.*

23) *Williams,* My Turn At Bat, *op. cit., p. 99. Mickey Cochrane headed up the baseball program at Great Lakes for three years. Kit Crissey writes in* Athletes Away *that "Many professional players specifically chose the Navy and Great Lakes so they could play for him, and thus he was able to field outstanding teams in 1942, 1943 and 1944." See Harrington E. Crissey,* Athletes Away *(Philadelphia: Archway Press, 1984).*

24) *Williams,* My Turn At Bat, *op. cit., p. 98, 99.*

25) *Michael Seidel,* Ted Williams: A Baseball Life *(Chicago: Contemporary Books, 1991), p. 118.*

26) *Ted Williams with David Pietrusza,* Teddy Ballgame *(Toronto, Sports Media, 2002), p. 53.*

27) *Williams,* My Turn At Bat, *op. cit., p. 99.*

28) *Williams with Pietrusza,* Teddy Ballgame, *op. cit., p. 53.*

29) Washington Post, *April 13, 1942.*

30) Boston Record, *April 13, 1942.*

31) *Linn,* Hitter, *op. cit., p. 129.*

32) *"Williams Pledges to Join U.S. in Fall,"* The Sporting News, *March 12, 1942.*

33) *Ibidem.*

34) *Seidel,* Ted Williams, A Baseball Life, *op. cit., p. 121.*

35) Boston Globe, *March 12, 1942.*

36) Washington Post, *May 27, 1942.*

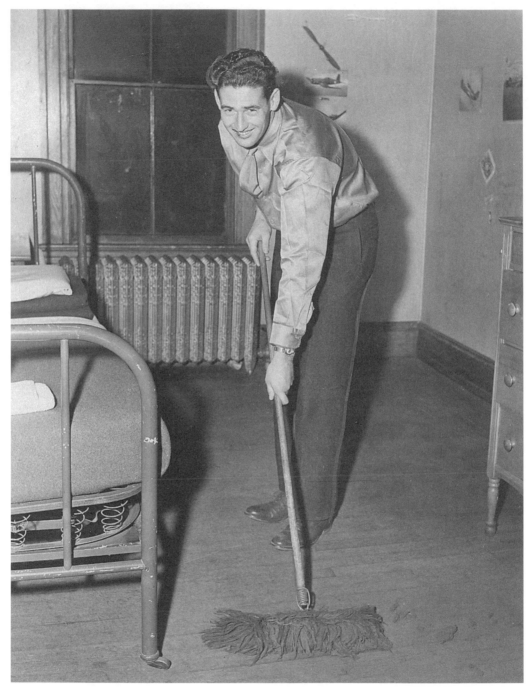

Ted Williams cleaning his quarters at Amherst College, December 1942.
Photo courtesy of the Cleveland Public Library.

CHAPTER 2 – WORLD WAR II: IN THE NAVY NOW

"Ted could make a plane and its six machine guns play like a symphony orchestra." Johnny Pesky [1]

Dave Egan's exclusive broke big on the front page of the May 23 *Boston Record*. Given how dramatically he'd written in Ted's defense, was it any surprise that he'd been rewarded with an exclusive? Ted had tipped him off and Egan was present at 150 Causeway. The main story began on page 3: "Ted Williams, without benefit of bat, hit the longest and hardest and loudest home run of his career yesterday, when he enlisted in the aviation branch of the United States Navy." The morning before, May 22, 1942, Williams awoke at the Hotel Shelton and made his way to the office on Causeway Street where he was sworn into the Navy by Commander Thomas A. Collins. A later public relations photograph re-enacted the oath-taking, Ted raising his right hand before Lt. Frank S. Donahue. When he walked out of the building, it was as Seaman Second Class Theodore S. Williams. He had, Egan wrote, "caught his detractors flat-footed off first base."

He didn't take the easy route, either. He neither signed up for public relations work nor as a physical instructor. "He wishes to become an active aviator in what is generally considered to be the toughest and most rigorous of all the branches of the service," wrote Egan. On the morning of the 22nd, Ted had taken both the physical and the mental examinations of the Naval Aviation Cadet selection

Ted taking the Navy oath in Boston, May 1942.
Photograph by Leslie Jones, courtesy of the Boston Public Library.

board for training as an airplane pilot in the United States Navy. He would undergo extensive classroom and field training as he prepared for combat.

Why would Williams choose the Navy, and why choose to become a Naval aviator? When he was asked, Ted quipped, "Hell, I've been up in the air for three years. Now I'm beginning to like it!" But why the Navy and not the Army? "My girl thinks I look sweet in Navy blue." Actually, the Navy was the service of choice for most ballplayers, as it turned out. How many of those choices were influenced by girlfriends has never been the subject of a Society for American Baseball Research (SABR) study.

The timing of Ted's decision may have been influenced by events in the news. The United States was not actively engaged in the European theater at this time. The war in the Pacific was, so far, mostly a Naval war and a war characterized by air battles – a war initiated by a surprise air attack on the American fleet.

Ed Rumill of the *Christian Science Monitor* later wrote that Ted had visited the Navy's air base at Squantum in Massachusetts before the game on May 6, at the invitation of Lt. Robert "Whitey" Fuller. When Dave Egan broke the story, he said the visit had been the morning of April 29 before the Sox dropped a tough luck game to the Tigers. Fuller drove Ted down and showed him around. Apparently a winning personality, Fuller had been a publicist at Dartmouth and on April 29 had been introduced to Ted by Sox publicist Ed Doherty (indicating that Bob Considine was probably wrong in believing that the Red Sox did not know of Ted's decision.) While at Squantum, Ted sat in the cockpit of a Navy plane, "pulled on a pair of goggles and toyed with the pilot's stick."[2] He made up his mind then and there, but waited until passing the examinations on May 22 before actually taking the final step, taking the oath.

When Williams first became interested, enrollment was limited to college graduates, but enrollment in the air service had recently been opened to high school graduates. "I don't know how I'll make out," he said, "because I never went beyond Hoover High School, and I understand you have to be pretty good in mathematics to become a pilot. But I'm going to give it a try. It will be tough. But that's the way I want it. I don't want any soft berth teaching gymnastics."[3] Arthur Sampson added a comment: "Playing baseball is Ted's first love. It has been all his life. And when he's playing baseball, everything else is secondary to it. But when he isn't playing baseball, The Kid goes into anything else just as intensely. That's true whether it is fishing or hunting. Or studying tax laws. He does nothing halfway or halfheartedly. It's whole hog or nothing with him. And that's the way it was when he finally put on a service uniform."[4]

By May 6, the Battle of the Coral Sea was raging in the Pacific. The battle lasted for several days. For the first time since Pearl Harbor, American and Japanese forces were engaged in direct and open battle. It was also the first battle fought entirely by aircraft, and they were U. S. Navy aircraft at that. The Naval Historical Center of the Department of the Navy explained the significance of the Battle of the Coral Sea: "An America hard-pressed by a dismal succession of nightmare stories of surrenders in the Philippines, battles lost, and great ships sacrificed, was to hear the statement that would thrill a nation. R.E. Dixon, second in command of *Lexington*'s dive bombers shouted into his microphone, 'Dixon to carrier. Scratch one flattop,' referring to the [Japanese] carrier *Shoho*. The Battle of the Coral Sea had taken place completely in and from the air. Torpedo planes dropped their blasts on enemy carriers while defensive planes and support ships fired on the enemy. It was the first Naval battle in which no ship on either side ever sighted the other."[5]

Williams told Egan, "I enlisted because the war has made everybody air conscious." He added, "I'm tickled to death to be in this thing. All I hope is that I can get up in the air in one of those ships. Man, I'll curve 'em!"[6]

Flying airplanes appealed to the more adventurous youths of the mid-twentieth century. The first aircraft he ever saw was the airship *USS Shenandoah*. In October 1924, the *Shenandoah* crossed the country from New Jersey to the West Coast, and was briefly based at San Diego. Ted was just six at the time, but it made an impression and he mentioned it to John Underwood when they were working on *My Turn At Bat*.[7]

Ted also had a model of sorts, Charles Lindbergh, who had been such an important figure in San Diego during Ted's youth. In February 1927, Lindbergh flew from San Diego to St. Louis in an airplane he'd helped design, and which was built by Ryan Airlines, Inc. of San Diego. Lindbergh and *The Spirit of St. Louis* set one record for flight time between San Diego and St. Louis, and then flew on to New York, setting a transcontinental flight time record. From New York, he made the first-ever trans-Atlantic flight, to France. Teddy Williams was almost nine years old, and Lucky Lindy's flight started in his hometown. It was no wonder that Lindbergh was the young boy's hero. Ted has said that his earliest hero was indeed Lindbergh, and not any baseball player.

Ted had seen Lindbergh at the stadium in San Diego one time when he was quite young. It was, he recalled, the day Teddy got his first barbershop haircut.[8]

Williams had told reporters in the weeks before that he would enlist after the season was over, or whenever he resolved the financial obligations he faced. True to his word, he had now done so, and sooner than anyone expected. Just as the controversy had died down, he joined up. The 22nd was an offday, and the team had traveled home after the road game against the Cleveland Indians on the 21st. With his appearance in Cleveland, Williams had played once in every American League park that year. He'd made the rounds, and he'd made his point.

Ted Williams and Johnny Pesky visiting Fenway Park.
Courtesy of the Boston Public Library.

He'd stood up to his critics.

Williams may also have been anticipating the Army and Navy relief fund exhibition game scheduled for the following day, May 23. The news of his enlistment no doubt helped sell a few more seats.

Dave Egan had kept up his support of Williams on the draft issue, though with a bit of humor, noting wryly on May 19 that Ted had nine dependents – "eight fellow Red Sox players and one mother." And Egan condemned the lengths to which the other Boston papers would go, in the highly competitive newspaper wars. Ted's manager James Silin was telephoned by someone posing as "Barnes of the *Globe*" saying that a story was due to break in one of the other papers implicating Silin in Williams being branded a draft-dodger. Half an hour later, a colleague of the first caller rang saying that a story was running that Silin "had finagled to keep Williams out of the draft, that it was known that Silin had profited to a certain extent from the career of Williams" and so on. Silin felt compelled to call a press conference in an attempt to clear the air as to his role in any of this. Egan also accused a "supposedly reputable Boston newspaper" of having hired an investigator to nose around San Diego and interview neighbors of May Williams about her financial circumstances. Boston was a tough newspaper town, and still remains a difficult media market for leading sports figures on the local teams. It's no surprise that Ted Williams so often found himself at war with the writers.

On May 22nd, all this became a non-issue. The train from Cleveland arrived at noon. Shortly afterward, Williams was at 150 Causeway Street where he announced that he had passed a Navy physical examination with flying colors, scoring well above normal. His exceptional vision was noted, an asset for an aviator as well as for a hitter. The Navy doctor, Frank Randolph Philbrook, declared that Williams was "in the pink and very steady."

It was a complete surprise for Collins, Yawkey, and Joe Cronin. Only Whitey Fuller knew Ted was coming in that day. Ted had wanted to make sure he passed the physical before saying anything publicly. Through arrangement with Fuller, Ted actually took the physical at the nearby apartment of a lieutenant commander in charge of the local flight board, to spare all concerned the hoopla and embarrassment had he not passed. He'd written his mother two days earlier to let her know of his plans.[9]

"I'm glad it's all straightened out now," Ted stated. "It's a load off my mind, even though I felt I was doing the right thing all the time. People, on the whole have been pretty swell to me, and I hope this will show that I appreciated their feeling toward me. I'm tickled to death and I'm hoping I'll get into the air quick to start some slugging against the Axis."[10] The *Monitor*'s Ed Rumill noted that within a few months, Ted could be fighting both for the people who'd cheered him, and for those who'd booed him.

Whitey Fuller said that Williams had not asked for any special treatment in terms of his ultimate call-up, and that he would be called routinely. It was understood, however, that the timing of his enlistment might be such that he'd be able to finish out the season, while he did classroom work three nights a week. At the time, with the flood of people entering the armed services, there was typically a lag of a few months between swearing in and reporting for training. Red Sox rookie Johnny Pesky informed his Portland, Oregon draft board by telegram: "Enlisted in Naval Aviation V-5, same as Ted Williams."[11] Pesky said years later that Fuller had told them that if they signed up in May, they wouldn't get called until October. "Williams talked me into that," Pesky said years later. "We got to finish the season." There were never any guarantees, but that's pretty much how it happened. "It's okay with me however it works out," Williams declared at the time. "I'm ready to go whenever they call me."

"We're proud he picked us," Fuller commented. "He couldn't have picked a tougher spot. He's going to be a flier, not a physical instructor or anything like that." Williams could have served Stateside, helping train recruits in physical education and conditioning. That was not the role he chose for himself.

When Williams was called, it was thought he would report to Squantum, receive his rating as Aviation Cadet, and be sent on for training.

The May 23 Army-Navy relief game pitted Boston against the Philadelphia Athletics at Fenway Park, and drew 12,216 paying customers. The A's won, 4-3, but Williams, who "received an ovation on each visit to the plate" banged a "towering home run wallop into the Red Sox bullpen in deep right field."[12] The *Times*' John Kieran wrote that "Tall Ted" had "made the greatest hit of his illustrious career when he signed the document that puts him on call to serve with the flying forces of the United States Navy... the day that sees Ted Williams walking off the diamond to begin basic pilot training will be a great day for Theodore Samuel Williams."[13]

There was another sacrifice involved in Ted's enlistment. A spokesman for the Naval Aviation Cadet Selection Board noted that "If a cadet marries before being commissioned he would be breaking his induction oath. The applicant must be unmarried, must never have been married and must not marry – openly or secretly – until he gets his wings."[14]

As the Sox played out the first part of the schedule, there were other appearances that Ted made. On June 24, for instance, he and Joe Cronin joined with Tigers Charlie Gehringer and Birdie Tebbetts at an event to help sell War Bonds in Flint, Michigan. Many ballplayers made many appearances throughout the war years to help raise money for defense.

Even before he'd received training, Ted Williams was on the minds of some Japanese soldiers.

Ted Williams' spectacular 1941 season received attention in another baseball-loving nation: Japan. The season ended two months before Pearl Harbor and the news of Ted's .406 season circulated in Japan. Ted's name cropped up in at least one unexpected quarter in mid-summer 1942.

Ray Makepeace graduated from high school in Minneapolis and had seen Ted play there during the 1938 season, while Ted was with the Sox' Minneapolis Millers minor league team. "We used to go down to Nicollet Park and we'd send one man up a telephone pole behind home plate, and in batting practice he would call the balls that were foul, telling us where they were going. There were 4 or 5 of us, and if you got a used ball, you'd get in for nothing." Makepeace played a little ball himself, some Class D in the Cardinals system. Well before war broke out, though, he'd signed up with the Army and sought a posting to The Philippines. He was there with an artillery contingent on Corregidor when the island surrendered to Japan in May 1942.

As a POW, Makepeace found himself in a labor battalion working in the port area of Manila, loading and unloading Japanese ships. At one point in June or July 1942, he was doing temporary duty in a Japanese kitchen and just outside the galley a group of Japanese soldiers was playing some ball. One of the balls rolled over by him, so he picked it up – and threw them back a curve ball. A soldier approached and asked, "You're a pitcher? You play baseball?" He replied yes, he did. Ted's 1941 season must have been fresh in the Japanese recruit's mind, since his next question was to ask if Makepeace knew Ted Williams. Yes, I did, Makepeace answered. "Then he asked me if I knew Babe Ruth and I said 'sure' and he said 'F--- Babe Ruth!' I showed him how to throw a curveball." Makepeace was given a pack of cigarettes and had to get back to his duties.

Interview with Ray Makepeace, December 15, 2002

Ted's 1942 season continued, and what a season it was. Sure, his 1942 average was 50 points below 1941's – but when you begin with .406 and lose 50 points, you're still hitting .356! Ted finished a full 25 points ahead of the second-best batter in the league, his teammate Johnny Pesky having a whale of a rookie year for himself. Pesky had been the clubhouse kid in Portland, Oregon when Williams came through town with the San Diego Padres in 1936 and 1937. Now, the two played on the same team, and by the end of the season, the rookie Pesky had hit safely 205 times.

There were several benefit games played throughout the year. A notable one took place the day after the regularly scheduled All-Star Game played at the Polo Grounds in New York on July 6. The winner of the July 6 game was to play a team of Service All-Stars. Since the American League beat the N.L. 3-1, it was the A.L. All-Stars against the Service All-Stars. It was quite a matchup.

Starting lineups and subsequent replacements were:

American League	**Service All-Stars** *(managed by Mickey Cochrane)*
Boudreau SS (Rizzuto)	*Mullin CF (Chapman)*
Henrich RF (Spence)	*McCoy 2B (Mueller)*
Williams LF	*Padgett LF*
DiMaggio, Joe CF	*Travis SS*
York 1B (McQuinn)	*Grace RF*
Doerr 2B	*Sturm 1B (Hajduk)*
Keltner 3B	*Andres 3B*
Rosar C	*Smith C (Pytlak)*
Bagby P (Sid Hudson, Tex Hughson)	*Feller P (Rigney, Mickey Harris, Grodzicki)*
	Morrie Arnovich and Johnny Lucadello both pinch-hit for the service team.

The American League won 5-0. Williams walked and scored in the first, and tripled and scored in the seventh.[15]

It should be kept in mind that Williams accomplished his success in 1942 while attending Naval classroom in the evenings. "We took classes during the summer, over at Mechanic Arts High School, three nights a week when we were at home. They were pretty good about it. Courses in Naval procedure."[16]

On July 13, Pesky and Williams both began classes at Mechanic Arts High School in Boston. Sitting at school desks, 250 students began the course work – four hours a night, three nights a week – that would prepare them for service in Naval Aviation. Williams was called to the front of the class to say a few words. Caught unprepared, he simply said, "I only hope I can prove myself worthy to go through with you. I give you my word I'll do my best." Then Lt. Donahue asked Johnny Pesky to mount the platform. Pesky said, "We're on a bigger team now – in the Navy – and I know I've got the guts to go through with you. When Ted and I get going in there with you, we'll give 'em hell!"[17]

A little bit earlier, after he had just registered for courses in navigation, aerology, physics, and advanced mathematics, and when not in front of the large audience, Ted had burst out, "Advanced math! I never had any of that. All I had was adding, subtracting, dividing and a little multiplying.

These birds will call me a meat-head – like they do in the left-field bleachers. All I want to do is get at that trigger." Several times on other occasions, asked why he had signed up, he answered with a bit of a joke: "I like to hit."[18]

Williams won the Triple Crown that year – leading the league in average, in home runs (36, 9 more than the #2 man), and RBIs (137, 23 more than the #2.) Despite the exceptionally rare accomplishment, and the margins by which he won each title, Ted was denied the award for Most Valuable Player. That went to New York's Joe Gordon. Gordon hit .322 to Ted's .356. He hit only half as many homers – 18 to Ted's 36 – and he knocked in 103 runs, to Ted's 137. Williams led in almost every offensive category – he scored 141 runs, Gordon scored 88 – but the Yankees second baseman won the award. Gordon did lead the league in some categories, though. Gordon's fielding percentage of .966 was not nearly as good as Ted's .991, but he did lead the league in errors by a second baseman. He also led the league in strikeouts by a healthy margin, whiffing 95 times, and he grounded into more double plays than anyone else that year, with 22.

Was this some kind of perverse joke? Not really. Gordon was a sparkplug with the pennant-winning New York team, but the fact that Williams was not awarded the MVP in '42 reflects the war between Williams and the writers. One voting writer – not a Boston one, as legend had it – didn't even include Ted in his top ten. Ted's enlistment had only resulted in a very temporary truce.

In November, after the season was well over, The Kid got called up. He'd joined the Navy's V-5 program, and so had a number of other ballplayers. Instead of reporting directly to Squantum, Ted was included as part of a group to undergo CPT – civilian pilot training – at Amherst College in Massachusetts. It was more or less an orientation course to see if the men might be good candidates. Meant to be a nine-week program, this became preliminary ground school and the group soon became merged into W.T.S., War Training Service, at Amherst. Ted arrived on November 17, and

he did so as part of a group of 30 cadets, in the company of Johnny Pesky, Joe Coleman, Buddy Gremp, Johnny Sain, and Paul Kluck, a catching prospect from the Sox farm club in Louisville. Had this not been November, with snow already on the ground, that could have been the nucleus of a pretty good ballclub.

Ted almost turned up late. He was due at 2:00 p.m., but apparently didn't quite have Amherst's location pinned down. Had he known Amherst was in western Massachusetts, he could have hopped off the train from Chicago when it stopped at Springfield.

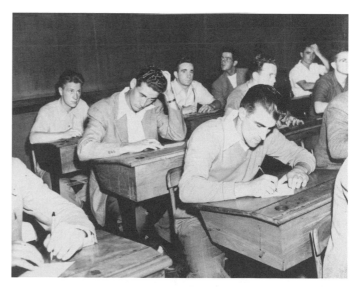

Ted Williams and Johnny Pesky studying in evening classes at Mechanic Arts High School, summer 1942.
Coutesy of the National Baseball Hall of Fame.

Instead, he came all the way into Boston, arriving at 3:00 a.m. After some sleep at the Sheraton, he went down to the breakfast room and ran into Duffy Lewis. Fortunately, former Sox star Lewis was now traveling secretary with the Boston Braves and was able to arrange a limousine for Ted – the only way he could possibly get to Amherst in time. So Williams showed up for military service by limo from Boston.[19]

Williams excelled in the classroom. He'd never been much of a student at Hoover High School in San Diego, but that's because he was always wanting to get out and play baseball. Now he was focused on his studies, and applied himself diligently even at difficult subjects like mathematics and physics. "Ted went through the program like a dose of salts," Pesky said. "He mastered intricate problems in fifteen minutes which took the average cadet an hour, and half the other cadets were college graduates."

Ted couldn't understand why Johnny was having such a hard time of it. "He called me 'dumb' and all this – which I was! Finally, I told him, 'Ted, I'm not you.'"[20] Williams achieved a 3.85 grade average out of a possible 4.0, according to Melvin L. Shettle, Jr., in his book *United States Naval Air Stations of World War II*.[21] In his Williams biography, Leigh Montville says Ted scored 2.98. Whatever it was, it was pretty good. Pesky was impressed. He told the AP, "Ted is going after this flying stuff as hot and heavy as he did about his batting. You know how hard and how long he practiced hitting. Well, he's bearing down much harder in this course than he ever did on his batting."[22]

Williams did well, warming to his new work, even if a bit unrealistically. He said, "I'm not batting .400 in this flying course yet, but I'm going to do it... I like it so much that I'd quit baseball for it. If I can make a success of flying, I'd just as soon stay in the service – provided I could get a month off once in a while to go hunting."[23]

Johnny Pesky explained a bit more, "We stayed in college dorms. We stayed in Genung House. Ted, Coleman, Sain, Gremp, and myself, we were all in this same house. It was nice up there. The students were still in school, but they just made room for us. It was great up there. We were there for about six months, to April 1943. Mostly classroom, but we flew out of Turners Falls. We had so many hours in a Piper Cub and then you soloed in the Piper Cub. Then you went to a Waco, which is a biplane, a little heavier aircraft."[24]

All of Ted's instructors agreed that he was determined to succeed as a Navy pilot. "Our instructors have been very patient with us," Ted enthused. "I crack that math book every time I get the chance. You have to know what mathematics are all about to be a Navy flier."[25] The cadets were applying themselves 15 hours a day.

It wasn't as though these were experienced air travelers. Johnny Pesky had only flown for the first time the year before, as a passenger. Williams almost didn't make it out of training alive. "I damn near killed myself in Amherst. Two of us were flying Cubs and I didn't see some power lines across a river – we were flying upriver – and I just barely cleared at the last second."[26]

All in all, though, Ted really enjoyed the experience. Expounding at length to Jack Malaney of the *Boston Post*, he said, "It's great here and I'm really crazy about every bit of it. I'll admit I dreaded coming here, because I never have had to take orders before and always did as I pleased, came and went as I wanted to and lived my own life. But I'm really stuck on it all, and I think you know me well enough to know that I'd say so if I didn't like it.

"The layout at the college here is great. We're much better off than the boys who have to go to camps. It's an experience worth having that I'd never get any other way. We work hard, but the food is good and there's plenty of it.

"Flying? I think flying as a whole, is easy. If a fellow listens, applies himself and thinks, he can fly. The flying doesn't bother me at all, though all of us were nervous the first couple of times. But the ground school, where we get math and that stuff, is something else again. That's tough!"[27]

Ted was known for his aversion to neckties, and he never owned a hat – other than the baseball cap that was part of his uniform. Now that he had donned another uniform, he often had to wear a regulation necktie and a military "overseas cap." Ted told Malaney, "It took me awhile to get used to the tie, but it doesn't bother me a bit now." Nor did the discipline. Malaney explained that Ted had become so accustomed to addressing officers as "Sir" that he made more general use of it. "It was odd for a scribe who had traveled with him since he joined the Sox to hear Ted say, 'It has been nice seeing you again, SIR,' as happened at Amherst."[28]

Though he'd said he enjoyed it all so much that he'd consider making a career of flying, that sentiment lasted about two minutes when asked whether he thought being out of baseball a year would make any difference in his ability to play baseball again. "Hell, no, I'd come back and lead the league in everything, if I could get a little longer spring training to get straightened out." The old self-confidence resurfaced – not that it was much below the surface to begin with, given his remarks on how easy it was to fly – and Malaney said, "It was nice of Ted to talk about staying, but...you couldn't keep him out of baseball when the war is over if they made him an admiral in the Navy."[29]

For the Christmas holiday, the students all went home, and most of the cadets did as well. "Everybody but the ballplayers," recalled cadet Lew Powers of Arlington, Massachusetts. "I stayed, too. I didn't have any money and there wasn't much point in it." Then he recalls a typical act of Ted Williams generosity. "I bumped into Williams in the fraternity house where we were living. He asked me in that big bluff way of his: 'No home to go to?' I just passed it off, something to the effect I was broke and let it go at that. He wouldn't let go. He forced money

Johnny Pesky and Ted Williams in airplane, 1942.
Courtesy of the National Baseball Hall of Fame.

into my hand, a couple of hundred dollars, and told me in no uncertain terms to get the hell out of there. I tried to tell him I might never be able to pay it back. But he was gone. He wouldn't listen." Poignantly, it was Ted Williams who had no home he really wanted to go to. A couple of hundred dollars was a large amount of money in 1942. Certainly, Williams helped Powers have a happier Christmas.[30]

After several months at Amherst and Turners Falls, it was time to further build up the recruits physically. They had done a lot of swimming at Amherst, including courses on resuscitation and life saving. They did a lot of exercise work and "as tough a session of calisthenics as could be given." Ted admitted he hadn't taken advantage of growing up on the West Coast: "When I was a kid, I was as tall as I am now, but I weighed about 40 pounds less. I was so skinny I was self conscious about it and the result was I seldom went to the beach. Here I've got to learn all over again as they are concentrating on the breast stroke, which permits you to know what is going on around you."[31] His swimming coach said he was working so hard at perfecting his stroke that he was usually the last to leave the pool.

Vincent X. Flaherty of the *Washington Times-Herald* told a tale that made one realize Ted was serious about his dedication to the effort. A couple of months after his callup, the organizers of the annual Baseball Writers' Dinner in New York wanted to present a bronze plaque to Williams honoring him for his Triple Crown. Ted declined, saying the Navy wouldn't let him attend. "He was sorry he could not be there, but the Navy was the Navy and that was that." The banquet committee wrote back, asking him to try harder – that there would be a lot of admirals and generals attending, that this was a major honor. "Again Williams came back with the same old bad news. The Navy didn't care how big an honor it was – he had to stay put, said Williams. Ted told the baseball boys he was terribly disappointed, but what was a guy to do but let the matter drop?" The committee did not. One of them got in touch with a Senator, who got in touch with James Forrestal, Secretary of the Navy. Forrestal wrote back saying that the Navy had no objection at all to Williams attending. Flaherty contacted the CO of the air station where Williams was based, and was told that it was the first they've heard of it. "It turned out Williams had concocted the story in the first place... When called on the carpet by the Navy, Williams said he didn't want to attend the dinner because he was in the Navy now. He wanted to be just another Navy guy, just like his bunkmates. Only when his commanding officer urged him to accept the honor did Williams go to New York."[32]

Williams was initially due to move on to Chapel Hill, North Carolina on April 15, 1943, but he pulled a hernia working out in Amherst and was transferred to Chelsea Naval Hospital in Chelsea, Massachusetts for an operation on March 17. Ted tried to out-do himself. "We were all trying to see how many chin-ups and push-ups we could do and how fast we could swim," Ted confided in *My Turn At Bat*. "That meant two months in the sack."[33] He was to stay in the hospital for a week and then return to Amherst for seven weeks of recuperation before undergoing the program at the recently-established Naval Pre Flight School in North Carolina.

Ted sent a letter from the Chelsea Naval Hospital to a friend in West Hempstead, Long Island named June Friest, who'd sent him some good luck charms. Dated March 25, 1943, Ted wrote privately (not for public consumption), "It won't be long and I'll be up and around again but I'll have to take it easy for a spell before I'll be able to get back to heavy duty. I really have enjoyed my experience in the Navy so far, especially the flying. I'm really crazy about that and I hope I can make the grade and earn my wings."[34]

The group was held up for other reasons and, while still in Massachusetts and before their scheduled reporting date of May 6, they were scheduled to play an April 29 game against Harvard University at Harvard Stadium. Ted Williams was named to manage the team. It would have been his first managerial stint. Alas, the game was rained out. The Harvard men were dismayed, too. "It was especially disappointing to the Harvard players when the game with the Amherst Naval Training nine was rained out. But it did not prevent their coach, Ted Williams, nor star shortstop Johnny Pesky, from working out in the Briggs Cage and giving some much needed instruction to the Crimson hitters."[35]

He joined up with the group later and spent the summer months at Chapel Hill. They were ready for him. He said, "I'll never forget getting off the train at Chapel Hill, just at dusk, and marching up in front of the administration building with the other recruits. The cadets already there were hanging out the windows watching us, and as we passed, one guy hollered, 'OK, Williams, we know you're there, and you're going to be sor-ry.'"[36] There was more classroom work, but also boxing and wrestling, some football and, of course, some baseball. It was good publicity for the Navy to have some celebrity ballplayers in the service and they took public relations photographs of Williams, Pesky, and Coleman

Some of the "Cloudbusters", Chapel Hill, North Carolina, 1943.
Rear: Johnny Pesky, Ted Williams. Front: Joe Coleman, Don Kepler, Johnny Sain.
Courtesy of The North Carolina Collection, University of North Carolina at Chapel Hill.

working out, at their duties, and while playing ball. Ted was back on the diamond before too long. On May 30, Ted hit a two-run homer (Pesky was on base) in the ninth inning of a game when the Navy Pre-Flight Cloudbusters faced the Norfolk Naval Air Station team. Pre-Flight fell just one run short, and lost the contest 5-4, before 6,500 people.

Ted wasn't completely happy about the experience, nor the obligation to play baseball while in the Navy. In another letter to June Friest, he complained about the heat in North Carolina and it was clear that the program was wearing on him. "Have been down here now for 6 weeks and wish it was my last ...this is the worst hole I ever got in – you have got one spare minute to yourself except possibly on Sat nite and Sunday afternoon and then we're usually playing ball here or away (I really wish I wasn't playing ball down here as it takes all your spare time what little you have.) And also I might add I'm having an awful time hitting these pitchers I've faced. I hit all the balls on the end of the bat and hit little grounders to first base. No kidding, I've been the out man so far."[37] With Williams, one has to wonder how much the poor hitting affected his overall mood. Nevertheless, it is evident that playing baseball for the Cloudbusters was not pure joy.

The hitting picked up, though, and both Pesky and Williams hit well in June. A June 29 report had Johnny hitting .460 and Ted at .390 for the Navy team in Chapel Hill.

On July 12, Williams even played a ballgame at Boston's Fenway Park, linking up with Babe Ruth himself in the Mayor's Field Day benefit game against the Boston Braves. It was the first time the two had ever met. In the day's game, The Babe was the manager and The Kid proved the hero.

During World War II, American access to rubber was curtailed by Japanese occupation of rubber-producing lands in Asia. In an effort to conserve rubber, baseballs were made without rubber centers. The wartime baseball was called the "balata ball".

Several days before the game, Gordon Campbell of the *Christian Science Monitor* had remarked that with the wartime balata baseball being used, "so far this year

**Williams, baseball coach Lt. Don Kepler, Johnny Pesky.
Cloudbusters Navy baseball team, Chapel Hill 1943.**
*Courtesy of The North Carolina Collection,
University of North Carolina at Chapel Hill.*

no one has been able to put a ball over or even into the bullpen in right field... Should [Williams] connect, it might indicate that the ball is not so dead as was first believed."[38]

Ruth, "fat and forty-eightish but still fabulous" (in the words of the AP dispatch), served as manager for a team of Service All-Stars, one of whom was the U. S. Navy's Ted Williams. Williams had arrived first. Signing baseballs before the game in his Navy uniform, Ted said, "I'll leave the honor space for the Babe." Then in strode the Babe. "Hiya Kid," he boomed, a black cigar in his mouth. "A very great pleasure indeed," said Ted, somewhat in awe. Ruth and Williams had a home run hitting contest before the game, which the young, fit Williams won 3-0. In the game itself, the Braves took a three-run lead, but Ruth's All-Stars came back with four runs in the top of the third, half of the runs driven in by a Dom DiMaggio triple with two aboard. The score went to 5-5 after five.

In the top of the seventh inning, Ted Williams' three-run home run into the bleachers off Dave Odom gave the All-Stars the lead. "And this time, when he crossed the plate and smiled up at the cheering thousands in the stands, he tipped his cap. He was happy to be back."[39] Ruth pinch-hit in the eighth but only flied out. Ruth's team beat the Braves, 9-8. WWII era teams were depleted of many of their best players. The Sampson Naval Training Center club even beat the Boston Red Sox once in 1944, by the score of 20-7.

Not all of the service team were ex-major leaguers, though. Walt Dropo was rookie of the year in 1950, but that was still a full seven years in the future. A student at UConn, he was drafted and stationed at Fort Devens. "They sent down a couple of us to that All-Star game to represent Fort Devens."[40]

Dom DiMaggio was the other star of the game for the All-Stars, hitting 2-for-5 with two RBI. Both Ted and Dom had to leave right after the game, because Ted's Pre-Flight team from Chapel Hill was scheduled to play DiMaggio and the Norfolk Navy team the next evening in Raleigh in a war bond benefit game.

On July 28, Ruth and Williams both played in Yankee Stadium in another benefit exhibition in front of more than 27,000 patrons. This time the two squared off on opposing teams, Ruth for the "Yank-Lands" (a team drawn from players of the Yankees and the Cleveland Indians, who'd played earlier in the day) and Williams playing left field for the Pre-Flight Cloudbusters. Ruth as manager worked 22 players into the lineup, including himself (he drew a walk in the sixth.) It was to no avail, though, despite a Yank-Lands 5-4 lead after six full. The Cloudbusters busted loose with seven runs in the top of the seventh en route to an 11-5 win. Ted went 1-for-4, singling and scoring a run in the frame.

In between the two ballgames, Williams had returned to Chapel Hill and a group of photographers gave him a real workout. With Navy p.r. officers as escorts, the men had Williams climbing a "commando-type obstacle... [and] crawling gingerly under barbed wire." Seemingly satisfied, they nonetheless made Williams run through the routine three times. Ed Rumill suggested that they worked him so hard, "they must have been thinking back to some of the verbal abuse Teddy, younger and untamed, had hurled in the direction of the lens boys when he wore a Boston uniform."[41]

A month later, Rumill suggested that the Navy was helping Ted mature. "Uncle Sam's Navy already has knocked a lot of the clowning out of Ted Williams and it will knock more out before the final shot has been fired in this war. This is no rap at the Kid. Any branch of the service changes every man who goes in. There is nothing better for the disposition – for what in baseball the boys call temperament – than a stretch with the military. They go in boys; come out men."[42]

Not that there weren't a few hijinks along the way. Phil Rizzuto tells of a story where the Pre-Flight team was in Norfolk for a game, but heavy rains caused a cancellation. Everyone was chewing the fat when suddenly Ted and several others grabbed Rizzuto and stripped him naked. Ted then "produced a bottle of indelible red mercury solution... and Ted was an artist at applying the solution to the body. 'I love you, Cora,' he printed on the Scooter's chest. 'I'm a Naval hero,' he painted on another part of the Scooter's anatomy. He printed a lot of other things that were somewhat less pretty, and needn't be mentioned, all over his body. And there was no way Phil could remove all that indelible red mercury solution. It would just have to wear away with time – two, three days, maybe a week." Rizzuto's wife Cora took it all in stride.[43]

Babe Ruth and Ted Williams, at war benefit ballgame.
Courtesy of The Sporting News/ZUMA Press.

Johnny Pesky had told Austen Lake that part of the object of all the intense physical training was "to find if we have a nerve-cracking point." Many wondered if Williams would crack. "But he never blew any fuses or got a single bad behavior demerit. If anything, he took a little stiffer discipline than the others, sort of stuff like, 'Oh, so you're the great Ted Williams, huh?'"[44]

The Cloudbusters were an excellent team, with a crack lineup. The 1943 team, with Ted in left and Pesky at short, and a pitching staff of Johnny Sain, Joe Coleman, Pete Appleton, and Ray Scarborough, won thirty games and lost only six. The infield also featured Buddy Hassett at first, Ed Moriarty at

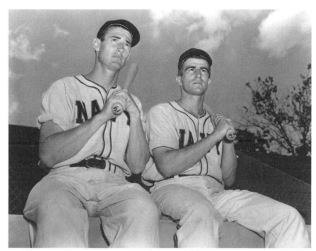

Ted Williams and Johnny Pesky, hitters for the Cloudbusters Navy baseball team, Chapel Hill 1943.
Courtesy of The North Carolina Collection, University of North Carolina at Chapel Hill.

second, and Buddy Gremp at third. Dusty Cooke played right field and Harry Craft played center. Catching duties were shared by Joe Cusick and Alex Sabo. They even had three major league veterans on the bench. Kit Crissey says that the team played military, collegiate, and industrial teams, but "nothing more ambitious could be scheduled because the aviation cadets had to conform to the regular training schedule – celestial navigation and aerology classes in the morning, military drill in the afternoon and intensive study at night." Moriarty, an officer, said that the cadets showed tremendous spirit, working to help each other with drill and their studies. "They had only one and a half hours of baseball practice a day, but a few players like Ted Williams and Johnny Pesky... sacrificed some meal time for extra batting and fielding."[45]

The team's manager, Don Kepler, said that Ted used to talk on and on about fishing on the long bus trips, and Ted "evinced a keen interest in his specialty of survivor training."[46]

Three weeks to the day after Ted Williams had enlisted (and quite possibly, the publicity attendant on Williams' enlistment played a part in the decision), another man was sworn in as a cadet at 150 Causeway Street in Boston. George Herbert Walker Bush became a seaman second class on the day he turned eighteen – June 12, 1942. Bush also joined the V-5 program of the U. S. Naval Reserve. Bush began training in August, reporting to the Naval Pre-Flight Training School at Chapel Hill on August 6, and both Williams and Bush found themselves at the Chapel Hill Naval Air Station at the same time, their tours of duty there overlapping. Bush watched Williams play a few games that summer of 1943. "I don't recall having met him," President Bush wrote this author in 2004. "The Navy was desperate to get trained pilots into the war zone. There was no time for socializing. As did Ted Williams, we all took our training seriously. Ted didn't receive any special treatment because of being a baseball star. I didn't get acquainted with him until much later in life."[47]

The stay at Chapel Hill lasted through most of the summer and then Williams traveled on to the town of Peru, Indiana and the year-old Naval Air Station Bunker Hill for primary flight training. Peru is about 20 miles north of Kokomo and NAS Bunker Hill is about halfway in between. The rapid mobilization of so many recruits given the exigencies of war sometimes created over-crowding, and dangerous circumstances. Ted's flight log book shows that he started the program at NAS Bunker Hill on September 12, 1943.

"The day we got there," Ted told John Underwood, "it looked like a flying circus. The air was black with planes. We'd been told, 'Always stay 1,000 feet away from any other airplane and 1,000 feet above the terrain, and make nice easy 45-degree turns.' But here we see about 150 planes in the air, all flying around each other, maybe 200 feet apart. There's a big round mat that everybody's landing on. It looked like flies on a garbage can. I said to Johnny Pesky, 'What the hell's going on?' They were all coming in at the end of their flying period. They'd gone out separately but they were coming in together. Awful."[48]

Ted Williams in football drills, June 24, 1943 at UNC Chapel Hill for Naval Pre-Flight training.
Courtesy of The North Carolina Collection, University of North Carolina at Chapel Hill.

By the time Williams and Pesky had arrived at Bunker Hill, on September 11, there were only a few games left on the base's baseball season. Ted Williams played four games for Bunker Hill. Fred Dickerson was a physical training officer at the station and he recalls when Ted and Johnny Pesky arrived with the detachment from Chapel Hill. "We knew when we got the group that those guys were on the list. It was somewhat late in the baseball season and our station team had probably five or six games to play. They were wondering about Williams and Pesky. Well, Pesky was anxious to play, and did. Ted didn't care about playing, said he had played at Carolina and didn't bring any bats with him, and that sort of thing. But the station commander was interested in seeing him play. He didn't actually contact him personally, but the word got down and so Ted decided to play. He did very well. They played out the season, and everybody was happy about it."[49]

How did Ted get along? Dickerson had heard that Ted had a bit of a reputation that preceded him, but says, "There was no difficulty here. He was well-liked; the cadets liked him and he got to be platoon commander. I had him in basketball and boxing and things of that sort. The guy was a tremendous athlete. He would have been great in sports other than baseball. He passed his tests and went on to flight training."[50]

Commanding officer Captain D. D. Gurley was among those who crowded around Ted as he was to leave the base, and called him a "regular Joe." He was such a good pilot that "his flight instruction was completed more than two weeks ahead of schedule and he was right up with his class in ground school subjects. He has an inquiring mind and that is a splendid piece of equipment for a flier."[51]

After six weeks at Bunker Hill, they were soloing and working on takeoffs and landings, navigation, night flying, and even aerobatics to develop their skills and become experienced pilots. They were accumulating hours, practicing until they had 100 hours of flying time. In six stages, Ted logged 33.5 hours of dual training and 59.5 hours of solo, with 9.5 hours of check time for a total of 102.5 hours. He completed the course on November 5, 1943.

Ted's United States Navy student jacket shows a final mark of 2.98. Major General Larry S. Taylor reviewed Ted's student jacket in late 2004 and reported that his "overall impression is that of an average to above-average flight student with consistently above-average grades in intelligence, enthusiasm, cooperation. Actual flying grades are mostly average, until he gets to the more advanced training. Then they are somewhat above-average. He received two 'downs' (unsatisfactory flights) on check rides in late '43. Most flight students receive at least one of these at some point during flight school."[52]

Ted Williams in football drills, June 24, 1943 at UNC Chapel Hill for Naval Pre-Flight training.
Courtesy of The North Carolina Collection, University of North Carolina at Chapel Hill.

The two "downs" were on 22 October 1943 and 19 December 1943. In October, check pilot Clark deemed Williams' work as unsatisfactory, his airwork "rough at times. Stunts weak. Pattern around pylons very irregular with too much rudder control. Wingovers too hurried with too much loss of altitude." A couple of months later, Williams took off in high pitch with flaps up. His throttle work was judged very rough, too. He was rated "not safe for solo", in his second check flight of the day (he passed the first one). Up again for another check the following day, Williams received a better rating, but instructor Patterson noted "student seemed over anxious."[53] Aviation Cadet Williams certainly didn't want to be washed out.

On December 6, 1943, Ted was ordered to Pensacola, Florida to begin intermediate flight training.

Ted at Bunker Hill looking ahead to going to Pensacola.
Official U. S. Navy photograph

NOTES

1) *Johnny Pesky quotation cited on the Internet at: http://home.sandiego.edu/~plucy/page4.html.*

2) Christian Science Monitor, *May 23, 1942.*

3) *Arthur Sampson,* Ted Williams *(NY: A. S. Barnes, 1950), p. 102.*

4) *Ibidem, p. 103.*

5) *Department of the Navy, Naval Historical Center, Internet posting.*

"*On the face of it, the Battle of the Coral Sea appeared to be a victory for the Japanese. The Imperial Navy had sunk one American fleet carrier and damaged another, sunk an oiler and a destroyer, while losing only Shoho and a large number of planes, and suffering severe damage to Shokaku and enough damage to Zuikaku to keep both out of the war for several months. It was a tactical victory for the Imperial forces. However, the battle was a strategic victory for the Americans. The Coral Sea meant the end of Japanese expansion southward. They would never again threaten Australia and New Zealand.*

"*The significance of the Battle of the Coral Sea was that the Americans had foiled the occupation of Port Moresby and the knockout of Australian air power. These were necessary before carrier strikes by the Japanese against Australia. In a few weeks the Americans would land on Guadalcanal, and the Japanese would eventually be driven out of the Solomon Islands after months of attrition warfare. There would be no more expansion, bases, or victories for Japan. Although both forces withdrew simultaneously, the Japanese had two less carriers for the Battle of Midway, and erroneously believed that the Americans had lost the Yorktown. Just as important was Admiral Yamamoto's determination to wipe out the American Fleet in the wake of the Battle of the Coral Sea. The American people must be convinced that the Japanese could not be defeated. Desperate for victory, the Japanese were marching down the road of defeat. The Battle of Midway [June 4-7] fought near the Central Pacific island of Midway, is considered the decisive battle of the war in the Pacific. Before this battle the Japanese were on the offensive, capturing territory throughout Asia and the Pacific. By their attack, the Japanese had planned to capture Midway to use as an advance base, as well as to entrap and destroy the U.S. Pacific Fleet. Because of communication intelligence successes, the U.S. Pacific Fleet surprised the Japanese forces, sinking the four Japanese carriers that had attacked Pearl Harbor only six months before, while only losing one carrier. After Midway, the Americans and their Allies took the offensive in the Pacific.*"

6) Boston Record, *May 23, 1942.*

7) *Ted is heard describing the Shenandoah visit and his admiration for Charles Lindbergh in the compact disc which accompanies the book* It's Only Me *(Chicago: Triumph Books, 2005).*

8) *Williams,* My Turn At Bat, *p. 17. At some point, Ted flew as a passenger in a plane while still in high school. He said, "I've never handled the stick but have flown a lot of planes of various sorts, including trans-continental ones, and have been awfully interested in them." (Jack Malaney, "Williams and Navy See Eye to Eye," The Sporting News, May 28, 1942.)*

9) *Jack Malaney, "Williams and Navy See Eye to Eye,"* The Sporting News, *May 28, 1942.*

10) New York Times, *May 23, 1942.*

11) Washington Post, *June 10, 1942.*

12) New York Times, *May 24, 1942.*

13) *Ibidem*

14) *Ibidem*

15) *Crissey,* Athletes Away, *op. cit., is the primary source for information on this game.*

16) *Interview with Johnny Pesky, November 16, 1998.*

17) Boston Globe, *July 14, 1942. The same newspaper provided biographical sketches of seven Navy men from New England who were reported missing after the torpedoing of the aircraft carrier USS Lexington.*

18) *Ibidem.*

19) *Howell Stevens, "Thumping Ted Off to a 'Flying Start'",* The Sporting News, *November 26, 1942.*

20) *Interview with Johnny Pesky, May 11, 1999.*

21) *Melvin L. Shettle, Jr.,* United States Naval Air Stations of World War II.

22) New York Times, *December 2, 1942.*

23) *Ibidem.*

24) *Interview with Johnny Pesky, May 11, 1999.*

25) New York Times, *December 2, 1942.*

26) *Williams,* My Turn At Bat, *p. 100.*

27) *Jack Malaney column printed in* The Sporting News, *December 10, 1942, p. 7.*

28) *Ibidem.*

29) *Ibidem.*

30) Mike Gillooly, "The Case for Ted Williams," Boston Evening American, *January 7, 1958.*

31) *Ibidem.*

32) *"When Navy Ordered Williams To Take Diamond Bow,"* The Sporting News, *November 23, 1944.*

33) *Williams,* My Turn At Bat, *p. 100.*

34) *Ted Williams, personal letter to June Friest, March 23, 1943.*

35) The Second Book of Harvard Athletics, 1923-1963, *Harvard Varsity Club, 1964.*

36) *Williams,* My Turn At Bat, *p. 100.*

37) *Letter to June Friest, June 14, 1943.*

38) Christian Science Monitor, *July 7, 1943.*

39) Boston Record, *July 13, 1943.*

40) *Interview with Walt Dropo, August 15, 2001.*

41) Christian Science Monitor, *July 22, 1943.*

42) Christian Science Monitor, *August 24, 1943.*

43) *Gene Schoor,* The Scooter, NY: Charles Scribner's Son, 1982, p. 79.

44) *Leigh Montville,* Ted Williams *(NY: Doubleday, 2004), p. 109.*

45) *Crissey,* Athletes Away, *p. 27.*

46) *Ibidem.*

47) *Letter to author from George H. W. Bush, July 19, 2004.*

48) *Williams,* My Turn At Bat, *p. 100.*

49) *Interview with Fred Dickerson, December 7, 2005.*

50) *Ibidem.*

51) Washington Post, *December 7, 1943.*

52) *Communication from Maj. Gen. Larry Taylor, December 27, 2004.*

53) *The comments cited come from Williams' U.S. Navy student flight jacket.*

Leigh Montville tells how the trainees at Chapel Hill were put through their paces in a number of sports. Johnny Pesky remembers the boxing instructor as a former professional fighter named, perhaps, Allie Clark. Clark noticed this one tall cadet named Williams who seemed to have exceptionally quick reflexes. As Montville recounts Pesky's story, Clark brought Williams into the ring near the end of one session and said, "Let's see if you can hit me." Both wore boxing gloves, and they squared off. "Ted was just swinging at first, and Clark got out of the way easy," Pesky told Montville. "He was a boxer! Then Ted started the get the hang of it. He fakes! And then he unloads. Pow! He hits the guy. Then he fakes again. Pow. He hits the guy again. When the thing was over, the instructor says, 'Hey, how would you like to have me help you make a fast million bucks?' Ted says, 'How would you do that?' 'I'll train you as a boxer.' Ted says, 'Oh, no, not me.' Clark didn't even know who Ted was."

Leigh Montville, Ted Williams
op. cit., pp. 109, 110.

Ted Williams boxing with instructor Swain, July 15, 1943 at UNC Chapel Hill for Naval Pre-Flight training, 1943.
Courtesy of The North Carolina Collection, University of North Carolina at Chapel Hill.

**Aviation cadet Ted Williams at Bunker Hill Naval Air Station, November 30, 1943,
listening to instructions from Chief Flight Instructor Duane M. "Red" English, USNR.**
Courtesy of the Cleveland Public Library.

CHAPTER 3 — WINNING HIS WINGS

It was at Pensacola that Ted Williams got his wings and got hitched, both on the same day. He also suffered probably his worst day ever at home plate but, more importantly, he served his country well as a Marine Corps instructor.

December 1943. The major league baseball season was over. Ted Williams had missed his first full season. He was to miss two more during World War II. When Williams reported to NAS Pensacola, the Red Sox team was smarting after the bruising they'd taken in regular season play. In 1942, Williams and Pesky had finished 1-2 in the American League batting race. Now both were gone, as were a number of other players. The Red Sox had been hurt the worst in the standings, plunging from 1942's second place finish (.621 winning percentage) to seventh place (.447, 29 games out of first).

Williams had led the league in runs with 141 in 1942. The leader in 1943 was Washington's George Case with just 102.

What if Williams had opted to keep on playing? There were only four batters in the A.L. who finished with averages over .300. And it's worth remembering that with many players throughout baseball now in the service, the pitching was weaker, too. It wasn't just that all the hitters were in the service. Luke Appling led the league with a .328 mark. The home run leader was Detroit's Rudy York with 34, but his slugging average was just .527 compared to Williams' .648 the year before. Appling's OBP of .419 paled beside Ted's .499.

Huck Finnegan of the *Boston American* visited Pensacola in December 1943 and chronicled some of Ted's time at the naval air station in a series of articles that began in early January 1944. "Teddy 'On High' in Flying Role," the series began. The newspaper created a special logo for Finnegan's series, entitled "Williams Wants A Zero" and depicting a Japanese Zero airplane in flames. Williams was stationed at Saufley Field, one of several in the Pensacola complex. Over 10,000 flyers were being turned out each year, and the population of Pensacola had ballooned from 35,000 pre-war to 100,000. Aviation Cadet Williams was in room 423 of Barracks 838.

Boston Red Sox outfielder Ted Williams (center) with some of his Navy and Marine flying comrades at a coffee bar at the Pensacola Naval Air Station.
Courtesy of The Sporting News/ZUMA Press.

Williams was out with the late squadron that day, so didn't get back to barracks until 6:20 p.m. He greeted Finnegan, but one of his bunkmates told him there was a 7 p.m. inspection. Williams hadn't had dinner yet, but said he'd sit down and talk with Finnegan. "Get up and grab a broom!" his roommates yelled. "Cleanup kid," chuckled Ted as he took a batting stance, broom in hand.

Williams had a lower bunk. The barracks was, of course, spartanly furnished, but Finnegan notes that Ted loved to rough it in the outdoors anyway, so the trappings of luxury were little missed. "This isn't the Shoreham," Ted remarked. Twenty minutes later, inspection over, Ted came downstairs wearing a black necktie with his khaki uniform and wearing his regulation overseas cap as well. By the time they reached the mess-hall, it was closed. Ted was famished. "This isn't the Shoreham," Finnegan reminded The Kid.

They set out in search of some grub, and a little brown dog followed close behind. "That's Scuttlebutt," Ted told the Boston reporter. "Here, Scuttle, old boy," he said as he picked up the puppy. Scuttlebutt slept on the second floor of Barracks 838. Ted brought him into the canteen, where flyers from England, France, and Australia joined the Americans grabbing a bite. "Gee, I miss baseball," Ted confided over his hamburg steak and fries. "You know I get the feeling sometimes that I'll never get the chance to play again. When I looked at my roomies, I realize I'm no kid. They're all 20 and 21. I'm 25. And this war won't be over in a hurry." But, he added, "I won't be satisfied with this life until I get myself a Zero. Boy, I thought I got the thrill of a lifetime when I hit that three-run homer in the '41 All-Star Game. Downing a Zero would cap that a hundred times. Lousy Japs, attacking Pearl Harbor and spoiling everything."

Williams was due to be commissioned sometime maybe in April. When he received his commission, he'd be offered a choice – to become an ensign in the Navy or a lieutenant in the Marines. On receiving their commissions, a lot of pilots became instructors. "If I wound up as an instructor," he said with a touch of sarcasm, "the wolves would say, 'I knew it. In the bag. He'll never leave the country.' That's why I want to make the Marines. I'll have no say in the matter. They can send me to the southwest Pacific, anywhere they wish. And whatever they do, I'll have a clear conscience. Ted Williams, Marine lieutenant, flying a fighter. Boy, wouldn't that be something?"

The officers on the base showed some pride in Ted Williams. When told that the Marines were looking for pilots, and they would only accept the top ten percent of the class of Navy pilots, Ted told fellow cadet Ray Sisk, "Let's put in for it." They did, and worked hard. It looked like Ted might make the grade. By the time pilots reached Pensacola, it was pretty clear they weren't going to wash out. "I love to fly," Ted went on. "Had my first taste of formation work this afternoon, and it was fun. You realize I've had over 150 hours in the air already? Yes, sir! Thirty five at Amherst, 115 at Bunker Hill and 16 here. We're flying some pretty heavy ships now."

"Williams Near Death On Take-Off Mistake" – so read the headline in the *Herald* on January 12, 1944. Williams had begun flying in Amherst, in a light plane weighing about 700 or 800 pounds. He had then moved up to a one-ton plane at Bunker Hill. Chapel Hill was all pre-flight work; there had been no flying there. Now at Saufley Field, Ted had a two-ton plane he was flying. "You know, I almost killed myself the other day," he mentioned to Finnegan. "Just about to take off when the instructor saw my wing flaps weren't down. If I had taken off, I wouldn't have been able to gain altitude, and the Sox would have a gold star on their flag. Wouldn't the newspapermen have loved that!" He howled in glee, Finnegan wrote, but then became serious once more.

"Boy, was I burned up at myself. I'm still in a 'D' league as far as flying is concerned. In baseball, you can make a mistake on a pitch, and you've got two strikes left. In this game, one miscue can be fatal. Instructor told me to forget it, that all beginners make 'em. 'That's why you have instructors,' he said. But I should have known better... Bet they're saying in Boston, 'Is Williams going to school forever?' Practice is what counts in flying, just like in batting."

Ted let drop that on a furlough mid-summer, he'd done some fishing up near Rangeley, Maine. He'd only been fishing once since getting to Florida, with the base athletic officer Herman Franks (a catcher with the Dodgers before the war) on the Escambia River. It was time to call it a night, so Finnegan asked about a photo session for the following day. "I'm just a drop in the bucket around here," Ted replied. "Few people know me. Less care. If they see me dropping out of recreation period to pose for a camera, they'll think I'm trying to pull that 'big shot' stuff, and I want none of that. It's tough enough getting by as it is." Ted tried to talk Finnegan into going fishing when he had time off on Christmas Day. "Christmas dinner. Escambia river bass, caught by Finnegan, cooked by Williams!"

If he made it into the Marines, Ted said, he would credit his roomie from Amherst and Chapel Hill, Lou Finger, and also Doc Ewen, his ground school instructor at Amherst. "Boy, was I a dunce when I enrolled at Amherst," he said. Ewen taught him all about wind velocity and the like – and "then he'd take me to the lab and explain why a ball curved, what made it curve. He's explain why a bat of a certain density would drive a ball farther than one of less density. Why a bat of medium weight, swung fast, would drive a ball farther than a heavy bat swung more slowly." So Ted Williams was still learning about hitting as a naval aviation cadet. "Are these professors ruining a .400 hitter?" Finnegan mused in his column. Would Williams "stop to think of wind velocity when trying to hit a curve ball out of the park?"

The day before Christmas, Ted received a package of brownies in the mail from his fiancee's grand-mother. Ted told Huck he didn't have time for evening movies over at the base gym. He always had navigation problems to work on, and was tired by day's end. "If I do get a free half-hour, I usually write to some kids." He got fan letters even on the base. And he kept in touch with kids he'd visited in the hospital back in Boston, kids like Donald Nicoll. He'd autographed a couple of dozen baseballs for the Christmas party for kids who lived with their families at the base. Finnegan shared Christmas dinner with Williams and his mates. Then it was back to business; reveille was at 5:30 the following morning.

Ted Williams coming off the baseball field, Bunker Hill, Indiana.
Collection of Bill Nowlin.

By the time Finnegan returned to the base, Ted had been up and was returning from his running. And Ted got soaked with his first demerits – five demerits and one hour of marching for not making his bed that morning. "Gee, I wanted to go through with a clean record," he groaned. "If a cadet didn't get a demerit once in a while, I'd think there was something wrong with him," said Lt. Cunningham, the man who'd written the notice.

Squadron commander Major Graham H. Benson said that he liked Williams' work. "I had heard of his pop-off reputation in baseball and was looking for some sign of temperament. But he's been here since December 12 and his conduct has been exemplary. He's had chances to pop off, too." He was above average in his studies and his work. "I know he had one 'down' on a solo check, but he went right up and turned in a grand flight." Then the major added, "I believe if you move around the barracks, you'll find Williams pretty well liked by one and sundry. He's in his room every night, plugging away. Never leaves the post, even on his day off. I'm delighted to hear he applied for the Marines, and I only hope he can serve under me as an instructor here after he's commissioned."

Ted had played "about 31" ballgames in 1943, he told Finnegan on the last evening of the visit. He didn't expect to play for Pensacola, though the base did have ball teams – albeit no "varsity.") If Ted didn't play in '44 or '45, did he think he could still come back? Yes, he thought so... he was, in Finnegan's words, "only 25 now, and a fellow doesn't forget all about hitting in a couple of years... 'Look at Hughey Duffy,' laughs Ted. 'He's older than Santa Claus but he can still hit the ball.'" Ted figured that with so many boys in the service, the postwar years wouldn't see as many youngsters entering the game, so returning veterans would have a leg up. "Boy! Wouldn't it be something to grab the East Indies back from the Japs and get that good rubber back again. What fun it

Bronson Bombers ballplayers, all former major leaguers, L to R: Bob Kennedy, Nick Tremark, Ray Stoviak, and Ted Williams. June 1944. The Bombers won eight games in a row in inter-field competition, but lost the ninth in extra innings. The .400 hitter was Tremark, at .413. Williams had the lowest average of the four, at .300.
Official U. S. Navy photograph.

would be to hit then! Give the balata to the Japs, I say!" Finnegan noted that Williams had been hitting homers at a Ruthian pace in 1942 "when suddenly the ball became mush."[1]

The news story resulted in some embarrassment for cadet Williams. Samuel Hynes, who was a cadet himself and later a Marine aviator who logged over 100 combat missions, had remembered Ted from when Ted played in Minneapolis in 1938 and Hynes had been a 13-year-old fan. Now the two were fellow cadets going through instrument training at Whiting Field, a few miles inland from Pensacola. "He was our first celebrity," Hynes wrote in his book *Flights of Passage*. "He didn't want to be that; he clearly wanted to be just another cadet and to live a military life of perfect ordinariness. but there he was, in the next barracks room or on the flight line, a tall thin guy in a flight jacket, one of us. We all wrote home that we were flying with Ted Williams, and felt a little more important because of him, even if we never spoke to him (I never did)."[2]

Nice enough, but for Ted Williams celebrity was not so easily set aside. Hynes recalled the Boston reporter Finnegan coming and getting from Ted "the quite reasonable statement that he wanted to be a fighter pilot." The series was printed after Finnegan had returned back to Boston, but at least one copy of the clippings made it to Whiting – probably from a family of one of the other cadets – and it got posted on the mess hall bulletin board. "That evening, when Williams entered the mess hall for supper, a chant began: 'Teddy wants a Zero, Teddy wants a Zero,' on and on, louder and louder, until Williams left his food uneaten and stalked angrily out." One can imagine his mortification, and anger. Hynes considered he himself had learned a "lesson in the hostilities of ordinary people." After all, he recognizes, "It wasn't his [Ted's] fault, and we all must have known that it wasn't. Sports writers did things like that to decent athletes. What were we punishing him for, then? For being famous? For having an existence out there, outside the Navy? Or simply for being somebody, a person with an identity, when we were all kids, just ciphers?"[3]

It was indeed serious work, training for air combat in which your life would be at stake. The lives of your fellow fliers could depend on you as well. It was work

---

How hard did Ted Williams play for Pensacola?

Ted Williams broke into the majors in 1939, setting a rookie record of 145 runs batted in, a record which has never been topped. In 1941, he hit .406, the last man to hit .400 in the major leagues. The year after that, 1942, Ted won the Triple Crown in the American League – leading the league in average, home runs, and runs batted in. In 1946, he came back after three years of military service and won the Most Valuable Player award, leading the Boston Red Sox into the World Series. He's gone down in history as perhaps The Greatest Hitter Who Ever Lived.

But in the summer of 1944, a 23 year old Naval cadet named Ezra "Pat" McGlothin from Coalfield, Tennessee held Ted Williams hitless for 19 innings in a wartime ballgame in Texas. The great Ted Williams went 0-for-7, and Mac McGlothin had himself quite a game. Not only did he pitch all 19 innings of the 5-4 win, but he drove in the second and third runs, scored the tying run in the 17th inning and then tripled in the winning run in the bottom of the 19th.

Ted Williams was one of three former major leaguers playing for Naval Air Station Pensacola. Buddy Gremp played first base and Bob Kennedy played short. Ted played center field. McGlothin pitched for the Corpus Christi All-Stars of the Naval Air Training Base in the Texas coastal city. The two Naval facilities played a series of games which began with the Corpus crew visiting Pensacola on a Saturday and Sunday. Pensacola took both games, 1-0 and 5-4. The following weekend, Pensacola flew to Corpus Christi for two games. The Saturday game was the long one.

Former major leaguers on the Corpus team were Sam Chapman in center and Johnny Sain (who played about half the game in right field, but pitched the following day).

Corpus Christi was certainly hoping to come back after a fruitless visit to Pensacola the previous weekend, and they took the Saturday game 2-1 with Johnny Sain holding Pensacola to just 4 hits. Gremp, Kennedy and Williams were the 2-3-4 hitters that day and not one of them got a hit, going 0-for-4, 0-for-4 and 0-for-3 respectively. It had been a tight pitcher's duel with Corpus Christi breaking the 1-1 tie in the bottom of the ninth when left fielder Bob Cowsar let Lt. (jg) R. Bergstrom's single get past him.

The ball rolled under the fence, a ground-rule triple. Sam Chapman then rapped a hard grounder between second and short to drive in the winning run. Chapman was also responsible for his team's earlier run in the seventh.

The Sunday game was even harder-fought. Bill Wagner took Cowsar's place in left, but that was the only change for Pensacola. Pensacola scored first, with one run in the second, but Corpus' Sylvester and Kalal both singled and then McGlothin's single brought them both home. Corpus added to its lead in the fourth, with one more run. 3-1. Pensacola added another run in the sixth and then Rurark tied it in the ninth, sending the game into extra innings.

Although Pensacola replaced starter Messina with Heinz and then Petrich – who had pitched the full game the day before – McGlothin threw all 19 for Corpus. The game might have ended in the 14th, but Sam Chapman's throw from center field to catcher Peer cut down Gremp at the plate to retire the side. In the 17th, an error allowed Bob Kennedy to reach base and he was driven in on a single by right fielder Neal, putting Pensacola ahead 4-3, but in the home half of the inning, McGlothin tripled and came in to tie the score on a sacrifice fly to Bill Wagner in left.

Finally, in the 19th, with darkness creeping in, Sain singled to lead off. He'd come in mid-game to play right field. Peer bunted to move him over, but the lead runner was cut down on the fielder's choice. McGlothin was up again. He ended it with a long drive to left center, between and over both Wagner and Williams. The rolled under the fence for another McGlothin triple, easily scoring Peer from first. In 2003, Bill Wagner still remembered the play. "I was playing left field, Williams was playing center, and it went between us. Williams yelled at me, 'You've got it, Wag!' I wasn't even close. That scored the winning run and it ended the game."

McGlothin walked 5 but struck out 13, and scattered 13 hits over the 19 innings. Bob Kennedy had done well off him, going 4-for-9, but Gremp was 1-for-7 and Williams 0-for-7. McGlothin sure showed some stuff. He made the majors briefly in the National League, appearing in 8 games for the Brooklyn Dodgers in 1949-50. His major league line reads 1-1 lifetime, with a 5.60 ERA. His one win in 1949, he jokes, was the margin of victory for the Dodgers, propelling them into the World Series. The Dodgers finished the season with a 97-57 mark, one game ahead of St. Louis, who

which really seemed to capture Williams' imagination. He even ranked baseball second, even though he played for base teams like the Bronson Bombers after he'd left Saufley Field for Bronson Field (both fields were part of the Pensacola complex). "I didn't have my heart in it at all and I played lousy. By this time I was more interested in flying."[4]

Fellow cadet (and ballplayer) Johnny Sain summed up his thoughts about Williams after the war. "I liked him better the more I knew him. I think he made the adjustment from civilian life to service amazingly well. It's not easy for a ballplayer who had been so much in the public eye as Williams to drop into almost complete obscurity suddenly, and I give Ted credit for making the change as well as he did. Only a superman could have done any better." Sain continued, "Williams is naturally smart and he was willing to 'play the game.' He was unjustly criticized in some quarters. What I noted chiefly about him as an airman was that he was never satisfied with himself. Ted was always trying to improve his technique. I imagine that is what makes him such a great hitter. I feel sure that Ted would have made an admirable combat flier and he would have had a chance to prove it had the war lasted another month."[5]

There were so many cadets being trained that a bottleneck of sorts developed – "there were more cadets than there were planes and the program dragged," Ted explained. Leigh Montville found that the Navy issued 61,658 sets of wings between 1942 and 1945. With the rapid mobilization and training, it's not surprising that personnel movement got backed up. At Chapel Hill and maybe again at Bunker Hill, he'd reportedly had the option to take the easier (and safer) route and join a service baseball team, but had declined.[6] There was indeed time to play baseball, but playing ball against other bases may have come to seem a bit obligatory, almost like another assignment. For relaxation, Ted sought rather to find some fishing from time to time, something he was better able to do after he earned his commission.

Ted's actual advanced flight training began on the SNV-1 on 13 December 1943. The first flights were with an instructor, and then Ted piloted flights on his own. By the end of 1943, he had logged another 18 hours.

In January, beginning on the first, Williams put in another 18.2 hours, finally completing 140 hours of link trainer time in mid-February. Beginning on March 1, he really began to build up the hours, primarily flying the SNJ-4 and SNJ-5. By the end of April, he had logged 256.5 hours and earned his rating as an instrument pilot.

INSTRUCTING

Ted made it into the Marines. Ted Williams earned his wings and was commissioned as a second lieutenant in the United States Marine Corps on May 2, 1944 at the Naval Air Training Center, Pensacola. Williams was an officer now. He was designated a "NAVAL AVIATOR (Heavier-than-Air.")

As a second lieutenant, Williams agreed that he did "solemnly swear (or affirm) that I will support and defend the Constitution of the United States against all enemies, foreign and domestic; that I will bear true faith and allegiance to the same; that I take this obligation freely, without any mental reservation or purpose of evasion; and that I will well and faithfully discharge the duties of the office on which I am about to enter; So help me God."

Later that same day, he married Doris Soule at the base chapel. She had taken up work in Pensacola at a beauty shop of some kind. The couple sent a telegram to Ruby Soule, the mother of the bride, in Princeton, Minnesota. Having won his wings, Williams was free to wed. The stricture against students marrying no longer applied.

The United States and its Allies were making good progress in the war, both in Europe and the Pacific, though victory was not assured. The very next month saw U.S. forces land in Normandy. D-Day was June 6, just five weeks after Ted Williams became an officer.

Commissioned on the same day was Raymond Sisk. Sisk and Williams had met as Naval cadets at Chapel Hill, then gone through primary flight school together at Bunker Hill, living in the same barracks. "I admired him going through as a cadet. He had never had algebra or any of this stuff. As a matter of fact, they took 30

were 96-58. Had McGlothin lost that game instead of winning it, the Cards and the Dodgers would have been forced into a playoff.

Ted Williams, as we know, returned to the majors, playing in the other league. Give McGlothin credit for a great performance. Maybe Ted's heart wasn't one hundred percent in baseball, but there can be no doubt that he always tried to blast the ball when he stepped into the batter's box. He was too much of a competitor to do otherwise. Bob Kennedy, asked if the former major leaguers got up for these games, said, "Oh yeah. It was a break from the doldrums of what we were doing. You know, when you get out on that field, you're trying to win."

Interview with Bob Kennedy, January 1, 2004. Thanks to Pat McGlothin and Bill Wagner for interviews on February 7, 2003 regarding this game.

Fellow instructor Jim Stygles remembers one ball Ted hit a long, long way. "Right in Pensacola itself," he explains, "the ballfield was adjacent to the airfield. Chevalier Field. During an All-Navy type game, he hit one ball off Johnny Sain. Sam Chapman was playing center field and he hit it over Chapman's head so far that Chapman was quoted as saying, 'Do you think I want to chase that ball and get run over by those airplanes?' The ball went all the way out to the runway."

Interview with Jim Stygles, April 6, 2004.

The Kid at bat for the United States Navy. Ca. 1943.
Official U. S. Navy photograph.
Courtesy of The Sporting News/ZUMA Press.

of us for the Marine Corps out of 300, and every one of us was a college graduate except Ted. We used to sit down with him and pound it through his head. He [made a real] effort to get through there. Flying... he had no problem flying the airplane. It was just the ground school, and so we'd go in the head after the lights went out and make sure he understood navigation. Ted was collaring a lot of us."[7]

During advanced flight training at Pensacola, each instructor was assigned six cadets and followed that group of six through the training program. Sisk and Williams were in the same group of six. "One of the cadets came up to us one day and said, 'They're looking for Marine pilots out of our class. They'll take ten percent of the class for Marines.' We both applied, and we both got taken. Instead of ensign, we both got commissioned as second lieutenants in the Marine Corps. I went on to advanced flight training over at Jacksonville, Florida and then up with the Marine Corps at Cherry Point. I ended up out in the Pacific. They grabbed him to stay at Pensacola as instructor – because they wanted him to play for the ball team." The next time Williams and Sisk met was to travel from Boston to report for recall into the Marines in 1952.[8]

Col. Edro Buchser flew 101 missions in the Pacific during World War II. He met Ted in Jacksonville, at the BOQ, but "we were never that good a friends in Jacksonville." Buchser and Williams became very close in Korea. He explained how it was about joining the Marines. "We were all Navy cadets, but once you got your wings, the Marine Corps would take you if you volunteered. You had to volunteer. If you didn't, you went in the Navy. Well, I volunteered. As a matter of fact, practically my whole class volunteered for the Marine Corps, but they only take the top ten percent. Same thing that Ted went through."[9]

Sisk, Williams, and the others trained at Saufley Field for three months, then went through a course of instrument flying at Whiting Field and eventually went on to Bronson Field, all fields being part of the same large complex at Pensacola. Sisk tells how it came to be that major league ballplayer Bob Kennedy wound up as their instructor. "As a matter of fact, one thing I always admired Ted for...when we got to Bronson Field, we got a Navy lieutenant and you'd think we'd never been in an airplane before! We came down from one flight and he started to read us up one side and down the other, and finally Ted walked right up to him, nose to nose. He said, 'Listen, you can't chew these guys out just because you don't like me, because I'm a ballplayer!' They went nose to nose, and finally Ted just heads right across the hangar – he's still got his parachute hanging behind him – goes across the hangar, up to the chief flight instructor's office to get rid of this Navy lieutenant. Three days later we got a new instructor. Who was it but Bob Kennedy, who played third base for the White Sox! He became our instructor. He was commissioned about three weeks before."[10]

Kennedy had played out the 1942 baseball season, too, a third baseman and occasional outfielder for the Chicago White Sox. His track through training had moved a little more quickly than Williams' and so he was instructing at Pensacola when Williams first arrived, he explained. "I had Ted as a student when he came down to Pensacola. He came through as a student, as a cadet. I was an instructor. I was in the Marine Corps at that time. He was a Navy cadet." Ted's former adversary in the A.L. was ready when Williams showed up.

"I had my goggles down, so he wouldn't recognize me. I made him carry my chute out to the plane. Then I told the mech, "Tie that big gangly guy in there so he don't fall out!" To stay off the radio, we had a thing called the Gosport where the cadets could hear... I could talk to him, but he couldn't talk to me. I had a little mirror and I noticed that he just had his helmet on and he had the ears all set. Of course, I screamed into that thing, "CAN YOU HEAR ME?" He jerked his head around.

Then I finally turned around and pulled my helmet off and, of course, you know Ted's language! The mechanic thought he was going to be court-martialed for swearing at an officer."[11]

Kennedy continued, "Anyway, we flew. I took him up and we flew. Ted was a good pilot. This was the SNJ. We took fighter tactics in that plane. It was the final stage. We instructed together, and then we went overseas right at the end of World War II."[12] Like Kennedy, Ted had a group of six that he shepherded through the process. "We'd teach the whole syllabus. Landings. Checking air speed. Formation flying. Some stunts to control the plane. Shooting at a fixed target. Shooting at a moving sleeve. Night flying. We taught everything."[13]

Williams put in about thirteen months of instructing at Pensacola, flying Navy SNJs. He was pleased to have the opportunity to work more with the aircraft. The time put in instructing would serve him well in combat, he reckoned.

He and Doris rented a room on Brainerd Street. A local 10-year-old, Ron Reinhardt, remembers playing softball on the streets with the other neighborhood kids. Ted would pitch to the kids. "He'd never hit. He'd pitch for both sides, just enjoying being out there with us."[14]

"He tried to keep to himself as best he could," Ray Sisk said. "He'd take off some weekends, if we had the weekend off, and he'd head up to Alabama fishing some."[15]

Jim Stygles instructed with Ted. "I was transferred over to Bronson. We went from an SNV – which was a fixed landing gear – to an SNJ, which you'd pick the wheels up when you take off and drop them when you're landing. I was 19 and it was like the blind leading the blind. He was already there at Bronson when I arrived. He was an instructor and the kids loved him. He was very, very easy to get along with, and he'd extend himself. He'd do more than most normal guys would. You can teach, and you can yell. I had a couple of guys that were no good. I had this Frenchman from Manchester, New Hampshire and all he did was – from the time you would salute him on the way out, all he would do is bark, bark, bark, bark. Some guys would get in the plane and take off and wouldn't even say hello. This is the way it was. He [Ted] had an excellent reputation."[16]

Stygles was from the Boston area, and met Ted while he was "just moseying around, walking from the BOQ over to the flight line... We went through it all: dive bombing and gunnery and navigation and night flying. Nobody was a specialist in anything."

Len Poth was a cadet, just a few weeks behind Williams. He had just two flights to go before he earned his wings. Both Poth and Williams had exceptional eyesight, and in Poth's case he had been excused from taking the full course of recognition training. Up to that point, in 18 months of training, he had perfect 4.0 scores. His squadron leader told him, "Hell, there's no use in you taking anyone else's time and taking up a seat. We'll just close your record on the recognition training." Poth came home from playing a game against men from Eglin Field, an Air Force base about forty miles away. The next morning, he found his name on a list of cadets being sent to Great Lakes (in effect, being washed out) – this, because he was given a zero on recognition training, having missed the final test. He tried to appeal but wasn't getting anywhere. The skipper wouldn't even see him. Ted saw that he was down, but didn't know why. "What in the hell is wrong with you?" Ted asked.

After he heard Poth's account, Ted swore a few times and then went to Nick Tremark, the officer in charge of the baseball field and asked to be excused to take care of something. About an hour later, Ted came back, grabbed Len and said, "Come on, let's go hit some damn baseballs. You're not going to go to Great Lakes."

Poth learned later that Ted had gone to the captain, unpinning his wings as he walked into the office. "I'm going to make it awful short, captain, because I know you're awful busy, but if Len Poth goes to Great Lakes tomorrow, I'm going with him." Poth chuckled later, "Of course, that was the end of that little episode. They weren't about to send Ted Williams to Great Lakes. If I'd been sent there, eighteen months of training would have been wasted. I didn't have a down."[17]

Poth earned his commission in the Navy, and flew 19 combat missions in the South Pacific before the war was over, including action at both Iwo Jima and Okinawa. Williams had stepped in, gone to bat for Len Poth and, in so doing, both made a contribution to the war effort and helped a fellow aviator fulfill his ambition and ultimately leave the service with a record that offered him justifiable pride in his service to his country.

When Ted became an instructor, he may have helped a number of other cadets win their wings as well. Writing for the California State Military Museum, M. L. Shettle, Jr. explains that "Due to an excess of cadets, instructors were mandated to washout one third of their students. Williams refused to washout good students for the sake of statistics and was called on the carpet for it. He stood his ground and replied: 'If I think a kid is going to make a competent flyer, I won't wash him."[18]

Pensacola and Corpus Christi were the two training centers for turning out Naval and Marine aviators. Lt. Williams was working with students who were still cadets. They'd followed a similar path to his own – already gone through ground school and primary flight. There was a regular curriculum, called Advanced Training. When a cadet finished that particular school, he would receive his wings. Most of the work was flight instruction, with a T-6 type aircraft called the "Texan," built by North American – a two-seat trainer. Students practiced takeoffs and landings, formation flying and gunnery. The aircraft was one of the most widely used aircraft in history. The plane was 29 feet long with a 42-foot wingspan. Cruising speed was 145 mph, and the propeller-driven plane had a maximum speed of 210 mph. It had a range of 629 miles, and a maximum altitude of 24,200 feet. It was the main trainer used by both the Army Air Corps (it was known as the A-6) and the Navy (where it was known as the SNJ).

Williams mostly instructed on the SNJ, but frequently on the N2S-3 as well. Beginning on May 23, he really stepped up the work, now an instructor, no longer a cadet. It was a rare day that he was not up and instructing. In June 1944, Ted flew 54 times. In July, he led 65 flights, and before August was over he'd flown in excess of 500 hours.

Williams felt that instructing helped him become "twice the flier" he might have been. "You learn most teaching others," he said.[19]

What was it like to study under Ted Williams the flight instructor? Another athlete gives us some idea. Frank Maznicki was a famous halfback at Boston College and later played football for both the Chicago Bears and the Boston Yanks. A former major league ballplayer himself – albeit in football – Maznicki also played outfield with Williams on the Bronson Field Bombers in 1944. He played right field, and Ted played center. Their team won the championship at Pensacola, and then went over to Corpus Christi and beat Johnny Sain and his team over there.

Maznicki was inducted into the International Scholar-Athlete Hall of Fame in 2002, and later that year remembered Ted Williams as his instructor at Pensacola. "He was my flight instructor, a very good flyer. He instructed me in instrument takeoffs. You're under a hood and then you line up and you take off. This was a skill that was almost at the end [of a cadet's training], after you've done everything else, then you did instrument takeoffs and stuff. He'd have different students and, one at a time, he'd take them up. He'd explain everything, what you had to do, and then say, 'Go ahead.' If something went wrong, he'd take over. I flew with him three or four times. He was a good instructor, too. He told it like it was."[20]

Bill Churchman instructed together with Williams at Pensacola. Bill had earned his wings over a year before Ted. "Everything about him as a pilot, instructing, was exemplary, because he was... had just great technique as an outstanding pilot, and gunnery in particular. He was older than most of the cadets. I was just 22. I was four years younger. As far as students going through flight training and instructing, he was in the upper tenth in the age category."[21]

Another cadet who had Williams as an instructor was Richard A. Ross, albeit for just one course, in formation flying. "He just told us what he wanted us to do. He said jump so you jumped. He just has this aura about him. He was this big tall, very thin guy, kind of shy, very low key, especially

Bronson Field baseball player Ted Williams signing baseball for fellow servicemen.
Collection of Bill Nowlin.

for a Marine. He was just a nice guy." As the flight was returning to base, Williams' plane broke off from the group of six ensigns. "All of a sudden, he said 'I'll see you later,' and he peeled down into the marsh. He was flying low to the ground, where you have more of a sensation of speed."[22] Ross added that Williams was a legend on the base for target shooting, both with bullets and with rockets. When the group assembled afterwards in the Ready Room, Ted simply said, "That was a good hop, fellas."

Doris Williams was now living in Pensacola, too, but Ted said, "I never see her. Don't even have time to make my bunk around here. They keep a fellow on the hop from 5:30 until 10 p.m."[23] There was time for baseball, though, and a little fishing. As for baseball, however, playing ball may well have felt like more of an obligation to Ted than a pleasure he sought. The brass expected him to play ball, and were pleased when Williams was on their base's team. "I didn't enter the service to play baseball," Ted later told Arthur Sampson. "I wanted to be a combat pilot. Actually, I would have escaped all the baseball in the service if I could have without getting into trouble."[24] When it came to Williams' Korean service, as we shall see, he was indeed able to avoid the pressure to play baseball.

One cadet who didn't meet Ted at Pensacola was Hank Evanish. "I look at the board – the flight board. There's Ted beside me, almost touching me at the shoulder. I was in awe of him. I didn't even say hello to him! There was the great Ted. He looked down at the board and his student flunked. If you pass, you get an arrow facing upward. If you flunk, the arrow goes down. This student's got a down. When Ted saw that, he turned around and there they were [his students] in the middle of the hangar and he went after them. I followed. He wanted to find out about this kid. He said, 'What happened?' 'Oh, this guy, he flunked us.' I'm right behind him. He turns around, back then he goes to the board by the instructor. I tried to get close, but I couldn't hear what he was saying. I can imagine. He wants them passed. The guy's shaking his head, 'No, no, no. I can't do it.' He went to the board, he erased the down arrow and he put down 'INC' – incomplete. Then he went back to tell the fellows that they didn't flunk. And then he walked away. I'm so sorry to this day that I didn't follow him. I should have gone to see him and asked him to get me in the Marine Corps. Everybody loved him, his superiors – he had a lot of influence. To this day, you can't believe how much I suffered [because I didn't take the opportunity to talk with Ted Williams]. Every day, all these years. Every day I think about it. It bothers me."[25]

Williams received a new posting across the state to operational training school at NAS Jacksonville – as it happened, the orders came on the first anniversary of D-Day, June 6, 1945. His posting to Jacksonville was announced on June 2, and from then into early August, Williams went through the Corsair Operational Training Unit at Jacksonville, an assignment in preparation for combat. By this time, though, events were progressing well. The war in Europe had been won – May 8 had been V-E Day. It was now a one-front war. The Pacific theater remained more of a naval war and it remained the Pacific where Williams expected to be sent. Japanese forces were yielding, an island at a time, but no victory was won without fierce resistance. There was every indication throughout June and July, however, that this would continue to be a bloody battle. Landing American troops on Japanese soil might well result in many hundreds of thousands of fatalities on both sides.

Lt. Williams began to take gunnery practice at Jacksonville, flying Corsairs, and his typically excellent hand-eye coordination came through again. Ted Williams set gunnery records that were never broken, and now never will be. The gunnery techniques today are so different that they are no longer comparable to those of sixty years ago. He learned how to fire his plane's guns from wingovers, zooms, and barrel rolls, setting records for hits, reflexes, coordination, and visual reaction time.

His instructor had wartime experience; he'd shot down one Japanese Zero, but bemoaned his own shortcomings: if he could have shot better, he believed he would have bagged eight or ten. "I just couldn't shoot," he said. Ted made sure that he could shoot.

Instructing wasn't any cushy job, Ray Sisk reminds us. "It's a dangerous job, because you're flying with cadets who don't know diddly sometimes. You couldn't tell how they selected instructors. Ted had a real high gunnery record, firing at the sleeve and so forth. [One plane towed a fabric sleeve serving as a target, and an attacking pilot would fire at the sleeve.] Those are the guys they headed out to the fleet, but I'm sure he got grabbed because he was a ballplayer. They had a good time down there."[26] After all, Richard Ben Cramer, asked, "What base commander would give him up as ornament and outfielder?"[27]

And yet Williams, if we take him at his word, found the obligation to play baseball a bit more of an obligation than something he sought. For others, though, baseball offered a refuge. Mel Brookey told Leigh Montville that for some of the young men on service baseball teams, "It was really life or death. Especially before the war ended. If you went 0-for-5, you could have found yourself in Okinawa or Guam."[28]

Sisk was probably right; it wasn't always clear why an officer was designated to serve as an instructor. Maybe they wanted to keep Williams on the air station's baseball team. Surely, though, you had to be very good to be an instructor. It was dangerous, and you had responsibility for the cadet, the aircraft and for yourself. Tim Cohane of *Look* magazine came to the conclusion that merit was central. "During his 38 months' service, Lieutenant Williams, of the Marines, flew 1,100 hours and set a new aviation gunnery record. He was kept out of combat because of his value as an instructor."[29]

Flight training was indeed inherently dangerous. Ted remembered a time in 1944 when three pilots who were in advanced flight training with him were returning back to base in Pensacola. "They tried some kind of hotshot landing, They went in and they were all killed. They were great guys. Young guys. Some of them were five years younger than me."[30]

Williams knew he was fortunate, though, to be serving Stateside. In June 1945, though, as the third season without Ted Williams was well underway, Williams cast a wistful eye toward baseball in a conversation with Lt. Furman Bisher. How did he feel about having to trade in his Red Sox uniform for that of the Marines? "It's a damned shame," he told Bisher. "But it's no more than is happening to anybody else's career. Sometimes I feel that fellows like Bob Feller and me have suffered most, career-wise. We were just before hitting the big dough for a sustained period and now we have had the very heart taken out of our baseball lives. On the other hand, Hank Greenberg and players his age had a chance to lay away a nest egg. I'm not complaining, though. This war is tough on everyone. I've still got two arms, two legs and I'm healthy. For that I'm thankful and I know I'm lucky."[31]

Course completed, Williams headed to the Pacific coast, and was stationed in San Francisco, due to head for the Hawaiian Islands, when war ended abruptly, following the detonation of two atomic bombs, one in Hiroshima on August 6 and the second in Nagasaki on August 9. The Japanese accepted Allied surrender terms on August 15, 1945. Ted was in San Francisco on V-J Day. Three days later, he shipped out for Hawaii. Doris did not make the move to either Jacksonville or Hawaii and remained at their Miami home.

Leigh Montville unearthed an article in the *Boston Globe* by Ruth Montgomery, which suggested that Williams' posting west out of Florida may have been prompted by a gung-ho Marine general.

"Late in the war," Montville writes, "Speaker of the House John W. McCormack, a congressman from South Boston, apparently had asked Marine headquarters in Washington for an appearance by Williams at an Irish event in Boston. A Marine general apparently had spotted the request, called for Williams' file, and discovered that Williams was still in Pensacola. 'We're not running a war to provide any pink teas for congressmen,' was the quote from the unnamed general. 'Why wasn't this fighter pilot sent into combat long ago?' That was how Williams wound up in Honolulu."[32] If so, this general would have been quite unaware of the prevailing practice throughout all the services. Very few ballplayers ever saw combat. It's always possible, though, that the rebuke reached Ted's ears and influenced his later determination to serve in combat when he was unexpectedly recalled to service in Korea in 1952.

His unit may have been scheduled to travel to Pearl Harbor, ultimately to serve in combat in the China-Burma-India theater, but, in any event, Williams was in a delay mode in San Francisco awaiting orders as a replacement pilot when the formal articles of surrender were signed on the *USS Missouri* on September 2, 1945. Three days later, he shipped out for Hawaii for what was now postwar duty.

In Hawaii, Williams trained as a replacement pilot. One Marine he met there was Col. Ben Robertshaw, a 1936 graduate of the U. S. Naval Academy. Years later, Robertshaw was the commanding officer of Marine Air Group 33 in Korea, headquartered at the very base where Williams was stationed. Robertshaw discussed first meeting Ted Williams: "I met him during World War II in Hawaii. He was in a replacement status and had to undergo carrier training before he went any further. I was in operations then, AirFMFPac, that's Aircraft Fleet Marine Force Pacific. We played volleyball almost every day after work, and he participated in that often, along with Ted Lyons. I just worked with him on rare occasions there. The next time I met him was in Korea."[33]

Ted qualified on carrier landings in August 1945, on the F-4U Corsair. By the time he completed his World War II service, Ted had flown an estimated 300 hours as an instructor and well over 1,000 hours in total.[34] Robertshaw was impressed with Williams' serious approach to flying. "He wanted to be assured that his training was qualifying him enough to go forward from there. He was primarily concerned about instrument flying. He approached his commanding officer and they both approached me about his adequacy. I demonstrated to him with other records that he had as much training as anybody else, and that satisfied him." There were intimations that maybe New York Yankees co-owner Dan Topping, in Hawaii at this time, had interceded in some fashion so that Williams could stay in Hawaii and play more baseball. Robertshaw never went to any of the games, he said, but asked directly whether Williams might have been seeking a way to avoid being sent forward, he replied, "Oh, no. No. If you're not well-trained, you let down your fellow pilots as well."[35]

Even though still in active training, Williams did have a chance to play a little baseball in Hawaii. And he was probably starting to get a little restless. After all, the war was over. Hank Greenberg was back playing ball. So was Bob Feller. Williams had put in three years and wasn't really needed in the post-war period. But Bill Dickey headed up the athletic program in Hawaii and the season wasn't quite over when Williams arrived. Ted didn't play much in Hawaii, but he did get into an All-Star Game. *(See next sidebar.)*

John Gunn passed on a report from Sgt. Maj. Bob De Villiers: "I was there on Ewa with Marine Corps aviation, and Williams flew in and landed. The higher officers met and greeted him, and requested him to play for their team that very day. I was close enough on the flight line to hear him say 'Oh God, no, I just flew in' or words similar to that. Anyhow, he really didn't want to. But, within a few minutes, he agreed to play.

"[I] don't remember where the game was, but for some reason the Sub Base seems to come to mind. The field had an extremely short right-field fence. Seemed only 150 feet or so behind first base. But, a screen must have been 60 feet tall.

"His first time up, he hit a screamer that would have been a home run in Boston, but hit the screen for a single there. Later in the game, he hit a high fly ball that would have been an out in Boston, but it was a home run there.

"He remained at Ewa a few months, and when not flying played on the Ewa Marines baseball team. I suppose the operations officer was under constant pressure not to have him flying the afternoon of ball games." [36]

He also did some flying in the Hawaiian Islands. Most of his flights in October were in the Grumman JRF-5 Goose, from Ewa to Kahuku, Ewa to Kahalui, Kahalui to Hilo, and back to Ewa.

Later in 1945, his forward orders canceled, Williams was transferred back to California. On November 19, 2nd Lt. Theodore S. Williams turned in his flight clothing to the 3rd Marine Air Wing facility. His flight goggles, headset, jacket, and gloves, all issued by NAS Pensacola, and all the optional items from flying boots to sunglasses and his carrying bag – even his official issue baseball cap – were all turned in and signed for, duly noted in Lt. Williams' log book. [37]

On December 5, 1945, he was reported to have arrived in San Diego, still in the service. Williams lacked the requisite number of points to have been mustered out immediately, but he expressed confidence that he would be out in time to join the Red Sox for the 1946 campaign. Ed Rumill, noting Ted's arrival back on the mainland, wrote that he expected The Kid to have matured while in the service, and perhaps become a "more likable character." Rumill said that Williams had already "changed considerably for the better just before he joined the Navy. Uncle Sam has probably added the finishing touches." [38]

Lt. Williams was discharged from the Marines on January 12, 1946 at Camp Miramar, not far from his hometown San Diego. He signed with the Red Sox – the first outfielder to sign – and the signing was announced on January 25. A month later, he headed east for spring training and arrived in camp on February 25, ready for the 1946 baseball season.

In June 1945, Ted had told Furman Bisher, "Flying is all right in wartime, and I like it, but when I get out of this uniform I'm NEVER gonna fly again." [39] Upon leaving the service, however, Williams signed up as a reserve in the Marine Corps. With both Germany and Japan suffering such resounding defeats, and with the A-bomb in America's arsenal, Ted could never have suspected he'd be called back to war just six years later.

"Although Ted did not make a contribution to the War in the form of combat, he did have an effect on the War. Every place Ted went he would raise the morale of the men he was with. When men saw the great Ted Williams working hard preparing to serve his country, it made the other men work that much harder. By Ted joining the fight, it showed that no matter how big the celebrity the United States needed to come together as a whole to win the war." [40]

Baseball at Bronson Field

One of the popular songs of the '40s was "Don't Fence Me In." The base newspaper *Gosport* said Williams spoke often of the song because the diamond at Bronson had no fences. He longed for the song "Fence Me In." Williams would hit into many 450-foot outs and go 0-for-4 from time to time.

"They don't come to watch me hit singles," Williams told [fellow aviator Leonard] Poth. "Would it be out of line to see how far I could hit it?" Williams asked Poth.

In a game, Poth said, Williams hit one foul over a radio tower 500 feet from home plate.

John Gunn

1945 ALL-STAR GAME – BASEBALL NAVY WORLD SERIES, HELD AT FURLONG FIELD, HAWAII

There was no All-Star Game in the summer of 1945. But in late September, the service stars of the American League and those of the National League squared off in what might be called a combination all-star game and world series. It was a scheduled, best-of-seven game series, played at Honolulu's Furlong Field in the 14th Naval District. Furlong Field had been built in 1943, right near Pearl Harbor where, less than two years previously, Japanese aircraft had wreaked such destruction.

World War II had ended with the surrender of Japan on September 2, but few of the ballplayers in the service had yet been demobilized. There was a high caliber of players participating, and the games included Ted Williams, Stan Musial, Billy Herman, Bob Lemon, Johnny Pesky, and Bob Kennedy. Gayle Hawes of the *Honolulu Advertiser* wrote that the Navy series would "present more individual stars than even the world series on the mainland... a titanic battle between some of the best known players in baseball." [September 23, 1945] Herman, Musial, and Dick Wakefield had all been selected for the 1943 All-Star Game.

The first game was set for Wednesday, September 26 at 3:30 PM. Additional stands had been erected, programs were printed and all military personnel were "invited to the battle." The National Leaguers worked out at Peterson Field's Aiea Barracks, under the leadership of manager Billy Herman. Herman already had 13 major league seasons under his belt, playing for the Cubs and Dodgers. A future Hall of Famer, Herman and his team were up against Schoolboy Rowe's squad of American Leaguers. Rowe's men drilled at the submarine base.

The announced starting lineups give some idea of the quality of play that could be expected. Most of the men were in decent form, having played a number of exhibition ballgames during their time in the service. The 14th Naval District baseball league season had ended on the 16th, and Billy Herman had been voted the league's MVP, with 83 points, with Johnny Pesky of NAS Honolulu coming in second, with 50 points. Charley Gilbert edged out Eddie McGah by just one point for third place. Leading vote-getter among the pitchers was the Aiea Hospital (and former Brooklyn Dodgers) star Hugh Casey.

The Naval District's All-Star team featured three unanimous choices: Herman, Pesky, and Ship Repair Unit's Stan Musial.

Ted Williams had played only in four games, as had fellow Marine Flyer teammate Bob Kennedy. Both had been transferred to Hawaii later than many of the others. "I'm still a little rusty, but I hope to be ready for this big series," Williams said. "I think every man on our squad is anxious to win, and every one of our boys will be ready to go Wednesday afternoon. It should be quite a series." Bill Dickey agreed. Dickey, the athletic officer of the district, declared that the teams were well-matched and that he was "looking forward to seeing seven games of the best baseball you'll have a chance to see anywhere this year."
Honolulu Advertiser, *September 25, 1945*

Ted was indeed rusty, as he told Vincent X. Flaherty of the *Los Angeles Examiner*. He'd played in about 40 games with service teams in 1943, and about 20 in 1944, but in 1945, he only played seven. "Between you and me, Williams didn't look very good," he told Flaherty. "I couldn't get started." The Sporting News, *February 14, 1946*

Game One (September 26): National League 6, American League 5

WP: Hugh Casey, LP: Bob Lemon

The Advertiser's Hayes picked the American League as favorites. The starting lineups were:

National League	American League
Charley Gilbert CF	Jack Conway 2B
Jim Carlin 3B	Johnny Pesky SS
Billy Herman 2B	Chet Hajduk 1B
Stan Musial RF	Ted Williams RF
Whitey Platt LF	Dick Wakefield LF
Wimpy Quinn 1B	Jack Phillips CF
Ray Lamanno C	Bob Kennedy 3B
Ray Hamrick SS	Rollie Hemsley C
Clyde Shoun P	Freddie Hutchinson P

An overflow crowd of around 26,000 fans watched Game One of the "All-Star Baseball Series." The matchup was a good one. Hutchinson was a key prospect for the Tigers, who had paid the then-enormous sum of $75,000 to purchase him in 1938. Shoun had thrown a no-hitter for Cincinnati against the Boston Braves the year before, on May 15, 1944. Ted Williams, incidentally, wore #23 – not #9 – and Musial wore #14.

Hutchinson started on the mound, the N.L. team batting first. Both teams went down in order in the first. The first scoring was in the second, when Stan Musial led off with a line drive home run over the right field fence. After two outs, Ray Lamanno "smashed a towering drive over the right center field stands." Clyde Shoun surrendered the 2-0 lead he'd been handed, walking Williams in the bottom of the second, giving up a single to Dick Wakefield and then Bob Kennedy hit the first pitch into the left center field seats for a 3-run homer. Both teams put men on base throughout the middle innings, but the only run scored was when the A.L. got one in the sixth. Williams singled to lead off, and moved up to second on a walk to Wakefield. Harris had not started in center for the Americans; Phillips had, and his single would have meant a run – except that Lamanno's throw from behind the plate picked off Ted at second.

Kennedy walked, to load the bases. Rollie Hemsley's single to left just scored one, and neither Hutchinson nor Conway could push a run across.

That score held, 4-2 A. L., until the eighth inning, though the *Advertiser's* Hayes noted a couple of "fancy double plays to halt budding National League rallies."

The N.L. tied it in the top of the eighth. After Charley Gilbert doubled to left, Jim Carlin doubled to right, but Gilbert had to hold at third. Herman hit a sac fly to Williams in right, and Platt lined a single to center, scoring Carlin. Bob Lemon came in to relieve, and threw one pitch to shut down the side. In the ninth, though, Lamanno singled off Lemon's glove, then took second on a sacrifice by Hank Schenz. Up stepped Hugh Casey, who'd come in to pitch the eighth, and doubled to center, driving in Lamanno. Lemon's wild pitch allowed Casey to take third, and he scored a few moments later on Gilbert's sac fly to Ned Harris, who'd taken over for Phillips in center. It was a close play at the plate, and Casey hurt his leg sliding. Lou Tost replaced Casey on the mound, and nearly gave it back to the American Leaguers.

In the bottom of the ninth, now down 6-4, Packy Rogers pinch-hit for Lemon and walked, but was forced at second on an Eddie McGah grounder. McGah was safe, and took second when Herman's throw to Quinn went wild. Johnny Pesky's Texas Leaguer moved him to third, and there were runners at the corner with just one out. Another National error, this time by Carlin, saw McGah score, Pesky take second, and Hajduk safe at first. Up stepped Ted Williams, who'd beaten the National League in the 1941 All-Star Game with a dramatic home run. This time, he hit the ball sky-high but straight up and Lamanno camped under it to make the catch. "In disgust, [Williams] hurled his bat 40 feet in the air, and it almost struck a photographer on the way down," wrote Joe Anzivino for the *Star-Bulletin*. Dick Wakefield struck out swinging on a pitch out of the strike zone.

Game Two (September 28): National League 4, American League 0

WP: Max Wilson, LP: Luman Harris

A.L. manager Schoolboy Rowe expected more from Harris. Pitching for Barber's Point in the 14th Naval District regular season, he had twice had no-hitters going until the eighth inning. The lefthander Wilson, though, had run off a string of seven straight victories for NAS Honolulu, and the A.L. had not fared well against either southpaw Shoun or Tost in the first game. Wilson won, and won handily, holding the A.L. to just one hit, a third inning single by Johnny Pesky which barely landed in front of Musial's glove in right; Musial's throw cut down Johnny as he tried to stretch it to take two bases. The Nationals scored twice in the fourth, once in the fifth and again once in the ninth. Both The Kid and Stan the Man posted identical 0-for-3's at the plate.

Game Three (September 30): National League 6, American League 3

WP: Lou Tost, LP: Hank Feimster

The third game was postponed a day due to heavy rains, but when the two teams played on September 30, it began to look like a National League rout, particularly when they scored four times in the top of the first. The four runs were enough to put the game away, and the A.L. stars didn't score until the bottom of the ninth. Lou Tost threw a complete game for the Nationals, the big blow off him being a Ted Williams two-run homer completely over the right field bleachers. Hajduk had singled before Ted. "We ain't whipped yet," Rowe announced. Even if the Nationals wrapped it up in less than the full seven games, the plan was to play all seven contests. Dick Wakefield had missed games two and three with an injured hand.

Game Four (October 3): American League 12, National League 1

WP: Jack Hallett, LP: Clyde Shoun

After another rainout, the A.L. seemed to summon up the bats and knocked out 14 hits, scoring three times in the bottom of the first to take a lead that pitcher Jack Hallett did not let them relinquish. Shoun had walked Conway and Pesky, and then intentionally passed cleanup hitter Ted Williams after Hemsley had moved both runners up with a sacrifice. Bob Kennedy's single to right center knocked in two. Leading batter on the day was Boston's Johnny Pesky, who went 3 for 3, with a single, a double, and a fifth-inning two-run homer into the right field bleachers. Barney Lutz also hit a two-run homer into right, in the same frame. Both home runs were hit off reliever Wes Livengood. Wakefield was back and went 3 for 4. Musial went 2 for 3, and Williams was 0 for 1. Rowe put himself in the game and banged a long single off the fence in center. Players in those days cared deeply about their league, so it was perhaps true that "the victory had a slight taint" since Hallett was Pittsburgh Pirates property at the time, despite having broken in with the A.L. White Sox.

Game Five (October 5): American League 4, National League 1

WP: Luman Harris, LP: Max Wilson

Now the silent bats were those of the Nationals. Luman Harris went the distance, doling out just three hits and one run, a home run by Carlin in the top of the ninth. He'd had a no-hitter going for 6 2/3 innings. The Americans scored three times in the bottom of the sixth on first baseman Ken Sears' three-run homer with Pesky on third and Kennedy on second (Pesky had bunted safely and Kennedy had doubled). Musial went hitless in four at bats. Williams did not play and, suffering from a bad cold, had lost his voice. The doctor confined him to quarters. Uncharacteristically quiet, Williams whispered that he hoped to be able to play in the sixth game.

Game Six (October 6): National League 4, American League 3
WP: Lou Tost, LP: Ed Weiland

This was a hard-fought game, with Lou Tost winning his second game of the series (and the series itself) over Ed Weiland. Scoreless through four, the N.L. scored once in the top of the fifth and once again the next inning. The Americans came back with one in the bottom of the sixth, and tied it with another in the seventh. After eight full, the score stood 2-2. Hamrick led off with an infield single to deep short, and Pesky's throw to first went astray, letting Hamrick take second. Tost sacrifice bunted him to third. Gilbert took four pitches and walked. Billy Herman had been 0 for his last 11, and after going 0 for 3 on the day, the manager had taken himself out of the game. Hence it wasn't Herman, but Hank Schenz who was up next. Schenz tried to squeeze Hamrick across but fouled off the pitch. The next pitch was a called strike, so he was hitting away on the 0-2 count and banged a two-RBI double into right center. The American Leaguers fought back in the bottom of the ninth. Al Lyons, who had homered in the seventh, hit a terrific drive to center but Gilbert hauled it in at the barrier. Phillips pinch-hit for Bill Marks, and was robbed by Quinn at first. Quinn had made a similar play on Pesky earlier in the game, squelching a rally. Down to their last out, American League manager Schoolboy Rowe put himself in, to hit for Weiland. A decent-hitting pitcher, Rowe connected and drove a home run over the leftfield bleachers. Conway, though, whiffed and the game was over.

Game Seven (October 7): American League 5, National League 2

WP: Bob Lemon, LP: Clyde Shoun

The Americans left feeling a bit better, scoring a decisive 5-2 win in the anti-climactic final game on October 7. Both Phillips and Joe Glenn homered for the A.L. The sole N.L. run was on a home run by Gil Brack, leading off the ninth inning.

Composite batting statistics, minimum 10 at bats:

American League	National League
Hemsley 6 for 15 .400	Lamanno 6 for 14 .428
Pesky 9 for 26 .346	Quinn 9 for 27 .333
Hajduk 4 for 12 .333	Carlin 7 for 25 .280
Kennedy 6 for 21 .286	Platt 6 for 24 .250
Sears 4 for 14 .286	Hamrick 4 for 20 .200
Wakefield 5 for 18 .278	Musial 4 for 20 .200
Williams 3 for 11 .272	Gilbert 4 for 27 .148
Lyons 3 for 12 .250	Herman 2 for 20 .100
Phillips 3 for 12 .250	
Marks 4 for 17 .235	
Conway 5 for 25 .200	

HR

(AL): Glenn, Kennedy, Lyons, Lutz, Pesky, Phillips, Rowe, Sears, Williams

(NL): Brack, Carlin, Gilbert, Lamanno, Musial

RBI

(AL): Kennedy 5, Sears 4, Lutz 3, Pesky 3, Glenn 2, Hemsley 2, Rowe 2, Wakefield 2, Williams 2, Lyons 1, Phillips 1

(NL): Gilbert 3, Lamanno 2, Musial 2, Platt 2, Schenz 2, Brack 1, Carlin 1, Casey 1, Hamrick 1, Herman 1, Quinn 1, Scheffing 1, Tost 1, West 1, Wilson 1

Thanks to fellow SABR member Duff Zwald for researching both the Honolulu Star-Bulletin *and* Honolulu Advertiser *at the author's request.*

POSTSCRIPT

Navy Lt. Jim Dodge was one of cadet Williams' instructors at Bronson Field, giving Ted instruction in both landings and formation flying. Dodge recalls, "He was an excellent student. I can remember that. He was good."

From Milwaukee, Dodge first followed Ted's baseball career beginning in 1938 when Ted played for the Minneapolis Millers. "I saw him play at Pensacola on the Bronson Field team. He was active, except sometimes we'd have to go looking for him. Most of the time, he was out on the bay fishing. In fact, when we played Corpus Christi for the title, he was nowhere to be found. We had all the admirals there, came to see the game, and particularly Williams. One of the chiefs in our squadron said, 'I know where he is. I'll get him.' And he got him out of the bay. He joined us about the third inning, I guess."

The day Ted got his wings, Ted married Doris Soule and Jim Dodge was among those who served as best man. "Nobody knew he was going to get married. There were suspicions. He came in the hangar. It was after his last flight and he was getting his wings. We were in the hangar. I remember somebody saying, 'Are you getting married today?' He said, 'Yeah. I want you all to be my best man.' I was one of about 15 probably. He went off by himself after."

Interview with Jim Dodge, August 7, 2006

NOTES

1) *All material from the Huck Finnegan series in the* Boston Sunday Advertiser *and* Boston American *ran beginning January 9, 1944. The one "down" Ted was assessed was one of only two he ever received. He tells a bit more about it in Williams,* My Turn At Bat, *pp. 102, 103, stating it was the only one he received. His Navy record shows one more.*

2) *Samuel Hynes,* Flights of Passage, *NY: Penguin Books, 2003, pp. 69-70.*

3) *Ibid., p. 70.*

4) *Williams,* My Turn At Bat, *op. cit., p. 103.*

5) Christian Science Monitor, *March 18, 1946.*

6) *See, for instance, Ed Linn's* Hitter, *p. 248.*

7) *Interview with Raymond Sisk, December 18, 2002. Ted's close friend, Gen. Larry S. Taylor, suggests that Ted may have wanted to go out for the Marines for the very reason that the Marines only took the top 10%. The fact that it was more elite may well have appealed to Ted. Communication from Larry Taylor, June 3, 2005.*

8) *Ibidem.*

9) *Interview with Ed Buchser, September 26, 2002.*

10) *Ibidem.*

11) *Interview with Bob Kennedy, January 1, 2004.*

12) *Ibidem.*

13) *Bob Kennedy, quoted in Leigh Montville,* Ted Williams, *op. cit., p. 116.*

14) *Bruce McLellan,* Decatur Daily, *July 2002. Reinhardt also remembered Ted's German shepherd. "He would put a cracker on the dog's nose, and the dog would let it sit there until Ted Williams gave him permission to eat it. Then the dog would flip it up and eat it."*

15) *Interview with Raymond Sisk, op. cit.*

16) *Interview with Jim Stygles, April 6, 2004.*

17) *Interview with Leonard Poth, June 2, 2003. Ted's eyesight was exceptional, by all accounts; though perhaps not that rare statistically, he was able to do exceptional things combining his sight and thought processes – be it spotting ducks in the air, reading the label on a fast-spinning 78 rpm record, or in aviation recognition. The tale of Williams being able to read a spinning phonograph record was said to be a myth, but Arthur Siegel told in the August 21, 1957* Boston Traveler *of a newspaperman named Steve White, who visited with Williams during training at Chapel Hill. White says Williams asked him to put a record on the turntable and then "read the label, all of it. That included the Spanish printing, because the record companies were making a pitch for sales in the Latin-American countries. It was the strangest and most impressive thing I had seen. Here was a man with vision so keen and quick it could slow down the speed, as far as Ted was concerned, of the record. I then could understand why he could swing late and yet generate power."*

18) M. L. Shettle, Jr., "Californians and the Military Ted Williams Baseball Legend, Marine Corps Aviator", *The California State Military Museum.*

19) *Seidel*, Ted Williams: A Baseball Life, *op. cit., p. 138.*

20) *Interview with Frank Maznicki, December 18, 2002. After the war, Maznicki went back with the Chicago Bears and the team beat the New York Giants for the 1946 World Championship – while Williams went back to the Red Sox, who came up just short in their quest for a World Championship of their own.*

21) *Interview with Bill Churchman, April 27, 1997.*

22) *O'Ryan Johnson*, Lawrence Eagle Tribune, *July 6, 2002.*

23) Boston Herald, *January 2, 1945.*

24) *Arthur Sampson*, Ted Williams, *op. cit., p. 104.*

25) *Interview with Hank Evanish, October 21, 2003. Hank Evanish commissioned two larger than life statues of Ted Williams, which were placed in front of the Ted Williams Museum and outside Boston's Fenway Park, both in 2004.*

26) *Interview with Raymond Sisk, December 18, 2002.*

27) *Richard Ben Cramer,* The Seasons of The Kid *(NY: Prentice Hall, 1991), p. 41.*

28) *Leigh Montville,* Ted Williams, *p. 118.*

29) *"Ted Williams, Baseball's Greatest Hitter,"* Look, *October 15, 1946.*

30) *Cataneo, David, "Ted Williams Remembers",* Boston Herald, *May 26, 1997.*

31) The Sporting News, *June 14, 1945.*

32) *Leigh Montville,* Ted Williams, *p. 155.*

33) *Interview with Gen. Louis B. Robertshaw, November 16, 2002.*

34) *USMC Officer Data Sheet completed by Capt. T. S. Williams, April 28, 1952.*

35) *Interview with Robertshaw, op. cit.*

36) *Communication from John Gunn, June 20, 2005. Thanks to Larry S. Taylor.*

37) *Ted Williams USMC Flight Log Book, provided courtesy of Claudia Williams.*

38) *"Teddy Williams in California,"* Christian Science Monitor, *December 5, 1945.*

39) The Sporting News, *June 14, 1945.*

40) *http://home.sandiego.edu/~plucy/page4.html. No author is attributed to this article.*

Lt. Theodore S. Williams and Mrs. Doris Soule Williams in San Diego, January 1946.
Courtesy of the May Williams Collection.

CHAPTER 4 – BETWEEN TWO WARS

For a month after his discharge, Williams and his wife Doris relaxed as both visited Ted's mother in San Diego. Ted got in some fishing, too, on the Salton Sea and on Lake Marina and Lake Otay, both at San Diego. Ted worked out at handball, to help get himself in shape. He'd played some baseball in the service, but Michael Seidel says that Ted did not play nearly as much as a lot of the ballplayers in military uniforms. He'd played about forty games in 1943, maybe twenty in 1944, and only seven in 1945. After becoming a civilian once more, Ted was offered $1,000 per game to play a series of ten exhibition games in the Caribbean in early 1946, but Sox owner Tom Yawkey reportedly countered and paid Ted $10,000 not to play. He didn't want to take chances with his marquee man. Ted got himself in shape, though, and was ready. So were the Red Sox.[1]

When Opening Day 1946 rolled around, President Harry S. Truman and the military leader of the European theatre, General Dwight D. Eisenhower, were both seated in the stands at Washington's Griffith Stadium. They watched Williams pounce on Roger Wolff's 3-2 pitch in the third inning and bang it deep into the Griffith Stadium seats. It was his first game back after three years away, and he hit a home run estimated to have traveled as far as 460 feet.

In 1946, right off the bat, Boston bolted out in front of the field with a stunning start to the season, winning 21 of their first 24 games, and the Sox fairly strolled to the pennant. The immediate post-war years were terrific ones for the Red Sox, but the team never realized its full potential.

Ted was the league's MVP, the first time he'd ever been so honored. The 27-year-old seemingly hadn't missed a beat despite 38 months in the armed services. Many Red Sox players had career years, but Boston failed to grasp the ultimate prize, losing to St. Louis in the seventh game of the World Series.

1947 was a bit of an off year for the team; so many pitchers had sore arms. Williams, though, won the Triple Crown – his second. Only one other player in history had ever won the Triple Crown twice, the National League's Rogers Hornsby. Nearly sixty years later, both Williams and Hornsby remain the only hitters to have earned this distinction.

In both 1948 and 1949, the Red Sox lost the pennant at the last possible moment. In 1948, they ended the regular season tied with the Cleveland Indians – but then lost a single-game playoff held at Fenway Park. In 1949, the Red Sox faced two games with the Yankees at Yankee Stadium to close out the season. It was another tight race, but all Boston had to do was win one of the two and the pennant was theirs. They lost both games.

May Williams and her son, San Diego, January 1946.
Courtesy of the May Williams Collection.

The notion of a curse began to take root. For three of the last four seasons (1946, 1948, and 1949), Boston had blown it, first losing Game Seven of the World Series and twice losing the pennant on the final day of the regular season. How did they summon up the energy to launch into the 1950 season? Refreshingly, Johnny Pesky said it was simple: all they had to do was win one more game than the year before.

Ted won the batting title in 1948, and in 1949 he just missed a third Triple Crown by the narrowest of margins: .0001557 of a point. A ten-thousandth of a point! He was first in homers and first in runs batted in, but was edged out for batting average by George Kell on the final day of the season.

1950 and 1951 were both years in which the Sox came close to another pennant, finishing just four games out of first place in 1950 and, though they faded in '51, they were competitive throughout most of the year.

By 1952, Williams knew he might be headed back to war. Ted was in the Marine Corps Reserve, and after Communist troops had advanced deep into South Korea in mid-1950, the reserves were being reactivated.

In 1948, there had been another event of note. On January 28, Ted first became a father – and that prompted a war of another sort, as the Boston sportswriters sharpened their swords once more. The problem was, Ted was in Florida, fishing, when Barbara-Joyce Williams came into this world in at Boston Lying-In Hospital. To be fair, he had planned to be in Boston for the birth, but Bobby-Jo was born two weeks premature. And the night of the 29th was Boston's annual Baseball Writers' Dinner, which Ted had declined to attend. That may have compounded the sin, in the eyes of the daily chroniclers of things Ted.

When first informed of his daughter's birth, Williams responded with coarse language and didn't react the way one would have hoped. It also took him several days before he finally made it to Boston to see his wife and daughter. That didn't sit well with folks, either. "The hell with public opinion," he told waiting writers when he finally did turn up. Writing about it years later, Ted was still angry (and probably more than a little defensive). "They didn't get word to me for a day. I couldn't get a flight out right away, and by the time I got to Boston I had been tried in the newspapers and found guilty. The crime of the century. One of the papers conducted a man-on-the-street survey to see what 'people' thought of Jack The Ripper. Harold Kaese wrote that 'Everybody knew where Moses was when the lights went out, and everybody knows where Ted Williams was when his baby was born – he was fishing.'"[2] Paul Gallico wrote, "You are not a nice fellow, Brother Williams. I do believe baseball and the sports pages would be better off without you." Far less was made of Ted's departure. "I left a few days later to get back to my fishing."[3] Ted was apparently not ready to be domesticated.

EVENTS IN THE OUTSIDE WORLD

There was baseball, and then there was the rest of life. In the world at large, military matters had never quite calmed down. The rise of Russia as a world power and the prominent role of U.S. forces on two continents (Europe and Asia) found the victors jostling to establish their separate spheres of influence. A new Cold War helped keep the military machine at heightened levels. This was probably good for the American economy, but it was a flawed machine.

At first, Americans thought they could relax and maybe slip back into the sort of isolationism that once seemed feasible to some, America being so well protected by oceans from the troubles of Europe and Asia. The United States was triumphant, the economy operating at a high level of efficiency, and fully and finally out of the depths of the Depression. America had nuclear weapons, and no other country did. Germany and Japan were in ruins, literally in the one case and militarily in the other. Who would dare challenge American supremacy?

Robert Pollard explained that the "pell-mell demobilization of American armed forces after the war demonstrated the underlying strength of neo-isolationism. James Forrestal and Secretary of War Robert P. Patterson, who had replaced Henry Stimson in September, warned Truman in October 1945 that demobilization jeopardized the American strategic position in the world. Truman agreed, but felt that he could do nothing to stop it. In January 1946, Forrestal noted in his diary, the 'Under Secretary [Dean Acheson] said [demobilization] was a matter of great embarrassment and concern to his own Department in their conduct of our foreign affairs.'

"The Truman White House could not contain the overpowering public and bipartisan Congressional outcry – accompanied by riots at overseas military bases in January 1946 – for the early return home of American soldiers... American armed forces shrank from about twelve million in June 1945 to one-and-a-half million in June 1947. Across-the-board cuts of specialists and experienced members of the armed forces eroded the military effectiveness of units even more than these figures would suggest.

"The annual rate of military spending plunged from $90.9 billion in January 1945 to $10.3 billion during the second quarter of 1947. The cessation of hostilities would have prompted defense cutbacks in any case, but the fiscally conservative mood of the country, which Truman and his advisers shared, caused what in retrospect appears a precipitous dismantling of the American military machine."[4]

Others have described demobilization as having occurred in "tidal wave" and "chaotic" fashion, and a lot

Front page of August 16, 1946 *Red Sox Ramblings* produced as free giveaway by Boston Red Sox. Ted Williams and Johnny Pesky posing post-war in a C-54 transport plane.
Collection of Bill Nowlin.

of work went into integrating all the returning servicemen into the domestic work force. Naval commander Guy G. Wooten said that the Navy scrapped or mothballed so many ships, and cut staffs so deeply that "for about two years following V-J Day, any serious overseas crisis would have found the fleet unable to respond."

A U.S. Army Center for Military History report states that "Truman wanted to retain a postwar Army of 1.5 million, a Navy of 600,000, and an Air Force of 400,000. But neither Congress nor the American public was willing to sustain such a force. Within five months of V-J Day, 8.5 million servicemen and women had been mustered out, and in June of the following year only two full Army divisions were available for deployment in an emergency. By 1947 the Army numbered a mere 700,000 – sixth in size among the armies of the world."[5]

There were any number of obstacles to be overcome in the years immediately after the war, from the blockade of Berlin and the resulting Berlin Airlift to "Red" takeovers in countries like Czechoslovakia. The Iron Curtain progressively descended, closing off Eastern Europe and drawing it fully into the Soviet sphere. By 1947, the policy of containment had already been enunciated – Communism was so expansive that it became U.S. policy to contain it within its newly current boundaries. Insurgencies in several countries, like Greece, threatened to extend the reach of the Reds and, if nothing else, proved destabilizing. Within a very few years, by 1949, not only had China become a Communist country, but the Soviet Union had developed and tested its own atomic weapon.

Domestically, someone had to be blamed for the "loss of China" – and Senator Joseph McCarthy of Wisconsin blamed it on traitors from within, on alleged Communists or on "Com-symps" in the State Department and even in the Army itself. The military had already drastically demobilized and, as Stanley Weintraub has written, "our intelligence services were woefully ignorant of the plans and ambitions of other governments. They were far more concerned with Soviet activities than anything in Asia, thus made little effort to trace policy evolutions in the two Koreas and China." Stanley Weintraub argues that the U.S. was also guilty of an "excessive confidence in our air power."[6]

This over-confidence in air power and nuclear deterrent combined to make it seem unnecessary to staff the services at anywhere near wartime levels – even in the very aviation service that purportedly merited such confidence.

The Marine Corps was shrunk substantially, and particularly in Marine aviation. There were thousands of Marines in the Reserves, but were the reserves kept active and in actual readiness? "No, not at all," reports ballplayer Bob Kennedy, talking specifically about Ted Williams and himself. "Neither of us had flown at all."[7]

During World War II, Marine aviation grew to comprise five air wings, formed of 31 groups, 145 squadrons, and 112,626 Marines – aviators and associated support personnel. In particular, Marine pilots had developed the techniques of close air support to produce a very effective component of modern warfare. Historians have written that "Close air support so effectively dislodged dug-in enemy on Okinawa that aviation planners placed more and more emphasis on that mission for the upcoming invasion of Japan." Okinawa had been, however, the last major battle of the war for the Marines. Despite this proficiency, after the war was over, this formidable force was scaled back dramatically. The Marine Corps, in toto, was reduced to 75,000 regulars – including the air units. "Marine Corps aviation was cut to two skeleton wings and barely avoided being absorbed by the new U.S. Air Force."[8]

As a fighting force, the Marines were now no longer active and, Peter Mersky writes, "with the Army taking direct charge, both administratively and physically, of the occupation of Japan, the Marines self-deflated. There were many retirees in the senior ranks; other chose to revert to a lower rank to remain on active duty. Pilots were ordered to serve tours of duty with ground units, unless they wanted to resign."[9]

There was a movement to unify the services right after the war, but it came to naught. There was some progress in preparedness. In 1948, the Marines acquired their first jet aircraft and also their first helicopters. Both were to become important elements in close air support missions in the years that followed. According to Mersky, the first jets were used in World War II, but the Marine Corps was not really furnished jets until between the wars, and basically relied on "outdated Corsairs."

The first Marine squadron with jet aircraft was VMF-311, based in El Toro. Colonel John P. Condon was the first commander of a Marine jet squadron, assuming command in April 1948. It received its "first real Navy jet fighter, the F9F-1 Panther" in February 1950.

And then shortly afterward, in June 1950, Communist forces from North Korea invaded and threatened to overrun the south.

Marines on the ground and Marine Air worked very closely and effectively together, and helped push the North Koreans back – before Chinese troops crossed the border and joined the fray, again driving south of the 38th parallel. It was a war which continued back and forth a bit, but then pretty much settled down to one of fixed positions and outposts, with just forays testing the opposing lines back and forth, back and forth.

A great deal of the carnage in Korea probably could have been prevented by better intelligence and by more appropriate disposition of forces. The inevitable demobilization following the Second World War had gone too far, and hostile forces tested the resolve of Americans to defend their vastly expanded position in world geopolitics.

All the services were under-strength, and still using equipment left over from the Second World War. "Those were cut-back years," said USMC Lt. Col. John F. Bolt. "The Secretary of Defense was Louis Johnson. He was running for the Presidency and trying to make a name for himself. He was not going to cut back the strength of the armed forces, but was going to cut out all the fat. He cut out supply parts, maintenance equipment and specialized tools, so it was really hard to keep the planes flying in those days. Then the Korean War came. We stumbled into it by some political blunders of the Secretary of State and President Harry S. Truman, who were drawing the line for the Russians. The armed forces were down below minimal levels when it started."[10]

A report issued by the American Security Council Foundation concluded that "Exactly one month after he took office Johnson cancelled the so-called 'super-carrier,' the USS United States, which was then under construction in Norfolk. The Defense Secretary took this action without consulting the Congress, Secretary of the Navy John L. Sullivan, or Admiral Louis Denfeld, the Chief of Naval Operations.

"Johnson also wanted to reduce Essex class carriers from 8 to 4; carrier air wings from 14 to 6, and Marine squadrons from 23 to 12. Furthermore, he taunted the Navy by proclaiming that it had 'built its last big carrier.' As the controversy about this decision developed in the newspapers, Johnson threatened to leave the Navy 'with only one carrier for joy-riding by the old Admirals.'

"He also announced that Marine aviation would be transferred to the Air Force. The Secretary of the Army, Gordon Gray, agreed with Secretary Johnson and said the entire Marine Corps should become part of the Army. Johnson's next move was to impose a 'gag order' on his military subordinates."[11]

Michael T. Isenberg explained what followed: "The Navy Secretary resigned. Johnson handpicked the successor. The successor had no qualifications, except that 'in 1948 he had helped deliver Nebraska for the President.' His loyalty was with Johnson, not the Navy. At a time when the Navy needed all the bureaucratic leverage possible, the service found itself on the hit list of the Secretary of Defense and without any protection whatsoever from its top civilian."[12]

Caught unprepared, with Marine aviation having been pared to the bone in the months after World War II, there was a need to call up the Reserves. By the end of the Korean conflict, a USMC History and Museums Division website outlines, the Marine Corps had expanded from the 75,000 cited above to a total of 261,000, "most of whom were Reserves. Complete mobilization of the organized ground reserve had been accomplished in just 53 days, from 20 July to 11 September 1950. Of the Marines participating in the Inchon invasion, 17 percent were reservists. By June 1951 the proportion of reservists in Marine Corps units in Korea had increased to nearly 50 percent, and during the war, 48 percent of all 1st Marine Aircraft Wing Combat sorties were flown by Marine reservists. Between July 1950 and June 1953, approximately 122,000 reservists, both recruits and veterans, saw active duty in Korea."[13]

It was virtually inevitable that Captain Williams' name would come up for review in the process of recall. He was enlisted in the Marine Corps Reserve.

Former Navy commander James Dolan, working as a civilian at Korean air base K-3 during Ted's tenure there, said, "The bad thing about the Marine Corps was that if you had those wings of gold, your ass was in the service in the Korean War. They called up everybody!"[14]

Ted Williams didn't know it, but he was about to be called to war.

NOTES

1) *Seidel,* Ted Williams: A Baseball Life, *op. cit., pp. 138-140.*

2) *Williams,* My Turn At Bat, *op. cit., p. 160.*

3) *Ibidem, p. 161.*

4) *Robert A. Pollard, Economic Security and the Origins of the Cold War, 1945-1950
    (New York: Columbia University Press, 1985), pp. 20-23.*

5) *Guy Wooten, "A Brief History of the U.S. Army in World War II," U.S. Army Center for Military History.*

6) *Stanley Weintraub,* MacArthur's War: Korea and the Undoing of an American Hero *(NY: Free Press, 2000)*

7) *Interview with Bob Kennedy, op. cit.*

8)   *Edwin Howard Simmons and J. Robert Moskin, editors,* The Marines, *(Westport, CT: Hugh Lauter Levin Associates, 1998).*

9)   *Peter B. Mersky,* U.S. Marine Corps Aviation
     (Mt. Pleasant, SC: Nautical and Aviation Publishing Company of America, 1997), third edition, p. 120.

10) Oral history of Lt. Col. John F. Bolt, *collected and edited by Lt. Bruce D. Gamble, USNR (Retired),*
     Naval Aviation Museum Foundation Staff Historian, 1993.

11) "Forrestal, Johnson and the Admirals' Revolt of 1949", *The American Security Council Foundation.*

12) *Isenberg, Michael T.,* Shield of the Republic: The United States Navy in an Era of Cold War and Violent Peace,
     Vol. 1: 1945-1962 *(New York: St. Martin's Press, 1993).*

13) *Information obtained from website of History & Museums Division, USMC.*

14) *Interview with James J. Dolan, February 3, 2003.*

"And the best of luck to both of you," Capt. Julius C. Early, senior medical officer at Jacksonville Naval Air Station, says to Jerry Coleman and Ted Williams after the two ballplayers passed their physical examinations, April 1952.
Courtesy of The Sporting News/ZUMA Press.

Ted Williams Day, April 30, 1952. Ted is
seen holding hands with Pvt. Fred Wolfe,
a veteran injured in the Korean War.
Courtesy of The Sporting News/Zuma Press.

"TED" WILLIAMS DAY

FENWAY PARK
WEDNESDAY, APRIL 30, 1952

Ted Williams Day Program, April 30, 1952.
Collection of Bill Nowlin.

CHAPTER 5 – CALLED BACK TO WAR

Here was Ted Williams, 33 years old with a wife and young daughter, having already devoted 38 months to military service – and when war intensified in Korea, he was called back to active duty.

If he'd enlisted in the Naval Reserve, he wouldn't have been called back, but in the Marine Corps, large numbers of Reserve officers were recalled. The Corps simply wasn't sufficiently staffed to address the need.

Williams had been going through a rough stretch, and this certainly didn't improve his mood. At times, it seemed that Ted was at war with the press or even the fans. In 1950, he'd been tearing up the league. Coming off the '49 season, when he'd just missed the Triple Crown but won the MVP, he was determined to do even better. He may have been trying to pump himself up, get the juices flowing, but on May 17, 1950, Ed Linn writes, he "achieved a pinnacle of boorish behavior, even for him, by responding to the braying of the fans with a time-honored hand gesture of contempt and insult followed by a sudden squall of expert expectorating."[1] It all started when he dropped a fairly easy fly ball. Fans got on him, and their mood grew surlier as the Sox sunk into a 13-0 deficit. Late in the game, in the eighth inning, Ted hit a grand slam, but a grand slam doesn't mean much if your team is down by 13 runs. Linn said "some of the fans seemed to view those four meaningless RBIs as a personal affront, and the abuse came raining down anew."[2] It was in the second game of the day's doubleheader, though, that Ted messed up big-time. The Red Sox were winning game two, and by the thin score of 3-1. It was the top of the eighth and Detroit had the bases loaded. Williams tried to aggressively field a single to left but the ball bounced badly and skittered past Ted, rolling all the way back to the Wall. Like a spoiled kid, Ted took his time chasing down the ball, and only "lobbed it lazily" back in, Linn explains. All three runners scored, giving the Tigers the lead. If there's one thing that Boston fans abhor, it is lack of hustle. The fans really gave it to him. On his way to the dugout, when the inning was over, Williams paused and made an obscene gesture to the crowd not just once but three times, addressing various segments of the crowd.

Ted wrote, after he'd retired, "I have no excuse for the way I acted, for the things I did at certain sensational moments when I couldn't stand it any more and just reacted. Blew up. I am sorry for them, and ashamed, and I would probably do them again if the conditions were the same. That's the way I am."[3] Ted knew himself. These were honest reactions, not premeditated, but they were also angry ones and childish ones. Referring to a later 1956 incident, Ted wrote, "Certainly it was my fault, but when I heard those boos I was steaming." And he explained how what he really couldn't stand were the people who would boo him one moment and cheer the next – in the ninth inning of a scoreless game against the Yankees in Boston, Ted dropped a high fly ball and Mantle was safe at second. Williams was booed. Moments later Ted made a spectacular catch on a Berra liner to end the inning. "Now they were cheering, and that made me madder still because I hate front-runners, people who are with you when you're up and against you when you're down."[4] This time, Ted spat at the fans and, after being walked at the plate, flipped his bat high in the air in disgust – even though his walk forced in the winning run! "Even that made me mad. I didn't want any walk, I wanted to hit the damn ball."[5]

Yawkey fined Williams $5,000 and several sportswriters wrote that Williams ought to quit baseball. Get out of the game. "I think they finally had me on the ropes," Ted wrote. "They really poured it to me." Williams often warred with the writers, and with the fans, or so it seemed. But the fans also came through for him, and the very next night, there was anticipation that the fans would "nail

Williams to the cross." They didn't. "The greatest reception I ever got was that night when I came to home plate. Without question, the greatest reception I ever got. I said to myself right then and there, Boy, these fans are for me. They're showing those lousy writers, and they're showing me."[6]

Gestures notwithstanding, Williams produced at the plate in 1950 and at the All-Star break, he already had 83 runs batted in, fueled in part by his 25 home runs. Project those stats forward and he would have had his most productive season. In the first inning of the 1950 All-Star Game itself, held in Comiskey Park on July 11, Williams crashed hard into the outfield fence as he hauled in a Ralph Kiner drive. He broke his elbow. Only thing was, he didn't know it and tried to play through the pain, playing for eight innings – taking in another Kiner liner in the third, and singling in the go-ahead run for the A.L. in the fifth. But the elbow was broken and he only played 89 games in 1950. His .317 mark would have pleased almost any other batter, but it was the lowest mark Williams had ever registered.

And 1951 didn't feel that much better. He played a full season, appearing in 148 games and led the league in walks, on-base percentage, and slugging, but his average was only .318 (which still placed him fourth in the league). He hit 30 homers and drove in 126 runs – wonderful totals, but it still felt like an off year by the standards he'd set for himself.

After 1951, things began to change. It was Bobby Doerr's last year with Boston. As it happens, Johnny Pesky was traded away mid-season in 1952, Ted went off to war, and Dominic DiMaggio pretty much played out the string.

Just eight days after Williams had broken his elbow in Chicago, the President of the United States authorized the activation of the Marine Corps Reserve. The next day, 20 July 1950, the first 4,830 reservists were recalled. The war proceeded, with more and more reservists being brought back. The Corps had a real shortage of trained pilots, so it began to seem inevitable that Williams would be called.

AN INVITATION

It was on January 9, 1952 that the Marines recalled Ted Williams. It was announced from the start that Ted's second tour of duty was expected to be for 17 months. He was ordered to report to Squantum for a physical on April 2. Squantum was the same base near Boston where he'd in effect been recruited by Whitey Fuller ten years earlier, in 1942. Were he to pass the physical, he would report to Willow Grove, Pennsylvania for eight weeks of refresher training.

Williams had been fishing in Florida when the news arrived. The only address the Corps had was c/o Fenway Park, and so their "letter of invitation" was sent to him via the Red Sox. It was Williams' business manager, Fred Corcoran, who informed Ted that he had been recalled. The exact words that Williams uttered are not known, but one can guess they were a little bluer than those released for public consumption: "If Uncle Sam wants me, I'm ready. I'm no different from the next fellow."

Though Ted had left the Marine Corps as a second lieutenant, he had risen in the ranks while in the Reserves. Williams was promoted to first lieutenant on 28 July 1947. It was an off day in the Sox schedule. He'd had a couple of good days, hitting two homers on the 26th and another one, plus a double, on the 27th. The day after he was promoted, he was up against Bob Feller and the Boudreau Shift (where most of the defensive infielders moved to the right side of the infield, to defend against the pull-hitting Williams) but bunted safely to third base in the ninth inning. Williams had been made a captain in the Corps on 1 January 1951. After his recall in January 1952, uncertain as to how events might unfold, his plan was simply to proceed to spring training and then to report in for his physical as ordered.

It was understood that the Red Sox paid Williams approximately $100,000 a year at the time. The Marine Corps pay for a captain would be $350.00 per month, though Williams would get supplements because of his dependent wife and daughter, his service in World War II, and for food and housing. As an aviator, he also received some additional money for flight pay. He was still taking a huge pay cut, coming at a time that he was worried about his longevity on the ball field. He was, after all, 33 years old and had just posted what were, for him, two sub-par seasons.

The Boston Red Sox team had been built around Williams. If he passed his physical and was taken, it would pretty much doom any hopes the club had to contend in 1952. They had just mailed his contract a few days earlier. Manager Lou Boudreau had said back in October that anyone could be traded, but that if it were Ted Williams, they'd want "at least four or five established stars" for him, and he realized that no club would make such a move. Boudreau declared in December that Williams would not be traded, and Ted expressed relief and gratitude, saying he wanted to finish his career with the Sox.

Now this: a new war! There was the question of whether he would pass the physical, given his shattered elbow from 1950. That he'd played a full season in 1951, and performed so well, made the question more or less moot. There was still some suspense. One can only imagine the feelings that coursed through Ted, or that were felt by Doris at the prospect of having her husband called off to war.

Why was Ted Williams recalled? Was it a simple mistake?

Lt. Theodore S. Williams was one of many Marines recalled, one of "hundreds" according to the first report in the *New York Times* on January 10, 1952. The next day's *Times* reported the recall of two other major league Marines – Jerry Coleman of the Yankees and Lloyd Merriman of the Cincinnati Reds. Coleman would come back as a captain and Merriman as a first lieutenant. Coleman was the 1949 Rookie of the Year in the American League – and it was his hit on the last day of the season which spelled ultimate defeat for the Red Sox.

Coleman was actually playing in a high school ballgame when news of Pearl Harbor arrived during the fourth or fifth inning. Only 17, he was too young to enlist, so he spent 1942 playing for Wellsville in the Yankees' system. He had been very impressed by a couple of Naval aviators who had visited the school earlier in the year, and the morning he turned 18, Jerry applied for the V-5 program. He received his wings on 1 April 1944. Coleman flew the SBD Dauntless in the Pacific and logged 57 missions as a dive-bomber pilot throughout Guadalcanal, the Solomon Islands, and the Philippines during World War II. His unit, VMSB-341, was the first Marine Corps squadron specifically designated for close air support missions.

Merriman, like Williams, had not seen combat but had served in the Second World War. "I was training all the way through in World War II. I went to different training schools but I never got out of the States. I was commissioned and then ended up at Opa Locka in Miami."[7] Like Coleman, Merriman's major league career only began after the war, in 1949.

Ted told David Pietrusza, "When the U.S. went to war in Korea – and it was the right thing for us to do – I was in the Marine Corps Reserves. I loved to fly, oh, how I loved it, and staying in the reserves was a good way to stay in the air. In 1952 they started calling up reservists. Not all of them, but I was on their goddamn list. I was going on 34 years old. I had already served in World War II. I had banged the hell out of my elbow back in 1950. It was a mess. In other words, I didn't think it was fair. I didn't think it was right, to be called up again."[8]

Bob Kennedy said that neither he nor Ted had actually flown while in the reserves. Nor had Jerry Coleman – not once. He'd never even done a weekend stint. And, of course, the point of having a reserve was to be able to recall those who were reservists. But Williams was in the inactive reserves. James G. Fox was a major in VMF-311, one of John Glenn's roommates at Marine base K-3 in Korea. He explained that Ted Williams had "some strong opinions about the politicians for letting the Marine Corps call up the… what shall we call it? The non-active reserve. As long as you're in the reserve, though, you can get called back. There's two kinds of reserves. There's the inactive reserve and then there's the people who fly on weekends, get paid for it, get promoted and stayed active. They got called back, too, but for some reason, they decided that the Marines' organized reserve at the time, if they took them in, they would take them in as organizations at that time and not as individuals. That's a key point. They needed pilots, so they didn't call up the organized reserve until they were going to call them as units. Instead, they called up individuals in the unorganized reserve. There was somebody way up who made that decision not to call up the organized reserve of Marine Corps aviation until they called them as whole units."[9] The policy makes sense; it's unwise to break up a unit. The result in this case, though, was that more individuals were recalled. Today's Marine Corps Reserve has called up far fewer individuals, and the only pilots sent as individuals are filling non-flying billets.[11]

Williams always felt he'd been called back in part because of his fame. Linn writes, "In point of fact, he had little doubt that he and Jerry Coleman had been called up solely for their publicity value."[10] A few years after his Korean service, Williams told a reporter, "If they had called back everyone in the same category as me, I'd have no beef. But they didn't. They picked on me because I was well known."[12]

Another pilot, "Banshee" Bob Johnson, who flew with VMJ-1 out of the same Korean base as Ted Williams, elaborated a bit. "You have to know the Marine Corps. They would use Ted like you wouldn't believe, for publicity purposes. If he'd gone into the Navy Reserve, he wouldn't have been called back, oh hell, no. In fact, when I got my orders, I had my wife and two kids. Really little kids. One had just been born a month before. The other one, we just learned he had to have his eye operated on. The dog had just gotten killed. I'd just torn the furnace out of the basement. And the orders came. Got that picture? I was 29. The orders came and I went to my local Congressman and I said, 'Hey' and I went through all the problems I had.

"So he said he'd get back to me. And here's what he said. Are you ready? He said, 'If you'd been in the Army, or the Navy, or the Coast Guard, I might have been able to do something for you. But you stupid ass, you were in the Marine Corps and I can't do a thing for you.'

"We weren't active at all. I had absolutely zero flight time between World War II and Korea. They had to dig deeper if they were going to accomplish the mission."[13]

John Verdi flew in Ted's squadron in Korea. Outspoken, like Ted, he explained that, "It was Regulars, holding their desk-jobs in Washington, who issued the lunatic orders which recalled Class III (i.e., inactive) Reserves before Class II Reserves (i.e., Drill-Pay OMCR) – many of these latter were not called at all (some, to their credit, volunteered nevertheless.)" Those in the Organized Marine Corps Reserve – the ones who were active and being paid to be in a more advanced state of readiness – were not the ones that were called; the inactive reserves were. Discussing Ted Williams in particular, Verdi wrote in his memoir of the war, "So the first thing you have to understand about Capt. Theodore S. Williams, USMCR is that he should not have been in 311 in 1953. Maybe recall of Ted and people in his MCR Class might have been appropriate by 1955 – had the campaign gone on that long. It was NOT appropriate in 1951-52-53."[14]

Throughout the war, many of the Regulars sympathized with all of those who'd been recalled from the inactive Reserves. They knew they'd been given a raw deal.

Ted was furious, though to his credit, he didn't pop off in public. The Marine Corps had featured Ted's face in a promotional campaign run circa 1949 or 1950, complete with a poster showing Ted in a Red Sox uniform and the words: "United States Marines – Ask the Man Who Was One." Ted felt he had been promised that he would not be recalled, perhaps more or less a tradeoff for allowing them to use his likeness in recruitment campaigns. He also felt that he'd been targeted because he was a noted ballplayer.

He wasn't the only one who objected to the method the Marines used to effect their recall.

Williams would have been pleased had his recall been voided. In *My Turn At Bat*, he tells of meeting "a big cheese man from Ohio, a baseball fan who told me he knew Senator Robert Taft." That didn't help. When the big cheese approached Taft, the word he conveyed back to Williams was, "I have some reservations as to the fairness of it, whether these fellows should be going back, but I don't interfere with a thing like that." Fred Corcoran, who handled Ted's business affairs, spoke with John F. Kennedy, then a Congressman from Massachusetts. JFK told Corcoran he tried to do something, but could not. Ted admitted, "In my heart I was bitter about it, but I made up my mind I wasn't going to bellyache. I kept thinking one of those gutless politicians someplace along the line would see that it wasn't right and do something."[15]

Taft was running for President, and Kennedy for the U.S. Senate. Neither interceded, nor did anyone else. In the 1988 revision of his autobiography, Williams spoke out against the inequities of selective service. If it were an emergency, fine. Everybody goes. "But Korea wasn't a declared war, it wasn't an all-out war. They should have let the professionals handle it. A lot of the professionals on duty for Reserves didn't go. The war in Vietnam was another undeclared war. If I had had a kid in Vietnam I'd have been screaming. The unfairness of the Selective Service is obvious when you know how the draft law and the exemptions work. There's only one way to do it, of course, if you're going to have a draft, and that's to draft everybody."[16]

It wasn't that Ted was against American involvement in Korea. He wrote in *My Turn At Bat*, "I felt we should have been in Korea, just as I later felt we should have been in Vietnam, and I think the Koreans themselves have shown their appreciation, they've been pretty loyal allies. They knew we never coveted any of their territory. That ought to be a message for some people. But I also felt we only half tried to win." He added, "The guys I met in the Marine Corps were the greatest gung-ho guys I ever met. I gripe, but there were guys in there with four kids, right out of the Reserves, too, and I'd hear them say, 'I'm not going to bitch about it, this is the right thing we're doing.'"[17]

And Williams did not bellyache about it, in public, until well after the war was over. He said all the right things for public consumption, though it was never any secret among his fellow Marines how upset he was. He carried it with him throughout his whole Korean War service, and some squadron mates thought he carried it way too far. At least one of Ted's commanding officers seems to have felt that his bitching crossed the line and was destructive of morale.

Was it a matter of singling out the athlete, as Williams expressed, or was it perhaps a mistake? Art Moran, Executive Officer of Ted's squadron in Korea the month Ted arrived and, later in Ted's service, the commanding officer of VMF-311, said that it was a mistake. A few days before Williams arrived in the squadron, Moran's personnel officer told him, "You know about that big hassle that we had in the Marine Corps when Ted got ordered to active duty? I wrote it. I wrote the orders." He told Moran, confirming Ted's understanding, "Hell, I knew that Ted Williams was not supposed to be ordered to active duty. He had been promised by the Commandant of the Marine Corps at the time, at the end of World War II, that if they would let the Marine Corps use his name occasionally – always with prior permission – the Commandant promised him that he would never have to serve another day of active duty. And Ted said, 'OK.' I knew Ted Williams [was] not to be called up, but I had all the cards of the folks who hadn't been called up yet, and here was Theodore S. Williams, and he looked pretty good to me."[18] The name Theodore Williams on an index card hadn't translated to Ted Williams, and once he'd been called, it would have been bad public relations to void the recall.

It was front page news when Ted Williams was recalled. John Gunn reports that "the Washington press corps descended on the Marine Commandant's office. He 'suddenly remembered' he had an engagement in Bethesda, Maryland. Why not speak to the selection board, he suggested to reporters." One of the board was Major Len Fribourg, who later told Gunn that he had served on the five-member board charged with recalling Marine aviators. "We went through 5,000 jackets to see whom to recall. The name Theodore Samuel Williams didn't mean anything to us." Fribourg added, "Even if it had, we would have recalled him."[19] So maybe it wasn't a mistake. Fribourg eventually became a general and served as technical adviser to the film *Sands of Iwo Jima*.

Moran knew there was a real need for trained pilots. Though his squadron was largely spared fatalities, Moran spoke of Marine Air generally, saying, "We lost quite a number of pilots in the Korean war. There were many that were not very well trained because, Jesus, after World War II we really got cut down. There were some times shortly after World War II when our pilots were performing crew chief duties on their own airplanes! And then when the Korean thing hit, naturally we had to call up the reserves again."[20]

Tom Ross, a pilot in sister squadron VMF-115, had gone through flight school with John Glenn. Ross flew 93 missions in Korea, and retired in 1970 as a colonel after 29 years in the Marine Corps. He said, "We didn't really need Ted. Jerry Coleman was another ballplayer that was called up. He wasn't flying jets in Korea; he was in a Corsair squadron. I don't know how many missions he got in, but he had a takeoff accident in a Corsair and was just lucky as hell to survive it. But we didn't really need those guys and I always was sort of ashamed of the headquarters of the Marine Corps for calling them into active duty. I don't know what was prompting them or motivating them to do that."[21]

Ernie Needham was a sergeant who was a flight line leader with VMF-115 from July 1952 to May 1953. He noted that the squadrons were "very, very rank-heavy in the pilots because most of them were Reserves... They called so many of them back and that's why we had so many captains and majors running around. There wasn't that many lieutenants. Right now there would be, but at that time they weren't training anybody. The military was down next to nothing. The younger ones that had been there had rotated home or were rotating back. Then they started digging in and getting these guys like Ted Williams and what's his name? The guy that used to be with Johnny Carson? Ed McMahon, yeah."[22]

The Marines had simply run out of pilots and had to draw on the Reserve. Larry Hawkins, who we will see below is the Marine pilot who saved Ted Williams' life in February 1953, was one of those rare lieutenants. He says, "When I was there initially, we had 13 majors and 14 captains and four flying second lieutenants and one or two first lieutenants. Everybody except the C.O. and probably the operations office and maybe the exec – oftentimes, those were the only regular officers in the squadron. When I first got there [Korea, in November 1952], 35 missions was the average. All of a sudden, somewhere around December or January, they realized that they were running out of pilots because they hadn't taken them for four years, from '46 to '50. And there they had the Reserves called up by this time, and the Reserves had already gone through their allotted amount of strikes. They were hesitating to call them back, so they upped our mission level from 35 to 100. If you got to 100, then you could get a waiver. Korea, there was more stress on you than Vietnam because of the fact that we always had a.a. [anti-aircraft fire] and we were doing a lot of close work. The mission was much longer, because we'd take off and then have to fly 175 miles [from K-3 at Pohang] to get north of the bomb line."[23]

Joe Mitchell was one of Ted's hutmates in Korea. He heard about Ted being recalled the day it happened.

Joe Mitchell, VMF-311, Ted Williams' hutmate, K-3. *Photo by Ted Williams.*

When the Korean War broke out, I was flying in a Phantom squadron down at Cherry Point, and instead of sending me over as a jet pilot at that point, they sent me over to Headquarters, Marine Corps. Headquarters, Marine Corps in those days was up in the Pentagon. I was in the Division of Aviation. We were car pooling in those days and two fellows I was riding with – Tom Tulapane and [Lloyd] Dochterman. Dochterman was on the G-1 end of the business and I was G-4, G-1 being personnel. One night we were getting ready to go home from the Pentagon and Dochterman was late getting out to go home. We said, "What the hell happened to you?" He said, "Gee, I had a heck of a day." He was running down the lists of Marine aviators who were in the reserve – either active or inactive reserve – for recall. If it hadn't been for the reserves, we wouldn't have done very well in Korea because there just weren't enough of us. And Ted Williams popped up on his list.

I don't know all the details or remember the specifications for these guys to be recalled, but anyway he was 35 years old or under. The other guy on his list that day was Tyrone Power, who had just turned 36, I think. Whatever the breakoff was, [Williams] was in the thing and this kind of got Dochterman's attention and he was afraid to just go ahead and mail one to Fenway Park and recall him without checking it out with the brass.

So he went in to see his boss, and his boss and he went in to see General Jerome, who was the Division of Aviation commander. General Jerome said, "Does he meet all the specifications?" "Yes." "Well, send him the... better still..." So he called the Commandant -- as I remember Dochterman's story – and let the Commandant in on it, and the Commandant said, "Well, if he meets all the qualifications, send him an invitation to come back to active duty."

Dochterman had quite a day that day, and I remember he was all rattled up about it. That was the first time I heard about Ted Williams vis-a-vis the Marine Corps. So it wasn't a surprise to me when I heard he had just joined the squadron and moved into my hut.[24]

Others who were recalled, like Jerry Coleman, simply took it as the way it was: "Our numbers came up in this bracket and we were called."[25] Simple as that – though had the Corps trained new pilots from 1946 onwards, they would almost certainly not have been recalled. Had they been in the Navy, they never would have been recalled. When World War II had ended, all Marine pilots were put in the reserve, though one could have taken active steps to be excused and, Coleman says, any such request would have been granted. Neither he nor Ted Williams nor Bob Kennedy, nor any number of other Marines, had taken those steps. They never thought there was going to be another war, nor that they would be recalled. When World War II ended, "I was not discharged," Coleman explained. "I was put on an inactive status. It took a lot of paperwork to be discharged. And if they had asked me, 'Do you want to get out of the service?' I would have said, "No."" And, in fact, after Korea, Coleman joined a VTU (Volunteer Training Unit) and helped do promotional work for the Marine Corps.[26]

The Marine Corps felt compelled to issue a statement exonerating itself, and in the process shifted a bit of the burden onto Williams' shoulders. The January 11, 1952 *Boston Record American* ran a story by Austen Lake saying, "The U. S. Marine Corps today publicly denied that Ted Williams was being 'exploited' in being recalled to active duty – and disclosed that Williams had personally sought the promotion which preceded his recall. Orders for Williams to report for a physical examination in anticipation of a return to duty as a Marine flier set up a howl of protest from baseball fans and led to charges he was being 'shanghaied' back into uniform for his athletic talents and 'name value.'"[27]

The article went on to note that Williams had been notified that in 1951 that he had been selected by a promotion board for advancement from First Lieutenant to Captain. He could have refused the promotion. In fact, he had to take affirmative steps to obtain the promotion – among them, he would have to submit to a physical examination. He did take the physical and "in his own handwriting penned an acceptance of the promotion." It should be noted that the war in Korea was well underway at the time; it's not as though he didn't know there was a war on.

Though it was agreed that Williams had not participated in any training while in the reserve, nor had he gone on active duty with reserve units, Lake continued, "it was explained that he has been active in one phase of Marine Corps activities, and has proved valuable in this respect." What service had he provided? "To aid Marine Corps recruiting, the Red Sox star has posed for recruiting photographs, has 'cut records' used in radio broadcasts to spur recruiting, and has taken part in radio interviews stressing his Marine Corps connection, it was stated officially. Newspaper clippings and other evidence of his activities in this field were sent to Washington, it was stated. Along with his excellent record while in service, these activities presumably aided in his selection for promotion to captain."[28]

So, Ted Williams took time out and lent his name to help the cause and, in part because he did so, he was deemed to have been more active than one might otherwise have concluded given his complete lack of any flight time or other participation. It's easy to understand why he might have felt a little betrayed. On the other hand, many other Marines were called back who had done even less.

The news that Ted Williams was being recalled was indeed a major story and newspapermen descended on the Florida Keys to try to get a few words from Williams himself. Austen Lake, Boston columnist, wrote that Williams rapidly moved about 25 miles further south on the Keys "to escape the hordes of newsmen, photographers and movie crews which are staging a manhunt" trying to locate him. Lake's source in Miami, someone close to Ted, told him, "Ted has been badgered by scores of newsmen for the last two days, and he's afraid he'll say something that will be misconstrued." Given Ted's habitual candor, this was probably a wise fear on his part.

NOTES

1) *Linn*, Hitter, *op. cit.*, *p. 231.*

2) *Williams*, My Turn At Bat, *op. cit.*, *p. 232.*

3) *Ibidem*, *p. 133.*

4) *Ibidem*, *p. 135.*

5) *Ibidem*, *p. 136.*

6) *Ibidem*, *p. 137.*

7) *Interview with Lloyd Merriman, November 16, 2002.*

8) *Williams and Pietrusza*, Teddy Ballgame, *op. cit.*, *p. 96.*

9) *Interview with James G. Fox, February 8, 2003.*

10) *Linn*, Hitter, *pp. 287. 288.*

11) *Communication from Gen. Larry S. Taylor, USMC (Ret.),*
    June 3, 2005.

12) *Ibidem.*

13) *Interview with Bob Johnson, May 31, 2003.*

14) *John M. Verdi*, First Hundred: A Memoir of The Korean War,
    1952-1953, *privately printed, 1989, p. 151.*

15) *Williams*, My Turn At Bat, *pp. 173, 174.*

16) *Ibidem.*

17) *Ibid.*, *p. 176.*

18) *Interview with Art Moran, May 8, 1997.*

19) *Communication from John Gunn, June 8, 2003.*

20) *Interview with Art Moran, May 8, 1997.*

21) *Interview with Col. Thomas Ross, October 1, 2002.*

22) *Interview with Ernest Needham, December 12, 2002.*

23) *Interview with Larry Hawkins, December 21, 2002.*

24) *Interview with Joseph A. Mitchell, February 3, 2003.*

25) *Interview with Jerry Coleman, June 8, 2004.*

26) *Ibidem.*

27) *Austen Lake, "Williams To Report to Training Camp,"*
    Boston Record-American, *January 11, 1952.*

28) *Ibidem.*

29) *Ibidem.*

Among the songs sung in the evening at the O Club at K-3 was "Reserves Lament." The lyrics encapsulate some of the feeling of the recalled reservists on having to serve and to fight in Korea. These songs were composed by Marines in Korea, and neither copyrighted nor published.

RESERVES LAMENT

I can't forget Korea,
I can't forget old Guam

For Syngman Rhee and Joe Stalin
have made me feel at home.

I flew across the bomb line
and got a hole or two

But all I get is a bunch of shit from you, and you, and you!

Chorus:

Oh I was called to risk my ass
and save the U.N., too

But all I get is a bunch of shit from you, and you, and you!

The A.A. was terrific, and the small arms were intense.

While the fly boys bombed the front lines,
the division did the rest.

While the regulars held their desk jobs,
the reserves were called en masse,

For the U.N. knew the Marine Reserves
were the ones to save their ass.

Chorus

I love you, dear old U.S.A. with all my aching heart.

If I hadn't joined the damned reserves,
we'd never had to part

But we won't cry and we won't squawk,
for we are not alone

And one of these days the regulars
will come and we can all go home.

Chorus

Now, we don't mind the hardship,
we've faced them in the past

But we wonder if our Congressmen
have had 40's up their ass.

We have to fight to save the peace,
that's what the bastards said.

But when you check the casualties, you'll find no
Senators dead.

Chorus

I hope to raise a family when this damned war is through.

I hope to have a bouncing boy to tell my stories to,

But someday when he grows up, if he joins
the Marine Reserve

I'll kick his ass from dawn to dusk,
for that's what he'll deserve.

Trading in his baseball uniform for a Marine Corps uniform. Ted Williams Day, April 30, 1952.
Courtesy of the Boston Public Library.

CHAPTER 6 – REPORTING FOR DUTY, AGAIN

Baseball's Opening Day 1952 was on April 15 in Washington. On the second of April, both Ted Williams and Jerry Coleman reported to NAS Jacksonville for Marine Corps physicals as scheduled. Ted took a cab from his hotel, picked up Coleman, and the two turned up together for a ninety-minute exam. Both were found physically fit by the medical board, meeting in the town of Yukon, Florida. Navy Medical Corps Captain Julius C. Early made the announcement. In Williams' case, there had been plans to have an orthopedic specialist check out his elbow, but the examination by the six-person board that Early supervised determined that the specialist was not required. Actually, the examination might have been a little less rigorous, as Jerry Coleman relates with good humor, "Ted started to raise the arm with the elbow he'd broken in the All-Star Game and say, 'Doc, I've got this...' and the doctor patted him a couple of times on the arm and said, 'You're OK.'"[1]

Out to meet with reporters, both Williams and Coleman were introduced to the press as captains in the United States Marine Corps. Williams said, "Well, I'm back in the Marines. I'll try to be a good one... I kind of expected to pass. The only thing I didn't know was if the elbow would meet the requirements. Evidently it does." Ted was instructed to present himself on May 2 at Willow Grove Naval Air Station, Pennsylvania, to begin refresher work. Coleman was to report to Los Alamitos, California.

Coleman said that he felt sorrier for Williams "than I do for myself. After all, if everything goes all right, I'll only be 29 when I get out and if I have to serve only the 17 months now required, I'll still be able to play ball. But Ted will be much older."[2] Ted would be 35.

Ted Williams was the highest-paid player in baseball, with a salary understood to be $100,000 at the time. His pay was now going to be that of a captain, somewhere in the $7,500 range, what with the various allowances. There was some question as to whether Williams might rejoin the Red Sox to play the remaining spring exhibition games and the fourteen regular season games in the schedule before May 2. Ted wanted to play, and both he and Coleman were even optimistic about playing after their scheduled 17-month tour of duty. "I'm praying for a quick truce," Ted remarked, tongue partially in cheek.

Jim Dobbins cartoon *from the* Lowell Sun.

Williams had announced earlier in the year that if he were recalled for active duty, he would probably quit baseball. Something changed, and Hy Hurwitz informed *Boston Globe* readers that "Williams believes that by keeping in good condition... as he always does... that he will be able to return to the Red Sox when he is released." Hurwitz noted that "If Williams loses two more years of major league baseball it will mean that one third of his potential 15-year span in the majors would have been spent in the service. That's quite a chunk out of any one's life, but such great players like Cobb, Collins and Ruth played more than 20 years."[3]

It was noted that neither Coleman nor Williams had flown an airplane in the preceding six years, despite being in the reserves.

Some of the Sox players spoke out. Billy Goodman said, "I can't see how they have to take a guy in who had already done his job. There's not enough written about this... You guys better get on the ball." Mel Parnell added, "I can't understand how they bring back guys like Ted and Jerry Coleman, after all they did before. Boy, it will be rough to come back at Ted's age." And Don Lenhardt chipped in, "Boy, when they take a fellow Ted's age, and a married man with a family, it's murder. We are going to miss him, make no doubt about that."[4]

Tom Monahan, writing in the *Boston Traveler*, had a different take than Hurwitz. Ted told Monahan, "People ask me if I'm through with baseball if I spend two years in the Marines. Offhand, I'd imagine that I'd be done. Oh, sure, I know that Johnny Mize of the Yankees and Walker Cooper of the Braves are crowding 40. But they don't have the same problems that I do. They can report for spring training late – and it doesn't matter if they play every day or not. But I have the responsibility of exhibition games. As long as I'm up there, people will expect to see me in the line-up, and I'll feel they have a right to expect me in there." Spring training becomes tougher as a player grows older. Ted said that he would "play as long as I can before going into the Marines. Then we'll let time take care of the post-Marine future of Williams."[5]

Ted explained that you never know what might come up. "Something might happen between now and May 2 that would postpone my return to the Marines. That's why I'll keep playing. If I stopped playing now and then found that I could continue in civilian life for a while, I'd have lost that much in preparing." And he added, "I'll play out the string before the May 2 reporting date because I'll make more for that than I'll get for two years in the Marines." A stretch of 17 months in the Marines would make him about $11,000 – and it was thought he'd be due about $12,000 for a two-week baseball season.

After the physical, Hurwitz had driven Coleman and Williams back to their hotels in Jacksonville. "We reached Coleman's hotel first. As he departed, Jerry said to Ted, 'Goodbye, Captain. I hope we can get some duty together. Good luck, anyway.' And after Jerry had disappeared into his hotel lobby, Williams stated, 'There goes a great little guy and a great ball player, too.'"[6]

Most fans had no shot at making the kind of money Williams made, but that still didn't prevent them from empathizing with him. "Fans Now Feel Sorry for Ted" read a *Boston Post* headline the day after he passed the physical. The *Post*'s Gerry Hern asked how anyone would think the Marines could have announced that they were taking everyone but the ballplayers. He understood that Williams resented the fact that any inactive Reserves were being recalled, but Hern also allowed that "the opinion here is that Williams would have resented the implication that he wasn't good enough to be considered on his merits as a reserve marine aviator."[7]

A Marine Corps spokesman said there was a strong possibility that both Williams and Coleman would be assigned to fighter squadrons in Korea by the time of the World Series. Lt. Col. William Frash couldn't say that it was certain but "they definitely are taking courses which will ready them for combat." Neither ballplayer uttered anything of a negative nature.

Williams may have had a fiery relationship with the fickle fans and with the "knights of the keyboard," but he never tangled with umpires and he always got along fine with his managers, too. A couple of days before he was due to report for duty, Ted was described by new manager Lou Boudreau: "I never met a more cooperative player in my life. Ted made it easy for me as Red Sox manager... The way he dug in and worked and played has been remarkable."[8]

Ted did fine in spring training, even hitting two home runs in one game during a City Series game against the Boston Braves. The season opened in Washington, and Ted tripled in the eighth inning off the right-center field fence – but maybe he should have pulled up at second. He both pulled a leg muscle and put a strain on his knee while sliding into third base. Mel Parnell shut out the Senators 3-0, letting up just three hits. A pinch runner took Ted's place and scored a few moments later. Ted was 1-for-3 on the day, but missed most of the next few weeks except for four scattered pinch-hitting appearances. One of them produced a hit.

On April 16, Ted pinch-hit for Ted Lepcio in the seventh inning, but struck out. On the 18th, he lined out in the fifth, batting for pitcher Ike Delock. On April 20, in again for Lepcio, Ted singled in the seventh. On April 21, he grounded out for Gumpert, in an eighth-inning pinch-hitting role.

A few days before he was due to report to the Marines, Ted told *Boston Traveler* writer George Carens, "If you ask me to sing a swan song, I'd say the happy memories never will disappear, whatever the future holds. I've never tried to hurt anyone, never criticized any player, and tried to help young players. It would be nice to wake up some morning and find that the whole world is at peace, but in the meantime, the deadline is getting closer, and I'll be ready to go."[9]

Ted's actual orders apparently arrived when he was in Boston. Russ Whipple was a Marine on recruiting duty in Boston, and the one charged with delivering the orders to Williams. "Russ went to Williams' home, knocked on the door and said, 'Captain Williams, I have your orders.' Ted took the envelope from Russ, said, 'Yes, sir,' thanked him and saluted, even though it was not required since the slugger was not in uniform."[10]

TED WILLIAMS DAY – A FAREWELL

When the idea of holding a "Ted Williams Day" was broached, for the April 30 game against the visiting Detroit Tigers, Ted assented to the idea, but said he didn't want any gifts for himself. Organizers of the event, which included Boston's Mayor John B. Hynes and Fire Commissioner Mike Kelleher, promised Ted they'd give Bobby-Jo a bicycle and maybe have a few modest gifts.

Things got a little out of Ted's control, though, and all sorts of well-wishers hopped in. Gifts began to arrive to committee chairman Kelleher from businesses and "leading citizens" from New England and New York. By the time it was all over, there was a "memory book" organized by the Boston Traveler, comprised of 400,000 signatures of fans. And a brand-new light blue Cadillac. Everyone was prepared to praise Ted, or so it seemed.

Except for one person, a sportswriter. Somewhat predictably, his old nemesis Dave Egan ("The Colonel") with the *Boston Daily Record* wrote a column headlined, "Ted Undeserving of Fans' Tribute." This is the same Dave Egan who defended Ted ten years earlier, when Ted was sticking

What they were fighting for: Ted greets Patricia Ann Lewis (3 1/2) at Naval Training Center, Pensacola. She was born at Pearl Harbor and evacuated with her mother after the attack.
Courtesy of the National Baseball Hall of Fame.

to his guns and refusing to cast aside his legitimately earned draft deferment. The same Dave Egan who Ted invited to come with him for an exclusive, when he enlisted in the Navy in 1942. It is rumored that Egan had a problem with alcohol, and he did have a propensity to stir the pot, particularly when it came to Ted Williams. Though he'd been supportive of Williams in 1942, Egan had become an antagonist. His frequent columns blasting Ted Williams – for a variety of reasons – seemed to sell newspapers, and kicking The Kid became his stock in trade.

In his column the morning of Ted Williams Day, Egan decried Williams as a model for youth, complaining that the lesson a young boy could draw from Ted's example was that "even the most indecent gesture will be overlooked, so long as he can hit a baseball with a piece of wood." Egan minced no words: "It seems disgraceful to me, that a person such as Williams now is to be given the keys to the city. We talk about juvenile delinquency, and fight against it, and then officially honor a man whom we should officially horsewhip for the vicious influence that he has had on the childhood of America."[11]

His article on Ted's "Day" never let up. He condemned those who would honor Williams. "Men who call themselves community leaders insult the decent and intelligent fathers and mothers in the community, lavishing honors on a man who, consistently and over a period of many years, has set the poorest possible example to our children, and if this is leadership, I'll have strychnine." He contrasted Williams to Babe Ruth who was no saint but, in Egan's view, at least comported himself well before the children.

"I shall pay no honor to Ted Williams," The Colonel concluded, "for the reason that I cannot honor a man whom I do not respect...Williams has stubbornly and stupidly refused to recognize his responsibility to childhood. The kid has set a sorry example for a generation of kids. He has been a Pied Piper, leading them along a bitter, lonely road. He has done much harm, and now it is one minute before midnight. If this is to be his final hour, then he should capitalize on it by apologizing to all boyhood everywhere, and by telling them that the social niceties are of the utmost importance, if only because they raise man above the level of the beast." So ended his diatribe. Ted Williams was evidently uncivilized and represented the beast, as against human civilization. And he deserved to be horsewhipped (presumably a civilized and appropriate response).

Is it any wonder that Williams warred with writers, when a ceremony honoring him as he went off to serve his country prompted a call for him to be horsewhipped instead? Most other sportswriters wrote the story straight, and credited Williams for returning to military service.

The ceremony at Fenway Park, however, was not marred by any ill will. Both teams, the Tigers and the Red Sox, lined up stretching all the way across the field from one dugout to the other, with Ted positioned at home plate. It was quite an emotional day and, after a number of speeches, all the players and all the fans in the stands all joined hands and sang "Auld Lang Syne." The Tigers and Sox players "joined hands extending across the field to the stands where spectators clasped hands with the players. Ted was in the middle and in this way, he 'shook hands' with everybody in the park."[12]

The lineup of players was configured to appear like a bird's wing, a visual reference to Ted's air service. To Ted's right was a wheelchair-bound veteran, Fred Wolfe, who had been injured in Korea.

Ted spoke to the assembled crowd and "appeared very humble and gracious as he stood there, cap in hand, pawing the dirt with his spikes, as the drama unfolded."[13]

Ted Williams Day saw The Kid enjoy his first start since Opening Day. Ted went 2-for-3. He singled sharply in the first inning. The game progressed and he found himself up again in the seventh with the score tied 3-3. There were two outs and Dom DiMaggio on first base. Dizzy Trout was pitching. Ted hit six home runs off Trout in his career. This was a big one, hit into Fenway's right-field grandstand and putting the Red Sox ahead, 5-3. He'd hit a home run up his last time up before heading off to what was supposed to be a 17-month stretch in the Marines.

On the season, he was now 4-for-10, a perfect .400 average. Though he fell 390 at-bats short of the number required to win the batting title (400), Ted had his second .400 season. He was to have one more in his career.

Ted hit a home run in what might well have been his last at-bat in the major leagues. Jerry Coleman played his last game in Yankee Stadium before a crowd that "stood and cheered long and loud on his final appearance at the plate," and Coleman hit a triple. Coleman planned to come back to the Yankees after his service time. For Williams, Ed Rumill wrote, "the great ovation and turnout for Ted's farewell yesterday may have influenced him to try a comeback when he returns."[14]

Ted hangs up one uniform. April 30, 1952.
Courtesy of The Sporting News/ZUMA Press.

Ted had waved his cap to the fans in several directions, and in the trainer's room well after the game, one of Ted's friends told him, "That was a nice thing you did, waving your cap to everybody especially when you turned and waved to the bleachers. When did you break down and decide to give the fans a break?" Ted replied, "They deserved it, didn't they, cheering me like they did? I never expected anything like that." The friend followed up, "Would you consider, then, that you had finally gotten around to tipping your cap?" "No!" Ted declared. "I'll never do it. I'm sorry, but I never will."[15]

When he left the park a couple of hours after the game, there were still around 500 fans outside, and he had to be led to his car while two mounted policemen helped keep order.

That evening, he invited a number of bellhops, garagemen, and others to a party and dinner – the sort of people whose company he most enjoyed.

Ted took May Day off – not realizing that before the next twelve months were up, he'd be shouting "Mayday!" into his radio as his jet was on fire, and be lucky to escape with his life. And then the next day, he drove to report for duty in Pennsylvania with two friends.

On the morning of May 2, Williams left his abode at the Hotel Shelton to meet up with Ray Sisk and Bob Scowcroft, two Marines from Medford and Needham who had also been recalled. Ted had offered to drive them to Willow Grove, the Marine base to which they were to report before midnight. Willow Grove was located just outside Philadelphia.

Scowcroft had met Ted very briefly once before, ten years earlier. Scowcroft was being sworn into the War Training Service of the Navy back in 1942 – and the swearing-in ceremony took place in left field at Fenway Park! Ted was there, though neither in his baseball uniform nor his own Naval uniform. "When I got called back into the Marines in 1952, we had to get new uniforms and he was using the same tailor I was using. Then he called on the phone to know if I would be willing to drive his car down to Willow Grove. I said, 'Sure, that's very nice of you to call me. My wife will appreciate it because she'll get to use my car.' We were in the same unit there. I was a pilot, too. We had dinner every night for the six weeks we were there. I went to Pensacola and he went to Cherry Point. I was in Corsairs. I never went to Korea. I stayed at Pensacola. I never saw him again."[16]

Ray Sisk had first met Ted as a cadet in pre-flight school in North Carolina back in 1943. They both trained together at Bunker Hill in Indiana and were both in the same flight through advanced training at Pensacola, one of the six cadets in the group. "You had six cadets with one instructor, and you flew with the six guys and the instructor trails you all the time. So I was in the same flight with him; we both got commissioned on the same day. I didn't see Ted again until it came out in the paper that he was being called back to active duty. It came out in the Boston papers that he was being recalled for the Korean War. I told my wife, 'Well, if they've got Ted, they've got me, too!' My orders were in the mail the following Saturday.

"So when he came back from spring training, he called me up and said, 'Hey, did they get you?' So we decided to meet, and we roomed together down there at Willow Grove Naval Air Station."[17]

Ted told Sisk he'd get rid of the reporters and to meet him out on Massachusetts Route 9, at a location near where 128 and 9 join. Did he drive the robin's-egg blue Cadillac he'd just been given at Ted Williams Day? No, that went to his wife Doris, and Ted took her Ford. Sisk and Scowcroft and Williams drove south, to report before midnight. Ted's celebrity preceded them. They stopped at a restaurant in northern New Jersey and were eating hamburgers when Ted was spotted. "Driving down, we stopped at a Howard Johnson's and some little black kid who was in the back room, in the kitchen, looked out and he recognized Ted. He come running out and he wanted his autograph. Ted said, 'Let's get the hell out of here. Everybody will want my autograph.' So we jumped in the car and headed for Willow Grove.

"He had me drive from that Howard Johnson's, because I had been stationed at Willow Grove before and knew where it was. As we came up to the Willow Grove main gate, he said, 'Just drive by, because these reporters down here in Philadelphia are the worst in the world.' We drive by the main gate and there's not a soul in sight except the sentry. So we made a fast U-turn and came back and entered the gate and, jeez, I don't know where the hell they come from but all of a sudden there's about fifteen photographers and reporters waiting for him to arrive."[18]

Sisk and Williams roomed together during refresher training at Willow Grove.

"He was just a regular guy. Hell, when we'd go out on leave – a night off – he'd always pick up the tab. It gets embarrassing. One night in Pennsylvania, about four of us went up to Doylestown for dinner, some place up there. Near the end of the meal, he said, 'I'm going to go call the wife.' We got the waitress and got the check and paid it. Well, he was bullshit! He didn't speak to us for about two days, he was so damn mad that we would pay the check."[19]

NOTES

1) *Interview with Jerry Coleman, June 8, 2004.*

2) The Sporting News, *April 9, 1952.*

3) Boston Globe, *April 3, 1952.*

4) *Ibidem.*

5) Boston Traveler, *April 4, 1952.*

6) The Sporting News, *April 9, 1952.*

7) Boston Post, *April 3, 1952.*

8) Boston Traveler, *April 30, 1952.*

9) *Dick Johnson and Glenn Stout,* Ted Williams, *p. 118.*

10) *Letter to author from Jack Halligan, April 27, 2004.*

11) Boston Daily Record, *April 30, 1952.*

12) *Murray Kramer, "Hollywood End Provided by Ted,"* Boston Record, *May 1, 1952.*

13) Christian Science Monitor, *May 1, 1952.*

14) *Ibidem.*

15) *Ibidem.*
Williams did later tip his cap on a few ceremonial occasions, the last time being at the 1999 All-Star Game, held at Fenway Park.

16) *Interview with Bob Scowcroft, December 20, 2002.*

17) *Interview with Raymond Sisk, December 18, 2002.*

18) *Ibidem.*

19) *Ibidem.*

Ted climbing into aircraft.
Courtesy of The Sporting News/ZUMA Press.

CHAPTER 7 – GETTING INTO JETS, PREPARING FOR COMBAT

As soon as he arrived at Willow Grove, Capt. Williams began an eight-week refresher course in flying. Like many reservists, he hadn't flown a lick since 1945.

Jets were the newest aircraft, the top of the line, and Williams put his name on the list requesting that he be assigned to learn to fly jets.

A very brief AP dispatch noted Ted's arrival back in the Marines. Datelined May 2, it read: "Ted Williams rejoined the Marines today, May 2. Williams, the great Boston Red Sox slugger who forced the opposition to devise a special defense to get him out, arrived at Willow Grove Naval Air Station base this morning to resume his role as a captain flying for the Marines. Williams, a native of San Diego, Calif., bowed out of baseball for at least 17 months and possibly forever."

Would the North Korean and Chinese troops have to devise a special defense against Ted Williams? Well, that might be expecting a little much, but it was noted just a week later that Williams, Jerry Coleman, and Bob Kennedy all expected combat roles. "We've been recalled because the Marines are badly in need of pilots," Kennedy explained. "I've done a bit of checking on my own and I've been told there hasn't been a new Marine Corps pilot commissioned since 1946. The way I understand it, the Marine Corps suddenly came upon a need of pilots in a hurry and found it quicker to recall the World War II veterans than to develop new ones. It looks like we're in it for business. That's why I think Williams, Coleman and I will be in combat within six months if the war still is going on."[1]

Jack McGuckin became commanding officer of Marine squadron 224. In his book *Split Second from Hell*, McGuckin tells of first meeting Williams at Willow Grove: "The orders came in to the detachment for other Marine pilots who had not been in the Reserve Squadrons and had flown no military planes since 1946. One of those to report to us at Willow Grove was Ted Williams, the greatest hitter baseball ever had. When I first saw his orders, my thought was, 'There goes 100,000 bucks a year.' I wondered if he would 'pull any strings' and try to get out of active duty. After all, he had not flown anything for

Jerry Coleman and Ted Williams signing baseballs while visiting base for their physical examinations. April 2, 1952.
Courtesy of The Sporting News/ZUMA Press.

years and could be in a lot of danger starting all over again. He reported as ordered and, as a matter of fact, went for the toughest test of all. He checked out in jets and went to Korea. When I met him there, I wondered why he had to prove anything. He was the best at what he did in baseball, and I suppose his pride refused to let him settle for anything less, even in a war. The drive of pride was more universal than I had ever suspected."[2]

Ted may have still been bitter about the recall, but he'd not unburdened himself with any unfortunate utterances in public. Major James M. Walley served alongside Ted in the same squadron in Korea. He first met Ted at Willow Grove. "As a matter of fact, I was the officer who greeted him when he reported in to the air station there in Philadelphia. Willow Grove. I greeted him, filled out all the papers and then he went back to where he was living. When he reported, he seemed reconciled to the fact that he'd been recalled and that was the way it was. He didn't complain too much to me. He tried to fit in with people very, very well."[3]

Jack Campbell worked closely with Williams at Willow Grove. Campbell had known Ted in Florida a decade earlier. While Ted was instructing at Bronson Field, Campbell was instructing at Saufley Field. Campbell had been recalled in December 1951 and went through refresher training himself, but was once again kept on to instruct others as he had done in the Second World War. He's pretty sure he gave Ted his first jet flight. "I was already instructing when Ted showed up. He wanted to get into jets and I took him up for some instruction. As a matter of fact, I feel certain that I gave him his first jet flight in what the Navy called a TV-2 aircraft.

"Somewhere along the line there, he went on over to another squadron and got him some time in the F9F and was assigned to a squadron. I went overseas fairly soon after that, and I was already in the squadron [VMF-311] when he showed up in Korea.

"I guess I've told 100,000 people that he was just a regular guy. He was an excellent pilot. He was a detail-type pilot. He wanted to make sure everything was exactly according to the book. I couldn't say anything less than that he was just a super-nice guy and, well, he was just accepted as another Marine Corps pilot."[4]

Another pilot Ted had instructed with at Bronson was Jim Stygles. He arrived at Willow Grove a couple of months before Ted, and he's kept a photograph of Ted and the squadron at Willow Grove. "I was the exec of that group. It was a recall, hurry-up, fix-em-up, twenty hours and then get out. That was the principle of the whole thing. You sit in the aircraft for an hour and figure out where everything is – including the relief tube. They had one just between your knees, just in case... long flight and so forth." (There were no relief tubes in jets, but the training at Willow Grove was still with the SNJ's. It was only at his next posting, at Cherry Point, that Ted moved up to jets.)

"We also had Ed McMahon. He was on television and he was telling the people that he was being recalled back to the Marine Corps. It was a rainy day and all the guys were in the BOQ. There was one fellow whose name was Toomey. His nickname was 'Slip It' – Slip It Toomey. He was sitting there and he had his handkerchief out and he was dabbing his eyes, and he says, 'Wait 'til we get ahold of him!'"[5]

Ted and squadron 224 at Willow Grove, PA. 1943.
Courtesy of Jim Stygles.

The Marines didn't waste any time getting Williams back up in the air. He reported for duty on May 2, 1952, was issued his uniform and other equipment, and was aloft for his first flight of refresher training on May 5. Jim Stygles took Ted up three times that day, twice in the SNJ-5 and once in the SNJ-6. Williams was just a passenger on the first flight but then took over the controls from that point forward.

Williams was credited with an even 1,000 hours of flight time brought forward, and began to build hours almost exclusively in the SNJ, except for one flight in the dual-propeller Beech JRB-4 Expeditor on May 8.

Bill Churchman had instructed together with Ted Williams for seven or eight months in Pensacola. Come the Korean conflict, they called back all the single-engine Marine pilots, and Churchman became Ted's instructor at Willow Grove. "If you got your wings at Pensacola or Corpus Christi," he explained, "you were either what was known as a single-engine pilot or a multi-engine pilot. They didn't need any multi-engine, cargo pilots, over in Korea. I had just returned from Korea and – would you believe – I was Ted's instructor at Willow Grove."[6]

In *My Turn At Bat*, Ted recalls how Bill Churchman was the one who urged him to take up jet training. "My old Navy SNV was practically obsolete," Ted wrote.[7]

Churchman recalls pushing Ted towards jets. "I said, 'Christ, you go into a target at 200 knots, come out about 250. In a jet, you can double that.' I gave him his flight instruction at Willow Grove. He was taking what we call retread training. Refresher training. He was, as he always was in everything, very adaptable. We used to horse around a lot, as far as that was concerned. He took about two or three hours of... he hadn't flown a plane since about 1946.

"It only took him two or three hours, sitting in the back seat before he got everything right, where he soloed. We used to practice dogfighting. You go up to about 7,000 feet, you go on collision courses about 1,000 feet apart and then you start scissoring and get up on his tail. The technique is that you fly your airplane almost at stalling speed so you get smaller circles, and then you pounce on the guy who you're fighting. I said to Williams [on the radio], 'Where the hell are you? I can't find you anywhere.' He says, 'Look in your goddamned mirror. I'm right behind you.' He was outstanding."

"Bobby-Jo, who was about a year and a half, two years old, then. She was there with her mother, stayed there. Doylestown, which is a town near there.

"He moved on to Cherry Point. I said, 'When you get down to Cherry Point, for God's sake, don't stay in Corsairs.' I didn't see him again until after the war."[8]

Jerry Coleman says that when he reported to Las Alamitos, he didn't really have a choice. They just told him he was going to be in Corsairs, and he moved on to El Toro. "The last thing we were going to do was play baseball, though," he said. Robert Ruark had written an article critical of the Marine Corps, suggesting that the Marines were trying to build itself a good ball team by recalling these players, and the Corps was very sensitive to anything along these lines. One time someone snapped a photo of Coleman playing for recreation and when it ran, he got the word not to let it happen again. When some Marines in Korea criticized Ted Williams for not paying ball on the base with them, they may not have realized that the Marine Corps itself may have frowned on the idea, and discouraged Williams from playing.[9]

By mid-June, Williams had completed refresher training and reported to Cherry Point, North Carolina for ground school work and a further 90 hours of flying time. He was assigned to an attack training squadron. His group of twelve reserve pilots was primarily training on the Corsair at this time. After one lengthy local familiarization flight in an SNJ on June 17, Ted was up the very next day on a "Fam and bounce" in the single-engine FG-10 Corsair – practicing takeoffs and landings. He also worked a lot on night flying and practiced section tactics and division tactics.

On July 15, Williams began to fly the Lockheed TV-2 and the Beech SNB Navigator. The TV-2 was the first jet aircraft Ted Williams had flown.

Major Jon Mendes instructed Ted at Cherry Point and, like Campbell, also ended up in VMF-311 with Williams in Korea. "I was a reserve officer, and in a reserve squadron and I got called back in September of '51. I had flown missions in dive bombers in the Pacific in the Second World War. When I was called back, I was sent to Cherry Point and I became the Operations Officer of the Fighter Refresher Training Squadron VMFT-20. We also did the transition training from props to jets. We gave five rides in a jet two-seated transition trainer, then they soloed and took a few more flights and a two months' course in flying the F9F Panther, which is the tactical combat plane, the top of the line for the Marine Corps at the time.

"John Glenn came through. He had orders for Korea and he didn't want to go back and fly Corsairs again. He wanted to fly jets. H. E. Smith, who was the C.O. of the squadron knew him and he gave Glenn his jet checkout.

"And then Ted came through. Apparently he had had fighter refresher training at Willow Grove. I first met him when he came to my squadron for jet checkout. I said to myself, 'Well, here's a name character. Since I'm the Operations Officer, I'll take him.' So I took him as a student and I gave him his first five rides.

"I told him on his first ride that I was going to demonstrate slow rolls. I said, 'Now I'm going to show you a slow roll. Remember, in the Corsair, when you get on your back, you've got a big engine up front so you have to push the stick forward to keep the nose up. Well, in the jet, the trainer, there's no engine up there. So you just push the stick over and roll it over and forget about it. It's easy.' The jets had no weight in the front, and if you push your nose forward – push the stick forward – then you break gravity and all the crap in the bottom of the cockpit falls down in your face. I told him about that and said, 'Don't push the stick forward.' Well, sure enough, on that first flight, I demonstrated a slow roll. When he did it, he pushed the stick forward and everything came down. All the dirt came down. But he checked out fine – the five rides – and he went on to fly the F9.

"I guess it was about six or eight weeks later – I'd been there for over a year – I got orders to go to VMF-224. I checked out and when I got to Korea I was assigned to the same squadron that John and Ted were in. 311. John was senior to me by a couple hundred numbers because he graduated six weeks ahead of me at flight school back in '43. Ted was a captain and John and I were both majors. John was the operations officer and I was the assistant. When he went up to fly F-86s with the Air Force, then I took over as operations officer." [10]

VMF-311 was indeed quite a squadron, including as it did both Ted Williams and John Glenn. Then there were Lloyd Merriman and Jack Bolt in sister squadron VMF-115. Bolt was a Marine ace from World War II, who became an ace in Korea as well. Merriman was, like Williams, a major leaguer. He had played over 300 games in three seasons with the Cincinnati Reds (1949-1951). There was also another pilot in VMF-311 who had a baseball connection. Captain Charles E. Street, Jr., the Communications Officer, had joined the squadron on 17 December 1952. His father was veteran major league catcher Gabby Street, who'd played for a number of teams from 1904 to 1912. He'd been Walter Johnson's catcher on the Senators in the years 1908 through 1911, and on August 21, 1908 he caught a baseball thrown from the Washington Monument.[11] The senior Street served in the U.S. Army in both the Spanish American War (1898) and in World War I (1918-19), and after his WWI service was known as "Old Sarge" throughout baseball, particularly when he managed the St. Louis Cardinals to pennants in both 1930 and 1931.

Jon Mendes knew that his training squadron was seen as a plum by many Marine aviators. He concluded that Ted "had enough pull to be sent to my squadron like Glenn did – to be checked out on jets. That's the top of the line." The transition trainer was the TV-2. Mendes explained that the five rides were for familiarization. "I was the operations officer and when he came into the squadron, I said to myself, well, here's a guy we don't want to lose or get hurt, so I better take him myself. I was in charge and I'd been doing it longer than anyone else. He reported and I got his name and put him on the board. We gave him sound ground school – the manual and checkout of the plane, let him walk around and kick the tires until he felt comfortable and then I took him out on his first flight. He responded just as well as any other pilot. There was nothing slow or fast or outstanding or bad. It's a regular routine. You demonstrate it and then they practice it. Dead stick landings. Gliding. It's not complicated but you have to be taught. Once you learn it, then you go to the F9. It's a heavier plane and more complicated, but you learn."[12]

Lt. Gen. Tom Miller agrees that the Ted Williams name might have helped him get placed in 311. "Most every Marine pilot – reserve and active duty – wanted to get into jets, because that was the new thing. I'm sure it was Ted's popularity that managed him to sneak into the jet program."[13]

Jets offered a fascination for Marine pilots who had never flown one. Jim Stygles tells a story of one pilot's risky self-instruction in jet aviation. "Chicky Whelan. He used to be a baseball coach or a scout for one of the major league teams. I guess Chicky got bombed one evening in the club and he went out and he warmed up one of the jets. He took off and he came back, and he comes back to the club. Everybody was looking for him, and looking at him. He goes, 'Those aren't any different from those propeller jobs.' He was very fortunate."[14]

Talk about VMF-311 gets us a little ahead of Ted's progress, though. He didn't join 311 until after leaving the States. Williams began to work with jets in mid-July, as noted, and took his first flight in the F9F Panther with a checkout flight on August 25, 1952. The Panther was the aircraft he would use throughout his combat service in Korea. For the first three weeks of August, he had worked on tactics, bombing and rocketry, and close air support, flying the World War II vintage F6F-5 Hellcat.

Ted was living off-base in Havelock, North Carolina with Doris and daughter Bobby-Jo. Another pilot who went through training at the same time, and wound up in VMF-115 (311's sister squadron in Korea) was Walter Roark, and he gives a bit of a look into Ted's friendship with his fellow pilots. "I was at Cherry Point at the same time. He had a car, you know. Didn't really the rest of us much have cars. The rest of us were lucky to have a damn bicycle to ride around on. But he was OK. I thought he was nice to say, 'Hey, listen, come on out.' I was never a close personal friend, but we'd go to the club for lunch. He'd say, 'You want a lift to the club?' And we'd sit in his car and listen to ballgames on the radio when we could.

Ted reports for duty, May 2, 1952.
Courtesy of The Sporting News/Zuma Press.

He had this Oldsmobile sedan and we'd load that up and go for lunch and listen to the ballgames. We'd sit in that car and talk and listen to the radio. He'd tell us, 'This guy's going to hit it.'"[15]

Ted enjoyed listening to ballgames, but he wasn't interested in playing ball. He was buckling down, trying to learn to fly jets safely and effectively. "They had a baseball team there," he said, "but I wasn't going to be playing any baseball. I had the word on that."[16] His position, very understandably, was that if he was asked to serve in the Marines again, he wasn't going to be playing the sort of exhibitions he had during the Second World War. Playing baseball was his livelihood. If the Marines wanted him, it had to be as a pilot. George Winewriter, a VMF-115 pilot said precisely that. "I used to go by his house down in Miami a lot, over there in South Miami. The big story about Ted was that when they called him back for Korea, they said we had a baseball team out at Quantico that was a very good team and was just about to win everything in the league and they wanted Ted to play baseball as soon as he got there. And he says, 'I get $100,000 for baseball. If I come back to the Marines, I'm going to fly!' That's what he was quoted as saying."[17] He did pose for a promotional photograph next to the famous recruiting poster showing him with the legend, "Ask the man who was one!" Ted held an index card with one word on it, replacing the word "was" with an "is."

After completing flight training with the F9, the group flew to Guantanamo Bay, Cuba, on September 25, and then on to the air station at Roosevelt Roads in Puerto Rico on the 29th for operational training. Williams may have been a day behind, as his log book reflects a flight from Cherry Point to Miami on September 30. In any event, he seems to have logged his next flight on October 15, a "fam flight," and then continued with some CAS (close air support) work. They followed the program there until October 26.

Bill Clem was another pilot who'd flown Corsairs in World War II. He never saw overseas service, spending much of his time ferrying planes coast to coast in the United States. Like Ted, though, he was in Hawaii awaiting forward orders right at the end of the war. He'd been recalled a week after Ted, and reported directly to Cherry Point. By September they were in the same group. There was a heavy training curriculum for these pilots being readied for combat.

"We had a lot of flights per day there," Clem recalls. "Familiarization. Bombs and rockets. Gunnery. CAP – that's combat air patrol. Carrier landing practice. We went on the field, with the wires and stuff. We were going to go out and do some carrier landings, but that's when they shipped us out.

"Section tactics. Dive bombing and rocketry. Vieques [Island in Puerto Rico] – we bombed the hell out of it! They're having a big to-do about that place now, but that's where the Marines would do their training. Landing. We'd go in for close air support practice in gunnery and rockets and so forth. He was good! He was pretty good.

"I remember one thing about being down in Puerto Rico with him. We went to a ballgame one night and, boy, the people went wild when they saw Williams there. It was a couple of local teams. We sat in the very first row. They announced it over the p.a. system. All the people were looking at us. They knew who he was. You see him at a ballgame, it was a big deal. They were big baseball fans down there.

"We went out to dinner a couple of times. He would always take a couple of guys with him. There was another ballplayer down there – Bob Kennedy. Ted gave me some good ideas of what fish to eat.

"Other than that, we just lived in tents on the side of the runway. Right on the edge of the runway. Four-man tents. With a cot. We had a mess hall in a tent. The only thing we had to worry about was the bugs. Practiced a lot of carrier landings. Then we flew back to Cherry Point. We worked there doing the same type of stuff. Helicopter support. Night familiarization. Field landings. Carrier landings. Instruments. Instruments. Instruments. Instruments. We did a lot of training there. And I know he did the same thing. We stayed there until December the 5th or 6th or something like that. At Christmas we had about two weeks off. Then we were out to California right after Christmas."[18]

Williams arrives in Puerto Rico for training, L to R: Matt Kenny, UPI; Ted Williams; Joaquin Martinez Rousset, El Mundo; Turin Lamas, El Mundo radio WKAQ. October 29, 1952.
Photograph courtesy of The Sporting News/Zuma Press.

Ted had a memory of Roosevelt Roads. "I almost landed in a sugar-cane field there one day. It was real windy and I was too high coming in so I just chopped the throttle, a perfectly natural thing for a guy who had been used to conventional piston-type engines. But I chopped too far, and the jet started settling in, and now the wind was pushing me back. I was getting low and I knew I was going to be short of the strip, so I poured the coal to it. What I had forgotten was that the fuel regulators on these jets aren't the same as conventional engines, there's a little time lag, a protective device so you don't flood it out. I was just about into that cane field when the power came and I got that little uumph that put me up. It would have been embarrassing."[19]

Late in October, Ted took a few hops, flying from Rosey Roads to Gitmo (Guantanamo Bay) on the 26th, then from Gitmo to Miami the following day, and Miami to Jacksonville the day after that, finally returning back to Cherry Point.

In mid-November, it was reported that Williams was to be detached from the jet fighter squadron at Cherry Point on December 8 and to report to Marine Corps Air Station El Toro in California by January 2, 1953. He had been "given strafing, rocket and bombing practice, ground schooling, drilling in close air support tactics and practice in oxygen chamber and bail-out trainer and 'dilbert-dunker' methods." Major General Thomas J. Cushman rated his progress as "excellent" and said that "Williams neither asked for nor received special consideration because of his national reputation."[20]

After Captain Williams completed one final flight on December 1, Lt. Col. H. R. Barr, the C.O. of VMF-223 at Cherry Point certified that Capt. Williams met the general requirements for assignment to the overseas replacement draft, qualified in the F9F. There was time off granted between completion of training and reporting to duty again at MCAS El Toro, not far from San Diego.

Soon after arriving at El Toro, the group started preparing for one aspect of life in Korea with a 10-day cold weather training exercise near Bridgeport, California. The Marine Corps Mountain Warfare Training Centre at Camp Pickel Meadows was established in 1951, set up to provide cold weather training for replacement personnel bound for Korea. Jon Mendes recalls, "He went to Pickel Meadows. So did I. Pickel Meadows was cold weather survival training, and every month all the pilots and all the enlisted personnel – replacements for the 1st Marine Air Wing – went to all-weather survival training at Pickel Meadows, which is still in existence today.

"They gave you heavy-duty winter survival clothing and they gave you three C-rations, and you climbed up to 13,000 feet. They gave you half a parachute to build a lean-to or whatever, and you had to survive up there for four days. There were maybe 35, 40 pilots and a couple of hundred enlisted men. I was the senior officer of this group. January or February of '53. This was a great deal. We climbed up with these thermal boots and clothing, and used our parachutes to make tents. We divided in teams of ten and then they had to decide, would they pool their rations to survive, or would they individually keep them? On the second day a transport came over and dropped three pounds of raw meat for each person. If you pooled it, you'd take it all together and make stews and survive. The idea was to let you understand that survival is a team thing, not an individual thing.

"As the senior officer of this group, I had them bring my ski poles and my ski boots up to the top of the mountain so I could ski. I'd been skiing on my way out west. Since I was a real mountaineer and a Boy Scout and all that stuff, this was duck soup to me. I really enjoyed it. It was a great experience, because when we finished up, all these guys realized that survival is a team effort. I have to tell you, when we were finished and we were going back in a bus – back to El Toro – I realized how fabulous that training was, psychologically. To let you realize what it was to survive. If I'd had to punch out over the mountains in Korea, I would have been prepared, somewhat."[21]

There were a couple of weeks at El Toro, before heading up to cold weather training, and Ted and Jerry Coleman shared a few dinners at the PX, but by December, Coleman was off to Korea. Following his transition training on the F-4U Corsair, he was transferred to service with VMA-323 and went on to fly another 63 close air support and interdiction-strike missions in Korea, until he was assigned duties as a forward air controller. As he understands it, Coleman was the only major league baseball player to see combat in both World War II and Korea. In all, he logged 120 missions. Upon retirement in 1964, Lt. Col. Coleman had earned two Distinguished Flying Crosses and 13 air medals. Despite playing as a major leaguer in six World Series for the Yankees, he still says, "The most important part of my life was my time in the service."[22] The next time Williams and Coleman met after El Toro was on the field at Fenway Park.

Ted reported for cold weather training the morning of 14 January 1953 and completed the course on the 23rd. The course was staged out of Camp Pendleton. At this point in Ted's training, the first note of a little discord crept into the recollections of Marines who had trained with Williams. Bill Clem said, "I got along with Ted pretty good. He was stand-offish of course. He didn't mix much with the guys. He didn't do that. He got a little bit of... better treatment, sort of. When we went up there in the cold, in the cold weather training, we had to make a snow hut and live in it all night. He went up and slept in the barracks with the sergeants that were giving us the training, and we didn't like that much. He got a little extra. And he could wear whatever he wanted to... and do all this... which we couldn't.

"Maybe we were too young; he was older than us a little bit. He was four years older than I was. Then in Korea, I flew 86 missions over there. We came over on the same plane, and he came back…he was home by the time of the All-Star Game. We were all mad at him. It was a big deal. He was the big hero being at the All-Star Game and here we're still over there fighting the damn war, and he's home. That didn't sit too good." Clem explained this without any sense of rancor in his voice.[23]

Other Marines, asked about Clem's claim, do not remember it the same way. Jim Stehle called the place "miserable" and added, "He was with us through all of that. I don't think Ted got special treatment."[24] Charles Baker had no recollection of Williams getting any special treatment. He recalled, "We had a break at Christmas, and then we went out to the cold weather just before we left for Korea. Our home base was El Toro, but we all met in San Diego. Some of us rode the bus from El Toro while some others took their own transportation. Ted had rented a car while at El Toro and he drove his car and left it there on the base in San Diego. We all had to ride the bus from San Diego. We were out at Pickel Meadows for the cold weather. That was when we went on our overnight excursion. During that time, he was with another group.

Fragment of F9F-5 aircraft which hit Korean mountain in fog.
Photograph by E. Buchser, who said, "This guy was on instruments in real low clouds - missed approach to K-3 and waved off. Didn't climb enough and hit mountain at approximately 3,000 feet, going approximately 500-600 knots."

"I do remember one time when they gave us parachutes – old parachutes to use for protection or shelter overnight. There were groups of four and in his group, when it was his turn to carry it, he ditched it! Threw it over the side of a hill out there. He said, 'What do we need this thing for? We can do something else.' He just got rid of it. He did come close to getting into trouble at that moment, but I guess as time went on, everybody forgot it. I don't think he kind of went along with cold weather…

"I don't know if my memory is correct, but when we were on the cold weather thing one night, I think Ted was in our group of four. We didn't use the parachute.

We dug a cave and made a cave in there big enough for four guys, and put a little hole up through the top. Before we left the camp, they said, 'If any of you guys want a deer roast, we'll give you one but you've got to take it; don't just throw it away.' This group we were in said, 'Yeah, we'll take it.' They gave us an onion and a venison roast, and we took turns carrying the darn thing. When we got up there the first night and we dug in this cave, we had some rations, mixed the rations and this roast and onion and cooked it in one of our nasty old helmets. Everybody.. that odor came out of this hole up above there, and everybody could smell it. 'Who's cooking that dinner?' In my memory, I have him there but I can't swear to it.

"We were there two nights. We got back the third night. We had to sneak through the security lines or something and got back. Without being captured. I think Ted was there, and that's where we made his acquaintance. Then he let us use his car.

"On the way back, after we finished that training, we were sitting together on the bus going back. As we approached San Diego, there were two of us – Jesse Baird and myself – and Ted, just kind of chit-chatting together. Ted says, 'How are you guys getting back to El Toro?' I said, 'On the bus.' He said, 'Well, I brought my car down. Why don't you ride back with me? Where do you live?' This was on a Friday. Both of us stayed at Laguna, off-base. He stayed at the BOQ at El Toro. He said, 'Well, why don't you just ride with me? Drop me off at the BOQ and you guys take my car and Monday morning when you get back to work, I'll see you.' So Jess and I, we did. We rode back with him and dropped him off. Jess lived in a different house than I did, so he kept the car. We both went back to the squadron on Monday morning and gave it back to him. I always thought that was really neat. Neither one of us had a car. We didn't know how we were going to get from El Toro to Laguna. So that always was a real pleasant memory of old Ted."[25]

Ted didn't have such good memories of cold weather training school. He recalls the days in the Sierras as "living on canned stuff, spruce sprouts for beds, parachute for a tent, and I almost froze my tail off. Sure enough, down with another virus. When we got to Tokyo, everybody went out on the town except me. I stayed in bed for two days feeling lousy."[26]

Korea wasn't going to be any picnic. It was early on in his second tour of duty that Ted had a first-hand reminder of how dangerous flying can be. "One Saturday afternoon, a real pleasant, clear day at Willow Grove, I was warming the top bunk when, swisssssssss, a plane came over the field. Little while later, swisssssssss. The plane again. Finally I got down and looked out and sure enough it was an F9 jet, zooming up the field and flying around raising hell.

"About fifteen minutes later, you could hear the sirens and the fire engines, everything beating it out of the base. I jumped in my car and went after the fire engines, not knowing what had happened. I've always been a fire engine chaser. When I got where the fire engine had stopped, they were trying to put out this fire where a plane had gone down.

"It was the F9. It had come in, exploded and was burning. There were people crowded all around. A big crane was pulling out part of the tail, pulling out part of the engine, pulling out a tire, pulling out this and that, making a hole about thirty feet wide and four to five feet deep. They'd found the canopy off to one side, but they couldn't find the pilot; he'd apparently ejected.

When they neared the bottom somebody said, 'Hey, it looks like the fellow got out; he must be over there someplace.' Then they dragged out a shoe with a foot in it. Oh, Christ, was he mangled. The worst thing I'd ever seen. I saw two guys spin in and crash one time, but they were in one piece.

This guy was crunched."[27]

There was one former major leaguer killed in Korea. It was Major Robert Neighbors of the U.S. Air Force, who was missing in action after his airplane was shot down over North Korea on August 8, 1952. Neighbors was a shortstop who had appeared in seven games for the St. Louis Browns in September 1939. He never faced Ted in a major league game. Neighbors was officially declared dead in 1953, after prisoners of war were repatriated to the United States. Several professional minor league ballplayers were killed. Among them were:

Erwin John Adamcewicz, November 21, 1952, an infielder in the Cardinals system.

William Edward Crago, July 26, 1951, who played for the Dublin club in the Georgia State League.

Leonard George Glica, May 26, 1951, an infielder in the Dodgers system.

James Hudgens, April 21, 1952, an outfielder with San Jose (California League).

Raymond Henry Jankowski, November 5, 1951, a pitcher in the Cardinals system.

Walter Koehler, July 28, 1953, a pitcher with Carthage of the K-O-M League.

John Lazar, September 7, 1951, a pitcher in the Browns system.

Marcel Poelker, September 25, 1951, a second baseman with Muskogee of the Western Association.

Beverly Fred Tschudin, March 14, 1952, a catcher and manager for Tifton in the Georgia-Florida League.

Carl Duane Tumlinson, April 6, 1953, an infielder with Elmira in the Dodgers system.

Charles B. Wilcox, October 8, 1952, an outfielder with Baton Rouge (Evangeline League).[28]

Ted Williams and Bob Kennedy, in the Marines from the Cleveland Indians, in Miami after completing training maneuvers on the F-9F in Puerto Rico, 1952. *Courtesy Transcendental Graphics.*

Ed Linn tells us that Ted wrote to several friends that "he had a strong premonition that he was not going to come back alive."[29] As most baseball fans know, he almost didn't. Columnist Frank Graham of the *New York Journal-American* quoted an unnamed friend from California as having talked to Ted on the eve of his departure for the Far East. "I had a nice visit with him, but I came away from it more than a little depressed. He said he was proud that he was being sent to Korea for combat, which he had missed during the war, because he felt it meant that he had kept up with the kids. Then he said – and this is what I can't get out of my mind: 'I expect to be killed, of course.' He wasn't being maudlin about it. He said it very calmly. He simply had accepted what he was bound to think was his destiny. When I protested, he said: 'Why shouldn't I feel that way? So many are being killed.' Then he laughed and said: 'Don't get me wrong. I'm going to give it a battle – and if I'm lucky, I'll see you in New York one of these days.'"[30]

NOTES

1) Christian Science Monitor, *May 9, 1952.*

2) *Jack McGuckin,* Split Second from Hell, *pp. 70, 71.*

3) *Interview with James Walley, December 7, 2002.*

4) *Interview with Jack Campbell, November 27, 2002.*

5) *Interview with Jim Stygles, April 6, 2004.*

6) *Interview with Bill Churchman, April 27, 1997.*

7) *Williams,* My Turn At Bat, *op. cit., p. 176.*

8) *Interview with Bill Churchman, op. cit.*

9) *Interview with Jerry Coleman, June 8, 2004.*

10) *Interview with Jonathan D. Mendes, November 13, 2002.*

11) Memphis Commercial-Appeal, *March 21, 1965.*
   Interestingly, Williams' childhood hero Charles Lindbergh is reported to have flown with VMF-311 as a civilian adviser during World War II. Montville, Ted Williams, *op. cit., p. 159.*

12) *Interview with Jon Mendes, November 13, 2002.*

13) *Interview with Tom Miller, February 7, 2003.*

14) *Interview with Jim Stygles, April 6, 2004.*

15) *Interview with Walter N. Roark, Jr., December 21, 2002.*

16) *Williams,* My Turn At Bat, *p. 177.*

17) *Interview with George Winewriter, November 28, 2002.*

18) *Interview with Bill Clem, December 23, 2002.*

19) *Williams,* My Turn At Bat, *pp. 177, 178.*

20) Christian Science Monitor, *November 15, 1952.*

21) *Interview with Jon Mendes, December 18, 2002.*

22) *Interview with Jerry Coleman, June 8, 2004.*

23) *Interview with Bill Clem, December 23, 2002.*

24) *Interview with Jim Stehle, February 1, 2003.*

25) *Interview with Charles Baker, December 28, 2002.*

26) *Williams,* My Turn At Bat, *p. 178.*

27) *Ibid., pp. 176, 177.*

28) *Phillips, John,* Baseball Goes To War *(Kathleen, GA: John Phillips, 2003), pp. 18, 19.*

29) *Linn,* Hitter, *op. cit., p. 248.*

30) New York Journal-American, *March 28, 1953.*

Receiving instruction on instrument panel, February 1953, K-3, Korea.
L to R: Capt. William Clem, Capt. Marshall Austin, instructor, Capt. Ted Williams, and First Lt. Robert E. Miller.
Photograph by Sgt. Curt Giese. Courtesy of National Archives & Records Administration.

CHAPTER 8 — ARRIVAL IN KOREA

Just transitioning from the U.S. to Korea proved a bit of a p.r. ordeal for Capt. Williams. Ray Sisk had talked about how even his house had been staked out by reporters back in Medford in May 1952. He and Ted were to meet up to drive to Willow Grove, and Sisk had to slip out the back door of his father's house to avoid being followed when he headed for his rendezvous with Williams. Now, on the hops over to Korea, Ted had to hide out to avoid being besieged by newsmen.

Ted was one of a group of 35 Marines stationed at El Toro who were given orders on 26 January to depart two days later, and (as his travel orders read) to "proceed via government aircraft to such place beyond the seas as the 1st Marine Aircraft Wing may be located, and report upon arrival to the Commanding General, for duty in a flying status involving operational or training flights." Major Alton McCully was placed in charge. On the 28th at 0800, they were detached and ordered to proceed. On the 29th, they arrived at Fleet Logistic Air Wing, Pacific in Honolulu, Territory of Hawaii and certified to leave the very next day. On 1 February, the group arrived at 1745 hours at NAS Atsugi, Japan. Eight years after the war against Japan, Ted Williams was on Japanese soil at an occupying base. He left the next evening, as the group progressed to Korea. They arrived 2 February, also at 1745, and the various Marines were assigned to different units.

The draft from El Toro flew across the Pacific on an old R5D four-engine transport aircraft, bound for Hawaii. Commercially, the R5D was the DC-4. The plane landed at Barber's Point, Oahu, and the men were there for a couple of days before continuing on. Charles Baker, a pilot assigned to VMF-115 after arriving in Korea, remembers the pressure. "While we were there at Barber's Point, the reporters just hounded him all the time. He stuck pretty close to the BOQ there. He didn't go into town or anything. When we got back on the R5D to continue our trip, we landed in Midway or one of those islands for that first stop after we left Barber's Point, he told us about those guys just bugging him all the time. He just disliked them. 'Why can't they leave me alone?' We stopped

at Midway and, darn, there were some people there – reporters. We just refueled and went in and got a sandwich or something, loaded back up and took off again. When we got back on the plane, he was really ticked! So on the next stop, and I don't remember which place it really was, he says, 'Would you guys just bring me a sandwich and a Coke or something? I'm just going to stay on the airplane and stay away from those bastards.'

"So every time we stopped from there on out, we'd bring a sandwich or a Coke or something. In those days, there were at least three fuel stops in those things. We landed at Iwakuni in Japan, and we spent a couple of

Ted on the base.
Photo by Jack Campbell.

days there. They were briefing us and everything before we went on over to Korea. When we got there, he was assigned to 311 and Jesse and I were to 115." Ted Williams arrived at the base in Korea on 3 February at 1445 hours.[1]

By the time they reached Japan, as we have read, the virus that had plagued Ted flared up again. While the others were enjoying a couple of nights on the town before heading for the desolate K-3 airfield in Korea, Ted stayed in bed.

Williams had been assigned to Marine Air Group 33. This unit was headquartered on an old Japanese airfield, the southernmost field in Korea, by a town known as Pohang-dong, dubbed by some "Pohang-by-the-Sea." MAG-33 was comprised primarily of two Marine jet squadrons, VMF-115 and VMF-311, a photo reconnaissance squadron VMJ-1, and the all-weather night fighter squadron VMF(N)-513.

The Commanding Officer of MAG-33 at the time was Col. Louis B. Robertshaw. He also served as Air Base Commander, and had served with MAG-33 since 22 October 1952.

Ted Williams' first day with his new squadron was February 3, 1953. His first task was to complete a one-week course to prepare him for combat. A few nice stories appeared in the newspapers. Bill Cunningham wrote in the *Boston Herald* that Capt. Ted Williams had reached his battle station and that Capt. Jerry Coleman had already been credited with destroying a couple of bridges. "Consider the sheer guts of those two ballplayers... Both were in it before. Both were called back and now they're in it again... Both these guys could have ducked it. Baseball should think up new honors for stars such as these. Maybe they couldn't have ruined the game if they'd ratted on this recall to combat, but they certainly made it a grander game when they didn't."[2] And Arthur Daley of the *New York Times* praised both – and the Army's Dr. Bobby Brown – in a column the next day entitled "Playing for Keeps."[3]

Williams was only negatively impressed when he arrived. Sick to begin with, he wrote, "I remember landing at Pohang in Korea, lousy old corrugated mat, crummy quarters, a real dog box. Cold and damp and awful." He griped, "I never felt the Marines got the kind of equipment they deserved." The four-time batting champion and two-time Most Valuable Player, the most highly-compensated player in the history of baseball was assigned to quarters and a home-made sleeping platform. "I inherited a bed one of the guys had made – a major who was going home. It was two two-by-sixes, three feet apart, and the springs on it were the rubber inner-tubing off a jet's tires. It was all bent up, curved on either side from being squeezed together so long... The weather was miserable, cold, foggy, misty. My nose and ears plugged up." It was not a pretty picture.[4]

The base at Pohang was one of 55 bases spread across Korea. Each one was assigned a "K" number, and Pohang was K-3, or King-3 in radio parlance. There were perhaps a couple of thousand personnel on the base. At full strength, there were more or less 35 pilots in each squadron, though they were rarely at full strength. Including all the mechanics, food service people, support staff, etc., each squadron comprised about five hundred people. K-3 was also the headquarters of MAG-33.

Marine Aircraft Group 33 was fully engaged in the routine of daily combat operations when Captain Theodore S. Williams arrived in February 1953. On the first day of the month, MAG-33's Commanding Officer Col. L. B. Robertshaw personally led 13 aircraft in an attack on a rail bridge. Other missions of the day attacked enemy supply buildings and a rail line. In all, 47 combat sorties were flown out of K-3 on 1 February.

The small photo squadron VMJ-1, also based at K-3, was grounded due to an unusual number of flameouts while the problem was being investigated.

Fifty-five sorties were flown on 2 February attacking enemy bunkers, mortar positions, personnel shelters, and supplies.

On his first full day, Williams found K-3 was bustling with activity. The squadron he'd been assigned to, VMF-311, flew 16 close air support sorties and 12 interdiction sorties. The first group of four F9F-2 Panther jets streaked into the skies at 0815, followed by four more at 1015 and another four at 1030. Four more fighter-bombers took off at 1225 (three of these were F9F-5's), another four at 1255 and a group of eight at 1411. The last mission returned to base at 1550, all aircraft accounted for. One plane on that last mission received some "minor damage in the left wing butt" from small arms fire over the target area. There were 28 departures and, fortunately, 28 safe landings by VMF 311 and an additional 20 takeoffs and 20 landings by sister squadron VMF-115. With several test and familiarization flights, there were over 100 takeoffs and landings the day of Williams' arrival.[5]

Ted had breakfast that morning, and fellow pilot Lt. George Winewriter recalls it almost 50 years later. Winewriter flew for VMF-115 and had been on the base since just before Christmas. "I had a pre-dawn takeoff and, after the mission, I was eating a late breakfast. Another man came in and we had breakfast together. We sat together and talked a while. He was mainly interested in how the flying was and how much instrument weather flying there might have been. We were the only ones in the mess hall. We had a good breakfast together. I went back to my barracks, to the squadron area and somebody said, 'You know, Ted Williams just came in today from the States!' I said, 'Oh my God, I had breakfast with him!'

"I knew he was in the Marine Corps, but Ted was a very unpretentious type of person. That's why I didn't recognize him."[6]

Ted formally reported at 1445 on 3 February, along with Captains Joseph M. Carruthers, William B. Clem and First Lieutenant Robert E. Miller.

In the mess hall that evening, surely there was talk of the plane that had been hit, the pilot telling what he noticed of the impact of the bullets on his plane, or marveling how he hadn't even known he'd been hit. Pilots on the late morning mission (Mission 3301, a prebriefed Group interdiction mission comprised of four aircraft from VMF-115 and four from VMF-311, led by Colonel Coursey of MAG-33) would have been buzzed about the two general purpose bombs they'd managed to skip into the mouth of a railroad tunnel. When the 500-pound bombs exploded, white puffs of smoke issued from both ends of the tunnel. It was an eventful day. This was war and Ted Williams had landed in the middle of it.

The C.O. greeted the fresh arrivals. He needed the new men. The squadron was a little low on pilots. Williams was fitted for his helmet and his flight gear, and assigned a bunk in a tin-walled, tin-roofed hut. Not exactly the comforts of home, but he'd been back in the Marines for nine months now and was getting used to different quarters. In a few weeks, the rest of the Red Sox would be reporting to spring training in Sarasota. Instead of looking at the lineup to see where he'd be batting that day, Captain Williams would be checking the Ready Room board to confirm his combat assignment. He wouldn't be batting cleanup, but he might be flying wing. Instead of facing a Bob Feller fastball or a Hoyt Wilhelm knuckleball, he'd be facing 37MM or small arms anti-aircraft fire. Instead of rounding third base and heading for home after driving another ball into the bleachers, he'd be delivering his ordnance and bringing home his Panther jet and then checking the board for the next day's flights.

Ted had been training for months, but now he had to learn base procedures at K-3, and get acclimated as best he could. This was not textbook stuff, not simple training anymore. This was combat readiness preparation. He got checked out all over again on field procedure, emergency procedures, how things were done at K-3, how the squadron handled realities in the field. He took a few test flights, and later recalled some practice bombing runs on an old bridge not too far from the base. In the process, he got to know the men, his squadron-mates, the pilots with whom he was going to be flying. These were men who he would depend on, and whose lives were to some extent in his hands as well.

Jack Campbell explained that he had taken a total of six familiarization flights:

"You practiced ADF approaches, GCA, and GCI approaches. These were done in a period of seven days. I assume Ted followed the same routine as I did.

"ADF = Automatic Direction Finding. A radio beacon/station that you could home to and then make a procedure turn to line you up with the air field, descending to a level to break out below the overcast.

"GCA = Ground Controlled Approach. Base radar that talked you down a flight path to break out with runway in front of you. Minimums could be 100' ceiling and 1/4 mile visibility.

"GCI = Ground Control Intercept. Another long range type radar that would control you down by furnishing you headings and turn you over to GCA at a certain point who in turn would control both your heading and altitude until the runway was in sight lined up for landing. GCI was designed to intercept inbound enemy aircraft."[7]

Campbell would lead Ted on his final "fam" flight, which (because they flew along the bomb line, in a combat zone) was also designated as Williams' first combat flight.

Fred Townsley arrived at K-3 about three months after Williams, but what he found waiting for him was pretty much the same, except that the weather was warmer and the ground wasn't frozen. "We all had the same thing," said squadron C.O. Art Moran, "Four walls. Korea is the coldest place I've ever been. And I originally came from northeastern Nebraska, where it really gets cold." Moran felt they got pretty good clothing and equipment, though.[8] Townsley wrote of his first impressions of the base: "We started circling for landing at K-3 Airfield Korea. As I looked at the dusty, dirty looking airfield my thoughts were, 'Why didn't I stay in school, I would have been preparing for my graduation as part of the class of 1953.' After the landing, someone from VMF-311, MAG-33, 1st MAW picked us up in a 6X6 truck and drove us to the Squadron Office where we were welcomed to Korea.

"We were quartered in the squadron recreation room until we could be moved into the regular barracks. The barracks were buildings made with corrugated metal about 16 feet wide by 32 feet long with double doors at each end and high windows along each side running about five feet above the deck to about four feet from each end of the building. The inside of the barracks was paneled with 1/4 inch plywood. There were two kerosene stoves in the middle aisle about eight feet inside the doors at each end. Canvas folding cots were spaced evenly along the walls under the windows, nine to each side. Shelves were built into the walls separating the cots and covered with some green (olive drab) material. The floors were concrete, there wasn't any insulation in the walls, and when the wind blew, you could feel it. In the winter we took masking tape and sealed the cracks as best we could. It was still cold, but beat the hell out of being in a tent.

"Since we were the new guys, the old timers wouldn't talk to us except to tell us what to do until we had been in country for a month or until the next replacement draft came in. The men (old timers) would come into the rec. hut and play ping pong until 2300 or 2400 hours each night to keep us awake, and then after lights out they would Klondike (throw large rocks onto the roof so we could listen to them roll down off the roof) the rec. hut. We were sure glad when the men we were replacing left so we could move into the regular huts."[9]

Early on at K-3, Ted himself met someone who would prove a notable figure in later years. Talking to Dave Anderson of the *New York Times* in 1998, a few days before John Glenn was to be launched in the space shuttle Discovery at age 77, Williams declared, "John Glenn is my idol in life right now." He explained that he'd known Glenn for more than forty years, and that they'd first met shortly after Ted arrived in Korea. "When I first got there, I didn't know anybody so I went to the pilots' room just to get acquainted. I looked over to the other end of the room and I saw two Marine majors there. I didn't know who they were, but they looked good to me. One was John Glenn. The other one, I've forgotten his name, but he became a major general."[10] John Glenn joined the unit on 15 February, just twelve days after Ted Williams.

VMF-311 was an elite squadron, and the forty pilots who served at one time or another during February 1953 included John Glenn and Ted Williams.

> "Shortly after getting off mess duty, I made Cpl. (E-3) and was assigned to Squadron Cpl. of the Guard. The night that I had duty, Capt. Ted Williams was SDO (Squadron Duty Officer.) It was just before he finished his tour of duty in Korea. He was the Squadron duty officer and I was his runner. As the runner, I just had to be available if he (SDO) needed me. He talked to me a little that evening, and when he started making up his cot for the night, he pulled out a set of sheets he had brought to the Operations Office to use since the squadron did not have sheets. People would not normally put sheets on a cot. Sheets were not issued at that time. He either had them sent from the states or bought them. He said that he was so poor when he was growing up that since he made it big in Major League Baseball, he wouldn't be without sheets if he had anything to say about it."
>
> *Communication from Fred Townsley, October 23, 2002*

NOTES

1) *Interview with Charles Baker, December 28, 2002.*

2) Boston Herald, *February 5, 1953.*

3) New York Times, *February 6, 1953.*

4) *Williams,* My Turn At Bat, *op. cit., pp. 178, 179.*

5) *All data on missions are taken from the squadron Command Diary files compiled monthly by the Commanding Officer, and since declassified. From this point forward in the narrative, we will use 24-hour military time.*

6) *Interview with George Winewriter, November 28, 2002.*

7) *Communication from Jack Campbell, December 28, 2002.*

8) *Interview with Art Moran, May 8, 1997.*

9) *Post by Fred Townsley on the VMA-311 Internet site. VMF-311 became VMA-311 in 1958.*
   New York Times, *October 29, 1998.*

Ted being strapped into F9F Panther by Roger McCully.
Courtesy of Roger McCully.

CHAPTER 9 – VMF-311 AND THE PANTHERJET

THE SQUADRON, VMF-311

Williams' squadron and sister squadron VMF-115 already had quite a history. VMF-311 was formed in December 1942 at Cherry Point, North Carolina to train replacement pilots for combat squadrons. The men flew the SNJ Texans. In April 1943, however, the unit was relocated to Parris Island and began flying Corsairs to prepare for combat. In August 1943, the unit headed to California and was stationed at Miramar. In 1943, VMF-311 became the first Marine squadron to catapult a Corsair from a Naval vessel. The unit first saw combat on 23 March 1944, flying out of the Kwajalein Islands. For a year and a half, the squadron hounded Japanese forces on various islands and atolls around the Marshalls, strafing and dive bombing and keeping the various island-based enemy forces from linking up with each other. VMF-311 was the first Marine squadron to use fighters as dive bombers.

The designation VMF-311 can be broken down as follows. This concise explanation is offered by a very close friend of Ted Williams, Major General Larry S. Taylor:

1st letter = V means fixed-wing aircraft, H means helicopter. (The V first meant heavier-than-air craft.)

2nd letter = M for Marine (the Navy just drops the 2d letter)

3rd letter = F for fighter, A for attack, etc.

Hence, VMF-311 is Marine Fighter Squadron 311, and Capt. T. S. Williams' full Korea unit "address" was VMF-311, MAG-33, 1stMAW, FMF. This translates as Marine Fighter Squadron 311, Marine Aircraft Group 33, 1st Marine Aircraft Wing, Fleet Marine Force. There are several squadrons in a MAG, several MAGs in a MAW, and 4 MAWs (3 active, 1 reserve) in the Marine Corps.

Moving onward to Okinawa, VMF-311 had its first aerial combat experience and hit 71 Japanese planes in just four months, while only suffering three fatalities of its own, none of them during dogfights. On one day alone (28 April 1945), 311's Corsairs destroyed 13 Japanese planes. During the Occupation, 311 was based in Yokosuka, Japan. In June 1946, 311 briefly moved to Tsingtao, China, but then pulled back the following month to the United States where it was temporarily deactivated for a few months.

Reconstituted in November, 1946, VMF-311 was just the second Marine squadron to receive jets, in April 1948. These first jets were the "Shooting Star," but by late 1949 the squadron was provided Panther F9F-2s. Photographs of VMF-311 aircraft show the distinctive tail marking "WL" and the group was informally known as the Willy Lovers, or Willing Lovers, from the radio call William Love (WL).

Deployed on short notice to Korea on 14 November 1950, the unit made its way overseas and began flying out of K-27; the airfield at Yonp'o was actually located in North Korea. It was from here on 10 December 1950 that VMF-311 flew the first Marine jet combat mission, providing close air support for Eighth Army units located near the Chosin Reservoir. The unit moved to K-9 at Pusan a few days later, until a more permanent base was established in February 1951 at a former Japanese airbase known as Yongil-man Airfield near Pohang. This base was designated K-3.

After a couple of times when pilots successfully scrambled to help out beleaguered ground forces, 311 was ordered to keep at least two pilots in the cockpit ready to roll at all times, if requested by TACC, the Tactical Air Control Center. VMF-311 was the only squadron based in Korea to be on this full-time CAP (Combat Air Patrol) alert. Rather than always attack pre-designated targets, some 311 jets were kept airborne, in effect on call for targeting assignments by the airborne tactical air controller who could respond to the exigencies of the moment. If not so assigned, each flight of four jets would move to pre-briefed secondary targets and deliver their payloads before they needed to return to base. Not only could they keep two pilots on the tarmac for CAP duty, but four jets could be in the air – and much closer to the front – during every daylight hour.

The weather often presented nearly impossible visual targeting, but advances in radar technologies led to the development of MPQ-14 radar-controlled bombing equipment and permitted bombing runs when pilots were unable to see the ground at all. Due to their superior speed, and despite the fact that K-3 was the base farthest from the main line of resistance (MLR) – also known as the "bomb line" – the Panthers often were on the scene and leading the attack in advance of the propeller-driven Corsairs. The Panther's flight characteristics were superior not only in sheer speed, but offered "a more stable firing platform offering better gunnery, bombing and rocket accuracy."[1]

There were occasional losses suffered by the squadron, but they were few and far between, particularly considering the number of sorties flown under the reconnaissance and round-the-clock in-air readiness mission. On 21 July 1951, Lt. Robert Bell piloted one of three VMF-311 jets attacked by 15 Russian-made MiG jets while returning from patrol work. Though downed, fortunately Lt. Bell was captured, became a P.O.W., and was repatriated a couple of months after the conclusion of the war. Even though the MiG was superior to the Panther in aerial combat, they rarely joined in combat because MiGs rarely dared leave the northern zone. Should they come under attack, the Panthers enjoyed a smaller turning radius and thus could typically evade MiG attacks.

There were pilots killed. On 10 August 1951, Major Frank S. Hoffecker's plane was hit during a dive bombing run and exploded in flame on ground impact. He had not been seen to eject and was thus listed as killed in action. On 3 October, Second Lt. Edward L. Frakes was also hit while attacking rail targets and his plane, too, exploded on impact. Major George N. Major was hit by anti-aircraft fire on 3 January 1952, and he, too, was lost when his plane plunged straight to the earth.

In February 1952, VMF-115 joined 311 at K-3 and MAG-33 doubled in size. A new photo squadron, VMJ-1 joined the Air Group in March.

A typical day started at 0415 when an operations clerk and an intelligence clerk began to annotate the Flak Situation Map to indicate targets for the day. The first CAP units were manned at 0500, one hour before reveille. CAP coverage was longer when the days were longer; they were to be on alert scramble from a half-hour before sunrise to a half-hour after sunset. Fortunately, those were the warmer months. Each pilot on CAP duty had to sit in his unheated aircraft for two hours; that was perhaps the single most unpleasant duty during the bitterly cold winter months. Breakfast was at 0630. By this time, some flights (the "early-earlies") would already be launched, and those pilots only looked forward to breakfast after the mission was completed.

On 10 May 1952, the squadron lost Captain John S. Bostwick when, per squadron history, "on the second pass at the target, [he] delivered his ordnance, made a left climbing pullout, rolled over on his back, and dove straight into the ground 150 meters behind enemy lines." The very next day,

Captain Malcom C. Hagan emerged from cloud cover while waiting for targeting from the airborne controller and crashed into a small observation plane. Both pilots were killed. There were other pilots captured and other severely damaged aircraft.

For several months, there were no losses at all, but then on 30 September 1952, Second Lt. Odyce W. Livingston lost his life when his aircraft flamed out during his landing approach and he crashed two miles short of K-3's runway. On 5 December, Capt. Donald H. Clark failed to respond to radio contact after an attack by 18 aircraft on an enemy supply concentration. He was listed as killed in action after one year had elapsed.

Soon after 1953 began, both 311 and 115 were supplied with the newer F9F-5 aircraft, the first F9F-5 mission being flown on 14 January. Increasingly the two squadrons joined in large joint flights.

In one month alone, June 1951, VMF-311 set a record, flying over 2,300 sorties. No other fighter squadron has ever matched that total. Some months were busier than others, but all in all, this was an experienced operation by the time Ted Williams was attached to the squadron in February 1953.

In all, VMF-311 flew 18,851 combat sorties during the Korean War.

For nearly two years after the end of active hostilities, 311 helped patrol the DMZ, from July 1953 until May 1955, at which time it was relocated to El Toro. In the years after Korea, the squadron saw combat in Vietnam (54,625 sorties) and Desert Storm (1,017 sorties) as well as work during Operation Enduring Freedom in Afghanistan.

Ted in cockpit with VMF-311 crew chief Roger McCully.
Courtesy of Roger McCully.

VMF-115

VMF-115 deployed to K-3 in February 1952, a year before Williams arrived. Though 311 flew more than twice as many sorties, 115 delivered more ordnance that any other Marine jet squadron. They also paid a price in casualties. VMF-115 lost 19 aircraft and had 14 pilots killed in action during the Korean conflict. Known as the Able Eagles, because of the "AE" painted on their jets, the day of September 10, 1952 was indeed a black day for 115. On that one day, the squadron lost six pilots and their six Panthers.

This was just 4 1/2 months before Ted Williams arrived at K-3, and it was certainly fresh in the minds of pilots on the base by early February '53. Twenty-four jets had left K-3 late that afternoon, 12 from 311 and 12 from 115. All the 311 jets returned, but only half of those from 115 returned safely that night. Due to inclement weather which had settled in over K-3, the mission was redirected to land at K-2. The first six jets landed safely, and the second six were due to land. They reported their fuel condition by radio, and then were never heard from again.

John Toler of the *Fauquier Times-Democrat* of Warrenton, Virginia has written the account "Catastrophe in the Clouds." He says, "It would be nearly two agonizing days before their fate was known." Other pilots waited in the "O" club. "Soon the club was filled with our guys, and those of VMF-311," said Lt. George S. Banks, the VMF-115 ordnance officer at the time. "No one said much, or talked about why we were there. But we all knew. We were waiting for 'the good word.'" The hope was that the planes had landed at some other base, somewhere. Calls were made, but there was no word. "Everyone was numb. No one left the club to eat, as though if we stayed together, the good news would come." 2

All missions were canceled the following morning, so that a thorough search could be conducted, but not a thing turned up. It was only the afternoon of the day after that when a helicopter located wreckage of all six planes on a mountain ridge about 23 miles southwest of K-2. Forty-one hours after the radio contact, it began to become clear what had occurred. The conclusion of investigators is that not one of the pilots had seen the mountains through the heavy overcast clouds and that they had all slammed into the mountainside.

THE AIRCRAFT

The aircraft for the two squadrons during the Korean War was the F9F Panther, made by Grumman Aviation. There was more than one model, and Ted flew both the F9F-2 and the F9F-5, but the jet that Williams flew most often was the F9F-5 Panther. It was powered by a single Pratt & Whitney J48-P-4/P-6A turbojet, and had a maximum speed of 604 mph at sea level, 579 mph at 5,000 feet, or 543 mph at 35,000 feet. Its cruising speed was designated at 481 mph. The "stalling speed" was 132 mph. This jet had an initial climb rate of 5,090 feet per minute, nearly a mile in one minute, and a service ceiling of 42,800 feet. Range was 1,300 miles.

The dimensions of the F9F-5 are: wingspan 38 feet 0 inches, length 38 feet 10 1/2 inches, height 12 feet 4 inches, wing area 250 square feet. Weights: 10,147 pounds empty, 17,766 pounds gross, 18,721 pounds maximum takeoff. Internal fuel capacity: 1,003 US gallons.

Armament: four 20MM cannons in the nose. Eight underwing hardpoints which could accommodate a total underwing load of up to 3465 pounds of bombs and rockets.

The somewhat older and smaller F9F-2 was not that much slower: 575 mph at sea level, though it had slightly faster cruising and initial climb speeds and it had a bit more range as well. The main advantage of the "5" over the "2" was in ordnance: the F9F-2 could only carry 2,000 pounds, where the F9F-5 could carry 3,465 pounds.

Compare the F9F to the workhorse F4U-1D Corsair that had seen so much duty in World War II, and which Jerry Coleman was still flying with his squadron, and one sees why many pilots might have preferred the Panther. The Corsair's maximum speed was 328 mph at sea level, giving the Panther almost a 250 mph advantage. Like the earlier Panther, the F9F-2, the Corsair was built to carry 2,000 pounds of ordnance. It was a single-engine three-bladed propeller-drive aircraft with a wingspan of 41 feet 0 inches and an overall length of 33 feet, 4 inches. A lighter plane, the Corsair checked in at 8,695 pounds. The climb was 3,210 feet per minute, and the plane had a 37,000 service ceiling and a range of 1,015 miles, though with a full one-ton payload, that range was limited to just 500 miles.

Ted liked flying planes, and he really enjoyed the transition to jets. He liked speed. "From my early days in baseball I always had brand-new cars and I'd zip up the highways from Minnesota to Florida at eighty or ninety miles an hour, getting the feel for speed, and I know enough to realize it wasn't the greatest transition in the world to airplanes... I was impressed with jets the minute I got in one. Easy to fly, easier than props because they had no torque, less noise, tricycle landing gear. Wonderful flight characteristics. Turn one over and it would just r-o-l-l, nothing to it."[3]

NOTES

1) Lynn Montross, Hubard Kuokka, and Norman Hicks, The East-Central Front – U.S. Marine Operations in Korea 1950-1953 Vol. IV. P. 64, published by HistDiv, HQMC, 1962. Much of the information contained in this chapter comes from "A History of Marine Attack Squadron 311" by Major William J. Sambito, published by the History and Museums Division, Headquarters U.S. Marine Corps. Washington, 1978.

2) Communication from John Toler, October 24, 2002.

3) Williams, My Turn At Bat, op. cit., pp. 182, 177.

Ted Williams right after arriving in Korea, in the K-3 flight operations briefing room.
Above Ted's head is a model of a F9F Panther shown ready to intercept a MiG fighter.
Photo courtesy of the Cleveland Public Library.

CHAPTER 10 – TED'S FIRST TWO MISSIONS

It was one thing to be targeting an old bridge no longer in use, but it was another thing indeed to be flying in harm's way with enemy anti-aircraft gunners pumping shells skyward, and even ground troops firing at the low-flying planes during dive bombing runs. This is what all the training and practice had been for. This was the real thing.

Between his arrival on 3 February 1953 and his first combat mission on the 14th, Williams got in his takeoffs and landings at K-3, learned base procedures, and soaked up stories from his squadron mates.

There were no missions on the morning of the 4th but a mid-afternoon mission attacked bunkers and artillery. One minute later, over another part of North Korea, 12 jets (four from 115 and eight from 311) attacked supplies, vehicle revetments, and bunkers. Captain Campbell led the only two missions flown on the 5th; the first departed base at 0920 and, flying in support of the KMC Regiment, attacked troops, trenches, automatic weapons positions, mortars, and caves. The other departed at 1310 and flew in support of the 1st ROK Infantry Division, attacking mortar positions and personnel shelters. The first mission encountered no opposition but the second attracted intense small arms fire, though without taking any damage.

Inclement weather pretty much shut down K-3 on the 6th, but the 7th was a very busy day with 15 interdiction sorties, seven close air support, and seven general support sorties. One plane received minor damage and another sustained major damage to the starboard wingroot as a result of the moderate small arms fire encountered over the target area, while the F9F-2s were attacking enemy supplies and personnel in support of the Capitol ROK Infantry Division.

February 8 saw 18 combat sorties, attacking caves and troops, supplies and a command post.

Ted Williams on R&R in Japan.
Courtesy of the May Williams Collection.

Another 16 sorties were flown on 9 February, though the larger of the two missions was unable to attack its prebriefed target due to bad weather conditions. The Group interdiction mission diverted to a target of opportunity and attacked a bridge, rail line, road, and village, dropping 48 1,000-pound general purpose (GP) bombs, two 500-pound GPs, 12 250-pound GPs, and firing 1,250 rounds of 20MM ammunition.

The bad weather settled in and no combat sorties at all were flown on the 10th, 11th, 12th, or 13th. There were a few operational flights, familiarization hops, and flight proficiency hops. Captain Williams made three familiarization flights in this time, two flights on February 10 and another one of February 11 for a total of 3.8 hours, all taken in the F9F-2. The weather on the 13th was so bad that no flights at all went out.

14 FEBRUARY 1953 – COMBAT MISSION #1

On Valentine's Day, the squadron was back in business, flying seven interdiction sorties, eight general support sorties, and eleven close air support sorties. There were also seven bombline reconnaissance flights and two familiarization hops. One of those flights gave Capt. Williams his first view of the bombline. It was the last flight of the day, departing K-3 at 1635 – just two aircraft, both F9F-2s, one piloted by Capt. Jack Campbell and the other by Capt. Ted Williams. The mission was listed in squadron records as "MLR fam" (main line of resistance familiarization) and each jet was airborne for 1.6 hours. Ted listed it in his flight log book as "RECON B/L" – reconnaissance on the bombline.

This was a fam flight, along the bombline (or as it was termed, the "main line of resistance" or MLR). Jack Campbell and Ted had worked together at Cherry Point, and so Campbell offered to take Ted up for his first fam flight. Campbell had already flown one mission that day. He'd led three F9F-2 aircraft on a close air support mission attacking enemy bunkers and trenches at Hyosongdong in support of the 2nd ROK Infantry Division. He'd returned to base at 1505, and then took Ted up, their two jets departing K-3 at 1635. Campbell led Williams up to the bomb line, then flew right "down the bomb line just to point out where the front lines were. That was our first mission – everybody – orientation-type. And I flew with him on that mission. Just a two-plane flight."[1] That gave Ted a first-hand look at the actual topography, so he knew where he'd be flying the next day. Williams' name was on the chalk board in the ready room. You knew the day before if you were going to be flying the following day. Ted Williams was due to fly his first active combat mission on the 15th.

This fam flight on the 14th is logged as a combat mission. Even though it was routine, it counted as mission number one. Each jet was armed with the standard 760 rounds of 20MM ammunition, though as it happened neither dropped any ordnance nor did they fire their weapons. The flight was intended to familiarize the pilot (Williams) with the look of the actual area along the bombline. Campbell explained the reasoning: "We were in a position that we could have been shot at. That's why it would count as a combat mission. We would fly at about 8,000 feet along the bombline just to see where the front lines were dug in. Small arms fire couldn't reach you at that altitude and since we were traveling pretty fast, the 37MM anti-aircraft probably wouldn't try to open up on us because that would give their position away to the ground troops. So that first mission was really easy, although you were in a position you could have been shot at. We were over enemy territory – not far, but we were over enemy territory."[2]

On Ted's first day at K-3, Pohang.
L to R: Bill Brown, Ted Williams, Joe Carruthers,
R. E. Miller. In front: Bill Clem, Bob Young.
Courtesy of Williams P. Brown.

VMF-311 squadron patch,
to be sewn on flight jackets.
Collection of Bill Nowlin.

Back in 1953, Campbell told Ed Hyde of *Sport* magazine, "Ted is eager to fly, and that guy can ask more questions. He wants to know everything about the Pantherjet because there are several different models. Since we fly all of the models at one time or another, we have to know what they're like. Some day our lives may depend upon this knowledge."[3]

15 FEBRUARY 1953 – COMBAT MISSION #2

Ted Williams' first mission with a payload was on 15 February 1953. It is noteworthy that on his very first such mission, one of his fellow pilots crashed his plane upon landing.

VMF-311 flew six missions on the 15th and Williams was on the fifth. Following standard operating procedure, he was in the ready room an hour before takeoff time and then proceeded to the intelligence section to be briefed by the flight leader. Once in a while, pilots would ask questions, for instance wanting to be clear who would make the flak suppression run. Normally the leader and maybe the number two man would make a flak suppression run, hitting the anti-aircraft or attempting to scatter enemy ground forces with their 20MM cannon.

Major Lloyd Dochterman was the flight leader on this mission; he'd been active at K-3 since 21 October 1952. After their briefing, the five jets which comprised Mission Number 3333 were airborne at 1430 on an interdiction mission. One hour and four minutes later, Major Dochterman gave the signal and Captains Joseph Carruthers, Bill Clem, Charles Street, and Ted Williams joined in the attack on a rail line. Street had been at K-3 since a week before Christmas, but both Carruthers and Clem had joined the squadron the same day as Williams. Dropping a total of 30 250-pound general purpose bombs, the Marine pilots cut the rail line in one place and two other probable cuts were identified. The flight returned to base at 1615. The aircraft piloted by Captain Clem, though, crashed upon landing. While he was spared injury, his plane suffered major damage.

Bill Clem had island-hopped across the Pacific with Ted, and both reported to the squadron together. They'd spent time together at Roosevelt Roads, in cold weather training out of Pendleton, and then from Miramar they flew out of San Diego. Clem recounts the trans-Pacific flights: "We traveled on that Martin Mars flying boat. We flew to Hawaii on that flying boat. We stayed over a day, and then we took a Navy plane from there to Japan. Itami. We were there another couple of days and then we reported to K-3. We went over together. There were maybe ten of us in that group." After settling in at K-3, "We all took those fam flights. My first flight in Korea was on February the 10th. I had four fam flights – three of them on the 10th, one on the 11th, and then one on the 12th. To get familiar with the area. Then on the 14th was my first actual combat mission. It was a recon mission over the main line of resistance – up there on the M.L.R." His schedule had basically paralleled Williams'.

"On the 15th. Sinwon-ni. I banged one up. It was damaged, but I was fine. I've got some pictures of it but I don't remember it. There was another time I landed at an emergency field. I got hit. My fire warning light came on. I didn't want to blow up, so I picked the nearest field I could find and I landed on this little strip that had metal matting like the old days. I put on the brakes and blew the brakes and skidded to a halt. Somebody flew me back."[4] Astonishing though it may seem that Clem can't remember banging up a plane on his first active combat mission, one can only hope to understand that after all the training, all the tension, and all the flights that followed, some of the experiences begin to blur after half a century.

Clem must have been shaken up, and so must have his fellow rookie pilots Joe Carruthers and Ted Williams. One of the three had already come very close to disaster. Williams noted in the "remarks" section of his log book: "I/D SINWON-NI" – interdiction, Sinwon-ni.

All three found their names on the board for the next day's mission, nonetheless. This was to be a "max effort" – a major mission involving over 200 aircraft, drawn from various bases. Sixteen fighter-bombers from VMF-115 and nineteen from 311 were scheduled to depart the next morning. Carruthers, Clem, and Williams were all among them.

If they hadn't had much sleep the night before the 15th, one wonders if Clem's close call might have spooked them further.

NOTES

1) *Interview with Jack Campbell, November 27, 2002.*

2) *Ibidem*

3) *Ed Hyde, "Ted Williams, Marine," Sport, July 1953.*

4) *Interview with Bill Clem, December 23, 2002.*

Topographic map of Kyomipo area, used by VMF-311 for the 16 February 1953 mission. AMS Series L851, Sheet 6330 III SE.

Courtesy of Map Division, Library of Congress.

CHAPTER 11 – A BRUSH WITH DEATH:
MISSION 3301, 16 FEBRUARY 1953

Another one of the three had a brush with death the following day. This time it was Ted Williams.

16 February 1953 was the day Ted Williams' own plane was hit and crashed. It was the first mission of two launched that day. Mission 3301 was airborne at 0932 and it was a large one. Thirty-five jets – 16 aircraft from VMF-115 and 19 from 311 – combined on a prebriefed interdiction mission, part of a much larger flight – a "max effort." All told, combining Air Force, Navy, and Marine aircraft, there may have been between 200 and 300 aircraft involved. The first AP report of the story – which in Boston prompted front page headlines – indicated that 200 planes had taken part in the daylight attack.

This was one of a series of large coordinated attacks. On 10 February, 300 planes had rained destruction on a huge rail and bridge complex near Sinanju, and five days later over 200 planes revisited the same area. MAG-33 took part in both attacks.

The *Pacific Stars and Stripes* termed the 16 February action the biggest strike of the year, "staged by four Air Force wings and two Marine air groups which hurled tons of bombs into the supply and troop area at Kyomipo, 23 miles southeast of the North Korea capital of Pyongyang. Pilots said they left the area blazing with fires and covered by a cloud of smoke that rose 5,000 feet into the air. They claimed the destruction of 96 buildings." The other Marine air group involved was MAG-12. Participating planes from the Air Force were Thunderjets from the 49th, 58th, and 474th wings and Shooting Stars from the 8th Wing. MAG-12 was flying Corsairs and Skyraiders.

Air Force F-86 fighters shot down three MiGs which tried to intercept the dive-bombers, and damaged eight others. Seven of the MiG claims were attributed to the 51st Fighter-Interceptor Wing. Other aircraft saw action on the day, including close air support and interdiction work by the Royal Australian 77th Squadron.

The activity continued after darkness fell, with B-26 and B-29 aircraft dropping explosives on other supply centers. By day's end, 985 combat sorties had been flown.

The flight leader for the MAG-33 pilots was Major Thomas M. Sellers of VMF-115. At 1052, they attacked supply buildings located at YC3688.

Pilots on the mission were, from VMF-311: Majors WALLEY, HOLLENBECK, MITCHELL, Captains KURTZ, ARMAGOST, NEWENDORP, CLEM, MONTAGUE, CAMPBELL, CARRUTHERS, WILLIAMS, McGRAW, and BROWN, Lieutenants DAY, JANSSEN, RUDY, HAWKINS, HEINTZ, and SAMPLE. VMF-115 pilots were Majors SELLERS, HILL, and ROSS, Captains JENSEN, BLANEY, TIVNAN, ROARK, SHARKEY, and IRELAND, and Lieutenants LeBLANC, WOODBURY, RHYKERD, Hollaway, BAKER, DAVIS, and BAIRD.

VMF-311 released a total of 241 250-pound bombs, and, in addition, expended 3,680 rounds of 20MM ammunition. VMF-115 contributed 128 250-pound GP bombs, and fired 2,150 rounds of 20MM. There was no flak and no enemy air opposition, but there was (per the squadron diary) "meager small arms fire" encountered over the target. All it takes is one hit in the right place, though, to down a plane – and one aircraft did receive major damage. That was the plane piloted by

Capt. T. S. Williams. Of the 35 planes which took off, seven returned safely to K-3. Two aircraft landed at K-14 due to low fuel, and 26 of them landed at K-13 (one of those being Williams'.) Damage was unassessed due to smoke in the target area.

Everyone was back on the ground before noon. Some were at K-13, some were at K-3, and maybe one or two were at K-6.

At 1608, 21 more jets were launched from K-3 – 12 from 115 and 9 from 311. Major Bolt's plane aborted due to mechanical reasons and had to return; as he was the flight controller, the flight had to circle for some 50 minutes while waiting for him to land and acquire a replacement plane. Major Sabot of 311 led this strike at supply shelters; damage was undetermined due to darkness. Sixteen of these aircraft had to land at either K-13 or K-14 due to low fuel. The remaining six made it back to K-3.

16 FEBRUARY 1953 – COMBAT MISSION #3

 Mission 3301 was, as indicated, a major air assault launched on targets in the north, involving aircraft from more than one base. Ted's flight left in the late morning and attacked supply buildings in north Korea, dropping 250-pound bombs. Ted's plane was hit – whether by ground fire or hit by his own bomb blast has never been determined. The Marine jets flew so low to drop their ordnance that occasionally fragments from the target being bombed would fly up and slam into the bottom of the aircraft. Whatever happened, it seriously damaged Ted's plane, which not only lost its radio and hydraulics but caught on fire when he first put his wheels down on approach to landing. More of the story of Ted's dramatic belly-landing of his F9F aircraft at an Air Force base in western Korea is told below. Suffice to say, Ted survived.

In the first mission of the 17th, Williams was airborne again at 0818 as part of a sixteen-plane strike led by Captain Blaney of VMF-115 (eight planes from each squadron took part), attacking an enemy troop concentration. Two aircraft had to land at K-13 due to low fuel, but Williams and everyone else made it back safely. His fifth mission on 19 February, though, was his last for several weeks. Ted developed pneumonia, for which he had to be treated off-base, so he was evacuated, and it was several weeks before he rejoined VMF-311 and resumed flying.

February 16 was not the only time Ted's aircraft was hit. At least one other time, in late April, he was hit so badly that it was noted in the squadron's command diary. There were no doubt a few other times he'd been hit more minimally. That sort of thing happened from time to time, and not all hits were deemed noteworthy.

Flying in combat is inherently dangerous, and you never know what might happen. Bill Clem tells of ammunition firing off before the planes even left the base that very morning; this occurred on more than one occasion. "We waited on the runway so long – it was so crowded – somebody got his nose too close to the guy in front of him and the ammunition started going off. The 20MM. Why did it start going off? He got his nose too close to the heat of the exhaust of the other guy. It got too hot and it started going off, inside the magazines." The lead pilot was being fired on, from behind, even before takeoff![1]

George Winewriter of VMF-115 told of another joint mission. "It was what we called a joint Army, Navy, and Marine mission. 350 planes. We were hitting the bridge complex up at the Yalu River. I had never been up that far before, but my squadron and I think maybe 311 also, we were assigned to hit the gun emplacements, and to escape out through the estuary – stay down low, right on the ground and go out that way; in case you had to land, you could land on the ice out there in an emergency.

"We went in there at about 20,000, 21,000 feet somewhere. Below us were the Corsairs. As I finished my run and scooted out over the estuary, they were shooting from the banks. The tracers were all above me. I had full bore on and everything and I was as close as I felt comfortable to the water, and I could hear the Corsair pilots hollering and screaming they were hit, they were going down. It was a terrible, terrible experience to hear on the radio. The Corsairs were really taking it. I don't know the statistics, but I know from listening on that radio that they took one hell of a beating. They came in lower than us, around maybe 12,000 feet and they were aiming at the bridges. We were supposed to knock out the gun emplacements but I don't think we got anywhere near all of them. As I remember it, there was a blanket of gunfire down around 12,000 feet where these guys were supposed to come in. We didn't get any anti-aircraft fire up at 20,000 feet."[2]

A division is a group of four aircraft that fly together on a mission, and Marvin Hollenbeck tells the story of Mission 3301. Hollenbeck was a regular; he'd flown transport planes during World War II and claims the distinction of landing the first airplane on Iwo Jima; he brought in 5,000 pounds of mortar ammunition on D plus 5 (the fifth day after American invasion of the island). Hollenbeck retired as a lieutenant colonel after 22 years of service.

Remembering the mission on the 16th with Ted Williams, Hollenbeck explained, "I was the division leader on that mission. Ted was my wingman. I had a first lieutenant as my section leader – Larry Hawkins – and I don't remember who his wingman was. It may have been Joe Mitchell. He was a tall fellow like I was. He [Ted] wasn't as tall as I am, but he was tall. I'm 6'5".

"That morning at the briefing, I told him that I dive real steep, and I dive real steep for a purpose – to get in to easier hit the target. The shallower you dive, the more trajectory your bombs have after you release them. When you dive straight down, there's no trajectory to your bombs and they go right straight down. Gravity pulls them right straight down to the earth. So I told him I dive real steep for that reason, and also because I dive just under the mach of the airplane. The mach of the airplane was .875 – almost .9 mach. I said, 'I don't care, Williams, if you hit anything or not. I just want you to drop your bombs and come home safe. And so when you see my bombs go, you go ahead and release and pull out right then, because I dive real fast and real steep and I don't want you going too low.'"

Hollenbeck also knew that this was one of Williams' very first missions. "Yes. Yes, that's right. So when we came off the target, we came off toward the south and we had agreed to turn hard left, to go to a point just to the west of the target a little bit, and then when we hit that point, why, we'd turn hard south and go south to the water, and close enough to the water where if you had to make a dead stick landing you'd be able to land in the ocean, in the mud flats. As soon as we hit far enough south where we could dead stick it into the water, we would head direct for K-13 because we're going to be low on fuel.

"We came off target, and I went hard right to the point, then hard left to the south. The flight leader hadn't called for a check-in yet. I couldn't see Williams or any of my section. So I called for my division to check in. Larry Hawkins came on the air and said '#2 is heading west towards Chodo and he's streaming fuel.' His [Williams'] radio was out. It was knocked out when he was hit. I said,

'Roger. Move up on him as fast as you can and head him south. As soon as you can dead stick it to the south in the water, take him to K-13 and get him on the deck as quickly as you can.' So he did. I never saw the three of my division until I got close to K-13 and then I spotted them. I let them go ahead first.

"He went in over the tower to brake and when he did, why then, there was two streams of smoke coming out of each wheel well. The doors over each wheel well opened, but the landing gear did not go down and lock because the hydraulics were shot out, were knocked out. He went on around, turned on the downwind leg and I came in right behind him – and tried to get his attention to bail out. He wouldn't look to the right. I was on the outside of the turn. He just went ahead and on down to the base leg and on in. The tower called while he was on the base leg, 'F9, the final, your landing gear is not down.' Of course, he didn't hear it. He went on in and landed, wheels up. It was either 8 or 10,000 feet of runway – a real long runway because it was an Air Force base. Just a ball of fire. There was nothing I could do about it.

"He slid down the concrete runway and off to the right-hand side of the runway in this slide because he was on his belly. It got hot as soon as he started slowing down because of the fire behind him, that ball of fire. So he pulled the T-handle to blow the canopy off, and damn if it didn't work. It wasn't knocked out. It blew the canopy off and he got out with his shoes on, and jumped off the leading edge of the wing, and fell and skinned his knee. That's all that happened to him.

"I had to go around and land. He seemed OK."[3]

Hollenbeck left K-3 soon afterward. He'd been there eight months, flown a total of 69 missions, and was due to rotate home. Ed Hyde's 1953 story in *Sport* magazine quoted Hollenbeck as saying that Ted was "a bit pale but calm. He told me that war suddenly became a wicked reality to him." Hollenbeck continued, "In the short time I'd known him, I never saw him as serious as he was that one time. Then he grinned, slammed me on the back and wisecracked, 'You son of a gun, they were shooting at you and they got me.'" Hollenbeck wound up, telling Hyde, "For a green pilot over here, Ted must have done everything right. He made it okay. He made the greatest play of his career." [4]

Ted wrote in *My Turn At Bat* about the February 16 mission. "Sure as hell, I got hit with small arms fire. When I pulled up out of my run, all the red lights were on in the plane and the damn thing started to shake. The stick stiffened up and was shaking. I knew I had a hydraulic leak. Fuel warning light, fire warning light, there are so many lights on a jet that when anything serious goes wrong the lights almost blind you. I was in serious trouble." His radio conked out. Ted was sure he was going to have to bail out, and worried because with his 6'4" frame, that would be an almost certain (and very serious) knee injury – not to mention landing in ice-cold waters or in enemy territory. He'd said, "It was the only real fear I had flying a plane, that if I had to bail out I wouldn't make it. I thought I'd surely leave my kneecaps in there."[5]

Ted's first C.O. at K-3 was Lt. Col. Francis K. Coss. He said that Williams was "just another pilot" but then amended his comment by adding, "He's a lot taller than most. And once in a while he has trouble fitting his big frame in some of the different Pantherjet models."[6] Was Ted too tall to eject? The question was posed to the 6'5" Col. Hollenbeck: "He wrote about how he didn't want to bail out because he was afraid he would chop his kneecaps off. You must have had a similar worry, then." Hollenbeck answered, "That wasn't really a concern of mine, because the seat ejection goes out about 30 degrees angled to the rear. It goes up at a 60 degree angle but tilted 30 degrees back from the vertical. You have a cord in back of your neck that sticks up like a 'U' and you reach with both hands up over your head and you grab the rope, and you bring it up and down over your face, keeping your elbows and your arms in real close as you can. When you get it down about your face, that releases the firing pin and it fires you out."[7]

Ben Robertshaw wasn't sure about the danger of being knee-capped in the F9F, either. "I never heard that of being a fault of that airplane, though when we got back to the States and got newer aircraft – the A4D – everybody that had any possible danger of losing kneecaps or feet had to pass an examination of clearance in the airplane by disarming an ejection seat and pulling the person up on a pulley overhead. It pulled the whole seat up just like he would be ejecting and then that would be ejecting. That would test his clearance to fly the airplane. I don't remember that as being a characteristic of the Pantherjet."[8]

Plane captain Bob Flanagan joined the unit about six weeks later, and questioned Ted's story, too. If it were true that he'd have been at risk of knee-capping, then he wouldn't be flying the airplane, Flanagan said. "If he didn't pull his legs back and put them on those two little plats there that you're supposed to have your feet on...you pull your feet off the rudder and pull down on the face curtain and out you go. If you had a leg sticking out or if you had your legs still on the rudder pedals, I could see possibly that happening. They made a big issue of it [recently] on ESPN, but I thought to myself, 'Come on!' If you thought you could get knee-capped, all you had to do was go in there and say, 'Hey, I'm too big to fly this airplane. If I have to punch out, I'm going to lose my knees.' And he would not be flying it. As if the Marine Corps would let him fly an airplane that would kill him!"[9]

Legend sometimes takes over a bit as stories are told and re-told. Senator John McCain once asked Ted Williams, "Why didn't you eject?" "I'd have rather died," he said, "than never to have been able to play baseball again."[10]

In 1954, writing in the *Saturday Evening Post*, Ted himself said, "I decided to ride my plane in. If I had known then that my ship was on fire, I damn well would have shot my canopy and jumped."[11]

Ted was flying an F9F-5. "It was a brand new airplane. We have F9F-2s and the F9F-5s were replacing the F9F-2s," Hollenbeck noted. Was Ted hit by small arms fire, as per the command diary? Or was he maybe hit by his own bomb blast, as some have suggested? Hollenbeck thought Ted might have been hit by his (Hollenbeck's) blast. "Whether he got bomb blast from my bombs – because he was behind me – or his own, I don't know. I don't know, but I'm just guessing that he probably went way too low."[12]

Whatever the cause, Ted's plane was hit, and lit up and shaking. "I started to call right away," Ted reported. "I had a plane in front and one to the side, but I couldn't pick anybody up. All of a sudden, this plane was right behind me. The pilot was a young sandy-haired lieutenant from Pine Grove, Pennsylvania named Larry Hawkins. He could see I was calling, nodding my head, and the last I hear was, 'I can barely read your transmission,' and the radio pooped out. Later he told me he was yelling for me to shoot the canopy and bail out, and if I'd known I was on fire I probably would have."[13]

Hawkins was in the section behind Ted. "At the time I picked him up coming off the target, I didn't know who it was. I didn't know it was him until after I landed and found out it was Ted Williams."

What Lieutenant Hawkins did know was that this was a squadron mate whose jet was beginning to go off course, and he flew to catch up to him, then steered him back in, giving hand signals to the radio-less Williams. To "Hawk," it was a Marine aviator in deep trouble. This appears to contradict Hollenbeck's recollection that Hawkins has radioed the word that Williams was heading off-course, but Hollenbeck's recollection was non-specific as to this point, whereas Hawkins is very clear in his memory.

Hawkins, who retired a Lieutenant Colonel, recalls the story:

"The day Ted crash-landed his jet, he was well ahead of me, probably about a mile and a half. As I was coming up off the target after dropping my bombs, I was pulling up and heading west, towards the Yellow Sea. That's when I spotted this aircraft going towards the north/northwest and I said to myself, 'That guy's going in the wrong direction.' Then I spotted the puffs of smoke coming out. I flew up alongside and looked over at him, and he looked over at me, but I didn't know who it was.

"Then I went back, and I saw this puff of smoke, this puff, puff, puff, just gentle puffs of smoke coming out of the tail section. I thought it was hydraulic fluid at first. Well, what I found out, it wasn't hydraulic fluid. As we went along, it still continued to stream and that's when it dawned on me it was fuel.

Lt. Larry Hawkins and Capt. Williams at K-3.
Photo courtesy of Larry Hawkins.

"That's when I thought, 'He must have been hit either in the main fuel cell or somewhere in one of the fuel lines.' And so I figured in my own mind at that point, this was probably about five minutes, I had turned him out over the sea and I had finally turned him southward. I had taken the lead by that time and I had given him the signal to join up on me instead of me being just on him. He had no radio. So it was just hand signals. I just patted my head and I said, 'I'll take the lead' and so he followed me. So I went out to the Yellow Sea. Anyway, I got him out to the west side of Korea and then I turned him south/southeast, following the coast line. Then it dawned on me that it was fuel, because it continued to stream. I said – this is all thoughts now -- 'Well, we've got a problem.' We climbed westerly to get above AA and also be over the sea; we climbed above 20,000 feet, maybe to 25,000.

"And as we were flying along, I said, 'I've got to keep him up at high air speed, because if I let him back off from 250 or so knots, that fuel will start pooling in the bottom of that fuselage. As you slow down a Panther, you start getting a back pressure up through there and it would start pooling the fuel underneath there, underneath the plenum chambers. That was a centrifugal flow engine, so you had air coming in around the engine, in addition to of course going through it. I thought, 'Well, as soon as I start slowing down, he's going to either catch on fire, and that fuel will pool underneath there if we don't keep high air speed.' So I kept him at that pretty good high air speed – not high in relationship to today's flying, but it was above 250.

"I set him up over the airfield, King-13, just south of Seoul. Suwon was the name of the base, an Air Force base. So we let down and circled around. I set him up at 7,500 feet, and I pointed down to the airfield. He looked and I'm sure he caught the picture because 7,500 feet at a certain spot in the air was part of the 'flameout pattern.' Had he flamed out – you know by this time, I figured if he's lost all that fuel – he'd have to deadstick it or eject, one of the two.

"So I set him up. Fortunately, I got him to that point. We had flown eastward after we went around the corner there of western Korea – it was North Korea but it was a corner, and we cut back in towards Seoul. I had called the tower all the way down from high altitude and quite some distance out to warn them we were inbound and so the runway was cleared for us when we arrived overhead. As we flew, I set him up there, I started circling and as we got down through the first circle, I gave him the 'wheels down' signal, which was a standard signal for that particular pattern. There's a standard pattern for a flameout pattern – a descending circular pattern from 7,500 over the landing runway – point down the runway and at about 3,500 feet abeam the runway you dropped your gear and flaps according to whether you were high or low on fuel. As I gave him the 'wheels down' signal, he put the wheels down. That's a cranking signal with your hands. He dropped the gear and as soon as he dropped the gear, the damn wheel well doors blew open. And of course by this time we were slowing down where we'd be under 200. We were down somewhere between 150 and 170 knots. And he broke on fire. A burst of flame from his wheel wells.

"So I hollered over the air, forgetting that he had no radio. I said, 'Eject! Eject!' Well, he didn't hear me, but he got the picture, that something had gone wrong. When the landing gear doors unlocked and the gear started down, the fuel that had pooled in the fuselage caught on fire. Williams must have heard a whooomp or felt the fire burst or something to indicate he had a problem, because he immediately pulled the landing gear back and dove for the end of the runway. So he slapped the gear handle back up. By this time he was burning slightly. As the gear came back up, the fire sort of...it was just keeping smoking, there wasn't that much fire coming out of him. So we turned back in the field at about the 180, he was about 3,500 feet, something around there. And then he came screaming across the end of the runway, doing about 200. I was, oh, about 150 feet in the air. He hit down, and by the time he slid 5,000 feet, 5,500 feet or something like that, I had slowed down. He had skidded, and I saw the canopy go off, and by the time I was just barely passing the aircraft and I was doing about 120, 130 knots, I looked over my shoulder and there I saw this big 6 foot 4 figure jumping out -- of course, I didn't know he was 6 foot 4 at that time. But I saw him scrambling out of that cockpit and he ran to the side of the runway. I never saw a guy move that fast in all my life.

"As you can imagine, this was all happening in seconds. He hits down the end of the runway, skids all the way for five thousand plus feet. The airplane comes to a stop. It's sort of pointing in a sideward position – the runway's pointing toward the west, but he's pointing slightly northwest by the time it's stopped skidding. And out over the side he goes, and over to the runway, and he's gone and off to the side of the runway. By the time I passed the end of the runway, and looked back, he was well out of the airplane. Must have been, I'd say a hundred yards away from it.

"That's the story.

"I landed there. They cleared the airfield. I landed there that afternoon. I had enough fuel to come back around a couple of times. It was only about a half an hour, an hour later because I walked into the debriefing shack and that's when...[I learned it had been Ted Williams.] I think the press people were there, or something. I remember there was a big hullabaloo."[14]

Hawkins mentioned how Williams "slapped the gear handle back up." That was good thinking on Ted's part. Hawkins had set Williams up so that he could shut the aircraft down and deadstick it in. Open wheel well doors allow the fuel to catch under the fuselage and so when fire broke out, Williams purposefully raised the wheels back up to squelch the flames. That he landed on the plane's belly was a deliberate action, not the simple failure of hydraulics. He skidded in on the plane's belly, wheels up, to reduce the likelihood of fire.

At least Williams had kept his wits about him. His training paid off. "I just hung on, didn't push the panic button and began to perform the way I was taught to fly in an emergency. When my fuel gauge read empty, I reached down and pulled my writing pad off the leg of my G-suit. I thought sure as hell I would have to bail out. But I wanted to make sure I was at least over our lines before I jumped." [15]

OTHER RENDITIONS

One of the more colorful pilots in the squadron, Tex Montague, said, "I remember the white puffs. They looked like cotton balls and those are 37MM. There were also tracers coming up from the ground. I remember very distinctly him getting shot down. Pinky Hollenbeck – he was the leader of the flight. I was on the flight. [Ted] got a real bad hit in his control system and his airplane was shaking and everything. They asked me to swing out and wait until he landed. I was behind him and watching him. He landed wheels up. I can see the sparks just flying; when that plane hit the ground, the sparks were just flying. Then he got halfway down the runway and the airplane swerved off to the right. Then we could see him climbing out, which was a relief to everybody.

"I pulled off to the right to get out of his way, to let him land first. I landed behind him. We talked. I don't remember all that he said, but I remember him saying that his control stick and all the controls were just shaking violently. I remember that very distinctly. He was pretty level-headed about it. The part that really upset him was how the airplane was shaking and vibrating after he got that hit. I'm almost positive it was 37mm. It could have been small arms fire. It could have been a combination.

There was so much damage to the airplane that I assumed it was 37mm. I don't think just a small bullet could have done that much damage. It's possible he could have been hit by his own blast. It's possible. That happened to several people."[16]

Ted himself wrote about the "wheels-up" landing. He recalled that he was coming in quick for a landing when there was a big explosion in the plane and "one of the wheel doors had blown off. Now there was smoke and fire underneath the plane. Why a wing didn't go was just an act of God... I came in at about 225 miles an hour, twice as fast as you'd ordinarily do it... With thirty feet of fire streaming from the plane, the villagers were running to beat hell... For more than a mile I skidded, ripping and tearing up the runway, sparks flying. I could see the fire truck, and I pressed the brakes so hard I almost broke my ankle, and all the time I'm screaming, 'When is this dirty S.O.B. going to stop?' ... Further up the runway the plane started sliding toward a second fire truck, and the truck tried to get out of the way, dust flying behind it. I stopped right at the end of the runway. The canopy wouldn't open at first, then I hit the emergency ejector, and the fire was all around me, everything on fire except the cockpit. Boy, I just dove out, and kind of somersaulted, and I took my helmet and SLAMMED it on the ground, I was so mad. There were two Marines right there to grab me. I came back and looked at the plane later, and it was burned to a crisp. They had doused it with foam, and the foam was all over it, and it was just cinders."[17]

In his first comments to reporters, the very day of the crash, Williams had explained that "the stick started to shake like mad in my hand. As I neared the base, the aileron started to get stiff so I turned off the hydraulic boost. I had to use both hands on the stick on the final approach. I thought I was going too fast, but when I looked at my indicator it wasn't working. It showed zero."[18] The wing flaps weren't working. The wheels wouldn't go down. "There wasn't anything to do but to 'belly in.' I hit pretty hard and went chugging down the runway. I thought I would never stop. I jerked the emergency release on the canopy and got it off, then I practically fell out of the airplane."[19] He told Ed Hyde of *Sport*, "I glanced out and saw smoke and flames behind me. I didn't waste any time. I just tumbled out and ran. I was scared stiff. I was afraid the tanks might blow. I was never more lucky."[20]

Williams estimated that when he'd landed he only had about 20 or 30 seconds' worth of fuel remaining. It was probably this very lack of fuel that prevented his entire Pantherjet from being engulfed in a fireball.

He reported that he hadn't even felt his plane get hit.

John Glenn was another squadron mate of Ted's in 311. Major Glenn was not on that particular mission that day, having only joined the squadron the previous day, but he sure heard about it. He explained, "The old F9 you have to understand a little bit about it to appreciate how serious that situation was. It's one thing to get hit and one thing to have some fire coming out the back in any airplane. That's a matter of some concern, needless to say...the thing doesn't blow. In the F9F, well, let me...all the jet engines now on fighters and on airliners and everything are what we call axial flow engines. It means that your air comes in the front of that engine and it comes straight back through the engine, through the compressors and on back and it comes back and the pressure is built up until the air is put into the burner and the fuel is injected and it burns and away you go. It flows along the axis of the engine. Now you had other engines that were centrifugal flow, and the air came in and you had a big impeller wheel that then was much larger but it slung the air out into a collector ring then and then that became your conduit for air under higher pressure going into the burners. Now this becomes a bit complicated, but in those centrifugal flow engines like we had in the F9 and which aren't...I don't think any airplane uses them now...but in that airplane they were fine for what we were doing except if you got hit and got a fire back around that engine, it was a rare circumstance when it didn't blow and blow the tail off the airplane. So that was the...Ted got hit and was coming back and there was smoke coming back and all this business and I don't think he... as I recall, he couldn't hear the radio transmissions, that was out. He knew he was on fire because I've talked to him about. I was down there about a year ago and talked to him about it, I was down in Florida and we were talking about some of those things. He knew he was on fire and didn't want to get out, and he was just lucky. He brought the thing around and couldn't get the gear down and bellied it in and it slid up the runway and he jumped out of the cockpit and ran off and stood there watched it melt down. He was just lucky the thing didn't blow."[21]

VMF-115's Woody Woodbury landed just ahead of Williams, and got himself into position to watch the wounded jet streak in. "I had landed and I heard all the conversation between Larry Hawkins and the tower. Ted, of course, didn't have radio. We had landed headed north. There was a stiff wind blowing and I had landed and I pulled off the runway. They had those Air Force 'FOLLOW ME' Jeeps – those Jeeps with the big sign that says FOLLOW ME. We had our designated parking area, but I wanted to see Ted 'cause I knew where he was in the air. I was just ahead of him a little way. They had us land first and they kept him up there. Every time he'd come into heavier air, his airplane would catch on air, and then Larry would take him up and with the lack of oxygen, the fire would snuff out. So then he finally had to come down; by then he was getting low on fuel.

"I had taxied off, turned to the right, headed back south on the taxi strip. I was supposed to head back to my designated area, but I gave the Jeep driver a 'thumbs down' thing like there was something wrong with my airplane, and I was going to pull off to the side. I indicated that to him and he nodded, so then he went back to pick up another jet, to bring another jet in. So I pulled off and I faced the runway. In other words, I landed north, turned around and headed south and then made a right turn on a little taxi strip there and sat there and watched Ted land.

"He came to a stop... I thought he was going to land on the rough grass, but he set it down right on the runway. The only thing he had out were his speed brakes. He had no gear, he had no flaps, he really had no hydraulic system. All he had was the engine, and he did get his speed brakes partially out. I remember, he hit and the sparks and everything just flew up the back of that airplane. He finally came to rest, I'm going to say, 75 to 100 yards from where I was sitting. I was like spellbound. His canopy was gone. He must have jettisoned it along the way. We had to open our canopies before we landed, anyhow, in most cases. He came out of that airplane a lot faster than he ever ran around those bases at Fenway!"[22]

Capt. Walter Roark from 115 had also landed and was taxiing in when he saw Ted's plane scream to a stop. "When that sucker came to a stop, he was out of that plane! I mean, he was out of that plane... it looked like it was still sliding a little bit. He went off the wing of that thing like a rocket! He didn't stay around. And it burned. Right there. It was all engulfed in flame. They retrieved him in one of the damn fire wagons, but I don't really think he went to sick bay. He might have come back over there and looked at the plane. You know, I just don't remember the plane after he got out of it. Hell, the plane was expendable. So what? The plane's gone. The man's OK. Let's go up and get debriefed and head for the damn club!"[23]

Leo LeBlanc was a lieutenant on the mission, and retired as a general in the Marine Corps. He recalled the max effort, or what he called a "group grope." "I guess each squadron had about 16 out. We were the lead group on that particular mission. We were up on the Haeju peninsula and there were supposed to be supplies and little huts and that kind of stuff.

"I didn't really see too much that was of any interest. I never saw or heard any firing, so I don't know what happened to him. He probably could have picked up 50 caliber or something, or maybe could have dropped too low and bomb blast could have got him. But anyway, he was sieved for sure, and the airplane caught fire. He's lucky that didn't explode on him, because that was a tendency of that airplane. Once you caught on fire, man, you didn't have too much time to get out. Well, Williams didn't know he was on fire. Everything was going blotzo in the cockpit, and there was a flame about 20 or 30 feet shooting right out of the back of that thing, as it came into the break.

"All our planes were landed. We were on the opposite end of the runway from which he touched down. We couldn't see him when he touched down, but finally as he come up the runway, he skidded about 3,000 feet at that point. There was crash trucks up and down the runway about 400 or 500 feet apart – and he was close right behind one of them and right in front of another one as he slid our way. We were stacked up trying to get parked. I don't know where I was in that whole gaggle but there was quite a few planes ahead of me, and we were stuck on the taxiway. We couldn't do anything. In the meantime, he starts skidding our way. Once he got to the dirt part, he just disappeared into this cloud of dust.

"The runway was concrete. It had a pretty good crown on it, so that's why when he touched down, he had no control. That thing was going wherever it wanted to. It's a wonder he didn't hit a crash truck! The airplane started turning a little bit – instead of going straight down and still holding the same heading, his nose was cocked to the right as he was sliding. No one knew who was in the airplane. All of a sudden, after this thing stopped – I would guess he was about 100, 150 feet from where I was – all of a sudden, you see this big guy come out with the chute on yet – that's hitting right between the knees – you can't run with it very well – but he was trying to lope as much as possible. It looked as crazy as the devil because he was a pretty big guy as you know. It was awkward as the devil, watching him try to... but he got out of there.

"They were right there pouring foam on him, or water. Whatever it was that they used in those days."[24]

General LeBlanc doesn't recall talking with Ted afterward. It was one of his last missions with 115, before going up to become a forward air controller with the First Division. "There was just a few people that could talk to him. He was sort of a private guy. Trying to get near him, he wasn't all that approachable."

It was foam that was used on the plane, according to Palmer Porter, the Air Force PFC who served as crane operator for the crash crew at K-13. "We got a call that he was coming in, a Marine F9F. We didn't know who it was. I was sitting on the taxiway about halfway down the runway. The fire department was right on the taxiway with me, and the ambulance. He smashed down on my left, and I saw him pulling that trout line to try and blow the canopy, pulling that canvas pull-down thing like a son-of-a-gun, but nothing happened. He slid past me and kept right on going.

"A Marine F9F, if you're going to bail out of the aircraft, you take your feet off the pedals and you put your feet in two pockets as if you were sitting in a chair, and then you put your elbows close into your body and reach right up to the top of your head. There's a ring there, and you pull the ring down with both hands. It's like a big heavy plastic shade. You pull it down to your chin, and then you straighten your arms out to your crotch and that blows the canopy. That canvas face cover is to block the wind blast from hitting your face.

"It was inoperative, but there's an inside crank handle and when he stopped, he cranked the canopy back, jumped up out of it, jumped out on the wing and started running back up towards the runway. The ambulance picked him up there. He just ran, and the guy out of the ambulance said, 'Get in' and they turned around and off he went.

"The ambulance took him off. I said to myself, 'I guess he's all right.' Nobody knew who it was.

"When he was coming in, he was blowing parts all over the goddamn countryside before he smashed down on the runway. He had no landing gear or nothing.

"It took a long time to put it out. I stood off to the side, sat in my crane."[25]

Jerry Coleman was serving on a different base, but this was a big mission and he followed the crash on his radio. "We were on that mission, the whole Marine Air was up in North Korea that day. We were listening to this as it developed. We all listened to it. When someone says 'Mayday!' it gets your attention immediately. We were all on the same frequency and were listening to this unpleasant situation. We were in the air, you know. The minute someone says 'Mayday!' your ears just go up about five feet. At the time we had no idea who it was, just a Marine pilot. And of course, we just listened to this, listened to it, listened to it and then of course, it ended. We don't know where it ended, or how it ended. And then a couple of days later we found out that it was Williams."[26]

"I would have done it for anybody," Larry Hawkins says, "because one of the things in North Korea when the snow was on the ground and everything – if you saw a guy get hit, too many times, sometimes we'd see an airplane go straight in the ground and you didn't know whether he came back out or not, you'd see a secondary or a big blast. Once in a while we'd lose a guy and we didn't know if the guy was with us until we got home. In this case, I picked him up right after we come off the target." We're lucky he did.

Had Ted Williams been killed, it would have been a great tragedy. We would have lost one of our greatest ballplayers midway through a stellar career. The Jimmy Fund for children's cancer research would have lost the man who, immediately upon his return from Korea, became its biggest fundraiser. Baseball would have lost the advocate who converted the occasion of his own induction into the Hall of Fame into a plea for recognition of the black ballplayers who had not had the same opportunities as he had. America would have lost a towering personality, who has gone on to touch and inspire countless thousands (fans and others) with his words, deeds, and example.

SECOND TAKES

A number of different Marines had different thoughts as to how and why Williams got hit. Jack Campbell thought it was small arms fire. "We kind of think it was small arms fire, because on a low-level run although you are bombing, you're at a low altitude at the end of the run. We probably started our bombing run from 18,000 feet. You would probably drop at around 2,000 feet – and by the time you pulled out, you were getting down to about 1,000 feet above the ground, and it was at an altitude small arms could hit you. Like a rifle. I think that's when he got hit. This was some kind of officer training school for the North Koreans. It was a big mission.

"I knew he'd been hit because we could hear that over the radio. We could hear Larry talking to him. Larry to start with indicated Ted, maybe you ought to bail out of that bird because it was burning just a little bit. Ted, that wasn't an option that he wanted to take. The Air Force base at Suwon, K-13, was at hand and, fortunately, it had the longest runway of any base in Korea.

"As we approached King-13, which was the base we landed at on the way back – a lot of our missions to the north, we would exhaust our fuel supply and then we would land at an Air Force base on our way back to our home base, and refuel. King-13 had a real long runway – probably a 10,000 foot runway. I was ahead of Ted, and as I landed he was the plane behind me landing and I could see through my rear view mirror that he was coming in. We knew he was going to be landing without any gear, without any flaps and we knew he was going to be hot when he touched down. I could see that red ball of fire – that's what it looked like – looking through my rear view mirror. As I rolled on down to the end of the runway, which was all the way down to the 10,000 foot, I could see that ball of fire still touching down. I knew that he was sliding down the runway and I would estimate that he slid 5 or 6,000 feet. At the very last moment, his airplane just sort of turned – and this was no gear, no flap, no speed brakes, either – and he kind of slid off the runway to the right. A big cloud of dust went up then, and that's the last I saw of that. The story was that some of the people in the fire trucks had gone to that point, which they figured was roughly halfway down the runway – I heard that some of the trucks had to back up simply because they thought that his airplane was going to slide into them.

"The humorous part of it – it was said – I don't know whether this was true or not – but I heard it then, they said that Ted came out of that cockpit and in about three steps, he was 150 feet away from that plane!"[27]

Major James M. Walley agreed with Tex Montague that it might have been anti-aircraft. "I think we were inclined to think that it was anti-aircraft fire. We were flying fairly low. What we tried to do, particularly in the wintertime when the jetstream from the Gobi Desert would come straight down the Korean peninsula, and it was very, very strong particularly when you got above 10,000 feet. We would expend maybe 2/3 of our fuel getting up to the target, and then jump back up to maybe 40 or 45,000 feet and pick up a 100 to 120-knot tail wind and come home using the rest of it. Most of the missions from Pohang were about two hours long."[28] Walley flew back to K-3 after the mission on the 16th. Surprisingly, no one recalls talking with Williams about the mission in the day or two afterward. Did Walley recall talking to Ted about it after he'd returned? "Not really. I think a lot of us tried to blank out a bunch of the stuff that went on."[29]

Pilot Charles Baker's logbook reflects the flight. A 2.1 hour mission to Kyomipo. It was a big flight, and he didn't see Ted get hit or land, and didn't recall there being that much fuss about it at the time. Baker had come over in the same draft with Williams, after they'd gone through cold weather training together. All he recalls, though, was "just the chitchat in the squadron that Ted was really shook up when it happened. Rightly so. He had every right to be. I got hit myself, mostly by small arms. On those close air support hops, you'd come back with a hole through the tail or through the wing or something. They'd put some tape on. I don't know if it was duct tape, but it was just like duct tape."[30]

Harvey Jensen was a captain with VMF-115, and led the first of the three divisions which hit the prebriefed target. "We were going after a supply dump that was fairly obvious, north of the bomb line by 10 or 15 miles. I have no idea what was stored there. It could have been anything. There was some small arms fire. There was always small arms fire when we were over the bomb lines. I led my division in and we hit it. The second division hit it. Ted was in the third division, back at Tail-End Charlie, and he came down and picked up his own bomb blast. That sort of thing happened more than we wanted it to. They got a lot of ribbing when it happened. We just weren't on the target. You just kept trying to get back on the target before you released, and it would tend to get a little bit too low. Probably somewhere between 800 and 1,500 feet [elevation.] That's what happened to Ted. He popped through his own bomb blast. Either that or he could have been close enough to the preceding planes, and gone through some of their shrapnel that had gone back up. That stuff flies a long way when it triggers."[31]

Jensen had landed just ahead of him at K-13. "Ted went off the runway. He went across the median and damn near got me. I was coming back the other way, having already landed. He kicked up a big cloud of dirt. They had the fire equipment running soon as he came in. He had a big ball of flame coming down the runway, because he was grinding off his speed brake. The speed brake was down and it was just grinding itself off on the runway, just like a chisel on the grindstone – only worse. Sparks and flames. I don't know whether his plane actually torched or not, because I was busy taxiing away from him. I know when the plane was surveyed, it was done.

"I did not see him then. I went right into the fuel pits and refueled and took off and went back to K-3. The only other thing I remember was the chaplain. He'd been out at the crash site. The chaplain came to me while I was refueling in the pit and said, 'I've been waiting my whole life to do that! As soon as Williams stopped and got out of the plane, I called him "Safe!" Baseball term. Then he put his arms out – 'Safe!'"[32]

Attempts to locate the K-13 base chaplain have proven unsuccessful. "I wouldn't have been a bit surprised if the chaplain would have been right there," Larry Hawkins said. "They knew he was coming. We called in. I didn't tell him to eject until we were down around King-13 and we were starting on the way down. I told him to drop his gear and gave him the signal, and he reached over and dropped his gear and that's when he broke on fire. I told you about trying to keep him at high enough speed to keep the fuel from pooling after I learned what was really going on. I didn't know I was that smart at the time [laughs.] Of course, having been an aviation safety officer and digging into holes for people, I'm pretty familiar with what happens when jet engines start to go."[33]

John Dager was an officer with the Air Force stationed at Suwon (K-13). "I was a jet fighter pilot with the Air Force, a first lieutenant. We flew F94 Starfires. We were the all-weather fighter interceptors; we kept the MiGs up in MiG Alley. I knew about Ted Williams from baseball, but I didn't even know he was in Korea until he landed that day. He was in the Marines. He wasn't at our base.

"We heard the crash when he hit the runway. We were in Quonset huts very close to the runway, in our little revetment area. When something like that happened, we could really hear it! When you belly-land a jet at a couple hundred miles an hour, it makes a loud screaming sound as the metal grinds on the blacktop runway. We all went out and looked. We didn't know who it was or what it was, but we knew somebody had bellied in.

"Pretty soon one of the boys came up from the Officers Club real quick and said, 'Hey, Ted Williams is down at the Officers Club. He was the one who just came in.' So we all rushed down. That's an experience to have someone like that come into your field. We were just plain old buck pilots doing our job. He just walked on over to the Officers Club and said he was okay, wasn't hurt. Obviously, he wasn't. I didn't hear him say it, but I heard…one of the boys said that he walked in there and said, 'Any of you Air Force types got a drink?' That's all I heard. You know, they gave us two ounces of whiskey for every mission that we flew. That was to calm our nerves after combat. I think he was a little bit shook up that day. Wouldn't you be? I couldn't get close to him because he was surrounded."[34]

The next day, Dager took a photograph of Williams' Panther. He didn't have to hurry; he had plenty of time. It wasn't going anywhere. "Over there, they didn't have parts and everything, and he was on our field and they didn't have any way of getting it off of our field. They picked it up with a crane and moved it over to the parking area. When you land on the belly, that plane isn't going to go up again! And the nose cone fell off. It was standing up beside it. They had it in the parking area, jacked up on 55-gallon drums. It was there for the duration."[35]

PFC Porter heard from the ambulance driver that he'd taken Ted to the O.C. and he'd belted down four drinks. Not before he had another look at the plane, though, and it may have been that look that shook Ted as much as anything. There were a lot of aircraft which landed hard at K-13. Because it had the longest runway on Korea, planes in trouble were often sent there – even B-29's from Okinawa and Guam. Porter, the crash crew crane operator, reckons he handled maybe fifteen or twenty planes a month.

Porter was ready to lift up the Panther and get it off the runway so the base could receive other aircraft, when the pilot returned to the scene. Porter recalls it clearly, "About 30 or 45 minutes later, the fire department got the fire out, so I backed up to the right-hand... the right corner of the wing and the fuselage. The mechanics got out and hooked the sling on, and I was just picking it up – I had it about two or three feet off the ground – and I happened to look to my left and the ambulance was coming back down the runway. I saw the pilot get out and I thought again, 'I guess he's all right' and I went back to lifting it up. The crane cab is about six foot in the air, and in a moment I felt a tap on my left foot. I looked down and my eyes bugged out! I thought, 'Oh my God. This is Ted Williams!'"

Porter was born and raised in North Weymouth, on Boston's South Shore. He recognized Williams immediately, having seen him play in Boston, and having seen his photo so many times in the paper. He read the *Pacific Stars and Stripes*, and knew that Ted was serving in Korea as a Marine pilot.

Then Ted asked him a question. "He said, 'Would you do me a favor, son?' I said, 'Yes, sir.' He said, 'Would you pick it up so I could walk under it and see what damage I did to it?' I said, 'Yes, sir.' I called the mechanics to get out of the way. I hauled it about seven feet in the air and he walked under it. It was dripping foam and everything else. I could see underneath it. Well, it was like an egg crate. You could look right up through the top of the cockpit and see the sky. Looking up from the cabin of the crane. Most of the bottom of the fuselage was stripped right off. You could look right up through the canopy and see the sky.

"That crane was an old Second World War crane. They had old junk over there at the beginning of the war – old Second World War stuff, trucks and everything else. Oh boy, when he asked me to pick it up, I picked it up about seven feet in the air like I said and I stood right up in the seat and stood right on that brake with my right foot and I put my left foot on top of my right foot, to make sure that... because the brakes were slipping on the goddamn thing and everything else, and I didn't know how old those cables were, and I says, Oh Jesus, that's all I need is this damn thing to come down on his head!"[36]

The crane held. Ted Williams was not crushed by having his plane dropped on him. He drove off in the ambulance again, and over to the officers' club. Porter lifted the plane onto the flatbed and took it back to the salvage area. The Splendid Splinter had left splinters of his jet strewn all down the runway, but Porter doesn't remember anyone keeping a single piece as a souvenir. He does add, "They said he got hit by artillery fire? Ground fire? He got hit by his own bomb blast. He was a gung-ho Marine and he wanted to see where his bombs hit. He flew right on the deck and it blew the bottom right out of the goddamn airplane."[37]

A DISSENTING OPINION

There were less charitable views expressed about the mission. Rylen Rudy is another 311 alumnus, and he disliked Williams intensely. "It was his fault that he got shot up on his third mission," Rudy argued. "We found out that the Koreans had never been duck hunting. They didn't know that you had to lead the duck or you're not going to hit him. Which made us happy as hell. They shot right at the Panther, and of course the Panther's made by the Grumman Iron Works. Man, it would take a lot of hits, without a problem. Most of the time, you didn't even get a scratch, because they were shooting at you. We went in. The first time was a shooting thing – they'd usually give you a couple of gravy hops where you know you're not going to get much, and then they'd start feeding you into the fire. His third mission was the one that Ted got all shot up on.

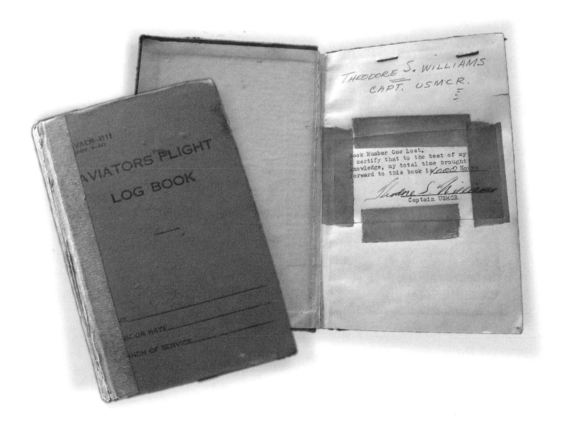

"Pinky Hollenbeck was the guy that was leading the flight and it was one of these gaggles where we had about sixteen airplanes going in on this target. Instead of taking his normal distance on the leader, Ted was so shook up that he was right up behind Pinky. All the way in and all the way out. Well, the theory was that they were all shooting at Pinky and what they were doing was hitting Ted. After we finally got back, in the debriefing, they asked, 'Pinky, did you see any flak?' Hell, no; he was the first guy in. He doesn't see it. Everybody else sees lots of it, but the first airplane in doesn't see it. Of course, that's where Ted got the living daylights shot out of him.

"He came off target and was smoking and Larry Hawkins pulled up alongside of him and tried to get him to bail out of the damn thing. Ted had tunnel vision straight ahead and, boy, he's headed south as fast as he can go. We got in to K-13. I landed before Ted did. When he touched down, he slid about 6,000 feet down a 9,000 foot runway, and then off to the side. And ended up with four 20MM cannons, loaded, and pointing right straight to the main base!

"As he slid down there, he finally slid off the side of the runway and ended up about 50 feet from an ambulance and fire truck that couldn't get their engines started to get the hell out of his way. They thought for a while he was going to go right straight into them. I'm taxiing around in front of him at this time. I saw the canopy come open and from what I gather, that's the first time he

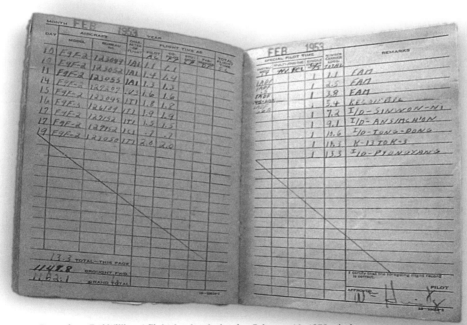

Pages from Ted Williams' flight log book showing February 16, 1953 mission.
Courtesy of Claudia Williams.

smelled smoke. He came out over the side of that airplane, with his parachute on, and I never saw a big man – especially hauling a parachute with him – run a 440 as fast as he did. He bugged out quickly, and headed back in. The fire truck was sitting there fifty feet away, so they put out the fire real quickly. A guy by the name of Chuck Hollaway and I went back out and de-armed his guns, because they were pointing right at the base. And still armed and ready to go. He didn't bother with anything but getting his ass out of there."[38]

Rudy had his own wheels-up landing on another occasion. "I got all shot up and had to belly it in at K-3 and went off the other end of the runway. 5,300 feet. With about a 70 foot drop off either end of it. So I took a Panther off the end of the damn thing and banged my back. Sixteen years later, I ended up having a back operation."[39]

Getting hit by bomb blasts or secondary explosions sometimes led to gruesome incidents. Rudy tells of the time Bill Armagost hit a Korean with his plane. "Army Armagost, he came in on a run out there one time and got a secondary explosion. Here's all this crap and crud and all this flailing around. Army, as he drops his stuff, flies through this cloud up there. About halfway through it, something hits his airplane and turns him almost sideways and then back out again, he comes out the other side and looks around and he can't find anything wrong with the airplane. He came back and landed it back at K-3 and the plane captain came around and says, "What did you hit?" And Army says, "I don't know, but where the hell is it?" Out on the end of the wing tank, the outside front of the tip tank. Army gets out there and here's a dent in the front of the tip tank. They took scrapings off it and it turns out it's human hair and blood. Some guy's sitting down there on that ammo dump or whatever it was that blew up and comes flying up in the air, and Army comes through and pops him in the head with the tip tank."[40]

Metal shop mechanic Elmer Plaetzer, a corporal with VMF-311 who served as a structural airframe mechanic at the time, says, "We didn't have many planes with bullet holes. The metal shop did those; we had four or five men working in the metal shop. We did have some planes that got too low while dropping their bombs and came back with parts of trees in them."[41]

What did Williams write in his log book after he returned from this harrowing mission, from which he had barely escaped with his life? Something colorful or memorable? A star, or an exclamation point? Not at all. The sum total of his remarks in the section provided: "I/D – AMSINCH'ON". In other words, an interdiction mission to Amsinch'on – and that's the only notation in his log book.

Marine Air Group 33 commanding officer Ben Robertshaw put Williams's mission in perspective, though. "Nobody has ever been sure whether he was hit by fragments of one of his own bombs or whether it was actually anti-aircraft. It doesn't matter, and it shouldn't be an issue. You're still putting your life on the line." And dive bombing put you right in harm's way, every time. General Robertshaw added, "After that mission, we all met that evening in the so-called O Club and we did a rain dance for the next day – that is customary, for pilots to get up on the table where they were imbibing and dance a little bit, and suggest that it rain the next day so that there wouldn't be any missions."[42] There was no rain on the 17th, though, and Ted Williams was on one of those missions, the very next morning.

Ted's understanding was that the target in Kyomipo had been a hand grenade factory.[43] One can only hope that the attack had saved the lives of a number of U.N. troops who might otherwise have been killed.

TWO POSTSCRIPTS

AN EYEWITNESS ACCOUNT

Joe Giaimo, Jr. wrote a letter home to his parents on February 16. He wrote:

"This morning about eleven, while working in the weather station, a very alert person yelled: 'An aircraft is on fire!' Immediately every one including myself ran outside, looking to the runway for a burning plane. Instead, we noticed some Panther Jets flying and circling over the field. One was on fire!

"Inside a minute, that plane was a ball of fire, burning from nose to tail. Any average pilot would have bailed out. But not this pilot. He was going to bring the plane in as she was. After circling the field, he brought the plane to the approach end of the runway and started to bring her down. We noticed her wheels wouldn't come down, that he was going to land her on her 'belly.' Believe me, he had a job on his hands. All of us were keeping our fingers crossed and praying for that pilot's life.

"Finally, the pilot banked her on the runway real gently and skidded down half the runway before turning right into the field. By so doing, the runway was clear for all other incoming traffic.

"At 12:30, I was sitting plotting a weather map when a Marine pilot (captain) approached. Like a bolt of lightning, I recognized him. I jumped out of my seat and said" 'Say, sir, aren't you Ted Williams?'

"He answered, 'That's right.'

"I grabbed his hand, shook it and said:

"'Glad to meet you, Ted.'

"Yes, mom and dad, Ted Williams, one of baseball's greatest players of all time, proved to be just as outstanding with his plane as with his bat." Washington Post, *March 27, 1953*

"GOLLY, I'M GLAD HE'S SAFE" – Doris Williams

The first that Ted's wife heard of the crash-landing was not from Ted himself, but from little Bobby-Jo who had "come running to her this morning, excitedly calling 'Mommy, Mommy, there's something about Daddy on TV.' She ran into the living room, but missed the brief news story. Later, Mrs. Williams said, she was in the kitchen and heard her husband's name mentioned again on the television broadcast. 'I ran into the living room again,' she said, 'but I only got the end of it.'" Apparently, the first time she got the full story is when an AP reporter read her the news over the telephone. Her response was, "O my gosh, I think it's awful. It's an awful close call – too close. And he just got there! It's enough to scare you to death. Golly, I'm glad he's safe."

Boston Evening Globe, *February 16, 1953*

TED'S AIRCRAFT

The plane Ted flew on 16 February was a Grumman F9F-5 Panther, made by Grumman Aircraft Corp. at Bethpage, Long Island, New York. Serial numbers for the aircraft were known as Bureau numbers, for the Navy Bureau of Aeronautics. These numbers were assigned sequentially beginning (in the third series of numbers) in 1940. Because the Navy procures aircraft for the Marines, the numbers assigned are Navy Bureau numbers. The Bureau Number for the particular plane Ted Williams flew on 16 February was BuNo 126109. The official loss is carried on the books as "hit by small arms fire and landed at K-13 on fire Feb 16, 1953."

The F9F-5 aircraft lost while in service with VMF-311 included:

> *125107 shot down by AAA – Aug 12, 1951. Pilot killed.*
>
> *125106 engine flamed out and crashed on runway at K-3 – Oct 16, 1951*
>
> *125087 in midair collision with USAF L-19 – May 11, 1952*
>
> *127192 hit by small arms fire and pilot bailed out 45 mi NE of Seoul – Sep 19, 1952*
>
> *127212 in takeoff accident at K-3 due to collapsed nosewheel – Sep 22, 1952*
>
> *126109 hit by small arms fire and landed at K-13 on fire – Feb 16, 1953*
>
> *126081 crash landed due to battle damage – Mar 23, 1953*
>
> *126189 ditched due to fuel starvation in bad weather near Kangea, Korea – May 6, 1953*
>
> *126002 fuel starvation due to bad weather and crashed near K-3 – May 6, 1953*
>
> *126006 pilot bailed out over Sea of Japan near Pusan, Korea – Jul 17, 1953*
>
> *126041 pilot bailed out over Sea of Japan near Pusan, Korea – Jul 17, 1953*
>
> *126073 ammo caught fire due to blast from another aircraft – Jul 17, 1953*

Of course, many other Panthers used by other squadrons were also lost.

BuNo 126225 appeared in the film *Bridges of Toko-Ri* which many Marine aviators say is the closest Hollywood has yet come to presenting what these missions over Korea were like.

NOTES

1) *Interview with Bill Clem, December 23, 2002.*

2) *Interview with George Winewriter, November 28, 2002.*

3) *Interview with Marvin Hollenbeck, February 3, 2003. There is a difference of opinion as to who led the mission for the jets from K-3. The 311 Command Diary credits Major Thomas M. Sellers of 115, but the 115 Command Diary reports that the flight leader was Major Robert H. Hill of 115. MAG-33 reports it was Sellers. At 1052, they attacked supply buildings located at YC3688 – or was it at YC355880? This time, 115 and MAG-33 agree it was YC355880 but 311 reports it was YC3688. At least they all agree it was an attack on supply buildings. The nature of the target seems to differ as well. In My Turn At Bat, Williams simply said it was "far above the thirty-eighth parallel." Linn quotes him, though, as saying it was "near Kyomipo." Ted says it was "an encampment, a large troop concentration." He told Ed Linn it was "a troop encampment near Kyomipo." [Hitter, p. 249] The three command diaries agree, though, that it was a complex of supply buildings, not a troop concentration. No doubt, though, that there were troops near their supplies. Michael Seidel says it was a "tank and infantry training school near Pyongyang." [Seidel, Ted Williams: A Baseball Life, op. cit., p. 249]*

4) *Ed Hyde, Sport, op. cit., July 1953.*

5) *Williams*, My Turn At Bat, *op. cit., p. 179.*

6) *Coss, quoted by Ed Hyde*, Sport, *op. cit., July 1953.*

7) *Interview with Marvin Hollenbeck, February 3, 2003.*

8) *Interview with Gen. L.B. Robertshaw, November 16, 2002.*

9) *Interview with Bob Flanagan, June 2, 2003.*

10) *John McCain*, Worth The Fighting For, *NY: Random House, 2002.*

11) *Ted Williams, "This Is My Last Year,"* Saturday Evening Post, *April 24, 1954.*

12) *Interview with Marvin Hollenbeck, February 3, 2003.*

13) *Williams*, My Turn At Bat, *op. cit., pp. 179, 180. Hawkins makes the point that Williams' plane only caught fire when he put the wheels down over K-13, prior to landing.*

14) *Interview with Lawrence Hawkins, June 2, 1997 and correspondence of April 21, 2004.*

15) *Hyde,* Sport, *July 1953.*

16) *Interview with Paul B. Montague, February 11, 2003.*

17) *Williams*, My Turn At Bat, *op. cit., pp. 180, 181.*

18) Boston Globe, *February 16, 1953.*

19) Pacific Stars and Stripes, *February 17, 1953.*

20) *Hyde,* Sport, *July, 1953.*

21) *Interview with John Glenn, October 1, 1996.*

22) *Interview with Robert Woodbury, October 1, 2002. The impression of a number of ups and downs to deprive the fire of oxygen weren't quite correct, according to Larry Hawkins.*

23) *Interview with Walter N. Roark, Jr., December 21, 2002.*

24) *Interview with Leo LeBlanc, December 27 and 31, 2002.*

25) *Interview with Palmer Porter, March 29, 2004.*

26) *Interview with Jerry Coleman, April 5, 1997.*

27) *Interview with Jack Campbell, November 27, 2002.*

28) *Interview with James M. Walley, December 7, 2002.*

29) *Ibidem.*

30) *Interviews with Charles Baker, December 28, 2002 and February 3, 2003.*

31) *Interview with Harvey Jensen, December 13, 2002.*

32) *Ibidem.*

33) *Interview with Larry Hawkins, December 21, 2002.*

34) *Interview with John Dager, December 20, 2002.*

35) *Ibidem.*

36) *Interview with Palmer Porter, March 29, 2004. Since Williams rarely drank, the hearsay regarding the four drinks is at least suspect.*

37) *Ibidem.*

38) *Interview with Rylen B. Rudy, February 4, 2003.*

39) *Ibidem.*

40) *Ibidem.*

41) *Interview with Elmer Plaetzer, December 27, 2002.*

42) *Interview with Louis B. Robertshaw, November 16, 2002.*

43) *Cataneo, David, "Ted Williams Remembers",* Boston Herald, *May 26, 1997.*

Pre-flight check, Ted in cockpit.
Photo by George Warnken.

CHAPTER 12 – FROM THE FLIGHT LINE TO A HOSPITAL SHIP

The day after he'd been shot down, torn up the Panther on the Air Force runway at Suwon, and nearly been killed in the process, Ted Williams was back up on another mission. He'd bellied in around noontime, but made it back to K-3 later that same day.

Darwin Glaese was in the same fighter squadron. He wasn't on the mission, but he's the one who brought Ted back from K-13. Glaese remembers, "The day he got knocked down, I picked him up. I happened to be up at K-13 to take two enlisted men up there, for them to go home on emergency leave. I had a twin engine Beechcraft up there and I heard all these sirens going off and everything... an emergency landing coming in. I looked up and saw two Marine Panthers coming in, one of them streaming a lot of smoke and some flame coming out of the back. Of course, I didn't know who it was at the time.

"So, anyway, it come in. Wheels-up landing, after they spread some foam down there real quick. It didn't take them long. It was about a two minutes job after the emergency signal, for the crash crew to put the foam down. He landed real hot, about 180 to 200 miles an hour, with his wheels up and he slid a long way on the runway and he come screeching to a stop. Opened up and out he jumps! Didn't have a scratch.

"I flew him back to the base that day. I brought these two men up there, but I was going back by myself. It was maybe 2 [1400 hours]. He went to sick bay, got debriefed, all that stuff. In a jet, it's only about 35 minutes back, but in a Beechcraft, it's about an hour and a half.

"He was a real independent kind of guy. He was real shook up at first but after a while he calmed down and he just sat there and rode home."[1]

Major Pat Harrison was one of Ted's roommates in the portion of the hut they shared with Joe Mitchell. Harrison picked up Ted after he was ferried back to K-3, and drove him back to their quarters. "My God, Pat, they almost got me today," Williams told the major. "Ted was gazing into the sky," Harrison (a lieutenant colonel in Norfolk, Virginia) said when he spoke with reporter Mike Gillooly a few years later. "He was thankful to be alive. He was the humble man I've come to know over the intervening years."[2]

And later that same evening, Captain Williams found his name on the board. The mission was to leave early, soon after 0800 the next morning.

17 FEBRUARY 1953 – COMBAT MISSION #4

The first flight of the day saw Ted Williams back in action again.

Mission 3301

Eight aircraft from VMF-311, eight from VMF-115 and two from HEDRON-33 were airborne at 0818/I on a prebriefed Group interdiction mission. The two aircraft from HEDRON-33, armed with only 20MM ammunition, served as Group Tactical Observers to observe and assess damage. Colonel ROBERTSHAW flying one of these aircraft also served as Tactical Officer (Airborne Commander.)

The mission, led by Captain Clive BLANEY of VMF-115, attacked a troop concentration, located at BU 4826 (Tong-dong). This target was hit at 0918/I, with 85% coverage being received. Four large fires were observed burning in the target area. Ordnance expended was 104 250-pound bombs and 1,995 rounds of 20MM ammunition. Negative opposition was encountered. Two of the flights landed at K-13 due to low fuel. The other aircraft returned safely to K-3 at 0956/I. The other VMF-115 pilots were Major THORPE, Captains LUNDIN, TIVNAN, IRELAND, ROARK, and SHARKEY, and Lieutenant Hollaway. The VMF-311 pilots were Majors FOX, WALLEY, Captains WILLIAMS, NEWENDORP, CARRUTHERS, CLEM, PETERSEN and MONTAGUE. Colonel ROBERTSHAW and Lieutenant VAN DUESEN flew the HEDRON-33 aircraft.

Ted was reported by the AP to have dropped two 500-pound bombs and four 250-pounders, but the squadron Command Diary does not reflect any 500-pound bombs being used on this mission. After returning from the flight, Williams was told that his wife had been informed he was safe, and he said, "I'm glad she found out that quickly that I'm OK. Thanks to the AP for giving me the message."

On the way back from the mission on the 17th, Williams landed again at K-13 – this base was sometimes used as a refueling stop – and he said that the operations officer there "told me that the plane which I crash landed yesterday was really clobbered and full of holes. They hit me in a good spot. They put my plane out of commission and they almost put me out of commission, too." He mentioned that his ankles were still a bit sore. He saw himself lucky to have survived, but also lucky to be flying jets with the Marines. "I got a good break in coming over here to fly jets. Every pilot wants to fly jets. I'm doing what I want to do. Getting back in the service is one of the nicest things that happened to me. I never saw combat in World War II. I was just an instructor at Pensacola." Would he return to baseball? "It all depends on how I feel and if I end up all in one hunk after this fight. There's no time for that over here [playing ball]. In my spare time I like to work around a little with photography. I rarely get off the base."[3] Williams said all the right things. He'd hardly had time to get off the base, though, since he'd been there just two weeks. After refueling, Ted took a quick flight back to K-3.

Another pilot who had flown with him this day said that Williams acted "like nothing had happened the day before."[4]

Asked about 17 February's flight duty, Ted replied, "It sure was better than the one yesterday."

Just as a rider thrown off a horse is well-advised to climb right back on again, so are pilots who are hit urged to head right back out again, so they have less time to brood about what might have been. Williams was uninjured physically, or only very slightly. It was probably salutary that he was strapped back in again right after breakfast the following morning.

Bill Clem's example may have influenced Ted. As recounted above, Clem crashed-landed his own plane on the 15th and it suffered "major damage" – but Clem was back up again on the first mission on the 16th, the one when Williams got hit. "That was kind of standard procedure in those wartime days over there, if you got shot at, maybe had an accident or maybe the plane even got hit. They just wanted to keep you going so you didn't have time to think about it. I didn't see him that day. I think I saw him the next day."[5]

Tom Miller was the executive officer of VMF-323. He is also one of John Glenn's closest friends; the two went through flight school together. Jerry Coleman was in Miller's squadron, and there was a time that Miller had to face the same issue with Coleman that Moran had with Williams:

do you launch him again? "Jerry flew many missions on my wing during the strikes there. Jerry had an unfortunate incident on about his 65th or 68th mission. He was taking off and the engine starting popping a little bit. Instead of going ahead and trying to go ahead and get it off, he pulled the throttle off but he couldn't get stopped at the end of the runway and the airplane ran over, and flipped over on its back. He was carrying a lot of bombs and the kind of bomb he was carrying we were very leery of because of their fusing. It was called a 260-pound frag bomb. Well, fortunately none of them went off, but it kind of tore Jerry up mentally. So I talked to the skipper and we grounded him and sent him to a ground job after that. But Jerry was a great guy and a hard charger just like Ted Williams was. That was the last time he flew in combat.

"It's been our experience all through the years, whether it's accidents or in combat, that if you are the subject that goes through the incident, sometimes it's better to put the guy right back in the air again real quick. Under the situation, we might have but on the other hand we might have had serious misgivings if he had have gone on and then he had got shot down. We were losing a pilot a week. We just finally decided, because of Jerry and because of his attitude – he was a hard charger – he didn't want to be relieved, but we went ahead and relieved him."[6] The philosophy was: send them back up again. But each case had to be decided on its own merits.

Apparently not everyone agreed with this philosophy.

Art Moran, Ted's commanding officer, got chewed out when he sent Williams back out the next day. Soon after the mission departed, Moran says, "the phone rang. It was the commanding general. He said, 'Moran, what the hell are you doing down there?' 'Well, General, is there a problem?' I said, 'I'm just trying to run a fighter squadron.' He said, 'Did you launch Ted Williams?'

"Ted had been launched through the system. When he got back [from the crash], I met him and talked to him about what most of us thought about having a problem with an airplane. If you want to continue to fly, you'd better get right back in another one. He agreed with that. I said, 'Well, let us know when you want to go again.' He said, 'What's wrong with now?' 'Great, go see the Operations officer.' When the general called, and said. 'Did you launch Ted Williams again?' I said, 'Yes, sir, I talked to him about it and told him what most of us thought about what trouble... your reactions after having a problem with an airplane. He said he wanted to go again.' 'Jesus Christ! Think of the publicity!' I said, 'General, down here he's just another Marine Corps captain doing his job.'

"I knew that a conversation had taken place between a couple of generals. The general grounded him when he got back from that second try."

As it happened, anyway, "Ted got a hell of a cold that kept [him laid up] for about a week or so."[7]

Woody Woodbury says Moran told him, "He was a Marine pilot and he was slated for the next flight, so I sent him on the damn flight." Woody adds, "Ted didn't object – and that really strengthened my admiration and respect for him. It was like hopping back on a horse. He got in a new jet for this mission – whatever one was assigned to him for the flight -- and he went and flew the mission. Art said, 'The general chewed me out. Do you realize that would have happened if that kid up there... oh boy!'"[8]

Moran was apparently not intimidated in the least. A couple of days later, he sent Williams back up again.

Almost immediately after returning from Korea, Ted Williams expressed some of his feelings to author John M. Ross for an article in The American Weekly *(August 23, 1953) entitled "Where Do We Go From Here?" The article was printed as "by Ted Williams as told to John M. Ross."*

Ted wrote the piece after attending the 1953 All-Star Game but before resuming play with the Red Sox.

He began, "It seemed strange standing there in Cincinnati's Crosley Field, a few weeks ago, while 30,000 fans cheered. Perhaps it was just being at baseball's All-Star game as Captain Ted Williams of the U.S. Marines – without a glove or bat in my hand...

Somehow it didn't seem right for me to be standing there alone, taking the bows. Tens of thousands of other young fellows – living, half-living, or dead – belonged there at my side, I thought. They would have liked the cheers, too.

It was good to be home again, back in a ball park. But I wonder if anyone ever leaves Korea, even when you're thousands of miles away from its filth and mud, and its nauseating stench no longer fills your nostrils.

The forgotten men who have stood or fallen there come home with you in spirit, I believe. And all the unanswered questions and confusion of this strange conflict – the war that is not a war – continue to haunt you, and you wonder if there is a solution at all.

I'm not bitter. Any guy who has been in combat knows that bitterness vanishes quickly when you gamble with death – and win. From there on, you are grateful to be alive.

Make no mistake about it. I am deeply grateful. I was lucky to get back in one piece and I know it.

I was lucky, too, to meet up with my buddies in the Marine Air Group 22, with whom I flew the F-9 Panther jets. I've never had more admiration for any group of men.

As a ballplayer, I've seen many heroes rise to the occasion – guys who give it the old college try when you need it most. The fans talk about them for years to come.

19 FEBRUARY 1953 – COMBAT MISSION #5

On the 19th, Lt. Col. COSS led an "ID" (interdiction) mission of eight aircraft from VMF-311. Airborne at 0717/I, this was an attack on buildings and shelters in the North Korean capitol, Pyongyang, which dropped 48 fragmentation bombs. Two lingering fires were noted, but it was impossible to assess further damage due to smoke and dust in the target area. There was no opposition and everyone was back on base by 0915/I. Pilots accompanying Coss were Captains WILLIAMS, STREET, CARRUTHERS, and CLEM, and Lieutenants RUDY, PARRISH, and Larry HAWKINS.

After the February 19 mission, Ted did not fly for the rest of the month, nor did he fly any combat missions at all during the month of March. He did take up planes on March 1, 2, and 3 – a test flight and two fam flights. His next mission was 4 April 1953.

Mission #5 was Ted's last mission, though, for six weeks. Going through cold weather training left Ted ill, and he was laid up for two days in Japan while in transit to Korea. Every account of Pohang in February 1953 indicates a frozen, miserable place. Jerry Coleman served elsewhere in Korea, but conditions were about the same on the whole peninsula. He arrived a couple of months before Williams. "Damn cold. Freezing, miserable, miserable country! I don't know what they fought over that country for. Hot in the summer, blazing hot. Miserable cold in the winter. The worst part of any mission was going from the ready hut to the plane! The winds across the runway... I froze to death out there. You couldn't wait to get to the plane to warm up."[9] Other pilots thought it was even worse sitting in the plane for a couple of hours on CAP. "You'd freeze your cookies off when you were standing alert. The Air Force was pretty fortunate. They had heaters in their 86s, but us guys in the Marine Corps, you're sitting there on a four-hour alert as air defense or something. You had no heat."[10]

First reports had Williams grounded with an ear infection which, according to reports from the First Marine Air Wing, interfered with Ted's flying. One way or another, Williams was down and out. "Almost immediately, he came down with a very severe cold, which turned into pneumonia.

I think somebody attributed that to the shock of the incident the day before that he maybe came down with that cold and pneumonia."[11]

Hutmate Joe Mitchell recalls, "He had a very bad nasal and chest involvement, and he had a problem with his ears. I guess they were pretty sensitive to altitude, and we were climbing to 20,000 feet, going up every day. The diving down. I don't know if he was bagging it or not, but he certainly appeared to be discomforted by this constant ear problem."[12]

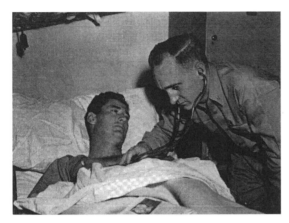

Dr. H. W. Jayne gives Ted Williams a checkup during sick leave stay on USS Consolation.
From book USS Consolation (AH-15).

After fighting it for a while, Williams was finally evacuated from K-3 and sent to one of the hospital ships the Navy kept anchored offshore. Ted was sent to the *USS Haven*, one of three ships in Inchon Harbor. Because of the very high tides at Inchon – the tides were over 20 feet between low and high tide – the ships could not be brought into a pier and tied up. They had to anchor offshore, presenting the problem of how to transport patients (some of them very seriously wounded) from shore to ship. Jan Herman, Chief Historian of the Navy Bureau of Medicine and Surgery, says that "the skipper of the *Haven* came up with this brilliant idea and he borrowed two pontoon floats from the Army. These were either cargo barges or pontoon barges. They towed them out with a tugboat and they strapped them, one on each side. It looked like two solar panels on a satellite, with two big yellow discs, one on each side. That was the target for the helicopter to land on."[13]

In Korea, the big play happened every day. Only the stakes were higher and the acclaim almost nil.

I must admit it was difficult for me to understand or match their amazing spirit at times. In my outfit, the average age was 32–33, and 95 per cent of the men were married and had kids. Most of them were reservists with service in World War II. You didn't have to ask any questions to find out how far from Korea they'd like to be.

Many people have said that one man shouldn't be called on to fight two wars in one lifetime. You wouldn't have put that motion to a vote over there. They'd kiss you on both cheeks just for thinking it. And then, maybe five minutes later, the same guys would be gunning their jets down the runway off to risks their necks again.

I hadn't been counting on another hitch in the service when I was called up by the Marine Reserves in April, 1952. I had spent three years in the Marines during World War II, and at age 33 and with four dependents, I thought I had reached the point where guys sit back and say, "Well, I guess they won't want me this time."

The recall wasn't exactly joyous news, but I tried to be philosophical about it. It was happening to a lot of fellows, I thought. I was no better than the rest. I'd miss that good Boston Red Sox paycheck, true, but I was no better than the rest.

But during the whole time in Korea it was hard for me to believe that it was the right thing to call back these fellows who were old timers by the standards of combat flying.

We had some laughs over there, too, just to balance the griping. An occasional party to break up the dull monotony. And did they know their baseball!

[Ted then retold the story of being shot down, the first time he'd put a scratch on a plane in almost four years of military flying.] I was a pretty lucky guy that day and I'll never forget it. I don't care how many times my line drives go smack at a fielder's glvoe hereafter, I'll never deny the fact that I'm a lucky stiff.

It was good to get back, that's for sure. But, I must say I was a little sorry to go off and leave behind so many good guys I had learned to like. Lloyd Merriman, the Cincinnati Red Leg center fielder, was at the same field with me and did a tremendous job over there. And, of course, there was Jerry Coleman of the New York Yankees. He had well over 100 combat missions in two wars before they grounded him – and twice he was almost a goner.

During her service on the *Haven*, Nurse Nancy Crosby took a number of photographs. Almost 50 years later, she offered them to historian Herman. He began to look through them and was startled by one in particular. "I get to the last one, and I say, 'Wait a minute! That's Ted Williams!' He's in his Marine fatigues and he's got his jacket on, and of course I see the baseball glove. It has 'H & W' on it, which is Health & Welfare, a committee every ship had. There's Ted Williams and I'm thinking, 'What the hell? How did he get on the ship?'

"They gave him the glove to pose with. They had softball games down on the pier. Next day I called her [Crosby], and asked her. 'Oh, he was one of our patients.' She didn't take care of him personally. She does remember how nice he was. He was very pleasant. He seemed to feel more comfortable on the ship among fellow Marines."[14]

Williams was on the *Haven* from 14 to 24 March 1953. Virginia Brown, Navy Nurse, says, "I'm sorry I didn't get to know him better. He was on the *Haven* twice. He had a URI [upper respiratory infection] the first time and an ENT the second time. I was not on the ward he was on, so we only met on the deck, but he was really a nice guy. He was a walking patient. He was mobile. When he first came, he was sick, but I don't think he had to spend much time in bed."[15]

It was Williams' first visit to a hospital ship. Toward the end of his posting in Korea, he spent time on another hospital ship, the *USS Consolation*. He was remembered among those who served there as well.

At the end of World War II, the *Consolation* was involved in evacuating and caring for ex-POWs and other Allied nationals. She was also the first Hospital Ship to arrive in Korea, in July 1950, to furnish medical support for United Nations Forces. The ship was fitted with a 60 foot by 60 foot helicopter landing platform and was the first hospital ship to ever receive casualties from the battlefield by helicopter. The first casualty arrived at 12:20 PM on 18 December 1951. Late in 1952, during a major Communist offensive, the *Consolation* – anchored in Inchon Harbor – received 62 helicopters in one 24-hour period. Over the course of its 31-month stay in Far Eastern waters, the *USS Consolation* served a total of 18,433 patients. One of them was Ted Williams.

One of the nurses who served on board recalls, "Ted Williams was a patient on Sick Officers Quarters (SOQ) on the *Consolation* on or about March 1953. If I can recall correctly, his diagnosis was upper respiratory infection. At the time I did not know he was a famous baseball player and never did he mention the fact. He was a cooperative, quiet and unassuming patient just interested in returning to his squadron."[16]

Major Hank Kirby, a hospital corpsman, recalls that the ship "had a special watch on him in officers' country, port side, when he came in with an upper respiratory infection thought to be bordering on pneumonia."

Did Kirby's ears perk up a bit when he heard that Ted Williams was on board ship? "Absolutely. There was sort of a scuttlebutt that came around and they said there were also special watches on him. I happened to receive a 12 to 2 special watch, which was merely to sit outside his door, let no one in, and then provide whatever medications were given. He had p.r.n. stuff – a decongestant. On the doctor's orders, it means whenever necessary given 4 hours apart or 6 hours apart – whatever they write.

"The next day I went in and just said hi. He was rather... Ted Williams-ish. He was brusque and curt and polite, but not particularly friendly. And it wasn't necessarily because he was an officer and I was an enlisted man. It was just his demeanor.

"He did a lot of reading. We had all kinds of books and older magazines and the US Armed Forces newspaper that were provided by relief agencies, primarily the Salvation Army and to a lesser degree the Red Cross. He complained of both stuffiness and hearing problems. That would be consistent with a eustachian tube infection, an ear infection which of course would give balance problems, most likely.

"I think, not wanting anything to happen to such a high profile person as Mr. Williams, that that special watch came about.

"Even an amateur such as I could detect that there was something wrong. The characteristic stuffiness and red eyes, talking as though you're stuffed up, were evident."[17]

Another Navy corpsman on the *USS Consolation* was John Bartlett; after the Navy, Bartlett went to medical school and became a surgeon. He later joined the reserves and served on the *Consolation* again in Vietnam and as chief of surgery aboard the *USS Mercy* during Desert Shield/ Desert Storm. "I was a corpsman on the SOQ. The sick officers' quarters. They were separated in those days. I think he had a room to himself. He was just a regular person, but he wasn't exuber-ant. He was a very quiet person and he didn't show a lot of fanfare. He was very...he wasn't a...he didn't talk much about his baseball then. I know he was a celebrity, but he was just like a regular pilot. I think they kind of kept him away from the other guys because they'd probably be pestering him a lot. I think he was in a room by himself for that reason.

"I just took care of him as a patient. He came and we treated him as a regular patient."[18]

Dale Purcell served in the photo squadron VMJ-1, which was stationed across the field from MAG-33 at K-3. He had a story to tell that tied into Ted Williams.

"A friend of mine [Charles Herrick] who had finished his missions, was flying an F-80, which was a utility plane. It used to be a fighter, but this had a second seat in there. A second pilot would often go up with you, and that's part of how you would get refreshers and re-training. Since we flew so much on instruments, every few weeks we would go up under the hood. This fellow would take you up, get you under the hood. Get you totally disoriented and get the plane out of control and tell you, 'OK, you take over on the instruments.' He would fly a mission – work a problem – get back over the field and into a landing approach. He would pop the canopy and you would solve the problem or you'd have to work it again.

"I had flown with him the day before and he had made a pilot error. Unrelated. When I was flying with him, he had exceeded the limits by a lot. He had totally forgotten that we had fully loaded tip tanks. There's a little sign on the dashboard of the F-80: 'DO NOT EXCEED 430 KNOTS UNLESS THE PLANE IS CLEAN.' So he was well beyond that and the plane was beginning to buffet. So I said, 'Charlie, chop the throttle. Reduce the speed.' He thought I was objecting to the problem, and he objected. I said, 'Reduce the speed or I will. We can talk about it then.' He did. We were the same rank, good friends.

"On the way in, I said, 'Chuck, you've flown your missions. You really ought to get Doc Eagleson to ground you for the weeks you have left.' He said, 'No, the only breaks I get in the day is to get to fly.' He was concerned about home and family. He, too, had been recalled and had a family and a life to live. I said, 'Well, why don't you ground yourself?' It's not a matter of saving face. You're preoccupied, worried about some things.' Neither of us did it [got him grounded].

"I was supposed to fly with him the next day, but when I got back to my barracks that day, I had a letter suggesting I go to Japan to make an emergency call home. So I took a weapon and flew into southern Japan where we had a staging base. I made the call and the situation was in hand, so I came to catch the flight back to Korea. I hadn't planned to stay there. This wasn't R&R. They had just gotten a load of replacement pilots from the States and they had to get them to Korea, so that the guys in reserve could go home. This was a Sunday. They said it'll be Tuesday before we can get you back there. Come at 2 on Tuesday. These replacement pilots are critical.

"When I got back on Tuesday, there was only one F-80 on the base and I was looking out the window and here it was standing on its nose, looking like an accordion. It had had a crash by the nose.

"I was met at the operations base and I asked the driver, 'What happened to the F-80?' He said, 'The adjutant wants to see you as soon as I can get you there.' I said, 'Sergeant, would you please answer the question? Was it Captain Herrick?' He said, 'Yes sir, but please let the adjutant tell you.' I got up there and he told me that the Seabee chief warrant officer who had extended the runways of this field was due to have a meritorious flight, be flown around Korea. This was the first time a combat pilot was not there for his instrument refresher so somebody else flew with him, and he landed short and hit the sloping ramp, that sloped down about 200 feet at about 45 degrees into a rice field on either end.

"The adjutant said he's aboard a hospital ship and the flight surgeon wants you up there. [The hospital ship was the *USS Consolation*.] It was 100 miles away, up in Inchon Harbor. Ted Williams was there on that hospital ship. There were three hospital ships there, with big red crosses on them. I went out in a small liberty boat. I came to the top of the ladder and the officer of the deck was there. I said, 'Permission to come on board?' And he said, 'Would you give me your weapon?' which I did. He said, 'Would you report to the chief medical officer?' I said, 'Explain.' He said it was the last liberty boat of the day. 'Now you're a non-combatant, the Geneva Convention rules for this hospital ship.' The lights were kept on, because helicopters were bringing wounded Marines right off of the front lines.

"I went to Charlie's little sitting area – there were four staterooms of two bunks each, two hospital beds one above the other. Captain Herrick was there and he was moaning and groaning. He had been there two days. His neck was broken. I was there with him for two or three days at the request of the medics and two psychiatrists aboard. They wanted to understand a little more about him and I knew a lot about him. We'd been on R&R together.

"Charlie had some problems in his head. He wanted me to get them to get him home. He and his wife had four sons and I could see her having to deal with a fifth child.

"I had time to hang out with him and Williams was there, sort of in uniform and sort of casual. He had pleurisy and was on antibiotics. He was sitting there chatting and one of the senior O.R. nurses happened to come in to the coffee break place. She had some blood on her scrub suit and Ted said, "Don't you think in the presence of Marines, Commander...? [Ted was suggesting she not show up with blood on her outfit, out of sensitivity.] She said, "Perhaps so. How are you feeling, Captain Williams?" He said, "I feel fine." She said, "If you feel OK and it's alright with the senior surgeon, would you be willing to come down to the O.R. and spend a little time? The Marines are taking a beating and we're getting a lot of guys coming in by chopper from the front lines. They're coming out [of surgery] with an empty sleeve or an empty trouser leg. It's kind of hard. We're so busy we can't do much to console them. It might mean something to them if you were to be there." He said, "Of course." So for several days there, whenever somebody would come out of anesthesia, the first face that he would see would be Ted Williams!

"This was never told, as far as I know, but I was there and I was part of it. It would cheer them up.

"I have read more recently that he had a great compassion for kids and for younger people. Well, that was coming out there on this hospital ship. He was about 33. I was 32. These kids were 18 or 19 year olds in a war and had these things happening to them. That was moving. I was there.

"I stuck with my friend Charlie, who was permanently paralyzed from the waist down. His is a great success story. He pulled out of it. Went to Yale Divinity School and he's had a remarkable life. He became a minister. A very delightful man."[19]

NOTES

1) Interview with Darwin Glaese, December 17, 2002.

2) Mike Gillooly, "The Case for Ted Williams," Boston Evening American, January 7, 1958.

3) Boston Globe, February 18, 1953.

4) Ed Hyde, Sport, op. cit., July 1953.

5) Interview with Jack Campbell, November 27, 2002.

6) Interview with Gen. Tom Miller, February 7, 2003.

7) Interview with Art Moran, May 8, 1997.

8) Interview with Woody Woodbury, October 1, 2002.

9) Interview with Jerry Coleman, April 5, 1997.

10) Interview with Larry Hawkins, December 21, 2002.

11) Interview with Jack Campbell, November 27, 2002.

12) Interview with Joseph A. Mitchell, February 3, 2003.

13) Interview with Jan Herman, December 17, 2002.

14) Ibidem.

15) Interview with Virginia Brown, December 20, 2002.

16) Communication from Rita Beatty, March 20, 2003.

17) Interview with Hank Kirby, January 10, 2003. Interestingly, Williams may have had a touch of tuberculosis as a child. So reports Leigh Montville in his book Ted Williams, op. cit., p. 57. Williams also suffered bouts of pneumonia in June 1954, September 1954, and September 1957.

18) Interview with Dr. John Bartlett, February 10, 2003.

19) Interviews with Dale Purcell, November 5 and December 12, 2002.

There was another time Ted Williams almost got shot down. John D. Knowlton was a young Maine boy in the 1940s. He'd seen Ted play once at Fenway Park in 1946, but lived in Greenville, Maine on the shore of Moosehead Lake where his father ran a family restaurant. Folsom's Flying Service and the Maine State Fish and Game Flying Service operated from wharves on the east side of the cove, and Mr. Knowlton was friendly with Flying Game Warden Bill Turgeon. Young John loved to see the single-engine airplanes take off or land on the waters of Moosehead Lake.

John also liked to play with fireworks in the days around Independence Day. Seeing those seaplanes come and go was too much temptation.

As he sets up the story, "Moosehead Lake's outgoing air traffic almost always took off up the lake away from town; the opportunist had only to wait for their return. Their gliding return to base brought them low over town, an area pockmarked with natural and man-made recesses and fringed by trees where an urban guerrilla could hide. The specialist could send up a whiz-bang and run to cover in one smooth motion. Of course we never aimed directly at a plane. Bracketing was the merit badge skill."

It was a few days after July 4, 1948, he was playing with some friends, hiding in a pit as a plane came in. They fired two homemade rockets in the direction of the descending aircraft – and then ran to hide. Late that afternoon, he heard the word that Ted Williams was in Greenville! When he came into the restaurant through the rear door, his mother pressed him into service: "Ted Williams is in the dining room. Put an apron on and go wait on him."

John peered into the dining room and saw Ted there, with three other people. Two of them he didn't know, but he did recognize the new Game Warden pilot. That's when he realized: "Oh my God, he came in on the State Fish and Game plane! I could have killed TED WILLIAMS! What would have happened if we had hit the plane? That was too grim to contemplate. I gave up aerial bombs forever."

John D. Knowlton
"How I Nearly Killed Ted Williams,"
Ted Williams Museum Magazine, 2001.

Papa-san.
Photo by E. Buchser.

CHAPTER 13 – LIFE ON THE BASE – K-3, POHANG

In 1953-54, Pohang looked like something out of the middle ages.
Fred Townsley

We had a lot of dogs on the field. They knew they were safe there, because out in Korea, outside there, they'd eat them.
Mike Canan

To better understand what daily life at K-3 was like during the months that Ted Williams was stationed there, we will shift gears a bit and present a patchwork quilt of impressions drawn from the many interviews conducted with others who served on the base. Some relate directly to Williams, and some to base life in general. All provide more color and context to the milieu in which Marine Captain Williams served.

Earl Traut, test pilot, Marine Aircraft Squadron 33:

It was very primitive. There were no paved roads, even in Pohang, which was a main city in that part of Korea. It was all dirt roads.

In winter, we'd see people going bare-legged and barefoot in the rice paddies when there was ice on the water and they were planting their rice. It was very primitive.[1]

James Dolan, ex-Navy tech rep, Westinghouse aviation gas turbine division:

When all those Marines came out of the mess hall, they'd bring out steaks and they'd throw them to the dogs. These steaks were being sent over – they were scarce in the States – but everybody had a damn dog. Well, COMFAIR Japan put out an order: no more individual dogs! They had to belong to a unit, like a squadron. Of course, the Koreans butchered the dogs.

Korean woman and child.
Photo by E. Buchser.

Korean woman selling fish.
Photo by E. Buchser.

As I remember, the officer I reported to at MAG-33 was Major Pat Harrison. He was a great guy. We went up to some very famous temple one day, some feast day for the Buddhists because everybody was dressed up. He was pissed off. There was a couple of light colonels with some good-looking Korean girls. He was really pissed off because it was a terrible example.

I understood that the Catholic Marines and the Protestant Marines each built an orphanage and bought rice paddies as a food source for orphans. We had Korean waitresses there, and nobody ever screwed around with them. They chaperoned them pretty well. Nice young Korean girls.

There was an old French priest that used to say Mass for the Marines on occasion, my understanding was he had a home for Korean women, a girls home. Now, in retrospect, I would guess these were some of those poor comfort girls: 100,000 were in Japanese army brothels from start of fighting in China the early 30s to August '45. The Japanese never even apologized for all those comfort girls.

In regard to duck hunting, I never did go out shooting with them but I know the guys would drive out where migratory geese and ducks came from Siberia. There were some huge snow geese. There was an awful lot of pheasant there. They would have a great time hunting, using Korean boys as retrievers, and they would give them to the kids! They were having a lot of fun shooting and they'd just give the pheasants or ducks to those kids.

The Koreans would take their night soil and make a pit, and keep collecting it until spring. They plant their seedlings in a small area of the rice paddy and then when the seedling is grown, they say OK, now we're going to waste a square foot of ground on you, now that we know you're viable. They have all this night soil – the whole flooded rice paddies. They had terrible hookworm. Can you imagine, that night soil there and you're walking around in it?

In the winter time you would see little boys and girls collecting grass for mother to use for cooking; they had to use rice also as fuel, Korea was completely deforested; the coal supplies were in the north.

The Korean home, it's like a mud home. The rice straw should be used for compost to go back in the field, but they were so short of fuel, they would save that. Mother is cooking but then the heat from the rice straw and/or grass and weeds goes under the floor, through a grid of channels underneath which transferred the heat to the floor, and then out the chimney.

One time around Christmas time, we went up around Seoul. The city was just wrecked. The only thing for sale in the market was empty whiskey bottles and beer cans. They'd take the beer cans and straighten them out. You'd see corrugated beer cartons, they'd build shacks with them but they also used them as raw material for cigarette lighters and things like that.[2]

 Curt Giese, fellow Marine at K-3:

Ted Williams was an exceptionally talented photographer. His father had been a photographer by profession. Sgt. Curt Giese of Wisconsin spent a lot of time with Williams, working with photography. "Ted and I have shot quite a few pictures of Korean kids in the village near the base. He always does his own developing and printing and he does very good work." Ted spent so much of his spare time hunting or photographing that "when Ted is wanted, a message is often sent to the MAG-33 photo lab where he is frequently found with his huge hands dipped in developing tanks."[3]

 Earl Traut worked with Ted in the darkroom:

I spent some time with him over the winter, in Korea. We never talked about baseball. He could borrow a Jeep – I was just a lieutenant – but he'd borrow a Jeep and the two of us would go out taking pictures around the countryside. I have a couple pictures of him where he's handing out candy to the kids. This wasn't at the regular orphanage that the Marines supported in Pohang. This was just driving out and looking around the countryside.

We mainly took pictures of the Korean people and the countryside, in different directions, different areas. The two of us took a Jeep up to Kyong-ju, the old Korean capital of hundreds or maybe even a thousand years ago. They had a very interesting museum there. They had an old temple. Many of the Korean people went up there for religious purposes. They had one temple there that we weren't allowed to go into. The elevation was over 1,000 feet and they had a beautiful view to the east.

We had different kinds of cameras and we debated about those, about which would take the better pictures. He had a Rolleiflex, I think, and I had a 35MM camera. We had a photo lab in our hobby shop, which was the end of a Quonset building – about the last maybe 15 feet of it. We'd develop our own black and white pictures, and had a little Bunsen burner, a cooking burner, to heat up the chemicals – we had to thaw out the chemicals to get them up to the right temperature. We had enough material there where we could develop the film and make the prints.[4]

Fred Townsley, VMF-311 runner

One day I was outside when the Korean garbage truck came to pick up the garbage. The truck was about a 1929 Chevy stake truck. The Koreans had tied rags around the tires through the spokes to keep from running on the inner tube. It looked like the truck was held together with bailing wire and bubble gum. The Korean men on the back picked up the garbage cans and emptied them into the back of the truck and one of the men reached into a can and pulled out a hand full of mashed potatoes and took a bite of it and laughed about it. Guess it was better than he had been eating.[5]

Louis Capozzoli, chief correspondent
First Marine Air Wing:

I was a master sergeant, in a replacement draft. The officers came over separately. I know Ted Williams. We both got there the same month.

We were on a picture taking tour down in the town. Pohang. I was a correspondent, but I was on my own. I was on liberty, then. We walked around together and took pictures. He was taking pictures of the town – the fishing boats, the people, the shops. I was doing the same thing and we just happened to meet and talk together. Somebody took a picture of the two of us together. I had a Jeep. It was a Sunday afternoon, as I recall. That's what guys did.

I talked to him at length when his plane came down with bullet holes in the wings [April 27 – Capozzoli arrived in February 1953].[6]

Ted with War Correspondent Lou Capozzoli.
Photo courtesy of Lou Capozzoli.

 Rylen Rudy, fellow pilot VMF-311:

The poverty level was down so low, you couldn't believe it. I don't know what a piece of tail cost when I was there in Korea, but basically 50 cents probably or a dollar. Anyway, when I got back over there in '60, the going price was basically a nickel. The people were so poor that we had boxes of those cheap cheap cheap candles, probably worth a nickel apiece and, hell, you could get a girl for a damn candle. They were that far off. Dogs were edible and so they had a hard time.

I went back again in '67 on another war game situation, and by this time the economy was up and the gals were running around in mini-skirts and things were really up and about. Completely different situation. Those were the only times I've been back.[7]

 Fred Townsley, VMF-311 runner:

In the H&MS-33, MAG-33 Group Photo Shop (a Quonset hut), the photographers had blown up a picture of Teague Cuttie's bosom. The door to the photo lab opened right between her boobs. She was a rather short Korean woman with a gigantic set of boobs. I mean big! During the winter of 1953-54, a bunch of us from the squadron went down to see her one week-end. I think it was about 76 miles from K-3 to K-2. The roads were not paved, and reminded me of the roads in Lincoln County, Oklahoma when I stayed with Uncle John in '47-'48-'49. We rode in the back of

Ted Williams with two houseboys, Edro Buchser in background.
Photograph courtesy of Tom Ross.

the Material Sections Weapons Carrier. It had a canvas top which was installed, and all except the driver and his shot-gun rode in the back. I think there was about six of us. It turned out to be about a two-hour or more like a three-hour ride down to Teague (south from K-3). It was cold and we all had on long johns, utilities, and cold weather gear. Even had on Mickey Mouse shoes (cold weather boots), only they didn't keep your feet warm unless you were walking. They didn't do anything to help keep your feet warm if you were riding in the back of a cold weapons carrier. After we found Cuttie's house, we all went inside the court yard (compound) and Cuttie just opened up the front of her coat and blouse and showed us her boobs. They were LARGE. We could avail ourselves of her services for $5, or one of her girls for $2. Then we still had a two-to-three-hour drive up north to K-3 and good old VMF-311. Don't remember much about the trip except for the bumpy roads and how drab the country looked.

I went through some of the same area in November 1984 when I went to the reunion in Korea to visit my son Stephen. The roads were paved and in good condition, the homes had electricity, and none of the houses had straw roofs. Compared to what Pohang looked like in 1984, in 1953-54 Pohang looked like something out of the middle ages. (8)

Leonard Waibel, line chief VMF-311:

We didn't have hangars. We didn't have any hangars. Not even for repair. We were right out there on the Marston matting, until they came in and gave us asphalt to fly off. The only thing that stopped us was weather. But we had to have the planes ready. We liked stand-downs, though. Give us a break. It wasn't that bad. I enjoyed it. You had to wear your boots, though. It was cold. We could see the ocean from where the runway was. We had a north-south runway, parallel to the coast. [9]

Bill Clem, fellow pilot VMF-311:

[Ted] had a little houseboy who took care of his hut. He called him "Jimmy." A little Korean boy.[10]

Mike Canan, fellow pilot VMF-311:

A couple of us went with him [Ted] one day and we went to the beach. We used to call it "Pohang-dong-ni by the sea." I'd say it was about three or four miles away. He was talking with these gals that would go out there and swim for seaweed and stuff like that. He was taking pictures of them. That's the only incident I ever had in being with him without being in a military sort of situation. Those girls could speak pretty good language [English], enough to get by.

He also had the same houseboy I had. Named Jimmy. He was about eight or nine, something like that. We hired them and they kind of swept our huts out. They'd put the trash out. We always gave them some money. That's how they existed. We gave them food, too. Ted was very, very friendly with this kid, and this kid liked Ted. Ted gave him a bicycle.[11]

Jack Bolt, pilot VMF-115:

I was in 115, yes. [Bolt joined the squadron 21 November 1952.] I had two contacts with Ted, other than just in the mess hall and the bar. One of them, I hunted with him four or five times, under the auspices of his very good friend Ed Buchser. Ed was Ted's best friend at K-3. The other thing, I was on a bathing schedule. Water and heat both were scarce. Bathing was scheduled. You took a bath every ten days or so, and I was on a bathing schedule with Ted, so I used to be in the shower room with him.

You would take off your inner pair of skivvies and maybe change your long handles, just depending on how cold it was. Normally, you'd have a pair of skivvies on plus two pair of long handles, and you'd change the bottom one, the inner one. And Ted would be there. Great complainer. Bitching all the time.

[Did you think he went too far with his bitching?] No. No. People sympathized with him, having to give up all of his prestigious place in the baseball world to go fight the war. He didn't like it. [laughs]

I was a regular. I enlisted two weeks before the war, before Pearl Harbor. I served 20 years. I made Lieutenant Colonel.

I was a member of what they called the Pohang-do Rod and Gun Club. Those of us that hunted – Buchser and Ted, myself, then there were a couple of others... a guy named Kenny... anyway, once a week, the mess hall would cook our game for us and serve it after the regular seating had been fed and left. Ted would regale us with baseball stories at the Rod and Gun Club meetings. He liked to talk. He would tell us stories about baseball. We had another professional baseball player there. He was not a member of the Rod and Gun Club but he would sit with us occasionally. Lloyd Merriman. Lloyd and Ted would tell us baseball stories. It was fascinating.[12]

Carrol Burch, pilot VMF-115:

Woody Woodbury entertained every night over at the club and I mean he's a real entertainer. Just fantastic. We needed a new piano so I went over with him when he went to Japan. We went over on R&R and I was with him when we brought that new piano back. I got up to Tokyo with him and we were in a place where they had a band. They took a little break and he got up and started entertaining. He had that crowd! He could take over a crowd and just have them in stitches in a minute. That guy offered him $1,000.00 a week if he'd come back and entertain at that club in Tokyo.

We didn't have any real drunks there, but with the entertainment – with Woody Woodbury on that piano every night... And the songs that we sang: "On Top of Old Ping Pong" and "Dark and Stormy Night" and all the songs we sang. Everybody joined in. I was talking about going up to the Yalu to get those bridges. We were out of K-13 and we opened the club. It was a brand new club. They just built it, and we opened it that night. Woody started entertaining and by about 1 o'clock in the morning, we had the group commander and the base Air Force commander up on the table doing the "rain dance."

[Sings] "Hey, zooba zoomba, zoomba zoomba. Hey zooma zoomba..." The weather came in and it held up our whole operation for two weeks. It closed us in. But they wouldn't let us go to the club anymore. Banned from the club!

[When you walked from the club back to the area where you had your huts, was there duckboard or just mud or a walkway of some kind?]

It was just graveled. Our area was kind of off to one side and theirs was kind of off to the other side. They were always throwing rocks on the roof. We always slept in sleeping bags, because it was cold out there and the fire always went out at night. My skipper was Jack Moss. He'd come in and throw me out in the snow about every night! He really wanted me to drink with him, and I drank with him a lot but I didn't stay as long as he wanted me to.[13]

 ## Banshee Bob Johnson, pilot VMJ-1:

We were all alone over there across the field. [115, 311 and MAG-33 were all across the field from VMJ-1.] We had our own little enclave. Our transportation across the field was our flight surgeon's ambulance. We had our own mess hall across on our side, but we had no officers' club. We'd run over there to invade their officers' clubs. Apparently we became so obnoxious, they refused us entrance. When we let Master Sgt. Vogel in our group know of our plight, he said, "Well, we can fix that." So he threw up half a Quonset hut and we had our own officers' club.[14]

 ## George Winewriter, pilot VMF-115:

We had good living quarters. I had a coal stove in the hut. I was right on waterfront property. The wind really whipped through there. By springtime, I was up at the division. We were in reserve. 2nd Batallion, Fifth Marine was Chesty Puller's first command and your first command as a Marine is usually a very sentimental thing. So when he got to Korea, the first place he went was to 2nd Batallion, Fifth Marines. I got to talk to him then. The most impressive man I ever met.[15]

Ed Buchser, provost marshal, K-3 and pilot VMF-115:

Ted got to be good friends with John Glenn. John Glenn's a good friend of mine, too. When I was in a position to lead the squadron and was designated as strike leader – as was John – we flew a mission together. He led his 16 airplanes and I led mine. I think we both got a DSC for it. I know I did and I think John did, too. That was to the capital of North Korea, Pyongyang. They could really throw up some flak up there.

John was sort of like Ted, he didn't really drink. So John and Ted got along real fine.

Ted in ready room with unknown enlisted man.
Photo by Jack Campbell.

The club was for the jet wing, which was the two squadrons and the photo squadron. It was an officers' mess. We were supposed to have 35 pilots and they were supposed to have 35. The photo squadron had maybe 12. Ted would come over there sometimes, but not like, say, Mooney and I. We were there nearly every night. No, Ted would come over. He'd sit and have a beer. And listen to Woody. We got Woody a piano. We had some great times in there.[16]

Tom Miller, Executive Officer VMF-323:

Ted was not his [Glenn's] roommate but he was in the same building. It was a wall between Ted and his bunkmates and John and his. The wall... they could throw things over to the other side. An interior wall.[17]

Woody Woodbury, pilot VMF-115:

There were no Korean soldiers [on the base] to my knowledge, although there were some at the gates. Like a detachment. I don't remember seeing more than maybe a half a dozen.

[There were workers on the base, though?]

They kept the huts. I still have a photograph or two of our Korean... we called them houseboys. Our little boy's name was Kim. He was terrific. Of course, he wanted to learn English and he wanted to come to the States. I still have letters from some of the waitresses. There was one girl named Ruby. I was just a young guy at the time, but Ruby – don't ask me why, because I'm not exactly Clark Gable – but Ruby fell in love with me and I'd get back to the States and she would write me these letters. They were hysterical [meaning humorous] – I mean, they were pitiable in a way because her English was so bad, but she was trying. She wanted to "come Stateside and live my house." Oh Jesus, it was unbelievable.

These were old Japanese huts the Japanese had constructed when they beat the Koreans in the war. We lived in these Japanese huts with tin roofs. Colder than hell in the winter. There's nothing colder than Korea in the winter. They have a wind there... oh, it was cold! Tom was a major. Edro was a captain; he made major over there... I was a first lieutenant and then became a captain.

They had oil stoves. Marines are pretty resourceful; they had those things working pretty well. Around the stove it was nice, but you get a few feet away, you'd freeze your butt. What the heck, we survived. Of course, we were young and when you're young, you move around a lot. I don't recall any windows. There might have been one window at one end or something like that. I have some pictures.

Ted adjusting Squadron Duty Officer armband.
Photo by Jack Campbell.

Screens were almost unheard of over there. They had apertures so daylight could get in. They had an opening like a window, but they had a board over it suspended by two hinges from the top. They would pull it open from the bottom and brace it with a stick. That let the light in. I don't think they had screens in Korea until the Americans brought them over there. There wasn't much snow. Not in Pohang.[18]

 ## Joseph Mitchell, fellow pilot VMF-311:

[The place you lived in, was it a hut that was connected to others?]

They were side-by-side, they were sort of like triplexes. They had partitions from one room to another. A door on the end where we were, and you went around to the left and the door to the next place opened up. They were kind of a framed hut. It wasn't like the old strong-back tents we lived in World War II.

[And they weren't real Quonset huts.]

It wasn't like a squashed little... no, it wasn't a Quonset hut. Originally, I was on a cot, but I think we advanced to something a little bit better than that. Springs maybe, I'm not sure. I don't remember that. Isn't it funny how you just can't remember that sort of thing? A wooden floor. There was a draft underneath. We had some kind of heating device. We used to be able to heat our water in the morning for a shave. It wasn't grandiose, but it was comfortable.[19]

 ## Rylen Rudy, fellow pilot VMF-311:

[Talks about some Korean friends he'd like to know about. Two women who worked on the base.] We had houseboys and then we had the young ladies who worked in the mess hall. Waited on tables. I got real friendly with two of the little gals that were in there. I've often wondered what happened to them. They came to me one time, about the time I was finishing flying the missions and all. They came and they had a dog-eared Sears catalog. I mean, this thing has been gleaned over so many times you wouldn't believe it. They came in and wanted to order some stuff and of course they couldn't do it. They wanted to know if I could order it. They wanted about $50 worth of stuff. Each wanted a pea coat. They wanted a set of blue jeans each. And then there was one of these "you tell him... no, you tell him... no, you tell him" type situations. Finally they flipped to the page and this one girl closed her eyes and stuck her finger on it, and what it was a package of seven-day panties. Monday, Tuesday, Wednesday, Thursday... each one a different color. They each wanted a set of panties. But they didn't know how to tell me about it.

[Rudy ordered them, and wanted to be paid in American money when it got there. About two-and-a-half or three months later, the package arrived. When he got back to K-3, they had the money.]

The thing that they did that was the most valuable, Sears had sent a brand new catalog with the thing. You never saw anybody so pleased in your life, and they were more pleased over the catalog than they were with the clothes.

These gals made about four and a half or five dollars a month, but they had the money in greenbacks. They went into Taegu or someplace and had gotten the money. I've always wondered what happened to those two little girls. Well, hell, they're pushing 70 years old now.[20]

Woody Woodbury, pilot VMF-115:

[How did Ted relate to other officers?] He was courteous. I think he was ticked off because of the ... a couple of Marine Corps officers of higher rank, who I don't believe even knew him, I think they wanted their ten minutes of headlines and I think they made some disparaging remarks. I guess subconsciously they figured their rank would protect them from anything. There were some derogatory things said about him by various people. I can't pinpoint any names but I can recall thinking, "Jesus, why would a guy say something like that for?" He wasn't there. He didn't know what was going on. He just expressed an opinion and some reporter picked it up and used it like it was a bona fide Bible, and it was not true at all. That used to hurt me.

When it comes to rank, I think Ted respected the man. There were a lot of these... we'd call them 90-day wonders early in the war. They were given a commission and, hell, they couldn't find their way out of a phone booth. Some of these guys were unbelievable. Andy Griffith once made a motion picture and it showed some of these inept people. *No Time for Sergeants?* I don't know if that was it or not. Ted, to me, was... if a colonel, let's say, was an s.o.b., Ted didn't mind telling him. Nobody did that in the military, and I don't really believe Ted did, either, but Ted had a way of letting people know that he didn't have much respect for him, and that's the way it was. I guess that's what I'm trying to say.

I think a lot of us liked enlisted men better. I used to play poker. I used to play poker with the officers and pilots. I don't think any of us ever referred to each other as officers. We were a young, scatterbrained bunch of young guys over there flying these new jet fighter planes and we were pilots. That was the main thing. Yeah, we were officers and we had to dress up when it came to formal things but we just had a job to do. We were just pilots. A lieutenant never called a captain "captain" – when you got up into the hierarchy – General Megee – you always called him "general." "Yes, sir, General" and this sort of thing, because that's respect for the rank and the seniority, whatever.[21]

Ted Williams "inside his hooch" lit by bare bulb.
Photo by E. Buchser.

Paul Janssen, fellow pilot VMF-311:

One of the things Ted would do, when he wasn't flying, he'd go out with the enlisted men on the ramp over there, and he'd hit fungoes to them with a baseball bat. He hit a lot of fungoes to them, and they loved that. He'd motion to one of the kids, and the kid wouldn't even move and the ball'd come right to him.

[I guess he always was more comfortable with the enlisted men than the upper rank.]

Yeah, because the upper rank was fawning on him to a great extent. Not too much in the squadrons, but in other areas. They'd ask him to have dinner with visiting generals. He didn't like that. He didn't like being over there in the first place! He didn't know he was in the ready reserves after World War II. But they called everybody up. We had ex-New York cops flying with us and everything.[22]

 Ed Buchser, provost marshal, K-3 and pilot VMF-115:

General Megee was a really fine man. Most guys automatically just don't like generals, but he was a fine guy. Anyway, I was a major and Ted was a captain. Don't get your feelings hurt if you're an Ivy Leaguer, but we have sort of a disdain for that type of person. His aide was a Harvard man. He was one of those kind of guys. We say they wear starched underwear. He called and he said the general would like to go duck hunting. I said, "Yeah, well, when?" No way I was going to say no to a general, even though I liked him – the general was a good guy. So, OK, we made the arrangements and Ted came down that afternoon, and I told him we got company. He said, "Who?" and I told him General Megee, and he said, "Aw, shit!" and started cussing and everything. "Goddamn rank!"

It didn't take long, though. Ted liked old General Megee, because he was just a regular guy and all he wanted to do was duck hunt. But his aide was another story. There was a long rice paddy and I knew there were ducks throughout – I'd called my roving patrol to find out where the ducks were – and I put the general on the downwind end, which is the best end. Ted about 200 yards up one side, and then I was about 200 yards further up. I didn't realize the aide was going to get in his blind with the general – I was amazed, really. Anyway, a big old flock of ducks came by and just as they were coming in, this aide stood up and pointed like a statue and shouted, "There they are, General!" I guess the general pulled him down. From Ted's blind, I could hear this rumble, rumble. The ducks flew off. It wasn't that long, maybe 5 or 10 minutes and another flock – it might have been the same flock came back – and the aide stood up again and pulled this shit again! Old Ted stood up and he cocked the pump gun – shotgun – and he yelled, "You son of a bitch! You do that one more time and I'm going to blow your fucking head off!" The general was not a dummy and so he sent the aide up to where the truck was parked and the aide just got to sit there and freeze his ass off all afternoon. In the meantime, we had a great duck hunt.

[Asked about the photograph with Ted wearing an SDO armband] He would have been the squadron duty officer for that day. It wasn't as much MP duty. You had a CO and an exec, but the duty officer stayed by the telephone in the ready room. If somebody would call or if they needed something, they would always call the duty officer. He sort of was the pseudo-skipper in a way. All organizations have an officer of the day.

He wasn't impressed with rank or anything. He was an officer himself, but I think he really preferred the company of enlisted men. Yeah. I think so. I know so! He'd be what you might call an enlisted man's officer. He didn't care if you were a colonel or what. And he didn't like it when people were kowtowing to him or bothering him for this or that because he was Ted Williams. He'd come down to my office sometimes just to get away from people trying to talk with him.

He was never impressed with rank.

I worked directly for the group commander, Robertshaw, a bird colonel. My little area was down under the hill, with 600 grunts. I would have breakfast and usually dinner with Col. Robertshaw. He was a really good guy, and he'd played football at the Naval Academy. He said, "Buck, I understand that you and Captain Williams are friends." And I said, "Yes, sir. We go duck hunting quite a bit." He said, "I wonder if he would mind eating with me." And I said, "Well, I'll see" and so I told Ted. Ted said, "Aw, sonavabitch, another goddamn brass…" But I said, "No, this guy is a good guy" so Ted said OK. Ted agreed, and we ate with the colonel. Ted, he didn't give a damn if a guy was a colonel or a private or what, and he got a little upset. The colonel and him got to talking about the war, and Ted had the same impressions that I did, and all the other pilots – that it was a bullshit deal that they could fly down over the Yalu and come down to our area, but we couldn't go up there. That was one of the things. He just really was loud, Ted was, cussing, really yelling at the colonel himself, and I'm trying to get him to shut up, you know, but the colonel… well, he was an athlete and he knew athletes and he was very tolerant of it. But if that had been some other colonel – and I can think of a lot of them – hell, they'd have taken action. Reprimanded him at least.[23]

Leonard Waibel, line chief VMF-311:

I remember taking a picture with him along an airplane. A lot of guys asked for Ted's picture with them, along the F9. I still remember, when he got ready to leave, he gave me a bottle of champagne. French champagne. He knew I was going back about the same time. He could buy it out of the officers' mess; they could buy anything they wanted. We couldn't get it. We could get beer, but… officers could buy hard liquor but we couldn't. We managed to get it if we wanted it.[24]

Bob Flanagan, plane captain (flight line mechanic) VMF-311:

I remember occasionally seeing him striding through the squadron living area with purpose on his face… just that kind of expression that famous people seem to have when they don't want to be bothered… Some of my fellow mechs on the flight line had the guts to strike up conversation with him when he was sitting a strip alert shift. We kept two aircraft with pilots aboard for emergency callup, usually four-hour shifts. We found out he liked to talk cameras and hunting and fishing naturally. Being an 18-year-old corporal, I just stayed back and listened. He was a baseball god to me. [25]

James Walley, fellow pilot VMF-311:

The other thing that I remember about him – I think he was allergic to neckties. If you went into certain areas, you had to wear it. In Korea, I never wore one.

[If a general would come visit, would you have to form up and put on a necktie?]

No, not really. We even received our decorations that we got in the field out there dressed in... almost dressed in flight clothing. That's how we spent most of our time.[26]

Roger McCully, crew chief, VMF-311:

He wouldn't take interest in any sports at all. I guess it might have been in his contract. I don't know. He wouldn't even participate in the games as an umpire or anything like that.

He was very, very friendly and he loved to talk fishing. I'd sit on the wing of the airplane when he had an early morning patrol, and they were all plugged in ready to go. I'd just sit on the wing or stand on the side of the plane and talk to him about fishing, because when he used to go to Spednic Lake between Maine and New Brunswick, my cousin was his guide for a year. Gerald Herron.

In March or April, we had a big draft of people going back [rotating back to the States]. It was the biggest draft of enlisted men that went over, and they were coming back. We were going to have a party. Of course, enlisted men weren't supposed to have party, anyway. But there was a few officers that would buy it for us. We'd pay them and they'd go down to the officer's country and buy a bottle for us. I was looking for this one particular captain and I went down to his particular hut. After dark. Knocked on the door and Ted Williams was there. That was his hut, too. He wanted to know what I wanted and I told him. He says, "Come on in, and I'll go down and get you a bottle." So he went down to officer's country and got me two bottles of VO. And he wouldn't let me pay him.

I thought that was nice of him. He wasn't too old in the outfit. He didn't know too many people, as far as enlisted men know.[27]

Leonard Waibel, line chief VMF-311:

We just heard a rumor that he was coming and then he arrived. There was another baseball player at K-6, Jerry Coleman. I met him.

The first contact I had with Ted Williams was the first time I helped him start an aircraft.

I didn't remember all the pilots, but I used to be the one to wake them up in the mornings. That was one of my jobs, too. I would just go in and raise heck with them! There was no other system. It was quite funny sometimes. I recall one time, they must have been out on a party – some of them liked to party pretty good. I was a technical sergeant that time. I had to wake them up one morning and went into the hut – that's when we changed from tents to huts, the first part of '53 – and when I walked in, I opened the hut door and it was all red like somebody had let off a flare in there. Those guys were all asleep. Four pilots in that room, and they were just covered with that light. It was so funny and weird. I remember I woke them all up and they couldn't believe it. There was always a joke. They were always joking. Somebody had sneaked in there. It was a flare. Somebody had opened the door and put a flare in, and it was still running when I got there. This was around 3 o'clock in the morning, 4 o'clock.

He had fun with the pilots and all the people. I got klondyked by him a couple of times. He could throw a rock! When he hit the side of my hut, I thought the whole place blew up! It was him. I told him the next day, "How come you klondyked me?" "Aw, you just needed it." The walls were made of corrugated metal. That was the thing. Oh, man. The walls and the roof were made of corrugated metal.

Another thing, they would sneak up and put a clothespin on the heating system outside your hut and cut off the fuel. Then we'd wake up freezing. They all did all kinds of things.

But, personally, he talked to me – I was enlisted at the time. He was super. He was a fine man. I don't know how he got along with the officers, but he got along with us enlisted... he was always cordial to me and all the plane captains all the time. He would stop and talk to us just like one of the troops. You'd never think he was a big star. He never acted any different. He never acted like it.[28]

Tex Montague, fellow pilot VMF-311:

I never went hunting with him. I never did go on R&R with him. You know, he had terrific eyes. He was a real good shot at skeet. I've shot skeet with him. He was real good at it. They had a practice skeet range there, to practice the lead... at Pohang. I guess he could see a baseball coming at 100 miles an hour, he could see it and he could see which way the ball was spinning.[29]

Jack Campbell, fellow pilot VMF-311:

I know Joe Mitchell. As a matter of fact, I have some pictures that I took of Ted and some he took of me, because we used to go out in the afternoon to visit some of the local village areas and take pictures. He had a 35MM Leica and I had a Rolleiflex that my parents had given me. We used to kind of challenge each other on who could take the best pictures. We developed some of our own film. We had a photo hut that we could use. Black and white.[30]

James Walley, fellow pilot VMF-311:

The only thing I remember distinctly about Ted was that he was quite a photographer and he taught many of us how to use the facility that we had – a darkroom – so that we could develop film, etc. He also was so taken with a couple of cameras over there that he bought a couple of extras and had them vacuum-sealed so that he could open them up every ten years. He was quite an individual.[31]

Ed Buchser, provost marshal, K-3 and pilot VMF-115:

Ed Buchser was provost marshal of the base and had his own office, where Ted could go for a little privacy. The two enjoyed hunting together, too, and they hooked up early on. "In the first few weeks that Williams was in Korea, he went hunting six or eight times with Buchser." [Sport, July 1953]

I was in 115. The two squadrons were sort of friendly rivals. You know what they say about the Marine Corps: if they can't find anybody else to fight, they fight among themselves. We used to throw rocks at each other – 115 and 311. If you were in a Quonset hut...it's actually from an ancient Korean game and we called it "krondyking." The villages in Korea used to pick up rocks and go along and have rock battles between villages. They didn't have anything else to do, I guess. It was a lot of fun but a lot of guys got hurt pretty bad so the general finally knocked it off.

I'd load up a couple of semi-automatic rifles. We'd go out 15, 20 miles. One time – and I've got a picture of this somewhere, too – an old papa-san, he had a load on his shoulders that looked like 20 feet in the air, a tall stack of firewood. Ted wanted to get his picture taken carrying that thing.

There was more to it than just brute strength. There was quite a bit of balancing to get underneath that thing. So I got a picture of the papa-san and I got a picture of Ted and he's starting to laugh just as the load is tipping over to one side.

He loved fishing, you know. I guess we could have somehow gone fishing there, but it was not convenient. So we didn't. Except Ted, he rigged up a damn piece of cane or whatever and he was fishing in a rice paddy. I don't know what the hell we did. He was fishing on the edge of this rice paddy. Shit, there were no fish in there, and I told him so. He said, "Well, you never know." He never caught anything.

I had met Ted once before, at the tail end of World War II, but I didn't really know him then. Jacksonville. The way it happened, I was the provost marshal – I'm talking about Korea now – I had roving patrols out, and the skipper and I would drop in to the sergeant-major's office and ask, "How many patrols have we got out today?" I would know that anyway, but he would show me on the map. I ran a raid on a suspected mountaintop that was supposedly giving fire as we were assembling to go on a mission... but anyway, roving patrols would tell me where the ducks were. So the word got around, if you want to shoot a duck, call Ed. Ed Buchser. The "drunken sheriff" was my nickname. I don't know how in the hell they ever got me for provost marshal, but they did. It was actually a pretty good tour of duty. I got to shoot a lot of ducks and got to do some things that I wouldn't normally have done. Ted, I met him at the club and he said, "Are you the provost marshal?" I think I had my badge on or something. He said something about how he wanted to go duck hunting. I said, "Yeah. Anytime."

One afternoon I came back after some kind of business, and the sergeant major said, "You've got a visitor over there" so I went over and it was Ted. I said, "Hey, how you doing?" He said something

Inscribed "To Buck. Hunting in Korea. Good Luck. Ted Williams 1953"
Photo by E. Buchser.

and how he wanted to go duck hunting. So we shot the shit. I don't intend this in any egotistical way, but we had temperaments that fit. I have a loud voice and I cuss a lot... so anyway we got along real good.

He was a hell of a camera buff. I didn't know that. I had a camera and I was trying. I knew a little bit about it – but he knew everything. Through his advice, I bought a new camera which was the Japanese version of the German Leica and the first picture I ever took – I wish I could find this photograph – it was in his hut. All the light we had was a single bulb coming down from the ceiling, and he stood... oh I don't know... four or five feet away and I got a hell of a good photo of him. Sort of in the halo of the light.

So then we started duck hunting together. We'd get the ducks! I'm from Kentucky originally. I've been hunting all my life. He could really shoot, too. He's the best shot with a shotgun I ever saw.

Sometimes we'd get like 125 ducks in three hours. Then other times, I wouldn't be able to stay long, or he'd just come in from a mission. He had his job to do, too. He flew 35 or more missions.

The Marine Corps would let you volunteer for missions. I liked it. The skipper of my squadron was a good buddy and a good man. He used to go duck hunting with me. So I would fly volunteer missions. If they had a spot open and had to call a supernumerary, and you were there you'd get that hop, that mission. I flew about a half a dozen or so and damn near got my head blown off and said, "That's it." There were guys that got killed even though they didn't have to be flying that mission. They were volunteering.

Old Ted and I got along real good. We used to go out in my Jeep – I had a Jeep and most pilots don't have their own Jeep, but as provost marshal I did. We'd take our cameras along and laugh and laugh and had a good time.

We'd get over 100 ducks and we'd get the Korean mess boys to cook them up and we'd have a dinner for all the pilots in the squadron. Ted really did not care for publicity. He – honest to God – he just didn't like it! He just wanted to be what he was – and that was the best frigging hitter in baseball.

There was an officers' mess and that's where all the officers would have their meals. The two fighter squadrons shared the mess, but the other squadron had their own little mess, but they'd come up once in a while. I'd even cook those ducks on the stove right in my hut, and Ted came over. That's where Woody and Tom Ross spent most of the time. I'd cook them on the stove. Mess would be served from 5 to 7 and I'd cook them after that. 9 or 10 at night, we'd have a couple of ducks and eat them.

He would always let me serve the big things. There would be a big mound of them as all the guys came by. I found two ducks that they had cooked and they looked just great – there wasn't anything wrong with them, except that they hadn't cleaned them. So a couple of buddies of mine, and one of them was from his squadron, they were shit-faced on martinis. They came in hungry and the mess officer told them they didn't have anything to eat, that the mess hall's closed. I saw them over there; both of them were pretty good guys. I yelled at the mess chief, "Send 'em down! I've got two ducks here." So I brought those ducks over there – and I'm reminding you that they hadn't been cleaned. So they were off by themselves and we were at our end of the mess hall, and I looked over and old Jerry Hendershot had his fork up the ass end of the duck and he's pulling out entrails like spaghetti and eating them. He was saying, "This is the best goddamn duck I ever ate in my life!" I didn't say anything to him that night, as a matter of fact for a couple of days, because I was afraid he'd get mad that I didn't tell him to quit.

Buchser talked about another kind of hunting.

One of the things that was really a serious business for the provost marshal was the whorehouses. Old Ted was really a skivvy honcho. He liked the girls. Skivvies are what we call our underwear. There's two connotations of skivvy honcho. One is you really like girls. The other is in relation to flying combat, that means that all he can do is piss his pants.

[Were there other women there, other than the prostitutes?] Where we were, there were none. But at K-2, which was only 35 miles away, they had a big Army hospital. My mother told me that a girl I'd gone to high school with was a nurse and was stationed there. I had to go to K-2 on business, something about prisoners. I don't remember what. I told Ted I was going and he said, "Oh Jesus! They got all those... what the hell did we call white girls?...I don't remember, but we had a slang term for them. I says, "Yeah, I'd planned on going to see this one girl." He said, "God, can I go with you?" "Well, yeah." So he arranged it with his squadron and he got two days off. He got in the Jeep with me. I was in a hurry and I got going pretty good. He said, "Slow down." I didn't. He said, "Goddamnit, slow down." And I just said, "Fuck you! This is my Jeep and I got to get there. I'm driving this Jeep. Just shut up!" Well, he just turned around and kind of...well, he kept silent. I don't know if he was sulking or not. Well, after about five minutes, we were talking, just good friends again. Whenever somebody would stand up to him and they was right, Ted could accept that.

We got over, and this is how things would go with Ted. I said to the nurse friend of mine – she was not any girl I was trying to get in her knickers, I was just friends. Ted was there, she told somebody, I guess, because that afternoon after working hours, around 5 or 6 o'clock, she said, "Would you come over to the mess hall?" I didn't say it to her, but I said to myself, "Yeah. That's what Ted wants. He wants to get him a girl if he can." Well, shit, there was a Navy captain – see, the Marines don't have their own medical corps – and he had all his shit out. [In other words, he set out a whole party spread of food and drink.] All the nurses were there – about 40 of them, it seemed like. Of course, I wasn't operating, but old Ted was. He was kind of pissed when he found out it was going to be a cocktail party. But he finally liked it. We ate dinner and had a couple of drinks. The girls I was with, I just said good night and I went to my room. Old Ted he had a nurse and she was good looking, too. So the next day we're driving back to K-3 and he's just silent over there in his side of the Jeep. I says, "What happened last night? Did you get laid?" He said, "Unhh." I said, "Well, you know...tell me!" "She had the fucking rag on." He was really depressed. The chance of his life and he missed out. I guess he could have had any one of them. He was a good looking guy to women.[32]

Virginia Tipps, Army Nurse, Taegu:

I was in the Army Nurse Corps at the 25th Evac Hospital at Taegu, a station hospital there [about 50 miles from Pohang]. I was like 23, 24, there for a year. We spent a lot of time in the Officers Club. He and his buddies used to come down to the Officers Club to see the nurses. There were very few women in Korea, you know. Only nurses. That's how I met him. He was very nice, very personable, a very nice-looking man. He wasn't a big drinker.

I danced with him at the Officers Club. I think we kissed a couple of times, but I really don't remember. I didn't know anything personal about him. He told me he was separated from his wife, which I thought was a big joke because everybody there was separated from somebody. I heard it about 10 million times. He was telling the truth (I learned later) but I did laugh at it.

I was engaged to a doctor further up the front line. He was very personable. Very nice looking man.

He was a celebrity by the time he got there. I knew absolutely nothing about baseball. The C.O. would ask him to speak to the enlisted men. He would talk with them about the game. They were all extremely interested, young GIs.[33]

Woody Woodbury, pilot VMF-115:

Down on the beach, we played touch football. Mixed up [not one squadron against the other] because some of us, we had the time off, we'd do something athletic while other guys were on missions. We flew from the "early-earlies" before dawn until late at night. It was a rotating type of thing. We'd go at 4:30, 3:30 in the morning. Awful early. There again, Ted was just one of the guys, and he flew those early-earlies like everybody. And he flew late missions and he got screwed out of meals like a lot of us did. When you come back from a flight, I can remember coming back and I was ravenous. And sometimes we couldn't get anything to eat and we'd have to fill up on candy bars. They had the Korean houseboys and Korean cooks and everything else, while it was run by sergeants overall. They couldn't have the dining rooms open 24 hours a day. It wasn't done in those days. Maybe they do it today.

Somebody's got some pictures of the guys throwing the ball back and forth on the beach. The beach was uninhabited totally. It was sandy. They had volleyball nets set up there, and some of the guys would play volleyball. Then they'd play touch football. It was heavy sand because it had never been packed down. K-3 was actually located on the south side of this bay that curved around. The water was cold 12 months a year. We just played touch football and a little football but it was no easy thing to do.[34]

Louis B. Robertshaw, Commanding Officer Marine Air Group 33:

It's possible that he didn't go over to the officers' club that much, but I didn't go over there that much myself. I think the presence of a ranking officer, particularly a commander, has an effect of monitoring, and I didn't want to project that. On the other hand, it could also give as image of over-familiarization, so it's better to go to scheduled events but not frequent them.

It was more than duck hunting. He hunted geese – these tremendously big geese – and I remember one that he shot, they put a nail overhead in a doorway and hung this thing by its jaws and chin, and its feet barely cleared the floor.[35]

Woody Woodbury, pilot VMF-115:

[Was there much friendly rivalry between the squadrons?] Oh yes. 311, their squadron insignia was a cat. WL, Willing Lovers. We were eagles. We were called Able Eagles. AE, that was our insignia. And they were willie love, in those days. Anyhow, it was a friendly thing. I wrote some parodies of some songs which we used to sing. I wrote one thing, which all the guys in the squadron sang it, even the guys in 311, because they didn't live in huts. They did, but we called them cathouses. It was that sort of nonsense.[36]

Walter Roark, pilot VMF-115:

Ted Williams... we all had empathy for him, but you know, we had to do...but as far as I know, he got his ass in that airplane and did the very best he could on every thing. I never saw him really goof off. But he didn't go out there and get the guys together, and play a little baseball and whatnot and so forth. He did kind of hang to himself a little bit. Nothing against the other pilots. Ted was just an individualist. He was a poor boy.

Ted, you'd never see him over at the bar. Those 311 boys, though, would come by our area and throw rocks on top of our huts. The 311 boys would come by our Quonset huts and throw those big rocks. They were about like a baseball, you know. You ricochet those off that metal roof, you goddamn know it.

We burned down their shithouse, though. Both squadrons had a four-holer out there. No, they burned down ours! I'd forgotten that. They burned down ours. That was made out of wood, that's right. Made by the Koreans.[37]

Carrol Burch, pilot VMF-115:

We had a guy named Woody Woodbury. He's A-number-1, top dog. He was great. Just fantastic.

Lloyd Merriman was just fantastic. He practiced with a bat. He had a bat and we lived in kind of a hut that had a floor and tin on top. It was a pretty nice place and there was four of us in each one of them. A piece of string that you turned the light on and off with, it hung down and he would always practice hitting the knot on the end of that string. Just a knot on the end. He practiced a lot with that bat, hitting the knot on that string. He was just a fantastic individual.

Ted, they lived in a different... we were all at the same place. They had their own...one thing that happened there, there was some, well, we captured their commanding officer one time. Art Moran. We captured him and brought him into the officers club and had a ball and chain on him and made a big deal of it. There was a little friendly competition between the two squadrons. Then one time, we had these outhouses that had lids – I forget whether it was a three-holer or a four-holer. The other squadron nailed down those lids!

Well, after breakfast, people started going out to go to their... each squadron had their own outhouse. So they nailed the lids down and we were really scratching for a place to go. And so, as soon as we got everything squared away there, we burned theirs down. We burned that thing down. [38]

Larry Hawkins, fellow pilot VMF-311:

[I heard that one time or another, somebody burned down the latrine.]

I'm not talking about that. [Laughs]

[Well, let me ask: was it 115's latrine that got burned down?]

Yeah. It was 115. I can't remember all the details of that.

[You don't want to remember. You were aware of this, though. It just somehow or other caught on fire and burned to the ground...]

Just somehow. Normally, you've got to remember one thing. Any time you clear out an outhouse in the field, you generally throw a bunch of lye in the bottom and then you put some gasoline in and you light a fire. That's what kills the bacteria and everything. You burn them out, really. Well, that's what could have happened then, but I'm not sure. I think it happened a little different.

[The Koreans took care of cleaning out the night soil, didn't they?]

Normally. When they didn't steal you blind. I had a little dog I found there in Korea. I kept feeding him and keeping him around my hut, and finally I called him Snowball. I sent a picture of him home to my mom and dad. All of a sudden, it's in the dead of winter, in January or February and that dog disappeared. They eat dogs. I didn't know.

After we got off the phone, I remembered another part of the story about the VMF-115 outhouse. A notice was posted that they could use ours, VMF-311's, at the off hours of around 1 a.m. to 2 a.m. daily.

Can't remember much more. It was quite a joke and of course the name was not Outhouse, the word started with S_ _ _ _ _r.[39]

Elmer Plaetzer, metal shop mechanic VMF-311:

He left maybe a month or six weeks after I got there. I got there in March. He was on a hospital ship and then he came back and then he was flying. Gary [sic] Coleman [sic – so many people say Coleman when they almost certainly mean Merriman] was flying with our sister squadron. He had problems with his ears. That was one of the medical problems that he had.

The only opportunity I had to meet him, so to speak, was we had a softball game with the officers against the enlisted men. That was the only time I actually saw him play baseball live. He actually played in the softball game. I was one of the enlisted men and I played right field and chased some of the balls he hit! It was just a scrub game. Whenever he hit them, they went over my head. It was just off of the airstrip, just a rough field. We were up on a plateau. It wasn't a regular ballfield. There was always a good camaraderie between the officers and the enlisted men. We used to throw rocks at each other. It generally started with the officers coming back from the officers' club at night. They'd pick up rocks and bounce them off of the butler huts, where the enlisted men were, which would get the guys out. We would wait until that calmed down and then we'd go out and bounce rocks off their huts.[40]

Carrol Burch, pilot VMF-115:

One kid, what was his name? Stubby! Stubby Stender. He was running one night. There was a group that went over and got pretty well lubricated every night and Stubby was one of them. He was krondyking and somebody came out and he was running as fast as he could, and ran smack dab into a light pole. It blacked both eyes. He had a great big knot in the middle of his forehead and both of his eyes were black. He couldn't even fly for a while until he got over that. [41]

George Winewriter, pilot VMF-115:

[Was there much rivalry between 115 and 311?] No, not that I know of. Maybe in the upper echelons. We had our own operations and our own operations officer. Bolt was our operations officer. I don't know enough about 311 to know who was theirs.

Yes, there was the krondyking. That was our squadron. There were lots of rocks around. Colonel Moss, our CO, we had a big ceremony – Col. Moss and Col. Lorne – we buried a great big rock out in the middle of that road between the two squadrons, and that was supposed to end all the krondyking.[42]

Leo LeBlanc, pilot VMF-115:

I left K-3 in February or early March. I would have to say that he didn't play [baseball], because I do know at Cherry Point that he wouldn't play. He would say, "If you want me to play, I'll get out and be all set." I don't think he played, where Lloyd Merriman did.

[I heard that some people resented that a little bit...] Yep. The kids...the guys who were fixing his airplanes. They would have a beer bust or something and they'd invite him, and the next thing you'd know they'd have a softball and out they'd go. Merriman always did it, but Ted Williams to my knowledge, never did it. He was pretty good after he got out, though.[43]

Leonard Waibel, line chief VMF-311:

We tried to get him to play baseball, but he wouldn't do it. He would hit a few balls, and he'd throw the balls but he would not play baseball with us. He said he didn't want to be around all us crazy Marines, that we might hurt him. There might have been some sort of contract he had. [44]

Bob Flanagan, plane captain (flight line mechanic) VMF-311:

Well, of course, these were thrown-together sandlot games. When those guys were playing in World War II – I'm familiar with military organized ball to some extent – and that's what they were there for – to play baseball. That went all the way up into the Sixties. A lot of the ringers [mentions some football figures who played on military teams]. Wes Santee, remember the miler? He ran for the Marine Corps. He was stationed at Quantico, and he didn't do a damn thing but run for the Marine Corps.

Remember, the guys that he was playing with when he was there at Pensacola were like Pee Wee Reese. He wasn't playing with a bunch of throw-together bang-ups like us. I was the organizer for the enlisted contingent, when the enlisted played the officers there at K-3. I think we had three or four ball games. We would play 115 and then we played one game with MACG-2, I think. They were across the field from us. And then we played our own officers a couple or three times. Colonel Ulrich used to come out to the flight line and confer with me to see when we could get a game together.

[I wonder if Ted ever went out and watched any of those games.]

I know he walked by one of them one time. He just kept right on going. Hell, could you imagine? Here's the king of baseball and he's going to play with us? Or, the simple matter of... Christ, the pitchers we had were wild! Why would he want to take a chance on going up there and getting beaned by one of them?

We were playing and he walked by, and that was pretty much it. The field that we used was actually the Korean Marine Corps parade grounds, down on the backside of the theater. Later on back there they built a Quonset hut and a beer hall. They had a bunch of tents. They would come down there on R&R and they were the external security. That complex would be on the northeast side of the base.

He may have been going... as I remember, the dental clinic was down there, and I believe the sick call was over in that direction, too. One of the guys, this colonel John L. Smith, he was the fellow that shot down five Zeros over Guadalcanal one day, got a Congressional Medal of Honor for that. He took over MAG-33 after the war was over. He was the air group commander. Hell, he came out and played with us. I can remember him knocking the second baseman ass over teakettle on a throw into second base.

The field we had there, I mean it was rock, stones and red clay. We had a few games there and they were pretty decent. We had bats and balls. We had shin guards, mask, and everything – Special Service came up with everything.[45]

Rylen Rudy, fellow pilot VMF-311:

The only thing I saw him do baseball-wise was that a group of us just happened to be walking up towards the squadron area from our quarters and there were some kids out playing baseball. Somebody knocked a ball over and it arrived basically where we were, and he reached down and picked it up, and a flick of the wrist was basically all the harder it seemed that he threw that thing. And that goddamned ball was like a bullet just at eye level straight in to wherever this kid was. I had never seen a ball thrown like that before! And I mean, he didn't put any effort behind it. It was amazing.[46]

Woody Woodbury, pilot VMF-115:

I can remember Lloyd Merriman, who played second base with the Cincinnati Redlegs over there, he was one of the pilots over there. He wasn't nearly as well known as Ted, but he and Ted got along great. When those two would get together, we'd just sit and listen and they'd talk baseball. Jerry Coleman was not with us. He was over across the country over at K-55 or K-8, maybe K-6, I should say. Edro knows Lloyd Merriman very well. I heard later that he had died, then I heard that he was alive and in some kind of a home and that he was mad at the world, didn't want to talk to anybody. He was up around Fresno. I can remember sitting around the chow hall and those guys would just banter back and forth and it was really interesting. There were not two-hour sessions. They'd talk for maybe half an hour, but it was really interesting. You'd hear Ted talking about Yawkey, and about different stars of that day. Casey Stengel, some of those old baseball names. He was not a name-dropper; he was more popular than any of them. It was spontaneous. I thought, gee, he knows all these people. These are people that you read about in the sports pages.

We were all rural kids from our original homes and, hell, we were never tied up with anybody like that. I think that's one of the reasons where a lot of us really liked Ted, because he was from San Diego himself and he didn't come off as a big star or anything else. He did have a temper but, hell, everybody has a temper. When you're a famous person and have a temper, that makes headlines but you take some country bumpkin like me out of the sticks, if I have a temper, who gives a damn? It's the same old story, I guess. As old as humanity, I guess.[47]

 Joseph Mitchell, fellow pilot VMF-311:

I had a couple of conversations with Ted about that. There was an appeal made through some of the enlisted people to get Ted out [to play]. He was reluctant for some reason or other to just willy-nilly to go out and play with the boys. It was just his thing. I'd say, "These guys, they really admire you not only for what you're doing here, but also as a baseball player, and if you were to throw these guys a little, you know, just back and forth – you don't have to play baseball with them – they'd write home and tell their mom and dad they played catch with Ted Williams. It would really be a morale builder."

He never said "yes"; he never said "no." He just kind of ignored me.

[He did play a number of games in World War II. He really hurt himself badly in the 1950 All-Star Game. Maybe he just didn't want to be in the spotlight there, even if it were just the local spotlight there.]

I don't know. I think maybe it was more that he didn't want to be fawned over more than that he didn't want to play catch with the boys. I didn't want to judge him on it.

[You could take that a couple of ways. Some people may have felt he was being snobbish, but then maybe he just didn't want to be on display. Maybe he just wanted to be another Marine pilot. But he didn't hold himself out as anybody special?]

No, he didn't. That's true. That's a valid point.

He used to read a lot. He used to go pheasant and duck hunting a lot, too.[48]

 Charles Baker, pilot VMF-115:

I didn't see too much of Ted those days, even though we were all right close together. We ate in the club – that was the dining room. He'd be in the club every once in a while, but not too often. He kind of stuck to himself.

On days that we weren't flying, we'd have our beer and go out and play softball or baseball. Just have rival games. Ted never showed up. We had Lloyd Merriman. He was in our squadron, and he was always joining in the fun and doing everything. But Ted never did.

[Did that bother people? They thought he was being unfriendly?] Yeah, yeah. They kind of thought he was kind of snubbish [sic], you know. One time we were talking over in his area, and I asked him why he didn't come out. I told him that people would really like to have him join us. He practiced his swing. He'd hang a ball down from the ceiling outside off of a framework and practice his swing.

He said, "I just don't want to play softball or anything just to have fun" because he was afraid it would ruin his coordination. His eye, you know. That satisfied me. It was the wrong atmosphere. He was concerned. It kind of made sense to me. It probably was a tennis ball or something that he just hung down, and he'd stand there and just swing at that thing.[49]

 ### Harlan Peacock, head, hydraulics section VMF-311:

My job with the Marine Corps was hydraulics and electrician at K-3. Whenever the birds go down, they would send somebody up. They would call us jet jockeys. Nobody ever heard of us. I don't fly, but I would go up with somebody else, in a TV-2. It was so cold over there that when they'd get ready to go on a strike, you would have to crawl into the air vent – they had one on each side – with a rubber mallet and beat on the engine-drive pump, the hydraulic pump, to beat the ice loose... the plane's running while you're doing this... and then they would tap you on the shoe to come back out.

Ted had a mystique about him that he doesn't have to say anything, but for some reason there's that respect and admiration... his demeanor demands that. But yet when you talk with him, he's just like you and me talking. That's the quality I saw in him. He never was stuck up or snobbish or any of that stuff. I talked to him just before he died and his main concern was that he'd outlive his dog. Slugger wasn't doing too good.[50]

 ### Lloyd Merriman, pilot VMF-115:

I got to know Ted over there. We put on kind of a clinic for the colonel of the base. He asked if we could put on a little clinic. Just talking to them. We tried to do a little demonstration, fielding ground balls and whatnot, and it worked all right, but there was sure a lot of rocks in the infield. Just one day. They might have played some ball, but I didn't see too much of that.

I went duck hunting with old Ted one time. He got a Jeep and a couple of shotguns and we drove out on to the levees on the rice paddy. He'd say "Here they come" and he'd count ducks before I could even see them.

Jerry [Coleman], he was up north. After he cracked up, he became a forward air controller.

We didn't really talk baseball there. We just didn't bunk together that often. The two squadrons were right together in one place – ate in the same place. Maybe we had different times of eating. There were a lot of missions. Then we were trying to learn, too. We wanted to know all that we could about what we were doing. You'd put in extra time. If they ran an overhaul on an airplane, you'd have to make a test flight. So we'd go out and fly around the sky and do the little things they wanted tested.[51]

A February 27 story in the *Boston Globe* reported "Ted's Too Tired to Play Baseball." He was doing some hunting off-base, but confided, "I understand the boys get together in intersquadron games after working hours, but I'm pretty well exhausted after flying on a mission, so I don't believe I'll be digging into too many ball games. I'm in pretty good shape, as all combat pilots are. I'm not doing anything in particular to keep in shape, other than a lot of walking."

At a later point, Ted told visiting writer Ed Hyde, "One of these days I'd like to bat a ball around or hold a scrub game, but something will always come up to upset our plans. The best thing for me is to get off the base with my camera or go hunting in out in the hills with a borrowed shotgun." He was captured by one image he'd recently shot. "I always like to carry a camera because there are some wonderful shots over here. The other day I caught one hell of a picture. A little Korean girl about six years old wearing a bright yellow blouse and red skirt with lipstick on her mouth and with a running nose. I had to pose her by holding out a candy bar. She made one fine picture." He concluded the thought by bringing it back to the seriousness of the situation, "That's about all a guy can do because this is a hell of a place to try to do anything. We're out here to fight and that's my job right now."[52]

Ted was also too busy to get together with the other major leaguers in Korea. Lt. Bobby Brown later served as president of the American League, but at this time the seven-year New York Yankee was a surgeon with the 160th Field Artillery Batallion. He had a film of the 1952 World Series in Korea with him and took his day off to travel to Seoul, where he hoped to show it to Ted Williams, Lloyd Merriman and Jerry Coleman. Coleman was scheduled for two missions that day and Williams drew combat duty, too, so neither were able to catch up with Brown. Merriman was free, but his plane to Seoul had to turn back because of adverse weather.[53]

The Yankees created a special film of the team sending their greetings to Coleman. Stengel, Lopat, Charlie Silvera and others had words for their former teammate, and Allie Reynolds added, "Jerry, if you see Ted Williams over there, tell him all the Yankee pitchers are glad he's so far away."[54]

The one extended portrait we have of Ted in Korea is contained in a newspaper report by veteran combat correspondent Jim Lucas. It appeared in a number of newspapers at the time. Because it provides such a good picture of Ted in the context of K-3, we reprint it in its entirety.

By Jim Lucas

POHANG, Korea, June 27, 1953

There are three names on the door at the south end of Hut 1-C, 1st Marine Air Wing:

MITCHELL, J. A.

SCOTT, L. L.

WILLIAMS, T.S.

Williams, T. S., flung his six foot, plus, frame down on his cot. Just as promptly, he got up again.

"Wise guys," he yelped accusingly, digging beneath the blankets and coming up with four cans of orange juice.

Mitchell, J.A., (a major from San Francisco), and Scott, L. L., (a captain from Ellensburg, Wash.), grinned delightedly. Capt. Ted Williams, late of the Boston Red Sox, doesn't sit on a bunk. He collapses on it.

"A present, Teddy boy," they chorused.

"Present, hell," Williams grumbled good-naturedly, stowing the juice in an improvised cooler which once was an ammunition can. "Since when you guys start giving me presents? And what's it doing in my sack?"

"We're afraid you might not find it, Bush," Capt. Jim Stacey of Chicago grinned from the doorway. He stepped in, stripped off wet flight jacket and took a playful poke at his friend.

Ted grinned and sparred back.

"I go to the top of the Big Time," he said, flexing his muscles, Tarzan-style, "and what happens? I come to this hole and these bums call me Bush Leaguer."

"You wouldn't even be big time in Japan," Jim Stacey goaded him.

"I was," Williams announced.

"Like hell," Jim retorted. "I was there."

When the argument subsided, I asked Ted for the answer to a question a lot of people were asking back home:

Will he return to baseball?

Ted's immediate reaction is a quick "I'm through." But after a bit of discussion of the subject he's not quite so emphatic. In fact, if Tom Yawkey wants him back in Boston, Ted's ready to go.

NOTHING THE MATTER WITH TED'S APPETITE

I'd run across Ted at dinner in Marine Air Raid Group 33's officers' mess just before dusk. Together we put away two man-sized meals – steak, French fries, creamed corn, hot biscuits, salad, coffee and ice cream. Ted suggested I wait for him in his quarters. He had some negatives in the "soup" at the hobby shop. I wouldn't, he promised, "take more than a minute."

I waited 45. Outside it was raining hard. Inside I had an opportunity to study the few square feet Ted Williams calls home in Pohang.

The Marines list 1-C as "hut, tropical, pre-fabricated, personnel." It sits in a sea of mud a huge sign proclaims as "Officers' Country." Ted and his two roommates share the south third of the building. 1-C has sandbags on its roof to keep it from blowing away.

Ted's cot is in one corner. Capt. Lee Scott sleeps in another corner and Maj. Jim Mitchell's bunk is toward the front. There's a table in the center. In still another corner there's a home-made combination bar, pantry, and washroom – a couple of Jerry cans of water, three tin wash basins and the usual assortment of toothbrushes, etc.

There's a copy of the 1953 All-Sports Almanac on Ted's bunk. On the metal beer cooler, he's painted:

GUNG-HO

CAPTAIN TED WILLIAMS

USMC

On the footlocker under his cot:

"T. S. Williams, 037773"

Ted roared in out of the rain, arms full of fresh prints from the darkroom.

"Old TSW scores again," he crowed. "Every one a masterpiece."

He spread them on the center table. Lee Scott, a camera perfectionist, examined each critically.

"Take a look at these," he said, shoving his own prints toward Ted, who eyed them cautiously.

"I learned something about developing tonight," Williams said mysteriously. "About Gamma. Be a good lad and I may tell you some day. You could improve on these, you know."

Capt. Scott snorted decisively.

"That'll be the day," he sneered.

Ted lowered himself onto his bunk, beneath a calendar picture of a pretty girl. It apparently was a gift from a Columbus, Ohio, auto accessory firm.

"Who's from Columbus?" I asked.

"Oh, her," Ted said. "She was here when I arrived. But I think she's nice. So I keep her. Wouldn't you?"

He settled back, comfortably, drawing his muddy field boots up on the blankets after him. He wore a khaki Marine shirt and a paid of wrinkled green dungaree trousers.

"I'm grounded, you know," he began. "Not permanently. I'll be flying in a few days. I've just come back from R&R (Rest and Recreation) in Japan and I caught cold. When I get a cold it settles in my ears. I don't know what's wrong."

NO ONE EVER HAD MORE LIES WRITTEN ABOUT HIM

He cocked his head slightly to one side and pounded gently on his left ear with the heel of his hand. Then he sat up, and there was a trace of belligerence in him.

"I suppose you've heard that I am deaf," he said. "I don't think there's a person living who's had more lies written about him than me."

He walked to his wardrobe – an old packing case into which he had hammered shelves – and came back with a magazine. He read aloud:

"Ted Williams will soon be retired by the Marines on disability. His hearing has been affected since he made a forced landing recently, bringing his jet down 3,000 feet per minute."

"There's not a man here," Williams almost yelled, "who doesn't bring it down 4,000 to 5,000 feet a minute every day. Where do they get that stuff?"

"You're a hero, Bush," Jim Stacey teased him.

"Can that," Ted growled, but his face relaxed in a grin.

"Just get this," he said. "I'm not deaf and I'm not being washed out. I got a cold and it settled in my ear. That's all. When you fly these babies, you've got to be I-A."

Shortly after this story was written the Marine Corps ordered Ted Williams permanently grounded and sent back to the United States for treatment of an ear and nose condition. After a checkup aboard the Danish hospital ship Jutlandia doctors recommended that he be removed from flying duty.

(Capt. Williams was scheduled to be released from active duty this fall but a Marine Corps spokesman said he might be kept on active duty for a longer period if his ear trouble doesn't clear up immediately. Capt. Williams' career as a combat pilot ended after 49 [sic] missions over enemy lines.)

I asked about the letter he'd written a friend saying he didn't expect to return from Korea alive. His face darkened.

"That!" He spat the word. He sat for a long time before he spoke.

"Made me sound like a fool," he said finally.

The discussion turned to his R&R in Japan with Jim Stacey. He said they'd gone to Osaka and Kyoto.

"I didn't enjoy it," he said. "I wasn't feeling good the first two days and the last three it rained. I couldn't take pictures."

TED'S PLANE HIT ON THIRD MISSION

Any day Ted Williams can't take pictures is wasted.

Did the Japanese fanatic baseball fans recognize him?

"Only once," he shuddered at the recollection. "One day in Osaka."

How many missions had he flown?

"Thirty nine," he said. "I've got about a month and a half to go before they give me staff duty."

Any more close ones?

"You heard about the first one, then." He was relaxed again. "It was on my third mission. The first one they send you along the bomb line to get acquainted. The second is up on the Haeju peninsula, where it doesn't matter much. The third is your big one. You're on your own.

"Funny," he mused. "I was the only guy hit. I still don't know what happened. I didn't feel anything. But they sure as hell hit me. We've gone over that plane with a fine tooth comb. It was small arms. No wonder they didn't hit anyone else. I got it all.

"I was on a strike near Kyomipo, after troops and supplies. It knocked out everything -- my radio, landing gear, everything. The stick started shaking like mad and my hands. I tried my radio but it was out. Then the aileron got stiff and I turned off the boost. I had to use both hands."

Ted ran his right hand through his hair thoughtfully.

"I figured I could never make it back, so I took her out to sea, like the book says," he said. "But one look at that water -- no sir, not for this boy. It was half frozen, and I could see myself breaking through and not getting up again. So I said to myself, 'Son, you're going down on land.' I heard later they were trying to tell me to ditch at sea. Glad I couldn't hear."

Ted put his wounded bird down for a belly landing at Kimpo [sic] that Feb. 16.

"I knew I was going too fast," he said, "but my indicator showed '0.' That struck me funny. There was nothing to do but belly in. I hit hard and went chugging down the runway. I thought I'd never stop. When I did, I released the canopy and almost fell out."

EVERYTHING ELSE HAS BEEN A MILK RUN

Any others?

"Yeah," Ted said. "a few weeks ago. Up around Chinnampo. You know what it's like up there. I was the fourth man on the target. We were going after a factory. I watched the first three, and I thought: 'This is easy.'

"I peeled off and, man, you never saw so much stuff! It was solid. It came up like a blanket. I got rid of my bombs and started weaving. I knew I was hit. I HAD to be.

"I looked out, and there was this big hole in my right tank. Big as your fist. I heard someone say he'd been hit and I chimed in, too. But my ship behaved, so I took her home."

He grinned -- obviously working up to his climax.

"Know what happened?" he demanded. "A big rock had bounced off the ground and gone right through my tank. It was still in there. They tell me rocks bounce 2,500 feet if they're hit right. But I had to see it to believe it."

Ted knocked on the wood of his cot.

"And that's all," he said. "Everything else has been a milk run."

Aside from flying, Ted has two interests – baseball and photography.

"My first season," he recalled. "I was hitting good and Joe Cronin – there's a real gentleman; ever meet him? -- took me to dinner at a high class place in New York. I remember he said, 'Ted, you're a great ball player and you're with a great team, but you'll never be as famous playing with Boston as you would be if you were here in New York. Just remember that and you'll understand a lot of things.' And he was right."

The discussion turned to his feud with the Boston sports writers.

"Don't get me started." he begged. "I get along with those who treat me right. But I don't want them in the club-house because they don't belong there. Ours isn't the only club that bars them. You can divide clubs into those afraid and that aren't. We weren't.

"I never refuse to talk to a writer after I've showered unless he's a bum who is always panning me. Then I tell him, 'Get away from me, you bum. I've got nothing to say to you.'"

OLD TSW KEPT SCRIBES OUT OF CLUBHOUSE

By this time he was pacing the floor.

"I'm going to read you something." he said, fishing in his locker for a letter. "This is from one of the guys on the club."

"'Dear Ted,' he read aloud. "'Got your letter and sure was glad to hear from you. Things are about the same here. (A lot of personal stuff, Williams explained, skipping pages.) Dom (DiMaggio) has retired. We sure did hate to see him go. Same thing as happened to (Earl) Combs. We don't vote on anything any more. The scribes come into the clubhouse whenever they want to.

"That's what's happening!" Williams flung the letter on the table. "Dom was our players' representative. He felt like I did. But know who it was who kept 'em out whenever the front office weakened? Old Number One. Old TSW."

Pressed again about the future, Ted said:

"I'm through. I may have a couple of years left in me, I don't know. But it depends on how I feel. Trouble with baseball is that you've got to be a politician. Always polishing the apple. I'm not that way. I figure I play good baseball, and that should be enough."

His friends hooted.

"You'll be back, and I'll be in the stands giving you a hard time," Lee Scott said.

"You'll know it's us – we'll be yelling, 'Hey, Bush'," Jim Stacey said.

"I won't even know you guys," Ted laughed. "You'll come around in your fancy Gyrene uniforms looking for passes and I'll say, 'Those bums? I never saw 'em before.'

"We'll sit in the bleachers," Major Jim Walley of New Orleans shouted, "and throw pop bottles."

"I'll throw 'em back," Ted promised. Then seriously: "I don't think I will go back. That little fishing tackle business of mine down in Florida is going to clear a million and a half bucks this year. Why should I lick anybody's boots?"

TED DOESN'T BLAME RHEE FOR HOWLING

He got up and lit a cigarette.

"Of course," he amended. "I might go back for Mr. Yawkey. He's the finest man I ever knew. I'd do anything for him."

Because he is a camera bug, Ted spends much of his free time touring southern Korea looking for pictures. He's just returned from a remote Korean fishing village.

"Trouble is," he said, "most GIs scare these people. They drive up in a Jeep, hop out, snap a few and drive off. The people don't know what's happening, but it scares them. You've got to take it easy. In the first two villages they turned their backs or ran, but these were happy to see us. They took us up to meet the village head man. He asked us to come back. We're going Sunday -- if it doesn't rain and we don't fly."

Ted asked about a truce. I brought him up to date on the situation.

"That'd be something," he said. "Personally, it can't come too soon. But I don't blame Rhee for howling. I would, too, if I were a Korean. It doesn't seem to me we've settled anything."

Has he enjoyed his tour in Korea?

"It's not something you enjoy," he said. "You're always under pressure, and you know something could happen. But you don't expect it. I wouldn't have wanted any special favors, and I've had a lot of new experiences. But I'll be glad when it's over.

"You and me," he said, "aren't getting any younger."

Two of the songs Woody Woodbury led the men in singing were *"On Top of Old Ping Pong"* and *"Old Number Nine"* (also known as "Dark and Stormy Night").

On Top of Old Ping Pong

On top of old Ping pong, all covered with flak,
I lost my poor wing man, he never came back.
For flying is pleasure, and crashing is grief,
And a quick triggered Commie is worse than a thief.
A thief will just rob you, and take what you save,
But a quick triggered Commie will send you to the grave.
The grave will decay you, and turn you to dust,
Not one MiG in a thousand an F9 can trust.
They'll chase you and kill you, and send out more lead,
Than cuts on a railroad or MiGs overhead.
So come all you pilots and listen to me,
Never go to Sinanju, or old Kuna-ri.
For the planes they will falter, and pilots will die,
You'll stay in Korea and never know why.
The moral of this story, can plainly be seen,
Stay east of old Diego, be a Stateside Marine.

Old Number Nine

'Twas a dark and stormy night, not a star was in sight,
All the Corsairs were tied down to the line.
When in mud up to his ears, stood a lonely volunteer
With his orders to fly old Number 9.

His ass was racked with pain as he climbed into his plane,
For his aircraft was hardly fit to fly;
And he whispered a prayer, as he climbed into the air.
For he knew this was his night to die.

As he flew o'er Haga-ru, he could see a school or two,
And the women and children very well,
But how was he to know, that he'd fly so Goddamned low
That his bomb blast would blow him all to hell.

In the wreck he was found, he was spread all o'er the ground,
And the crunchies, they raise his weary head.
With his life almost spent, here's the message he sent,
To his buddies, who'd be said to see him dead.

I used an 8 to 10 delay, but it didn't work out that way,
And without a tail, an F9F won't fly,
Tell the skipper for me, that he now has twenty-three,
He can roll up the ladder, Semper Fi.

NOTES

1) Interview with Earl Traut, September 23, 2004.

2) Interview with James Dolan, February 3, 2003.

3) Quoted by Ed Hyde, Sport, July 1953.

4) Interview with Earl Traut, op. cit.

5) Fred Townsley, posted on VMF-311/VMA-311 website.

6) Interview with Lou Capozzoli, May 31, 2002.

7) Interview with Rylen Rudy, February 4, 2003.

8) Fred Townsley, posted on VMF-311/VMA-311 website.

9) Interview with Leonard Waibel, December 19, 2002.

10) Interview with Bill Clem, December 23, 2002.

11) Interview with Mike Canan, December 31, 2002.

12) Interview with Jack Bolt, January 9, 2003.

13) Interview with Carrol Burch, February 6, 2003.

14) Interview with Bob Johnson, May 31, 2002.

15) Interview with George Winewriter, November 28, 2002.

16) Interview with Ed Buchser, September 26, 2002.

17) Interview with Tom Miller, February 7, 2003.

18) Interview with Woody Woodbury, October 1, 2002.

19) Interview with Joseph Mitchell, February 3, 2003.

20) Interview with Rylen B. Rudy, February 4, 2003.

21) Interview with Woody Woodbury, October 1, 2002.

22) Interview with Paul Janssen, December 23, 2002.

23) Interview with Ed Buchser, September 26, 2002.

24) Interview with Leonard Waibel, December 19, 2002.

25) Communication from Bob Flanagan, November 25, 2002.

26) Interview with James Walley, December 7, 2003.

27) Interview with Roger McCully, December 5, 2002.

28) Interview with Leonard Waibel, December 19, 2002. The word "krondyked" is spelled differently throughout this book, trying to keep with the pronunciation of the person being interviewed.

29) *Interview with Paul B. Montague, February 11, 2003.*

30) *Interview with Jack Campbell, November 27, 2002. Ted had more than one camera in Korea.*

31) *Interview with James Walley, December 7, 2002.*

32) *Interview with Ed Buchser, September 26, 2002.*

33) *Interview with Virginia Tipps, August 12, 2005.*

34) *Interview with Woody Woodbury, October 1, 2002.*

35) *Interview with L. B. Robertshaw, November 16, 2002.*

36) *Interview with Woody Woodbury, October 1, 2002.*

37) *Interview with Walter Roark, December 21, 2002.*

38) *Interview with Carrol Burch, February 6, 2003.*

39) *Interview with Larry Hawkins, December 21, 2002, and follow-up e-mail later that day.*

40) *Interview with Elmer Plaetzer, December 27, 2002.*

41) *Interview with Carrol Burch, February 6, 2003.*

42) *Interview with George Winewriter, November 28, 2002.*

43) *Interview with Leo LeBlanc, December 27 & 31, 2002.*

44) *Interview with Leonard Waibel, December 19, 2002.*

45) *Interview with Bob Flanagan, June 2, 2003.*

46) *Interview with Rylen Rudy, February 4, 2003.*

47) *Interview with Woody Woodbury, October 1, 2002.*

48) *Interview with Joseph Mitchell, February 3, 2003.*

49) *Interview with Charles Baker, December 28, 2002 and February 2, 2003.*

50) *Interview with Harlan Peacock, March 27, 2004.*

51) *Interview with Lloyd Merriman, November 16, 2002.*

52) *Ed Hyde,* Sport, *July 1953.*

53) The Sporting News, *March 18, 1953, p. 18.*

54) The Sporting News, *ibid., p. 27.*

"Ted had just received his mail at mail check." Somewhat less than three sacks full!
Photo by Jack Campbell.

CHAPTER 14 – CELEBRITY, GRUMBLING, AND GRIPING

Ted Williams was a celebrity, no matter how hard or how well he may have tried to blend in, and celebrity brings with it a number of problems. Ted also griped a lot. Just about all the reservists griped, and no doubt many of the regulars did, too. Sharing gripes and bitches can help build esprit de corps amongst a group of men serving together in any environment, and perhaps more so in one fraught with peril. Many felt Ted went too far with his grousing, though. To expect Ted Williams to be a model gung ho Marine would have been unrealistic; it's likely true that his very celebrity magnified his words, and seemed to give them greater force. How did he carry himself in Korea? Was he hounded by the press? And did his griping cross over the line from time to time?

 George Winewriter, pilot VMF-115:

[So people didn't really talk about him a lot, Ted Williams? He was a pretty famous guy at the time.] Well, he wasn't [famous] in our squadron. No, I don't remember him being treated like a celebrity or anything.

He was just another guy to me. There's all kind of guys... I hate to say it, because I like Ed Buchser very, very much, but he's one of them that if there's a celebrity there, he'll be right with him – so he knows a lot more about Ted Williams than I'll ever know. I wouldn't doubt there were some newspapermen there from time to time, too.

[As far as you know, he didn't hold himself out as any different from anybody else?] Oh, no. No. No, sir. He did a good job.

[Did you run into Ted Williams other times?] Only to hang around. If he had hung around the happy hours, though, I would know him real well! [Laughs.] I don't remember Ted at all in any of that social stuff.

There was a bar there and I was very active in it, but I don't think Ted was. John Glenn was there [on the base, not in the bar] and he's the exact different type of person, too [meaning that Glenn didn't hang around the bar, either].

I don't remember ever socializing with Ted in Korea.[1]

 Woody Woodbury, pilot VMF-115:

[You're in the entertainment business. When you first met Ted, did you notice a lot of commotion around him, him being a celebrity?] You could tell he was important because people would say, "There's Ted. That's him, that big guy over there." Ted was a big guy.

He had a lot of press in Korea.[2]

Walter Roark, pilot VMF-115:

[Some people had a difficult time with Ted, I guess.] Well, it might be that way, but it sure didn't bother me. He was a nice enough guy. It seemed like he was probably a nicer guy the first time he was in than when he got called back in for the Korean War, but that's understandable. Why would he be happy to be called back? Right in the middle of his career. His profession was baseball player, not a fighter pilot. He was a reservist. I was in as a regular. I stayed in 22 years. I said, "Hell, I can't make a living out there any other way. I might as well stay here and fly these airplanes." He was a reservist that got called back in.[3]

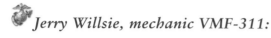 *Jerry Willsie, mechanic VMF-311:*

I remember the magazines was always coming over and taking his pictures and having write-ups. We got a big kick out of that. I would say that being he was going to go back to baseball as soon as his tour was up, I imagine that he liked the correspondents. I don't know if he got along with rest of the officers or not, because us enlisted men wasn't allowed in the officers' club and the officers' country. They were separate from the enlisted personnel. Their barracks and huts and recreation and that sort of thing. I don't know of any of us enlisted men that he was overbearing with. None that I know of. Very professional. Just too big for the airplane.[4]

Ted Williams on base in Korea.
Courtesy of Claudia Williams.

Roy Harris, electrician VMF-311:

We were extending the airstrip. I done the electrical system. When I first went over it was steel matting, and they just kept extending the base. Originally, it was a Japanese air base in World War II. We extended the strip for the jets. I was there for a year. When I got there, they were all generators. I built up a power system with Japanese transformers and American generators, and stepped the voltage up to 3,300 volts, and then stepped it back down so that they would have base power that way, and then generators for emergency backup.

I don't think Ted was playing. It was Lloyd Merriman. Ted Williams didn't play over there with us. He kind of stayed by himself. Ted Williams was there, but I didn't pitch against him, but I did against Lloyd Merriman. We were playing softball. He was a good hitter. I played fast pitch here in town. I very seldom saw him [Ted]. He kind of stuck more to himself. We didn't see much of him in the activities as far as that was concerned. We'd see him come in, fly in after a mission. One time he had a couple of holes in the airplane, probably from ground fire. I never heard why, but everybody said he was kind of a loner. That's what they told us there, and we just took it as that. It's always nice, though, to know that there were some celebrities around.[5]

 Marsh Austin, fellow pilot VMF-311:

He was really not a happy camper when he got there. He had mixed emotions. One, he didn't get into combat during World War II. And every aviator... if you never play in the game, you know, it's like if you practice baseball all your life and never play the game. That aspect, he was happy to be there.

He didn't talk about his personal life, but at the time, being the highest paid baseball player in the country and to be yanked out of his career, for the second time, it was pretty difficult. And of course had he stayed in baseball all through those two periods, why, there'd be records that... I don't know... they'd never be broken.

[I guess you just relaxed in the ready room after a mission and got ready for the next day. I see from some pictures that you would play backgammon or board games like that.]

We called it acey-deucey, essentially the same [as backgammon].

[I guess neither Ted nor John Glenn ever really drank or smoked cigarettes at all.]

No. I remember sitting one day with Ted and we were looking at a *Life* magazine and his picture was on the back cover with, I think it was Lucky Strikes. Cigarette advertisement, and we got talking about it and he told me, "I got $25,000 for smoking that cigarette, but I never took a puff."

[There were Korean people living right near the base?]

All around the base. The serving people, in the mess hall were Korean. A lot of the base maintenance.

[Who took these photographs?]

Sometimes we shared. If I took one that Ted would like, he took copies of it, so I can't say for certain which of these he took and which I took.[6]

James G. Fox, fellow pilot VMF-311:

I never had any problem at all with Ted. Ted and I got along pretty good. He had a view for the regular Marine Corps and I had a joking response to him and called him "Bush."

[Did you see many reporters around him, trying to get a story?]

Well, a couple of times, yes. They came around the ready room and I got sharp with them a couple of times. They were bugging me while I was trying to brief a flight where people were going to go out and risk their butts. [7]

 Louis Capozzoli, chief combat correspondent First Air Wing:

[Did your duties involve dealing with reporters and photographers who wanted access to him?]

Yeah. One time he told me, "Keep them away from me." He didn't like the reporters. When he came in one time with his wings shot up – he had holes in his wings from a blast from his dive bombing. The debris came up and hit his wing from the blast because he was so low. Well, the press got ahold of that and they flooded the place. There were 6 or 7 of them [reporters].

He was friendly. He didn't like to be disturbed all the time. I sent them down to MAG-33 then. I had a man stationed down there. I had the Wing, and MAG-33 was right next to us. He told me, "Keep those guys away from me." [8]

 Bob Flanagan, plane captain VMF-115:

Every time he flew, it was a P.R. event. When I say a P.R. event, Christ, there were people following. The cameras from the information office and so forth. It was sort of a pain in the butt.

[That's interesting, because some people say they hardly ever saw newspeople around Ted and some other people say that he was almost being hounded.]

Well, I thought he was being hounded, because every time I saw him, there was a Speed Graphic following him, and usually it was the Marine Corps. I had seen him sitting out there standing the CAP – the combat air patrol –- that's where they go out and sit them in an airplane for 4 hours at a whack. We used to have one fellow there from Chicago that used to go out and yak with Ted Williams all the time. He would go out there and lean up and they would yak yak yak a good portion of his tour. And then of course, we would pull him over in the corner: "What'd he say? What'd he say?"

But I felt sorry for him. Basically, I felt sorry for him. I think he was being used by the Marine Corps. He was 34 years old.

He was like, "I don't want to get bothered. Let me alone." [9]

John D. Beck, pilot VMF-115:

He was a nice guy. Big fellow. Good sense of humor, and as I remember some of the guys used to call him "Bush." He didn't play any baseball there.

When you came back from your hop, 115 – we were in one spot and 311 was in another. We were right across from each other, yes, but you saw each other at meal time. And maybe in the O Club, if you did that kind of thing later in the evening. I remember Woody.

I didn't think he was stand-offish. If you were in the same place at the same time, he was just like everybody else. If you didn't know who he was, you wouldn't realize he was a baseball star.

He just came and was one of the guys, that's all. I didn't hear him bring anything up about baseball, about how he was on the ball team or anything like that. He just came and did what he was supposed to. The day he left Korea and headed back home, at that time I was Operations Officer for the base. I talked to him at Operations. He just wanted to get the hell out of there. He was alright when I saw him last.

He got hit over there and made it back to one of the other fields. We knew what happened to him. Even then, we didn't see him except at meal time. Your flights didn't correspond to eating together all the time. You might have been up and back, or waiting to go. We all ate together and they joshed around at the time, but you didn't eat at the same time every day and sometimes you wouldn't see some of the guys for two or three days at a time because they were out while you were eating and vice versa.

[Did you ever hear people being critical of him?]

No, not in our squadron. We figured he was losing a lot more than most of the rest of us over there. And if he hadn't been in there and spent so much time in the military, nobody'd ever reach his record. He was in World War II and in Korea and some of these guys that have all these fancy records never were even in the service![10]

VMF-115 skipper "krondyking."
Courtesy of Russ Kelly.

Dale Purcell, pilot VMJ-1:

Among other things, I'm a psychologist. One of the things that happens anywhere, if there's a big shot ballplayer there a lot of people tend to – I don't use the term "suck up" – they tend to want to get acquainted. I think pros such as Williams would have his problems with the press and could spot a phony a mile away. I had never seen him until I went over there for dinner a couple of times. One night I was going to say something out of courtesy, because I had met him at a very fine restaurant in Tokyo near the International Press Club where I was a close friend of a former college friend, a White House correspondent... I went over there one night, I went across the field...you could eat wherever you wanted to... I went over a couple of times to eat with some friends who I had known from World War II. I'd gone over there a couple of times and encountered Col. Robertshaw. I didn't know which of those guys was Williams. I said to one fellow, "You're from Boston." He said, "No, sometimes the mistake is made. I'm from Oklahoma." I said, "Thanks." The meal was ending and I was about to leave. He did not stand out. This wasn't a ballgame. This was a war and there were other achievers. Spence Moseley. Lou Conti was now a major general and a very close friend of mine, who lost a son in Vietnam. Lou Conti and Spence Moseley, and Charlie Herrick and I used to go on R&R together to Japan. We would do a little photos, play a little golf, see the sights.

We weren't bowlers, we weren't chasing women.

Williams didn't stand out to me. In Glenn's book, I thought he got short shrift. He said we called him "Bush" because it bugged him. He was called "Big League" because that was a code name among some of his friends. Occasionally, a few of us would get a few steaks and cook them on a grill behind somebody's quarters, and if Williams happened to be one of them, fine.[11]

 Robert Sabot, pilot VMJ-1:

The publicity people were on his butt all the time. He was trying to do his job and keep to himself and the publicity guys were always after pictures and stories. Marine Corps. [Not regular commercial newspaper reporters – Sabot is specifically talking about Marine Corps publicists.] He roomed with a couple of my good friends. He was in the next hut. Ronnie Bruce was one of them. He died in a helicopter accident in maybe '61 or '62. He got out of jets and he was instructing a guy and they crashed and burned. He had serious burns and died.

[When you first met Ted, what was your impression of him?] Just a very normal, kind of a quiet guy. I think I flew a couple of hops with him. There's nothing you could say wrong about him.

We had three in our hut. Normally, there would be three or four. Stuck-up? No! God, no! He was just trying to keep to himself, do his job and Christ, I guess get back to baseball.

Where our mess hall was, you went up there and you had a drink at the bar and then the mess hall was right there. I don't recall him personally up there. I wasn't a friend of his. He was friendly with a few people, I think the people in his hut. Just normal stuff. He did his service in World War II and then got nailed again for Korea. He lost a hell of a lot of ground as far as baseball goes.[12]

Chuck Ingle, staff sergeant VMF-311:

I do remember his ego was bigger than he was. Also once his plane was riddled as he made the big error of being blasted by his own bombs; however, he did make it back and rode the plane down to a belly landing. Give him that.

The correspondents wouldn't leave him alone. He was almost as big as Bob Hope as far as they were concerned.

Williams personally, I only know what I observed when I did see him. As I say, at times, when I did see him, the news media and the correspondents, they were clicking cameras all around him. I think it was mostly the foreign correspondents themselves [as opposed to Marine Corps photographers].

[Did he seem to be enjoying that, or putting up with it?] Oh yes. He loved it. Did you ever hear of a guy chewing out the photographers because they're not getting it right to suit him? [Laughs]

[His father was a professional photographer, so he may have had his ideas...] He had an ego, too, though. I think if you traced his background, you know he had a pretty good ego. One time I was passing and he was sitting there in the cockpit and they were snapping pictures, and he was just waving his arms at them and this and that and pointing at this... like giving orders, you know.[13]

Rylen Rudy, fellow pilot VMF-311:

I think he was the biggest asshole the world has ever known.

You went to the O Club at night, and if everybody in the place knew who he was, he'd sit in the corner and have a drink and there wasn't any problems. I don't know what the hell he was drinking; I didn't care. If there was a new group comes in – of course, every month we had a new draft, they called it, new kids on campus. Well, if there was anybody in the O Club that did not know exactly who he was, he was loud and boisterous and made himself a pain in the ass, until they understood that this was the great Ted Williams! At that point, he calmed down and went on about his business.

He was always going to the clinic and checking himself in, instead of flying the damn missions. He walked in one day over there, and the corpsman was sitting in one these chairs like you used in high school – it's got this arm that's the writing desk portion of it all at the same time. This corpsman is sitting there and Williams walks up beside him. The corpsman looks up and sees that he's a captain and says, "Name, Captain?" Williams looks down at him and says, "Williams. T.S. The." That's a true story.

[That's funny. You could take that one way or another, of course.]

That's just the way he was. However, on another occasion, one of the things we used to do, we used to have to stand what's called runway duty. Any time you got airplanes airborne and you could see – which meant you didn't have to do it after dark – we had a pilot at the end of the runway, and the idea is he [a returning pilot] might be shot up, he might have had other problems, and he's forgot to put his gear down. So you've got flares and stuff to either wave him off or remind him to put his gear down before he tries to park this thing. And you've got an enlisted man out there with you. You've got a radio Jeep. Mostly, especially in the wintertime, you'd sit up on the hood of the radio

Jeep because it's running all the time and it keeps your ass warm. The way we used to work it, it'd be a four-hour shift out there. So you're there for two hours, when the enlisted man switches. You get a new guy, and then two hours after he shows up, you get a new officer shows up. Well, I went out one time. It was my turn to stand runway duty. And Ted Williams was out there. He and this kid were sitting up on this Jeep and they'd been sitting there two hours, shooting the breeze. So I pulled up. Ted took the Jeep I rode out in and Ted went back to the squadron office. I pulled up on the hood of the Jeep with this kid, and I said, "Well, what did you and the captain talk about?"

He said, "We talked about baseball. You know, that guy really knows about baseball! It's 2 up and 3 out and 3 crosswise and the ball goes out to the right field or the left field and where do you throw it next... " And he goes on and on and on about this whole thing, and about how much this guy knew about baseball. All of a sudden, I realized he didn't know who in the hell he was talking to! I finally said, "You know who the captain is, don't you?" "Ahh, I don't know. He's some Marine captain. What the heck." I says, "No, that was the great Ted Williams." This kid was absolutely floored. But Williams had never understood that the kid didn't know who he was. Or he would have sure as hell told him.

He was the biggest morale-buster I ever saw in my life. For one, mail would come in and for the whole squadron, there would probably be four bags of mail. Ted Williams would get three of them, and the rest of us would get one.[14]

Banshee Bob Johnson, pilot VMJ-1:

One of the highpoints of my military career was meeting Jack Benny at a casino in Las Vegas.[15]

Jerry Goldberg, S/SGT in charge of the radio shop VMF-311:

We didn't really interact with the pilots. Enlisted and officers, you know you don't have a... a business relationship is what you have. You answer, "Yes, the radio's working" or "No, the radio's not working" or whatever. I worked on repairing the radio. Making sure they were in good working order. I heard that his radio had gone out.

We had a photo hut and I was there developing some film one night and we got to talking a little bit. He was unhappy, that I remember.

[He was called back at age 34.] Yeah, that was old! They weren't prepared for the Korean War. It's fifty years ago [so I don't recall everything he said]. He wanted to play baseball. Those were his best years.

[Do you have any pictures of Ted Williams?] No. I wasn't his buddy. You don't go up and take his picture and then get lambasted for it![16]

Mike Canan, fellow pilot VMF-311:

He never showed up at the club. He was just in the ready room one day and that's how we met.

He was sort of a loner. He had a hut by himself, which they gave him. The press was after him all the time, and to accommodate them, they would put them in with him. He was with them all the time. He had press all around him all the time. These were magazine writers, mostly. I don't know too much about it, but they had some press around him. He was with them more than he was with us.

He never was alone. He was never lonely, even though he lived alone. He had these people who were in and out of there.[17]

Charles Baker, pilot VMF-115:

[When he talked, was he loud?] No. I sure don't remember that. If anything, he was the opposite. He didn't really talk that much. Unless you got into conversation with him. In the squadron when we were getting checked out and getting enough flight time there in El Toro, of course, most of your time was devoted to briefing and de-briefing and flying. Learning the new airplanes.

I never did go with him on R&R.

We went duck hunting and we did a lot of pheasant hunting. We'd shoot pheasants and bring them back and some of the mess people would feather them and cut them up and cook them for us. We'd eat pheasant.

Guys talk. One guy, one sour apple, will start spreading a rumor and the rest of the people pick it up and pass it on. Me, as an individual, I thought he was a hell of a guy. They'd talk about the fact that he didn't like the press and he'd give them a bad time. Nothing serious. The guy didn't like newsmen. He spoke his mind. I liked the guy.

[Did you see them much at K-3?] They kept them away pretty good. They weren't allowed on the base. They followed him in Japan, though. Another thing, kind of to his disadvantage, we had Jerry Coleman in the same draft going over and he was really a likable guy. He came in the club and boozed it up with us when we had parties. He really mixed in, and Ted wasn't like that. I can recall seeing him in the club, but he wasn't hanging on like the rest of us...And then Lloyd Merriman, he was another one that mixed with everybody. Go to parties and whatever. He'd mix with everybody. And I suppose some people compared those three guys, and Ted wasn't like that, you know. He was the smart one! He was protecting something, you know.[18]

Paul Janssen, fellow pilot VMF-311:

I liked him.

[He didn't hold himself too aloof or anything?] Not with us, he didn't. With the newspaper people. He hated them with a passion. I saw what they did to him over there. They were hounding him all the time. We were running cover for him. We just wouldn't tell them where he was at. We'd tell him when they were coming and he'd bail out.

He didn't have any problem with the Marine Corps press. These were civilian. A lot of them came over from Boston. Well, from the States. He told us about a few encounters he had in Boston. We got to laughing about it.[19]

 Jack Gross, Korean War combat correspondent:

I was a Marine combat correspondent there. I worked out of the air wing. I got into MAG-33 a lot of times, because of Ted Williams and there was another baseball player by the name of Lloyd Merriman. I was a staff sergeant. He was always awful nice to me. He was nice to everybody. He just didn't like to have anything to do with the press. I kept them off his ass. I'd tell them he's gone.

He was an international star. Everybody that found out he was there, they'd go up and they'd want to see him. He was low-key. He just wanted to fly his airplane then relax and get the hell out of there. Everybody wanted to go home!

I couldn't tell you anything personal about him. I was there when that picture was taken in Pohang-dong. He and another guy were there. They were doing a thing for an orphanage. The air wing had founded an orphanage. We were doing a... Ted Williams... I used to know that pilot he was with, but I can't remember it. He said, "Hi" and we said, "We got your picture, sir." and he said, "Oh, oh!"

[So you only ran into him once in a while?]

Only in the O Club once in a while. I was a staff sergeant. I could go in and get a cocktail once in a while. I'd get those guys' pictures in the paper, and then they'd be nice to me.

We'd send out a lot of news releases. He'd come back with holes in his plane and we'd take a picture of it, and stuff like that. We did that on all the pilots. We didn't make an exception.

Parents and family are very important to the Marine Corps. That was our job every morning. No matter where I was, I had to do 20 what they'd call "Joe Blows" – truck driver, people like that. They'd send that to hometown papers, and then you'd get a real nice letter back from a mom or dad. The kids would never write them. You'd get it in a little rural hometown paper and you'd get a front page three truck picture, and you'd get a headline. The Marine Corps still does that.

[You remember him being fairly nice to you, in your interactions with him?]

Ted Williams? No, sir. Have you ever been around the Marine Corps? Well, that's a different story when he's in the Marine Corps and you're in the Marine Corps, but you don't fraternize much. You might be nice to each other, but you don't bullshit and talk. I was a staff sergeant. [Ted was an officer.]

You know how people are with a celebrity. I can't stand phonies. Everybody pretends they know somebody. Sure, I kept the reporters away from him. He didn't like to be bothered. He was gun-shy. Not that he was afraid of them. He just didn't want to be bothered. He'd go out and kill the hell out of those guys [Communist troops, presumably] and then come back and sit down and have a drink. Williams hated phonies, too. He was terrifically honest and straightforward. He was sure no bullshitter, and he never had time for bullshitters. He didn't do very many interviews.

Wherever I was, the press guys knew that I could get them anything they wanted, and so they'd kind of make my tent their headquarters. I always had empty racks and stuff and they could just latch on there and relax. If I liked them, I kept them out of minefields. If I didn't like them, I aimed them into a minefield.[20]

Dale Purcell, pilot VMJ-1:

I was asked to drop by General Megee's office one night. I was a psychologist and was teaching and he said, "I have a couple of non-military questions." Jerry Coleman was on a forward field in his Corsair. He did everything right. He had three 1,000-pound bombs hung under the plane. He was about midway down the field [in the air] when his engine quit. As soon as it quit, he salvoed the bombs. You don't arm your bombs until you get over the bomb line, because if you have to salvo then you don't want to drop them on friendlies.

Coleman flicked his salvo button. He already had his gear up and partial flaps. He also had his cockpit locked open. He let the plane settle fast to do a wheels-up landing because there was no way he could get his wheels down. He slid down the runway – the bombs were tumbling but they didn't go off. It was a big four-blade prop and he slid it to the end and it dug into the dry dirt at the end of the runway. It flipped him over and it slid upside down until it stopped. The medics and the crash crew rushed down and dug away with their entrenching tools. The cockpit was full of all this silt. They cut his straps loose and pulled him out.

All of his orifices were full of this dirt. They got him over to sick bay and got him some oxygen. Since the canopy was locked in the open position, it filled up. Had it been locked closed, they might not have been able to get him out. When he salvoed his bombs, he also cut his master switch which reduced the likelihood that the fuel would catch on fire. He was up later that day and walking around.

Williams and him didn't drink. They didn't care at all about the happy hour at the end of the day.

The next evening I was asked by General Megee to stop by his quarters. He said I understand that Captain Coleman does his job, is a class act, doesn't say much and is doing the job here. I said, I agree with that. He said he's had just about the normal number of flights – he's one or two short of the normal 40 which is the standard cutoff for combat flights, after which you go into reserve. I had just finished my combat flights and gone into reserve and I was training senior non-commissioned career officers in leadership and I was alternating that with training a few Forward Air Controllers. Pilots that had been flying ordnance but who were needed on the front lines to call in air strikes. I had just finished a two-week stint at that.

It was no picnic – nor was it a picnic on the ground, being with the First Marine Division.

I said not only that, but by the end of the day we'd be hunting ducks on the river. As a photo pilot, I could usually tell where they were by my last flight before the light faded. We'd get a houseboy and a Jeep and some shotguns and away we'd go. He said fine.

"Now the other situation's different," the general said. "I refer to Captain Williams. The word to me is that he's sounding off a lot to the press about the money he's not getting in Boston." I said, "Well, General, I'm not sure it's true. I'm not over at that group's mess a lot, but I've had two or three instances with him and I just don't believe that that's the way he's behaving here." He said, "Well, illustrate."

I said, well, whenever the ducks are up in the mountain lake, we get the air-sea rescue helicopter, which sits right next to our squadron. They have to fly anyway and they would fly us up into the mountains – whoever wants to hunt ducks – and pick us up in an hour or so. They can't get there by Jeep but I know exactly where they are.

One day, one of the people in the three-man group was Captain Williams. We set down up there and it was far enough away from any U.S. base that a lot of the kids up there have never seen any G.I.s or had never been fed our food. Near our base, we had created two orphanages – one Protestant and one Catholic. Often at the end of a noon meal when we had hot food left over, our mess sergeant would get a trailer and would take it over. We'd play hit ball with the kids. The kids, we in turn got them equipped [with a church group] and bought them some rice land and an ox to till the soil.

When we landed up at this small village by a lake where the ducks were, the little kids crowded around out of curiosity. They looked terribly cold in the winter. We forgot all about the ducks. We were looking as these kids, freezing. No G. I. clothes. Just freezing, and in pretty tough circumstances. We just sat around and visited with them until the helicopter came back.

En route back, we were talking about those kids, away from any hot food, no G.I.s to get them into an orphanage and not likely that we would be up there very often. Williams was saying we've got to do something. He said, I wish we could find a way to get some warm gear and get somebody to get it up there. I said, well, I have a group in my home town. I'll take care of that [having this group round up the gear]. And he said, "Well, I'll pay for it, but on the condition that no one will ever know about it." I told him, "Well, not in your lifetime." I didn't realize that 49 years later he would die and I would tell that story. This is the first time I've told that story, other than when I told it to General Megee.

If you've watched MASH, you know there's a lot of heart that goes into situations like that. So I was sitting with General Megee Sunday night and I told him about Williams and these kids up on the lake with no clothes, and about the foul weather flight, and about that episode on the hospital ship. I said, "General Megee, there are more press than there are pilots at MAG-33. Those guys don't go anywhere. They don't get shot at, but they're filing these stories back to their publications." He said, "Precisely. What would you do?" He wanted an answer. I had met Colonel Robertshaw the same day I had met General Megee back at El Toro. I said, "I'd call Col. Robertshaw and suggest that any more sports stories out of the First Marine Air Wing, that reporter and that organization is going to be off limits for the duration." That dried it up.[21]

L. B. Robertshaw, *Commanding Officer Marine Air Group 33:*

We had another big league ballplayer in the group [Lloyd Merriman]. I imposed on them to teach baseball on Saturday afternoon. It was kind of funny. Ted Williams agreed, provided he could teach the infielders – he being an outfielder – and the other guy took the rest of the team over. It was something for those young enlisted men, to meet and talk to and work with Ted Williams. A good morale factor. It wasn't as much a matter of playing as it was teaching. They would hold these classes on Saturdays and we would relieve them of their flying duties to do so. He did his share, though.[22]

Lloyd Merriman, pilot VMF-115:

We had some good times, too. Old Woody, he kept things going. He'd play the piano and sing, just about every night. Ted didn't hang around there.

I played in '54 and '55 and then on the retirement deal, they gave me two more years for the service.

We weren't really that close. We knew each other. Kind of like John Glenn. You knew him, but...

There weren't any reporters there, but one or two probably came in special and saw him and left.

[Do you remember people coming around to look and see the famous Ted Williams? Did you ever see that?]

No, I didn't, but then again he might have been just dodging it, heading back to the tent. Nobody came to talk to me about being a ballplayer. Which was fine. You still get them in the mail even now, though.[23]

Jim Tyler, metalsmith, VMF-115:

When I went in the service from Tennessee, I wasn't a big ball fan. When I met Ted Williams, he was just really an ordinary guy. You would never know that he was an officer. I don't mean that literally, but he was just a happy go lucky guy.

I first met him one night when we was having a party. I just played guitar and sang. Lead singer, if you could call it that. My band was playing there in the officers' club and we were taking a little break, and he said... he called me "Tennessee Toddy." He loved "Your Cheatin' Heart." I bet I did it a hundred times for him.

[Ted's favorite kind of music was jazz piano.]

Oh yeah, but I mean, he was limited to me, there! [Laughs.] He didn't have no choice to go down the road. You know how it is when you get together, let it all hang out and you all sing.

Jim Tyler entertaining Korean orphans.
Courtesy Jim Tyler.

He would talk and play and stuff, but I was a country boy from Tennessee. I wasn't really impressed with him as a ballplayer, because we wasn't involved with ball. I just remember him as a nice guy. Hey, he never did brag about who he was or what he was.

He said, "Hey, Tyler, I've got an orphanage I go to and I'd like you to play for them. We go visit them every week and why don't we make it a Sunday deal?" I said, Sure, so I went on the truck with him the next Sunday. It was just lines of houses and we kind of pulled off the road. Pohang wasn't a very big city back then. This was 1953. I don't know if you'd call it a city or not. I do know that we had a lot of fun with Ted and the kids. It was sad about the kids, you know. They had just lost their families and some of them had lost an arm or a leg.

We brought anything we could get. Candy bars. Extra clothing. Just anything. He got extra stuff, too. He had a way of getting stuff, you know. We had our own bakery there at K-3 and he had the privilege of going down to the bakery. He could go down and get big quantities of doughnuts and fresh bread and stuff like that.

[Tyler explained that there were about 300 boys and girls in the orphanage.] We all pitched in, but Ted was in charge. Looking back, he must have spent thousands on the kids. It was hard to believe after all they had gone through they could still laugh and sing. Ted knew how to make them forget, if just for awhile.

You could tell him being around the kids, he had a way about making them probably forget what they'd been through. There was kind of an air about him. If everybody was like Ted Williams, we wouldn't have problems.[24]

 Elmer Plaetzer, metal shop mechanic VMF-311:

He was fine. If there was one thing, he was upset that he was recalled to service. I think that hung with him. Well, none of the guys that had served in World War II and had been recalled were very happy about it. Of course, he was at the peak of his career. Then to get called back and lose two years... but he did what he was supposed to do, so...

I can't recall Ted Williams being demeaned in any sense, or being criticized. I never heard anything derogatory about him. Everybody was belly-aching. I was belly-aching because I was drafted into the Marine Corps. I never enlisted; I was drafted into it. There was a lot of belly-aching going on and griping going on, but that was normal. If you didn't gripe, something was wrong with you.[25]

Ted on the flight line, canopy open.
Courtesy of Claudia Williams.

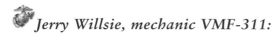
Jerry Willsie, mechanic VMF-311:

He was there when I was there. I was a mechanic. I stuffed him in a few – not many times, but a few times. He griped a lot. Yeah. He should have been in a bomber instead of a fighter, but he was all right.

[Did he gripe more than most?]

No, no, not really. I called it griping. He liked everything right up to snuff, you know. He wasn't overbearing or anything like that, but he was particular. I never did ask him any questions. We'd just get him strapped in and get him cranked up and that was it. At the end of the flight, if he had any criticism with the plane or if he thought anything needed attending to, they would write it down and then we would go from there.

They would make a walk around and inspect it, and if they seen something that they had a question about, they would call your attention to it.

[So he might do that more than most?]

No, not that I recall.

[Oh, OK, because you mentioned him being particular, so I just...]

Yeah, yeah. No, he was all right. He was particular, which I'm sure that if I was in their position and their seat and their mission, I would want everything up to snuff myself. He never gave anybody any trouble or anything like that.

There was a first lieutenant – and they're the hardest to get along with that there is – he called me out to the plane before one mission. This wasn't right... this wasn't right... that wasn't right. I had problems with him before, and I said, "Wait just a minute" so I went in and got our engineering officer, who came up within the ranks to the lieutenant position. And I told him the situation, and he went out and they had a few words. Yup. But you'll find that the older officers and pilots, the more years they have in service, are easier to get along with than the ones that just got out of flight school.

Ned Offner, oxygen and pressurization corporal, VMF-311:

He was one of our pilots. I've got a picture of him standing up in his plane. I think he just came back from a mission and he was standing up there ready to go get out.

I worked with all the oxygen equipment on the plane, for the face masks.

I know he was a little bit on the bitter side, because they recalled him.

[More so than other people?] I know one time they had organized athletics for everybody and he wouldn't participate. An order came out for everybody and an order came out from the colonel saying "This includes Ted Williams." I can't remember the colonel's name any more. It was a written order. That's the way I understand it.

[But did he seem worse than other people. Everybody grumbles.] I guess not, but you've got to consider he was making a lot of money. I think he was in the Second World War, too.

[Do you remember hearing anything about why he left?] No. His time was up, I guess.

[Did he seem friendly enough, though?] Yeah. He waved. They didn't do too much saluting over there. It all depends who was around.

I never saw him with too many newsmen. He had his buddies. A little stand-offish, though.[27]

 ### Lt. Col. Patrick Harrison, one of Ted's hutmates at K-3:

Ted never asked any favors. He avoided places where they'd point him out as a baseball star instead of a captain in the Marine Corps. He wanted to be the captain, the jet pilot, and not live off his baseball reputation.

If some of the people who called him names in stories ever knew him, they'd write differently. I know that. I know him from breakfast, lunch, and dinner, and from the toughest situations a man ever faced."[28]

 ### Harold Breece, assistant electronics officer, K-3

I was at K-3. [One day] the warrant officer says, "Let's go over to the O club" – to get a few beers. I'm in there and I'm talking to a guy I don't know. I'd been introduced to him as Ted Williams, just a pilot that had the wheels-up landing. I was definitely not sport-minded. I'm in there and we were drinking a couple of beers and I mentioned fishing. Boy, we started talking! He'd been to every place I'd fished, and then he'd been up to Alaska. Obviously he was a fisherman.

Well, lieutenant colonels and colonels would come by and interrupt our conversation, and talk baseball. Something about baseball. Well, I was only a captain. I'd interrupt and get back to fishing. On the way home from the club after a couple of beers, the warrant officer asked me, "Do you know who Ted Williams is?" I said, "Sure, he's the pal that made that beautiful wheels-up landing." But he said, "Do you know who he is?" No, I didn't, so he explained to me he was ichiban baseball player – number one.

A few days later, I bumped into him. We met on the flight line or someplace, just going our different ways. I go up to him and apologize for not knowing who he was. He said, "I didn't mind. I'm up to here with baseball. I go to the club and that's all they want to talk about!" He says, "I'm full of it. That's my occupation. I love fishing." That was Ted Williams. I talked fishing with him in between being interrupted about baseball.[29]

NOTES

1) *Interview with George Winewriter, November 28, 2002.*

2) *Interview with Woody Woodbury, October 1, 2002.*

3) *Interview with Walter Roark, December 21, 2002.*

4) *Interview with Jerry Willsie, December 27, 2002.*

5) *Interview with Roy Harris, January 3, 2003.*

6) *Interview with Marsh Austin, May 8, 1997.*

7) *Interview with James Fox, February 8, 2003.*

8) *Interview with Lou Capozzoli, May 31, 2003. Lou never did any writing about Ted Williams.*

9) *Interview with Bob Flanagan, June 2, 2003.*

10) *Interview with John Beck, December 13, 2002.*

11) *Interview with Dale Purcell, November 5 and December 12, 2002.*

12) *Interview with Robert Sabot, December 13, 2002.*

13) *Interview with Chuck Ingle, December 21, 2002.*

14) *Interview with Rylen B. Rudy, February 4, 2003. Other Marines from the squadron disagree with the characterization of Williams as a "morale-buster".*

15) *Interview with Bob Johnson, May 31, 2003.*

16) *Interview with Jerry Goldberg, November 27, 2002.*

17) *Interview with Mike Canan, December 31, 2002. No one else interviewed suggested Ted lived alone.*

18) *Interview with Charles Baker, February 2, 2003.*

19) *Interview with Paul Janssen, December 23, 2002.*

20) *Interview with Jack Gross, May 31, 2003.*

21) *Interview with Dale Purcell, November 5, 2002.*

22) *Interview with L. B. Robertshaw, November 16, 2002.*

23) *Interview with Lloyd Merriman, November 16, 2002.*

24) *Interview with Jim Tyler, August 5, 2004.*
    In the summer of 2004, Jim Tyler launched a campaign to name his local VFW post in Tullahoma, Tennessee after Ted Williams. He mused that the orphan kids ranged from maybe three- to sixteen-years-old, and they'd be in their 50s or 60s today – but he'd bet they remembered Ted Williams and the Marines he brought with him to the orphanage. Some of the information here comes from comments Tyler made to the Tullahoma News, *reported on www.zwire.com, August 5, 2004.*

25) *Interview with Elmer Plaetzer, December 27, 2002.*

26) *Interview with Jerry Willsie, December 27, 2002.*

27) *Interview with Ned Offner, December 27, 2002.*

28) *Mike Gillooly, "The Case for Ted Williams,"* Boston Evening American, *January 7, 1958.*

29) *Interview with Harold Breece, August 7, 2004.*

Ordnance to be loaded on the flight line, K-3.
Courtesy of Frank Cushing.

CHAPTER 15 – MISSIONS #6 THROUGH #39

Where once he exploded base hits for the Boston Red Sox, he switched to blasting the North Korean and Chinese Communist armies with bombs, rockets and napalm (flaming jellied gasoline) for the United Nations. And he belly-landed a badly shot-up jet last February as skillfully as an old pro hooking a slide into third base... Williams is still part of a team. But it's not the Red Sox any more, it's [VMF-311] flying out of southeast Korea. And his fellow Marines see few signs of the terrible-tempered Ted of baseball fame who once deliberately aimed a line drive at a heckling fan. Instead, they respect him not only as a fine pilot, but also for his evident ability to give and take a ribbing good-naturedly. The respect is deepened because they know the smiles must come hard. [Williams was giving up $100,000 a year during his service.] His new teammates call Williams "Bush" – short for "bush leaguer." It's all in good fun; and the nickname is not meant as a reflection on Ted's stature as a pilot or as a comrade in arms. As one of his fellow pilots said: "There's nothing small about Bush. He's a big-leaguer any way you look at it." [1]

Ted Williams was not sure he'd ever be able to play baseball again. He did have other opportunities. In the early 1950s he had invested in a fishing tackle business named Southern Tackle Distributors, "the biggest fishing tackle distributor in the South," he told Ed Hyde. "I'm in the damn thing and I'm as enthused about it as a kid in his first year of spring training. Right now, four wonderful guys – my partners – are taking care of my interests." [2]

Capt. Williams was laid up with illness for several weeks. News reports datelined March 24, 1953 have him recovering from pneumonia on the *Haven*, having arrived on the 12th or the 14th, depending on the report. "He should be ready to go back to duty soon," a doctor said. "He was up and about yesterday." A report a day later characterized him as "up and around" and said that he was visiting war wounded aboard ship. After being hospitalized 22 days, he was returned to flight status on April 1. He flew three fam flights to become re-oriented, and then had his name added to the board for combat.

He flew several combat missions, and then had a week off for R&R in Japan. For some, R&R proved strenuous in its own way – the old story about coming back from a vacation all worn out. Fred Townsley joked, "R&R stood for rest and recreation leave, but it was called Rack & Ruin, Rum & Rack, I & I (Intercourse & Intoxication), and many other things." [3] Williams didn't really drink, though, and he wasn't that long out of hospital, either.

Jon Mendes said one of the reasons Ted Williams and John Glenn hit it off was that "they both were boy scouts, in regard to drinking. They were 'temples and shriners.' They went to see temples and shrines – all the beautiful architecture – when we went on R&R to Japan, where the rest of us..." [4]

Bill Clem added, "When we'd go over to Japan for R&R for a couple of days, he wouldn't bum with the rest of the guys, but Glenn would. Of course, everybody knew Ted. That was tough on him over there. That was tough. Of course, all the brass were kind of kowtowing to him... I guess I don't know what to say."

[So you went on R&R a couple of times, but you just went your separate ways?] "With Ted? Yeah. I thought I was getting to be friends with him when we were in Puerto Rico and then early days, going over that trip, but that kind of went by the wayside, I guess."[5]

Ted might not truly have been such a boy scout when it came to women, though. "Old Ted was really a skivvy honcho. He liked the girls. Ted didn't really drink much. I was the drunken sheriff. I never knew him to drink. He just didn't care for it. But he sure liked the ladies.

"I had a picture. We were out taking pictures. Ted wanted to know what this place was with the big red Marine Corps sign on it was. I said, 'It's a whorehouse.' He said, 'Oh Christ, let's go in' and I said, 'No, Ted. No way!' He said, 'Why not?' I said, 'Man, they've got diseases they haven't even learned how to spell the names of.' He walked over – he's a big tall lanky guy – and I got a picture of him squatting down with his hands on his knees looking under the gate – the gate was like a salon gate – I got this picture of him. Him and Sammy Snead were good buddies, and I knew Sammy a little bit. I lived in the racquet club after Korea and I got to know Sammy a little bit. He saw this picture and he wanted to pay anything to get that picture! I knew how Ted felt. Even though he was a friend of Sammy's, I said I'm not going to sell it. He would have had fun with it, but there's no telling: Ted's liable to get mad. Ted had a hell of a temper.

"Those women, though, boy, they did have some stuff! That was one of my MAIN roles, to keep guys from getting infected. The other main duty was security for the air base." [6]

Before studying the actual missions flown by Capt. Ted Williams, let's pause for a few vignettes, each shedding a bit of light on either the missions or Ted himself. Our study of the missions will present summaries of each mission, drawn from the VMF-311, VMF-115, and MAG-33 Command Diaries. Some additional information has been gleaned from Ted Williams' own flight log books.

VMF-311 line chief Leonard Waibel explains his duties:

"The line chief oversaw all the maintenance and getting the aircraft ready for the flights. We have twelve aircraft and we had that many plane captains. We assigned each plane captain to one aircraft. Overall, I was to see that the maintenance was proper, that they were fueled, et cetera. There was always one or two in for repair.

"I would oversee all takeoffs. I would sit there in my Jeep and make sure they all got off. We'd have to get the aircraft ready. We'd start them all. We'd get everything ready. The ordnance would get them all loaded. I would give the operations officer the aircraft that were ready to fly, and he would assign them. I wouldn't assign them. I would just take it in there and I would watch him while he's putting it on the board.

"We always had early flights. I would put on the board what aircraft they would fly. It was very seldom that a given pilot would fly the same aircraft. Except the C.O. Sometimes the C.O. would tell you that he wanted this one or that one. Most of the time it never was. I was the one who would designate which ones. I would come into the flight room and put on the board the number of airplanes. The operations officer would assign them once he saw whatever airplanes I was going to give them."[7]

VMF-311 pilot, Major James Walley discussed one element of preparation:

[When you went out on a flight, you strapped some sort of data on your leg?]

"We had all kind of things. We had what was called a 'blood chit' – if we were shot down and we were captured by somebody in North Korea or what have you, they guaranteed them a certain amount of money. I think at that time it was $100,000 or something, if they would return you safely to the South Korean areas, then they would be able to collect that bounty. I think it worked one or two times. But you see, the thing was if you were shot down over there in the wintertime you had to have on thermal boots, you had to have all kind of stuff on – rubberized suits...

"The only data we carried was a little knee pad that we had strapped to our leg that would give us the target we were looking for and what have you. We didn't put anything on there that would jeopardize the war or anything. It mainly gave us the coordinates of where the target was that we were going to hit if it was an interdiction mission, let's say up around the capital of North Korea or towards the Yalu River, but most of the work that we did with 311 – I would say half of the flights that we did in 311 – we were flying close air support, which was fairly close to the front line."[8]

Did Ted look for any special consideration? His hutmate Joseph Mitchell joked: "Yeah, he said, 'Don't schedule me with Glenn... '"[9]

Lloyd Merriman recalled one minor accomplishment Ted sought in Korea.

"One time we were talking and he always wanted to see if he could complete a loop at 300 knots – at the bottom, you know, going in. He kept messing with and stalling out and messing with it, but he finally made it. This 300 knot loop. Now, why he wanted to do it, I have no idea. It was something he was going to get done. He'd be going in at 300 and then pull the nose up. I don't know why he wanted that. It wasn't all that fast in a jet, when you'd get up to 450 or so. It was in the States when he started talking about it. He was just interested in what the airplane could do."

[Did you have the same aircraft each mission?] "No, you had whatever came up. When it would come in, they'd go over it and service and have it ready to go."[10]

Jack Gross, Korean War Combat Correspondent, acknowledged that this was never easy work.

"Those guys had a terrific amount of pressure on them. Ask one of those pilots. I've seen them sit in a ready room with tears coming down their cheeks, because they weren't allowed to do close air support. That was because MacArthur hated Marines and didn't want them to get any glory. He used airplanes like the Army used artillery. To get an airstrike, they'd have to go clear to Tokyo – Eighth Army or the Air Force or somewhere to get permission. Meanwhile, the guys are getting killed. Like I say, it was really bad, especially the last six months in 1953. They were under as much pressure as any infantryman on the line, because the guys depended on them so."[11]

Back at K-3, Williams readied himself for a return to combat, taking three fam flights on April 2, 3, and early on April 4, 1953.

The first mission Williams flew after his long absence was the squadron's third and final mission of 4 April, a large interdiction effort involving two dozen aircraft from VMF-311 and VMF-115. Ben Robertshaw led the strike.

4 APRIL 1953 – COMBAT MISSION #6

Mission Number Intake 02

Colonel ROBERTSHAW, MAG-33 Commanding Officer, flying a VMF-311 aircraft, led a prebriefed Group interdiction mission composed of 13 aircraft from VMF-311 and 11 from VMF-115. Airborne at 1513 hours, the flight split into sections and attacked the following targets in the area of Ch'och'u-ri:

1615 hours, YC 0944, troops and supplies. Damage unassessed. Twenty four napalm were expended. [Note: the designation YC 0944 refers to the tactical pilotage map coordinates for the target.]

1620 hours, YC 0893, troops and supplies. Several fires were left burning. Twenty eight napalm and 800 rounds of 20MM ammunition were expended.

1620 hours, YC 0793, troops and supplies. Two buildings were observed with smoke preventing any further damage assessment. Ordnance expended was eight 500-pound bombs, sixteen 260 frags, forty two ATARS and 450 rounds of 20MM ammunition.

The flight encountered meager to moderate small arms, heavy weapons and automatic weapons anti-aircraft fire over YC 0792. No damage was received by the friendlies. Six of the aircraft landed at K-13 due to low fuel. The remaining aircraft returned safely to K-3 at 1720 hours. The other VMF-311 pilots were Lieutenant Colonel COSS, Majors WALLEY and DOCHTERMAN, Captains

Williams posing with a 1000-pound Easter gift for the enemy.
Courtesy of the May Williams Collection.

NORDELL, PETERSEN, RITCHIE, WILLIAMS, and LOVETTE, Lieutenants MILLER, HEILAND, and HAWKINS. Lieutenant Colonel DILL of MAG-33 flew with VMF-311 on this mission. The VMF-115 pilots were Lieutenant Colonel WARREN, Majors ELDRIDGE, THORPE, and SELLERS, Captains DUSENBURY, BURCH, IRELAND, and F. WILLIAMS, Lieutenants HATCH, BAIRD, and GODWIN. [Note: Captain T. S. Williams served in VMF-311, and there were two captains named Williams in VMF-115. Both of those Williams joined the unit on the very same day: 21 February 1953. They were Robert Williams and Frank L. Williams, Jr.]

6 APRIL 1953 – COMBAT MISSION #7

(There were no combat sorties flown on 5 April – Easter Sunday – due to inclement weather.)

Mission Number Intake 01

Captain RITCHIE of 311 led a prebriefed Group interdiction mission of eight aircraft from 311 and eight from 115, which took off at 0815/I*. The flight's destination was Sariwon, but it was diverted to other targets due to inclement weather. At 0910/I eight of the aircraft made a "free drop on an unknown target" located at YC 4168. Each aircraft was loaded with four tons of napalm. In all, the mission dropped 32 napalm and fired off 600 rounds of 20MM ammunition. At 0921/I, the remaining eight attacked a vehicle park, located at CT 5219. They estimated 12 buildings destroyed. There was negative opposition and all returned safely. The other VMF-311 pilots were Major SKINNER, Captains HENDERSHOT, CLEM, AUSTIN, WILLIAMS, PETERSEN, and HAGANS. The VMF-115 pilots were Majors BOLT and BERNARD, Captains R. WILLIAMS, SHARKEY, DUSENBURY, CASSIDAY, and THOMAS, and Lieutenant HATCH.

There were four other missions that day, including two close air support, one of which encountered intense small arms fire. There was also one recon mission and one other interdiction mission, which encountered moderate ground fire. One plane was hit but without serious damage or injury to the pilot. Later in the day, Williams took up a Panther for another fam flight, listed as FAM-CHASE.

*The designation of time in the Command Diary was also indicated as 0815/I or 1320/I, rather than 0815 hours. We will use that convention from this point forward in the chapter.

7 APRIL 1953 – COMBAT MISSION #8

There were five missions this day. Ted Williams was on the second of the day. Other missions attacked caves, trenches, mortar positions and troops.

Mission Number Intake 01

This was a prebriefed group interdiction mission led by Lieutenant Colonel COSS, composed of eight aircraft from 311, seven from 115, and two from HEDRON-33. It was airborne at 1320/I. The flight split up into sections and hit four different supply areas at 1408/I. The target was located at YC 3840 (Sang-doma). In all, 44 napalm were expended, along with 12 fire bombs, 24 500-pound incendiary bombs and 1,700 rounds of 20MM ammunition. At least 14 lingering fires were counted. Colonel ROBERTSHAW was Tactical Air Commander with Lieutenant SHUTT of MAG-33 flying as his wingman. The other VMF-311 pilots were Majors SKINNER and MITCHELL, Captains STREET, WILLIAMS, and McGRAW, and Lieutenant BROTHERS and SPENCER. The VMF-115 pilots were Lieutenant Colonel WARREN, Majors ELDRIDGE and BOLT, Captains THOMAS, GREEN, and F. WILLIAMS, and Lieutenant DAVIS. All returned safely at 1501/I.

8 APRIL 1953 – COMBAT MISSION #9

Williams took part in the fourth of the five missions flown this day. Again, it was the largest mission of the day. Three missions had been launched and returned, with one aircraft – that piloted by 311 pilot Marsh AUSTIN being hit by minor small caliber anti-aircraft fire. The damage was not detected during the flight and only discovered after debriefing. Shortly after the third mission returned, Williams and his fellow pilots were airborne.

Mission Number Intake 01

Airborne at 1348/I, this was a very large prebriefed Group interdiction mission led by Lieutenant Colonel WARREN. There were 12 planes from each squadron, the target a supply area at CU 6110 (Okchong-ni.) There was one secondary explosion so large that it obscured the rest of the target with smoke. There was "inaccurate meager automatic weapons anti-aircraft fire" but no damage recorded. It was a powerful attack: forty 500-pound bombs were dropped as well as 112 250-pound bombs, and 4,510 rounds of 20MM ammunition were expended. VMF-115 was represented by Major ROSS, Captains IRELAND, R. WILLIAMS, GREEN, WINERITER, and BURCH, First Lieutenants WOODBURY, PURVIS, and HUNTER, and Second Lieutenants HOLLAWAY and BAIRD. VMF-311 pilots were: Lieutenant Colonel MORAN, Majors WALLEY, DOCHTERMAN, and SKINNER, Captains WILLIAMS, CAMPBELL, RITCHIE, HAGANS, STREET, and HENDERSHOT, and Lieutenants MILLER and SPENCER.

Flight line of VMF-311 F9s at K-3, with Jeep used to load ammo.
Photos by George Warnken.

NAVALN-2700 (NEW 10-30)

NAVAL AIRCRAFT FLIGHT RECORD
(YELLOW SHEET)

PART A—PRE-FLIGHT *(Retain at place of take-off)*

MAINTENANCE FILL IN FIRST TWO ITEMS BELOW. OTHERS FOR USE IF NO OTHER CLEARANCE FILED.

CERTIFICATION

DATE	FUEL ABOARD (GAL.)	OIL ABOARD (GAL.)	ACCEPTANCE

4-7-53 *Full*   26 PTS

AMMO. LOADED   OTHER ORDNANCE LOADED

4 - MAPS

I accept this aircraft for flight.
I (have) (have not) examined discrepancy report for last flight.
For VP-VR aircraft: I have presented a Weight and Balance Clearance Form F, Form DD-365F, to the clearance authority as required.

MODEL OF AIRCRAFT   F9F-5

BUREAU NO.   126159

ETD / ETA

DESTINATION

I certify that this aircraft has this day been inspected by me or under my supervision in accordance with existing instructions and that the aircraft is ready for flight, fueled and armed as stated above.

SIGNATURE OF PILOT:

Williams

SIGNATURE OF MAINTENANCE CREW LEADER OR PLANE CAPTAIN

PILOT'S RANK   PILOT'S UNIT

PURPOSE OF FLIGHT

CLEARANCE

IF NO OTHER PASSENGER LIST IS FILED, LIST NAME, RANK, UNIT OF CREW AND PASSENGERS ON REVERSE

(DETACH HERE WHEN REST OF FORM IS TAKEN IN AIRCRAFT. ALWAYS TAKE PARTS B, C, AND D ON NONLOCAL

AVIATORS FLIGHT LOG BOOK

9 & 10 APRIL 1953

There were 28 interdiction sorties flown on these two days, but Captain T. S. Williams did not participate.

11 APRIL 1953 – COMBAT MISSION #10

Mission Number Intake 01

Ted WILLIAMS took part in the first mission of the day, airborne at 0927/I, a mission led by Major BOLT and composed of 12 aircraft from 115 and 16 from 311. The prebriefed interdiction mission attacked supply shelters located at BU 7952 (Pyolch'ang-ni.) Twenty-one 500-pound bombs were expended, along with 58 250-pounders and 125 rounds of 20MM ammunition. Two minutes later, they attacked other shelters at BU 7853 with another 32 500-pound bombs and 63 more 250-pound bombs. There was intense but inaccurate heavy weapons and anti-aircraft fire nearby. Most of the flight returned safely to K-3, four landed at K-14, and eight landed at K-13. Ted's was one of those that landed at K-13. He later flew back to K-3. The VMF-311 pilots were Lieutenant Colonels COSS and MORAN, with Majors DOCHTERMAN, MITCHELL, and MILT, Captains HENDERSHOT, ARMAGOST, WILLIAMS, BAILES, NORDELL, PETERSEN, LOVETTE, McGRAW, and STREET, and Lieutenants MILLER and BROTHERS. The other VMF-115 pilots were Lieutenant Colonel WARREN, Captains R. WILLIAMS, WEBB, WINERITER, SHAFTER, MOONEY, and THOMAS, Lieutenants SCHWINDT, HUNTER, and DAVIS. Lieutenant Colonel McSHANE of MAG-33 flew with VMF-115 on this mission.

Other missions that day included attacks on mortar positions, trench lines, bunkers, troops, caves and supply areas.

12 APRIL 1953 – COMBAT MISSION #11

Mission Number Intake 37

WILLIAMS' mission this day was a prebriefed main line of resistance reconnaissance mission comprised of five aircraft, led by Captain PETERSEN and airborne at 1430/I. The mission only lasted five minutes over the MLR after beginning at 1500/I, due to inclement weather. The other pilots, all of whom returned safely to base, were Major MILT and Captains NORDELL and BAILES.

13 APRIL 1953 – COMBAT MISSION #12

Mission Number Intake 47

The final mission of the day for 311 was airborne at 1515/I, a prebriefed interdiction mission of four aircraft. Major FOX was the flight leader and Major SKINNER and Captains LOVETTE and WILLIAMS were the other pilots. They attacked buildings at YC 4112 with eight 1,000-pound bombs and eight 500-pound bombs. The effectiveness of the use of ordnance was reported as 100%, with further damage unassessed. Earlier in the day, Williams had had to abort a flight for reasons unknown, but it was not a scheduled mission.

14 THROUGH 20 APRIL 1953

Ted Williams did not fly any missions for this week. Reports from Boston had it that "Williams is nearly deaf from an ear injury and would be discharged from service."[12] In fact, a First Marine Air Wing spokesman stated, Williams was "physically fit" and was in Japan for R&R. Just in time for Red Sox Opening Day, he sent a telegram from Toyonaka addressed to Lou Boudreau. It was read to those assembled in the Red Sox clubhouse before the April 16 game. "Best of everything to you and all the boys. – Ted Williams." Boston won that game 11-6.

On 21 April 1953, Williams returned to ready status. He was about to fly 10 missions in a seven-day span. It was a stretch that ended with another "brush with death."

21 APRIL 1953 – COMBAT MISSION #13

Mission Number Acme 24

The final mission of the day was a close air support mission of three aircraft led by Captain MONTAGUE, airborne at 1625/I. At 1717/I, under the control of MOSQUITO ADVERB SIXTY SEVEN, the flight attacked bunkers and mortar positions, located at CT 2028 (Nolgun-dong), in support of the 1st ROK Division. Two heavy weapons positions and 25 yards of trench line were damaged and one secondary explosion was observed. Six 1,000-pound bombs and five 500-pound bombs were expended. There was meager automatic weapons fire over the target area, but no damage, and all were back at base by 1750/I. Captain WILLIAMS and Lieutenant SPENCER were the two pilots flying with flight leader MONTAGUE.

WILLIAMS was up early the next day.

22 APRIL 1953 – COMBAT MISSIONS #14 & #15

Mission Number Acme 33

Major John GLENN led the second mission of the day, an "early-early" three plane "road recce" interdiction mission airborne at 0525/I. Captain LOVETTE was forced to abort due to radio failure, so the mission was comprised of just Major GLENN and Captain Ted WILLIAMS. At 0607/I, the two aircraft attacked a road bridge at CT 5155 with two 500-pound bombs and 75 rounds of 20MM ammunition. At 0631/I, they attacked another road bridge, dropping two more 500-pound bombs and twelve ATARS. There was meager automatic weapons anti-aircraft fire, but no damage was received. The aircraft returned safely to base at 0705/I.

Mission Number Acme 02

There was a second mission that day for WILLIAMS, who was airborne again at 1323/I as part of an interdiction mission composed of eight aircraft from VMF-311 and nine from VMF-115, led by Lieutenant Colonel WARREN of 115. The planes attacked buildings at BT 7969 (Sangnung-dong) with 65 napalm and 1,400 rounds of 20MM ammunition; they destroyed five of the buildings, leaving numerous fires burning. Other VMF-115 pilots were Major THORPE, Captains SHAFFER, WINERITER, MOONEY, and WESTFIELD, Lieutenants Hollaway, TAYLOR, and GODWIN. Representing VMF-311 on this mission were Majors MITCHELL, MENDES, SKINNER, and CANAN, Captains ARMAGOST, LOVETTE, and WILLIAMS, and Lieutenant KECK.

23 APRIL 1953 – COMBAT MISSIONS #16 & #17

Mission Number Acme 14

At 1015/I, Captain STREET led for aircraft on a close air support mission, flying in support of the 9th ROK Division, attacking trench line located at CT 6347 (Taedok-san). Captains CARRUTHERS, KURTZ, and WILLIAMS were the other three Marine pilots. The attack was at 1100/I and 25 yards of trench line were damaged, with the expenditure of eight 1,000-pound bombs, six 500-pound bombs and 175 rounds of 20MM ammunition. All aircraft were back at back at 1155/I. Williams just barely had time to grab some lunch before heading out again.

K-3 Marines with 20MM ammo belt.
Photo by George Warnken.

Mission Number Acme 37

The ninth mission of this busy day was a prebriefed main line of resistance reconnaissance mission, airborne at 1430/I under the command of Captain CLEM. The other pilots were Captain YOUNG, whose aircraft was forced to abort due to oil or gasoline fumes in the cockpit, and Captains FAUCHIER and WILLIAMS. The aircraft returned safely to base at 1545. There was apparently no ammunition expended, and the MAG-33 Command Diary reported "negative observations by flight as they followed the MLR from the West to East Coast."

24 APRIL 1953 – COMBAT MISSIONS #18 & #19

Mission Number Acme 46 Special

Lieutenant Colonel Art MORAN led a close air support mission to assist the 1st Marine Division. The mission was composed of six aircraft, piloted by Major MENDES and Captains WILLIAMS, and KURTZ, and Lieutenant SAMPLE, as well as Colonel STACY, MAG-33 Executive Officer who flew with VMF-311. At 0902/I, they attacked supply shelters located at CT 0106 and the flight's controller, PACIFY SIXTY, reported two caves sealed and 25 yards of trench damaged by the expenditure of twelve 1,000-pound bombs and twelve 500-pound bombs. One aircraft had to land at K-13 due to low fuel (his log book shows us that it was Ted's), but all others returned safely at 1000/I hours.

Mission Number Acme 20

Airborne at 1420/I, this was a prebriefed interdiction mission led by Lieutenant Colonel WARREN of VMF-115. There were twelve aircraft each from 115 and 311, and two from HEDRON-33. Captain WEBB of 115 had to abort due to radio trouble. Colonel ROBERTSHAW with wingman Lieutenant Colonel ADAMS, both flying HEDRON-33 aircraft, served as Tactical Air Coordinators. At 1507/I, the flight attacked supplies located at CT 3869 (Sajang-dong). There were eight buildings damaged, one large secondary explosion and one lingering fire. The VMF-115 summary reported four lingering fires. All returned safely to base at 1605/I. During the mission, 24 500-pound bombs, 16 500-pound incendiary bombs, 106 250-pound bombs, 4 frags, 10 100-pound bombs and 1,365 rounds of 20MM ammunition were expended.

The other 115 pilots were Major BERNARD, Captains DUSENBURY, WESTFIELD, Hollaway, BLANEY, and BURCH, Lieutenants GODWIN, PURVIS, SCHWINDT, and TAYLOR. VMF-311 pilots were Lieutenant Colonel MORAN, Majors CANAN and MENDES, Captains SMITH, ARMAGOST, FAUCHIER, SCOTT, LOVETTE, WILLIAMS, and KURTZ, and Lieutenants KECK and SPENCER.

25 APRIL 1953 – COMBAT MISSION #20

Mission Number Acme 01

Lieutenant Colonel MORAN led 19 aircraft in a prebriefed interdiction mission; 12 aircraft from VMF-311 joined 7 from VMF-115 and attacked supplies located at YD 5503 (Chungwa) at 1413/I. In this mission, 69 napalm and 2,025 rounds of 20MM ammunition were expended. Flak was reported but it was "meager and inaccurate." Two planes had to land at K-13. The remainder of the flight returned to K-3. VMF-311 pilots were Majors SKINNER, MITCHELL, and GLENN, Captains FAUCHIER, WILLIAMS, SMITH, LOVETTE, SCOTT, and STREET, and Lieutenants BROTHERS and KECK. VMF-115 pilots were Lieutenant Colonel WARREN, Captains WESTFIELD, WINERITER, MAIK, and BLANEY, and Lieutenants HATCH and MERRIMAN. This was a mission featuring two major league ballplayers and one future astronaut.

26 APRIL 1953 – COMBAT MISSION #21

Mission Number Acme 03

Twelve aircraft, led by Major FOX, were airborne at 0905/I for a prebriefed interdiction mission. This mission was coordinated with Mission Acme 04 and other missions from VMF-115 and MAG-12 to hit targets in the same general area. Colonel ROBERTSHAW, MAG-33 Commanding Officer, with wingmen Lieutenants Colonels DILL and ADAMS, both of MAG-33, served in the capacity of Tactical Air Coordinator. At 0955/I the flight attacked buildings and bunkers, located at BT 7996 (Chuam-ni). Ordnance expended was 48 500-pound bombs and 325 rounds of 20MM ammunition. The other pilots were Lieutenant Colonel MORAN, Major SKINNER, Captains FAUCHIER, HAGANS, WILLIAMS, McGRAW, SMITH, and CARRUTHERS, and Lieutenants SAMPLE and KECK. Lieutenant Colonel McSHANE of MABS-33 flew with the squadron on this mission.

Note: Acme 04 was a four-aircraft mission led by Major MITCHELL with Major GLENN, Captain SCOTT, and Lieutenant BROTHERS.

27 APRIL 1953 – COMBAT MISSION #22

Mission Number Acme 03

Twelve aircraft from VMF-311, nine from VMF-115 and two from HQ SQ-33 took off at 1340/I on a prebriefed interdiction mission. The flight, led by Major BERNARD of VMF-115, attacked three different supply areas at 1435/I. Colonel ROBERTSHAW was Tactical Air Coordinator, with Lieutenant Colonel DILL as his wingman. The three targets were at YC 0988, YC 0989 and YC 0888 (Chinnamp'o). Fifty six 500 pound bombs, 36 250 pound bombs, four 500-pound incendiary bombs and 1,335 rounds of 20MM ammunition were expended. Damage was unassessed due to smoke. The flight encountered moderate small arms fire and meager automatic weapons anti-aircraft fire over the targets. Two aircraft were hit. One aircraft received minor damage to the left tip tank; the other received major damage to the left wing area and fuselage from this fire, but both pilots were uninjured. All returned safely to base at 1535/I. The VMF-311 pilots were Majors GLENN and KELSO, Captains HAGANS, WILLIAMS, SCOTT, ARMAGOST, LOVETTE, and MONTAGUE, and Lieutenants HAWKINS, HEILAND, KECK, and MILLER. The other VMF-115 pilots were Major THORPE, Captains WEBB, DUSENBURY, LEWIS, BURCH, and BROWN, and Lieutenants TAYLOR and SCHWINDT.

The aircraft suffering the left tip tank damage was that piloted by Captain WILLIAMS.

This incident rated just the one mention in the Command Diary summary, but a five-column headline on the front page of the *Boston Globe*: "Flak Hits Ted Williams' Plane." The subhead read, "Sox Slugger Lands Safely After Raid." The port city of Chinnampo at the mouth of the Taedong River was a heavily defended target, and the tip tank on the wing was hit by anti-aircraft fire. "It wasn't important," Williams commented. The tip tank fuel was the first fuel tapped by the jet engines, so the tanks were empty by the time the Pantherjets had begun their run. Had the defenders had even more luck than they did, it would have become a very important hit for them. It was, the Associated Press reported, Williams' "second brush with death in 2 1/2 months."[13]

This time Williams was not launched again the very next day. Neither was just about anyone else, though. Due to inclement weather on the 28th, there was only one mission with just three aircraft. Captain Williams was not involved, though he took a plane up to get in some instrument familiarization work.

He did go up the day after that, though, despite the ongoing weather problem.

A number of Marines kept diaries of their own. Captain Carrol Burch flew this mission with Ted, and it's interesting to read his notes from the mission:

Flew one of Mam's old kites on a strike at Chinnampo on an ammunition factory. I pumped 200 rounds of 20MM cannon into the number one building in our area. She didn't blow so I strung my scotches (250 #ers) across it. Looked like an abandoned warehouse to me. I looked back and saw my bombs hit the building but it didn't blow.

Col. Robertshaw was the fouled up controller.

Came back on the gauges at 33,000.

Movie "Road to Bali" tonight.

We are getting new F9F-5s.

We got some pictures back today taken after we hit certain targets. Amazing – a big hole in a bridge on which we'd claimed a possible cut.

One village 95% burned out – 47 buildings.

Others 64 out of 78 buildings. 76 out of 94 buildings.

29 APRIL 1953 – COMBAT MISSION #23

Mission Number Acme 42

Again, due to inclement weather, there was only one mission that day. Four aircraft led by Lieutenant Colonel MORAN carried out a prebriefed MPQ mission, airborne at 1126/I. The other pilots were Captain WILLIAMS and Lieutenants SAMPLE and BROTHERS. The drop of eight 1,000-pound bombs and eight 500-pound bombs was made over an unknown location. Despite his aircraft having been hit on the 27th, Williams was right back up again.

30 APRIL 1953 – COMBAT MISSION #24

Mission Number Acme 01

The first mission of this day featured two Captains WILLIAMS. It was a prebriefed group interdiction mission composed of fourteen aircraft from VMF-311 and seven from VMF-115. The flight was airborne at 1038/I. One aircraft, piloted by Captain THORPE of 115, was forced to abort due to mechanical reasons. Colonel ROBERTSHAW was Tactical Air Coordinator, with Lieutenant Colonel DILL as wingman. The flight attacked the following targets in Oeam-dong:

1103/I, YC 1571, target #6, buildings; 60% coverage was received and two buildings were left burning. 24 napalm and 60 rounds of 20MM ammunition were expended.

1130/I, YC 1460, target #7, buildings. Sixteen buildings were left burning, with 50% coverage of the target being received. Thirty-six napalm and 675 rounds of 20MM ammunition were expended.

Three napalm were jettisoned in the target area, four were jettisoned in the K-3 jettison area and one napalm fell off an aircraft at YC 3840.

Three aircraft from VMF-311 landed at K-13 due to low fuel. The remainder of the flight returned safely to base at 1230/I. The other VMF-311 pilots were Lieutenant Colonel MORAN, Majors KELSO, MILT, and GLENN, Captains CARRUTHERS, WILLIAMS, SCOTT, and SMITH. The other VMF-115 pilots were Lieutenant Colonel WARREN, Captains BLANEY, IRELAND, F. WILLIAMS, and BROWN, and Lieutenant BAIRD.

This last flight in April brought Capt. Ted S. Williams' total flight time to over 1,200 hours.

2 MAY 1953 – COMBAT MISSION #25

Mission Number Acme 10

Captain CAMPBELL led a close air support mission of four aircraft, which were airborne at 0635/I. At 0740/I, the flight attacked personnel shelters, caves and mortar positions located at DT 0444 to DT 0544 (Pangdong-ni, per squadron records; the Williams flight log book records it as Puniisu-ri). The flight controller reported two mortar positions damaged, one cave sealed and twelve personnel shelters either damaged or destroyed, and 150 yards of trench line damaged. Eight 1,000-pound bombs, eight 250-pound bombs and 1,650 rounds of 20MM ammunition were expended. The flight leader pointed out that Captain WILLIAMS and Lieutenant HAWKINS had direct hits on peaks given as target coordinates. At 0740/I, while over DT 0545, the flight encountered intense small arms fire, but received no damage. The other pilot was Captain LOVETTE.

4 MAY 1953 – COMBAT MISSIONS #26 & #27

Mission Number Acme 10

Captain CAMPBELL again led four aircraft, departing at 0655/I, on a close air support mission flown in support of the 1st Marine Division. The flight damaged three automatic weapons positions, one bunker, and 75 yards of trench line, destroyed two mortar positions, and cut two communications trenches located at CT 0908 (Hangdong-ni). Eight 1,000-pound bombs, eight 250-pound bombs and 1,325 rounds of 20MM ammunition were expended. The other pilots were Captains WILLIAMS, CARRUTHERS, and ARMAGOST.

Mission Number Acme 12

Captain T. S. WILLIAMS flew a second mission on 4 May, one led by Captain CLEM. It was another close air support mission, airborne at 1310/I. The attack was initiated at 1345/I. Trench line, personnel shelters, mortar positions, and caves were attacked, with the flight receiving 100 yards of trench line damage, five personnel shelters damaged, one cave damaged, and one mortar position damaged. Eight 1,000-pound bombs and eight 250-pound bombs were expended. Map coordinates were not noted in the summary, but the destination indicated in the Aircraft Mission Log was Utkkaemugi. The other pilots were Captain CAMPBELL and Lieutenant VERDI.

5 MAY 1953 – COMBAT MISSION #28

Mission Number Acme 11

Four aircraft, piloted by Captains McGRAW (flight leader), NORDELL, and WILLIAMS, and Lieutenant RUDY, took off on an MPQ interdiction mission at 1350/I. At 1430/I, the flight made their drop on a target of unknown composition and location, with unassessed results. The flight encountered no enemy opposition and all the aircraft returned safely to base at 1515/I.

6 MAY 1953

One of Ted's squadron mates was killed in action this day. There was just one mission on 6 May, a close air support mission of four aircraft led by Captain ARMAGOST. Two of the aircraft were lost while trying to land. One, piloted by Captain CARRUTHERS was ditched in the ocean about two miles east of EQ 2589. The pilot was rescued about one hour after ditching. The second aircraft, piloted by Captain BAILES, crashed at EQ 4887. The crash was investigated, the wreckage located and the scattered remains of Captain BAILES were found on 7 May. Both Captains ARMAGOST and CLEM returned safely.

There were no flights on 7 May or 8 May due to inclement weather.

9 MAY 1953 – COMBAT MISSION #29

Mission Number Acme 03

An eight-aircraft flight, led by Major GLENN, took off at 1410/I for Tokch'on. Captain WILLIAMS was forced to abort because he could not transfer his fuel. Other pilots on this mission were Majors CANAN and MILT, Captains SMITH, NORDELL, and STREET, and Lieutenant HEILAND.

On 11 May 1953, Williams took another fam flight, but then had several days without flight activity.

16 MAY 1953 – COMBAT MISSION #30

Mission Number Acme 18

Four aircraft led by Captain LOVETTE took off at 1410/I on a close air support mission. At 1505/I, the flight attacked personnel shelters, bunkers and trench line, located at CT 7050 (O'dang-ni), in support of the Capitol ROK Infantry Division. Six personnel shelters, two bunkers, and 75 yards of trench line were reported as damaged. Eight 1,000-pound bombs, eight 250-pound bombs and 80 rounds of 20MM ammunition were expended. All returned safely to base at 1545/I. The other pilots were Major GLENN, Captain WILLIAMS, and Lieutenant KECK.

17 MAY 1953 – COMBAT MISSION #31

Mission Number Acme 02

Captain LOVETTE led seven aircraft on a prebriefed interdiction mission. The flight took off at 1045/I and at 1135/I attacked supplies, located at BU 5329 (Han-dong). Lieutenant Colonel WARREN and Major ELDRIDGE served as Tactical Air Coordinator and wingman, respectively. Six to eight buildings were destroyed, with further damage unassessable due to smoke obscuring the target area. Twenty-eight napalm and 2,210 rounds of 20MM ammunition were expended on this mission. While over the target, Captain LOVETTE's aircraft received a hole in the bomb rack from moderate small arms fire. There was also moderate but inaccurate heavy weapons anti-aircraft fire. All the aircraft returned safely at 1225/I. The other pilots were Major GLENN, Captains WILLIAMS, FAUCHIER, and NORDELL, Lieutenant HEILAND, and Lieutenant Colonel McSHANE of MABS-33.

18 May 1953 – combat mission #32

Mission Number Acme 15

Airborne at 1432/I, Lieutenant Colonel MORAN led a close air support mission composed of four aircraft, piloted by Captains LOVETTE and WILLIAMS, and Lieutenant SPENCER. The mission attacked personnel shelters, mortar positions, and bunkers at CT 6542 (Songamnyong) at 1520/I. The damage was unassessed due to smoke and intense cloud coverage over the target.

19 MAY 1953 – COMBAT MISSION #33

Mission Number Acme 02

Major FOX led eight aircraft on a prebriefed interdiction mission, airborne at 1322/I. At 1414/I, the flight attacked a rail bridge, located at YD 4107 (Chunghwa), and achieved three definite cuts. Sixteen 1,000-pound bombs and 625 rounds of 20MM ammunition were expended. The other pilots were Captains WILLIAMS, LOVETTE, and KURTZ, Lieutenants MILLER, HEILAND, and SPENCER.

20 MAY 1953 – COMBAT MISSION #34

Mission Number Acme 11

Captain CLEM led four aircraft on a close air support mission with destination Mundung-ni, taking off at 1055/I. At 1120/I the flight started reporting and checking and switching channels. MOSQUITO FILTER FOUR (the flight controller) had the flight's prebriefed target coordinate of DT 0342 to DT 0343, but marked the wrong target at DT 0742. The weather was getting bad and the flight was short on fuel. Because Lieutenant Colonel MORAN had been on a target at DT 0842 the day before, he knew that the target marked was in enemy territory so he led the flight in. The first drop was made at 1156/I at DT 0742 receiving 11 personnel shelters destroyed, four mortar positions damaged, and one cave damaged. Eight 1,000-pound bombs and eight 250-pound bombs were expended on this target, in support of the 20th ROK Infantry Division. The other pilots were Captain WILLIAMS and Lieutenant MILLER, and all landed safely at 1240/I.

21 MAY 1953 – COMBAT MISSION #35

Mission Number Acme 03

Major GLENN led a prebriefed interdiction mission composed of 10 aircraft which took off at 0932/I. At 1010/I the flight attacked personnel shelters located at CU 2934 (Yongp'o-ri). Thirty-two 500-pound incendiaries and 400 rounds of 20MM ammunition were expended. Two aircraft landed at K-13 due to low fuel. The other pilots were Lieutenant Colonel MORAN, Lieutenant Commander HARRIS, Majors SKINNER and MENDES, and Captains WILLIAMS, HIMES, and ARMAGOST. Lieutenant Colonel DILL, of MAG-33, and Lieutenant Colonel McSHANE, of MABS-33, flew with the squadron on this mission.

23 MAY 1953 – COMBAT MISSIONS #36 & #37

Mission Number Acme 14

Four aircraft led by Major MITCHELL took off at 1145/I on a close air support mission. At 1235/I, in support of the 5th ROK Infantry Division, the flight attacked an enemy stronghold, bunkers and trenches, located at CT 9247 (Oun-ni). One hundred yards of trench line and two automatic weapons positions were damaged. Eight 1,000-pound bombs, eight 250-pound bombs and 1,150 rounds of 20MM ammunition were expended. The other pilots were Captains CARRUTHERS and WILLIAMS and Lieutenant HEILAND. All returned safely at 1315/I.

Mission Number Acme 10A

At 1700/I, four aircraft led by Lieutenant MILLER took off on a close air support mission. At 1735/I, the flight attacked personnel shelters and trench line, located at DT 0343 (Kajang-dong), in support of the 20th ROK Infantry Division. Twenty-five yards of trench line were damaged. Sixteen 500-pound bombs, of which eight had 6- to 8-hour delay fuses, and 700 rounds of 20MM ammunition were expended. The other pilots were Major MITCHELL, and Captains CARRUTHERS and WILLIAMS.

24 MAY 1953 – COMBAT MISSION #38

Lieutenant Colonel MORAN led a prebriefed close air support mission composed of six aircraft which took off at 0719/I. At 0800/I, the flight attacked personnel shelters, mortar positions, and trench line, located at DT 1744 (Tong-myon), in support of the 45th U. S. Infantry Division. Three personnel shelters were destroyed, fifteen personnel shelters were damaged, four mortar positions were damaged, and 100 yards of trench line were damaged. Twenty-four 500-pound bombs and 1,200 rounds of 20MM ammunition were expended. Meager and inaccurate small arms and an unknown type weapons fire was encountered over the target area. The other pilots returned safely to base at 0855/I. The other pilots were Lieutenant Commander HARRIS, Captains CARRUTHERS, KURTZ, WILLIAMS, and ARMAGOST.

10 JUNE 1953 – COMBAT MISSION #39

Mission Number Acme 04

Lieutenant Colonel McSHANE led a prebriefed interdiction mission composed of 12 aircraft, which were airborne at 1035/I. Captain CLEM's plane experienced radio failure and he had to abort.At 1120/I, the remaining planes attacked personnel shelters and supplies located at YC 3758 (Tangjang-ni). Thirty-two napalm, 12 500-pound incendiaries and 2,175 rounds of 20MM ammunition were expended. Two aircraft landed at K-13 due to low fuel. The others returned to K-3 at 1210/I. The other pilots were Majors PEINE, MILT, and MENDES, Captains WILLIAMS, [Walter] ROSS, BROWN, and FAUCHIER, and Lieutentants SPENCER, BROTHERS, and KECK.

Mission Number Acme 06

Major MENDES led a prebriefed interdiction mission composed of seven aircraft, again targeting Tangjang-ni. The flight took off at 1528/I. The aircraft piloted by Captain WILLIAMS was forced to abort almost immediately due to the fire warning light coming on. At 1609/I the remainder of the flight attacked supply and personnel shelters. Small arms fire was moderate, and two aircraft were hit. Captain [Walter] ROSS' plane suffered a shattered windshield on the port side in front and the pilot received cuts under his left eye from the fragments of the windshield. Captain SMITH's aircraft received a hole in the leading edge of the starboard wing. The other pilots were Major MITCHELL, and Lieutenants KECK and EUSTER.

Note: on a June 1 mission, Major GLENN's plane had received a hole in the tail section. ROSS was hit again on 15 June.

The June 10 missions were, as it happened, the final missions Ted Williams flew in combat. His final scheduled mission, resulting in an abort (not noted in Williams' flight log book, but noted in squadron records), stands as a bit of anti-climax to the 39 completed missions Captain Williams flew while in Korea. Unlike his major league baseball career, which ended with a home run in his final time at bat, the final flight from the runway at K-3 was far less dramatic. Sometimes reality doesn't work out the way we might like to script it.

Two other flights out of K-3 were recorded in his log book. Neither were combat missions. One was a one-hour flight on 16 June in a HO35-1 aircraft, and the second was a 1.8 hour flight in an R4D-8. The first was a Sikorsky-made helicopter. It's not clear why Ted Williams was piloting a helicopter at this point, six days after his last combat mission, and it's unlikely it was a joyride offered him by another pilot since Williams recorded it in his log book and listed himself as pilot; no passenger was indicated. Remarks indicate this was a local fam flight. The second craft, the R4D-8, was known as the Skytrain. It was a large two-propeller transport plane normally used for moving military equipment and normally carrying a crew of three – a pilot, co-pilot, and navigator. Williams is listed as pilot in his log book. There were no remarks entered that might provide a clue as to the purpose of this last recorded flight.

In all, Williams was credited with having logged 1,227.8 hours of flight time, or over 51 days of 24 hours each.

NOTES

1) Marvin Koner, "Still a Big Leaguer," Collier's, May 1953.

2) Ed Hyde, Sport, July 1953.

3) Fred Townsley, posted on VMF-311/VMA-311 website.

4) Interview with Jon Mendes, November 13, 2002.

5) Interview with Bill Clem, December 23, 2002.

6) Interview with Ed Buchser, September 28, 2002.

7) Interview with Leonard Waibel, December 19, 2002.

8) Interview with James Walley, December 7, 2003.

9) Interview with Joseph Mitchell, February 3, 2003.

10) Interview with Lloyd Merriman, November 16, 2002.

11) Interview with Jack Gross, May 31, 2003.

12) Washington Post, April 19, 1953.

13) Boston Globe, April 28, 1953.

Ted Williams being "ordered to report to Fenway Park, Boston" by Col. Kenneth B. Chappell, USMC, Commanding Officer, Marine Barracks, Naval Gun Factory, Washington DC, July 28, 1953.
Courtesy of National Archives & Records Administration.

CHAPTER 16 – MUSTERED OUT OF THE MARINES

The time came when Ted Williams left Korea. The war was clearly coming to an end. He'd flown 39 missions, but he was having a rough time physically. Armistice negotiations had been going on for months, but it was pretty evident by mid-June 1953 that they weren't going to drag on too much longer. There are a number of theories advanced by his fellow Marines as to why Ted was sent back to the States. There was the official version, of course – that he had been sent back for treatment of a serious ear problem. Some were skeptical that this was the real reason. With Ted Williams, there is hardly a move he made that didn't engender question and comment.

Leaving Korea was not without comment, though it's also quite remarkable that many of the Marines at K-3 didn't know he had gone until sometime afterward. There was no farewell party. Though his voyage home was chronicled by reporters step by step along the way, it's quite remarkable that many of the Marines at K-3 didn't even know he'd departed. Through interviews, we find that several of them had not noticed his absence until some time after he'd gone.

Williams was mustered out of the Marines, but how and why are questions that prompt a considerable range of speculation. As in so many other areas, controversy seems to cloud the story. It seems there was never such a thing as a simple answer. There are stories, and then there are stories. Let's look at several, all recounted by USMC pilots who served at K-3.

We do know that the last time Ted took out a plane, he had to abort. He didn't go out in a blaze of glory, shot down at last. He didn't go out after dropping his payload on a major ammunition dump and setting off one of the largest secondary explosions ever seen in the Korean theater. No, as we have seen, he flew one mission on 10 June 1953, but on his second mission of the day, the aircraft piloted by Captain WILLIAMS was forced to abort almost immediately when the fire warning light came on.

Jon Mendes was the mission leader that day. As we noted, both Walter ROSS's and Floyd SMITH's planes were hit that day. Asked about it fifty years after the fact, Mendes didn't recall Williams' abort, though he recalled two people being hit. This was, however, the last time Ted suited up for combat.

The official explanation for his separation from the squadron was that Williams had suffered a "lack of ventilation in the ear and nose that causes interference with jet flying." He'd been bothered for over a month and hospitals in the war zone were not equipped to treat the condition.[1]

Why did Ted get sent back to Japan for treatment, then on to Hawaii, to California, and finally back to Walter Reed Hospital in Bethesda, Maryland? Bill Clem suggested that things were not as they appeared. "I'm going to tell you something. It's up to you to follow this if you want to, but I don't think you'll get very far with it. The reason he came back... the reason he got off... it wasn't because he was sick. We had a mission one day. We had two types of airplanes over there. We had F9F-2 and the F9F-5. He was scheduled to fly a -2 one day, which was a slower and not as good airplane. He was assigned to a -2, and he came into the ready room and he said, "I'm not going in the -2." He went back to the hut, and he wouldn't come back. He wasn't afraid or anything, but it was an inferior aircraft. So they had to assign someone else to it. They took the mission. The next day, the C.O. transferred him to the group, out of the squadron. MAG-33. I've never seen that in print. That's the truth. But it was awful quiet. I think the Marine Corps covered it up, because they didn't want that to happen. So then they made up this deal about his being sick. They sent him out to a hospital ship and then they sent him home. He did have some ear problems. A lot of people had ear problems."[2]

The command diaries reflect that Clem himself had to abort on the first June 10 mission of when his aircraft experienced radio failure. His log book confirmed it. "Yeah, I had to abort that. It shows an abort here. I went again that same day." Williams flew the first mission. Ted had to abort the second mission, but Clem was able to fly his second mission of the day, that evening. Told that Ted had aborted due to the fire warning light going off, Clem remembered a time like that himself. "That scares you. That scares you. I remember that. I landed at K-13 rather than K-3."

Ask if he remembered Williams ever complaining about ear conditions, he said he did not, but he added a personal note: "I remember one time when the canopy of mine went out and my ears haven't been the same since. Damn. Rapid decompression." Clem also volunteered, "Now, I don't want to take anything away from Ted. He was a good pilot. I guarantee you that. But that was pretty hairy right there when that happened with that plane, when he wouldn't take that. It's not well known."[3]

Was this really possible? Ted Williams had refused an aircraft, and in effect been sent home because of it? "He always was a stickler for doing things right," Clem had said. No pilot would want to go up in an unsafe aircraft about which they felt uncomfortable. That could endanger their lives and the lives of others on the mission.

"You'd have to check with somebody in maintenance about that, if he turned down the aircraft too often, but I was a flight leader and the squadron S-4 officer [supply officer] and I don't remember hearing about that at the time. That must have been somebody that had a tangle with him or something. He was kind of his own man, and I guess he was easy to tangle with."[4]

Before considering this further, let's look at another suggestion regarding Ted's final day. Milton Rugg became the Education Officer of VMF-311 in June 1953, but he only arrived on 15 June, 1953. That was five days after Williams' last missions. Rugg never met Ted, either before, during or after Korea. Not surprisingly, though, he heard stories about the four-time batting champion who was leaving the squadron around the time he was joining it. Rugg heard, "He came back from a mission and he put an airplane in a creek bed and I guess they figured he'd flown enough, and they sent him home."[5]

Asked about the fire warning light, Rugg replied, "It means that he had a fire in the engine compartment, not associated with the thrusters and the compressors. You're going to have a fire in your engine compartment. You have thrusters that thrust fuel in. You have the rotors that compress the air and then ignite the air and fuel mixture, which gives you your thrust. He had an abnormal light in there."

So then he aborted and returned to base? "No, he didn't make it to base. He put it in a creek. If you have a fire, you don't have a lot of time to think." [You just want to put it down as fast as you can?] "Yes."

[Was this near K-3?] "I don't know how near it was. Maybe a few miles... All I know is that the Marine base sent out a recovery team and they took out everything they thought was essential, and by the time they got back to the main base, the Koreans had the rest of the fuselage at the main gate to their village.

"It was written off. They sent a crew out and they took all the essential equipment out – radios and radar and gunsights and things like that. They left a shell of an airplane there. The Marine Corps just left it because they didn't think they could get it back, but with just physical manpower, the Koreans got it to their village.

"He'd served his time. It was time for him to go home. The war was winding down."

Was this likely? Landing in a creek bed? That's a little different from refusing an aircraft, but perhaps if he'd landed his jet in a creek bed, and then been asked to go up in a -2, he'd then refused that.

Rugg said he was not aware of any ear problems Williams had, or anything related to that. He was also not aware of any disciplinary rumors regarding Ted, nor had he heard the story that Ted had refused an aircraft. And, though he was Education Officer of the squadron, he couldn't recommend anyone else who might confirm the story. "After he left, nobody discussed him. We had other agendas. I'm sort of exorcised from the Marine Corps. I left under adverse conditions. The commanding officer said I was not compatible to the Marine Corps because I couldn't separate myself from my family. I was having a child born while I was there. When we signed up for World War II, we didn't know we were going to get called back for another war. I was 30."[6]

Trying to consider Clem's story first, a search of the command diaries indicated that there were no flights of any F9F-2 aircraft by VMF-311, even for familiarization purposes, at any time in June of 1953. There were also no F9F-2 flights, even for familiarization purposes, in May of 1953.

Working backward, one finds that in April, there was a test flight of an F9F-2 on 17 April. There was also, earlier in the day, a Combat Air Patrol flight. The last combat flight of an F9F-2 in the squadron was on 14 April.

One had flown on April 12th, two flew on the 7th, three on the 6th, two on the 5th, and two on April 2nd. Most of these flights were fam flights or CAP flights. In terms of taking an F9F-2 into combat, the only time this happened in April was the flight on the 14th.

In March, at the beginning of the month, there were quite a few combat missions flown with F9F-2s, but after March 6 when six F9F-2s flew an interdiction mission to Chokkun-ni, there were only two more times – on March 16 and 27 – when a sole F9F-2 flew on a combat mission. It doesn't seem that Williams had refused an F-2 at any time in his last three months at K-3. They simply weren't being used.

It could have been that Ted refused another aircraft (perhaps even an F9F-5) which he considered to be in sub-standard condition, though. I did exchange an e-mail with a sergeant who said, "he had the reputation of only taking out perfect planes." That sounds like Ted Williams – and also sounds very prudent! Clem's account has not been possible to verify, is not reflected in the official record, and seems unlikely.

What about Rugg's understanding that Williams had crash-landed his plane in a creek bed and the plane was scrubbed? It seems doubtful that this ever occurred. As one pilot pointed out, you don't land jet planes in creek beds. In any event, the squadron did have to account for lost and damaged aircraft, and there was not even one aircraft reported as lost or damaged beyond repair at any time during all of June 1953. The Aircraft Mission Log, which was filed monthly as part of the Command Diary, contains a separate line for each and every mission, completed over the signature of the commanding officer of the squadron. The Command Diary also had to receive a first endorsement by the commanding officer of MAG-33 and a second endorsement by the commanding general (sometimes signed by the assisting commanding general) of the 1st Marine Aircraft Wing.

The Command Diary was submitted to the Commandant of the Marine Corps via the Commanding General, Fleet Marine Force, Pacific.

For June 1953, the C.O. of MAG-33 was Colonel A. R. Stacy, and the assisting commanding general of the wing was A. W. Kreiser.

The Aircraft Mission Log detailed each and every flight in a given month – including familiarization flights. In the 30 days of June, 1953, there were 210 such flights.

Separate notations were made of the time of takeoff, aircraft model and configuration, number of planes of that particular aircraft type taking off, the mission purpose, and its destination (which might be "FAM" or "CAP SCRAMBLE" or an actual location – be it "K-3 TO ITAMI" or a targeted destination). The number of total aircraft hours, measured in hours and tenths, were tallied. Any aircraft which aborted had to be accounted for, with an indication as to the reason for the abort – weather, mechanical, electrical or "other." Needless to say, the "number of aircraft lost or damaged, all causes" was an important element. If an aircraft was damaged, the log had to indicate the reason for the damage. Four choices were provided: L indicating "failed to return to a friendly base," D1 being "Jettisoned or salvaged after return because of damage sustained," D2 being "Damaged beyond local repair; transferred or held for repair elsewhere," and D3 being "Damage from this mission repaired or reparable on board."

There was a final column for "Pers. K or M." Killed or missing. Fortunately, VMF-311 lost very few pilots or other personnel.

During June 1953, there were no losses whatsoever. There was only one damaged aircraft, and it was in category D3 "repaired or reparable on board." That damage was sustained on June 1 by Major John Glenn's aircraft, which received a "hole in the tail section" but was able to return to base safely. There was no other damage reported to any squadron aircraft.

Of the aborts, one was for weather, nine were for mechanical problems, one for electrical and two for other reasons.

For 10 June 1953, there is a discrepancy. There were ten entries indicating takeoffs that day. Four of them were fam flights. There were five missions recorded. The remaining flight was a movement of two aircraft from K-13 back to K-3. Only one abort was reported on the Aircraft Mission Log, and no loss or damage was reported there, though the Command Diary indicates two aborts and four planes receiving some degree of damage. The abort indicated was that of Captain Clem, an abort due to radio failure (this was listed as mechanical) on Mission Number Acme 04. The Command Diary for Mission Number Acme 06 states that Major Mendes led a prebriefed interdiction mission composed of seven aircraft which took off at 1528/I. "One (1) aircraft, piloted by Captain WILLIAMS, was forced to abort due to the fire warning light coming on." The Log shows the departure of six aircraft. A logical explanation would be that the fire warning light came on prior to takeoff, so Williams' aircraft was not included among those which took off, and thus not indicated as an abort of a plane which had taken off. The mission, which would have been Williams' 40th, was not recorded as such in his flight logbook.

It was a good mission to miss, as it happened, though one could not know that in advance. The target was a grouping of supply and personnel shelters at Tangjang-ni and it was the third mission of the day to target Tangjang-ni. No enemy opposition was noted on the first mission. The second mission, however, reported "moderate and accurate small arms fire while over the target" and in fact two aircraft were hit. The aircraft piloted by Lieutenant Euster received a small hole in the tip tank, while that of Lieutenant McPherson received a hole in the fairing cover in the fuselage under the horizontal stabilizer. Neither pilot was injured and all aircraft returned safely to K-3.

Mission Number Acme 06 also reported moderate and accurate small arms fire. Two aircraft were hit. Captain Walter Ross' plane received a shattered windshield on the port side in front. Ross suffered cuts under his left eye from fragments of the windshield. Captain Floyd Smith's plane received a hole in the leading edge of the starboard wing. Both planes returned safely, as did all the aircraft on the mission.

Oddly, neither of these incidents cited in the Command Diary narrative was reflected as damaged aircraft in the Aircraft Mission Log. There are a number of times during June 1953 where the two seem not to match, leading one to question the accuracy of record-keeping during this period.

In addition to the Aircraft Mission Log, the Operations section filed a written report. For June 1953, the report begins by stating, "There were no aircraft lost during the month. One (1) aircraft was slightly damaged when the nose wheel collapsed on contact with the runway."

The Engineering section also filed its report, reporting battle damage to 15 aircraft with three aircraft receiving major damage. The major damage was repaired overnight and all aircraft were ready for combat the following day. There was one accident reported and, the same day, one flame out.

Had an aircraft been forced to land in a creek bed, a salvage crew sent out to retrieve essential equipment, and the fuselage abandoned, this would almost certainly have been noted. Though there are discrepancies here and there, the total loss of an entire aircraft would be very hard to overlook – or, to think conspiratorially for just a moment, to cover up – and no other pilots have been located who can confirm Rugg's story – which is indeed a story he himself heard secondhand.

Some Marines thought Williams had left the squadron earlier than he should have, before he'd really flown enough missions. He'd flown 39, though, fewer than some but more than others. James Walley explained that there was supposed to be an upper limit: "The squadron allowed us to fly 100 missions and then if you wanted to fly more, you had to go see a psychiatrist. They wanted to find out if you were mentally competent before they let you go on more flights. It was a serious concern. You'd get a little fatigued after a while."[7]

Dale Purcell, of the photo squadron, said that "Not many pilots ever flew near 100 missions in Korea, that I know of. Not because of psychiatric reasons but because we had enough pilots there.

Now and then someone would get 40 or 50 in the Marine Corps and those who were career-minded might make the request to transfer fly with the Air Force to fly Sabrejets. That's what John Glenn did. I don't recall any particular instances where people had to leave early. Later, some may have had some stress – not because of the flying but because of being separated for so long from young families. Possibly some of the stress was back in the States with the families."[8]

Purcell, a doctoral candidate in audiology, explained how Williams' ears had become damaged. "The thing that happened here was that a flight went out and Tom Sellers was bringing his flight back and the weather hadn't blown off of the coast and they had to land in thick stuff. They normally would have been able to go directly in and take their intervals and come in at about 10-12 second intervals, [but with the bad weather] they had to keep the altitude all together over the field and corkscrew down.

"When they were spiraling down at this extreme rate of descent – especially for Williams who had his ears plugged up – it was because of weather. Not a stormy jet stream across the field, but because it was weather so thick you had to overlap wings in order to stay together. He did not stand out there. He stayed at number two position. He was off of Sellers' wing and people were taking their intervals off of his plane. As they came down – Sellers, knowing that this was a left-hand landing pattern at K-3 and one strip, and they would have about one chance if the weather was still messy – he had to get them down below the weather so that they could take their intervals and so the Tail End Charlie – the guy who was out of fuel – could land on the first patch. Williams stayed in. No one said 'Hey, Williams is staying in there.' Williams didn't say anything. The non-conspicuousness of the man is what I was telling you."

[You know from personal experience about the damage to his ears, as a professional audiologist?] Yes. What happened was that he had... the eustachian tubes, he couldn't relieve them. They were coming down too steeply and you couldn't adjust your eustachian tubes so your ears would... the changing pressure... you could slow down your rate of descent, but Williams stuck with him [Major Sellers] and it must have been excruciating pain. I know the pain. When they broke out, they were just underneath us, almost down to the field. The leader, Sellers, was being guided by ground control approach. The task of the rest of the flight was to stick with the guy in front of him and Williams was sticking with Sellers. It happened to be that he was on his wing that day. When they got together, they didn't line up and say, "You do this" – they simply slid into a right echelon so that when they came across the field in a long straightaway, Sellers asked "What's your state?" And Tail End Charlie said, "I'm on the fumes." The field had complete control – the tower. As they passed the end of the field, of course Williams being number two followed... his 5 or 6 seconds count after Sellers broke, Williams would have counted about 5 or 6 and then made his tight turn to the left. Then he would turn again downwind parallel to the field, then he would turn base leg. All that was taking a proper interval to be able to get down and onto the field behind the fellow in front of him. Williams did all that. Sellers would say, "One... .two... three... four... five... six... seven... eight." [polling all the aircraft in his flight to let anyone comment if they were on fumes or needed assistance]. At no point did he make any complaint. I was behind him. I had been out there sort of as safety. I had plenty of fuel. When they landed, I came in and landed. I turned left at the end to get to my VMJ-1, and they turned right off the runway. There was no medical alert about it, but I was told that evening that Williams couldn't get out of his airplane. Or he didn't. The plane captain hopped up on the side and the canopy was opened, I was told that his eardrums were ruptured and that they were bleeding. I'm not sure that eardrums bleed when they are ruptured under those circumstances – rather unusual – but I know that for the rest of the time when I would see him occasionally, he was simply not hearing well.

"If he was trying to avoid flight duty, I don't know that. I do know about the acute loss of hearing. I was getting my doctorate in speech and hearing at Northwestern, as well as teaching at Ottawa College, when I was recalled. Later I became president of Westminster College, but this is not about me. I think it has to do with my bona fides."[9]

There were only two missions on which Sellers and Williams both flew, and the first was that of 16 February 1953, when Ted was forced into his crash landing at Suwon. The other was Williams' first mission back after the prolonged stay on board the hospital ship with pneumonia. The 4 April 1953 mission also resulted in six of the aircraft forced to land at K-13 due to fuel shortages. This would have to have been the mission to which Purcell referred. And this meant that for almost all of his missions in Korea, Williams suffered from the effects to one degree or another.

Lt. Col. Patrick Harrison corroborates Purcell's story. Harrison had been a major at K-3 and was one of Ted's hutmates, along with Joe Mitchell before Lee Scott arrived. Mike Gillooly of the *Boston Evening American* interviewed Harrison in 1958, and Harrison asked about Ted, "Didn't somebody once say he wasn't a team player? Well, let me tell you about team play and maybe a doctor could later explain the intense pain that went along with his determination to be part of the Marine team. This happened in Korea, when Ted's division was at a high altitude orbit, waiting to come down and the four jets screeched out of the sky, preparatory to peeling off for their individual landings. They always come down in tight formation at a terrific rate of speed.

"Now this is a drop that demands No. 1 physical condition. Tremendous pressures build up in such a rapid descent. You feel it even slightly in a commercial flight. You're slightly out of line, you feel it. Ted got it in his ears. It led eventually to his discharge. But he never moved out of that formation, although he was in intense pain. He did it despite unimaginable suffering. That was team work and under great physical anguish." Harrison added, referring to the post-war Duplantier controversy (see chapter 22), "Sure, he pretends he's an antagonist of the Marine Corps. But he never missed an assignment in Korea; never missed a flight no matter what the weather. When the chips were down, he was there."[10]

Tom Ross came across Ted on the hospital ship, after an incident of his own. "I landed on a gravel airstrip just behind the bomb line. I got hit pretty badly and I was burning. The engine finally quit but I couldn't get enough altitude to bail out. It did hold together and then one of my wingmen picked up that gravel emergency strip and I plowed it in on the gravel. Just barely on our side of the bomb line. It was right behind an Army regimental headquarters and so a couple of Army pilots took me back to K-3 in a little airplane. I had a tremendous whiplash because I had to put the bird down at 130 knots and I just spiked it down, and so the deceleration was pretty severe. After a week in traction in the hospital, I resumed missions. It was a hospital ship, I believe it was the *Consolation*, at anchor at Inchon harbor. I went there in a helicopter.

"I saw Ted in the hospital ship when he was there for that tremendous sinus infection that he had, and I was there with my head in traction after having had a crash landing. I talked with Ted there briefly, in the hospital ship and I asked 'Are they going to send you home now?' and he said 'I sure hope so.' I just think of all that he could have done had he not taken all that time out of his baseball career. He did his duty." Ross knew that Ted had been a "reluctant warrior."[11]

Jerry Coleman understood that Ted's VIP status might have played some role in Ted's being mustered out. "Ted was sick when he was over there. He had an infection in his ear. I was 28 or 29 and he was six years older than me. I would think that it was much more difficult for him at his age, with his name and his impact on the entire Marine Corps. It must have been a hellish time for him. Eventually it got so bad that they decided that with his persona, his name and everything to get him out of there before he ended up killing himself without the enemy contributing. So he was sent back."[12]

Coleman himself may have paid a bit of a price because of his own fame. M. T. "Cotton" Schuerman, a pilot in VMF-311, told a Memphis reporter years later that "Coleman had finished all his missions and was rubbing it in to us about going to Japan to serve as athletic officer. Then a reporter in the States wrote an article about some of the big sports stars getting preferential treatment and Coleman spent the last three months in Korea as an air control officer with the troops on the front line. He wanted to meet the reporter who thought he was getting preferential treatment."[13]

Persona counted. Steven Bullock noted, regarding World War II, that over 90% of all major league players on rosters at the close of the 1941 season saw one form of military service or another, but "it seemed to be an unwritten rule during World War II that Major League stars and other celebrities were to be exempted from exposure to dangerous situations. Although the death rate for American military personnel approximated 3 percent, no active Major League player lost his life in combat, and only a handful were injured. Moreover, many of these injuries were either training mishaps or non-combat-related accidents." After all, he asked, "Who wanted to be the general or admiral who authorized combat duty for Joe DiMaggio or Ted Williams only to see them perish on a South Pacific island or over the skies of Germany?"[14]

As we have seen, the number of major leaguers who served in the Korean War could be counted on the fingers of one's hands.

When Williams finally did leave, he flew the first leg back to Japan with Woody Woodbury of 115. Woody remembers the hop, about a two-hour 30-minute flight, and remembers Ted's candor about returning to his marriage back home. Was Ted leaving one war only to enter another combat arena?

"Going from Korea on that flight... that was the day Ted left Korea for the last time, and he and I rode together from Korea to Japan. Of course, they didn't have any jet transport planes in those days. They had propellers, so it was quite a ride over the Sea of Japan to Itami where we landed. On that flight over there, Ted sort of opened up to me. He was having a terrible marital problem and told me pretty much about it. I've never told anybody about it and I don't really want to... but he just opened up. A lot of people don't realize that, for all of the stardom, the guy was a really humble guy. If they [only] would have left him alone! He wanted to be known as a great hitter. He wanted to be a good ballplayer and a nice guy, but he had a problem with his wife while he was away. A lot of guys did. A lot of wives, I guess they were lonely or whatever it was – I was not married at the time – it was a very upsetting time in his life. He was angry and he was frustrated. People were sending him clippings out of the *Miami Herald*, newspaper things saying Ted's wife was seen here and yaddidy yaddidy. It was an unsettled time for him. He was saying, 'How can she do this? God knows I'm having enough trouble with this sportswriter in Boston' – one who was on his case all the time. He had this infection on top of everything. He was really uptight about her. He was upset. He wasn't ranting and raving, because he ain't that breed of cat, but he was just upset. We were good enough friends that... His personal life, he never divulged that to anybody, including me. He just told me that he was having this terrible problem with his wife in Miami and he didn't appreciate what was going on, and of course I don't know how much of that was blown out of proportion, either. But when you're the wife of a celebrity, if you go out – even with another girlfriend – and if you're spotted, oh oh. Maybe he succumbed to that. Maybe none of it was true. Maybe all of it was true. I have no idea. I know this – he was in that R4D – that airplane – and they didn't have side-by-side seats like they have in jets, you know – they had like pews in churches along the sides of the airplane. So we sat there and he was down, he was depressed and he was ticked off. He was flying back to the States, and [going to] get it all straightened out."[15]

SPEAKING OUT ABOUT U.S. POLICY

As Williams left the war zone and was heading home, there was some anticipation in the Boston papers about the welcome he might receive and about what might be expected of him once he was back Stateside. Bill Cunningham of the *Boston Herald* wrote a column detailing some of his concern:

"Speaking of Williams, the Red Sox slugger may be back on American soil by the time you're reading this and on his way to the West Coast Navy hospital for the treatment of his ear and nose trouble. It's going to be interesting to see whether the Marine Corps confines its attention to his ears and nose exclusively or whether it will also try to do something about his mouth.

"Williams spoke in strong and characteristic language to war zone reporters of his disgust with the way the Korean action is being run. He said that American G.I.s are dying, and have died, because we haven't tried, and aren't trying to win, and he said 'the United States should be ashamed of itself.' He's telling the truth and it's all been said before – by General Van Fleet, among others. Some Congressmen and Senators, however, seem to have paid no attention until a baseball star spoke, and the repercussions in Washington have been considerable.

"The wondering about Williams now is if they won't try to crack down on him for speaking his mind, and how far they'll get if they do. We Boswells of the ball yards have all been through that many times with the gentleman, but the Marine Corps hasn't. At last understanding, the Armed Forces had a very strict rule against its members, especially officers, sounding off on controversial matters without official clearance. They'll be foolish to try to gag Williams because, first of all, he's telling the truth, and second of all, they can't do much, if anything, to him. He's a hospital case now, only sweating out his discharge.

"They'll have ways of halting reporters as long as he's on government property, but there'll be other times and it will be interesting to watch the trend of the Williams statements, if any, to the press from here on. Don't think the journalistic fraternity won't be after him with pencils poised, and not entirely upon the subject of his future in or out of baseball."[16]

There was a bit of follow-up in the July 4 paper.

"It's hard from this distance to pass any judgment on what Williams has said (if he did indeed say it) except to say that he ought to know what he's talking about. He sounds right to me in every instance but his seeming insistence that we long since should have used the A bomb. The rest of it's straight MacArthur – Van Fleet – Frank Lowe prescription, and charge that Americans have died, and are dying, because we – meaning Washington – haven't tried to win.

"If, however, you want a clearer picture of what Williams has, and, in fact, all fliers have, been through in Korea, your attention is respectfully called to a 30,000 word novel featured in this week's copy of *Life* magazine, and entitled 'The Bridges of Toko-Ri.' James A. Michener, the Pulitzer Prize winning author of other works about the Pacific, fictional and otherwise, is the writer of this one. Although it concerns the life, combat and reflections of a Navy jet pilot operating from an aircraft carrier, once they're over the target, they're all the same. This is really the story of all jet pilots in action... a picture of what these young fellows go through you'll find impossible to forget. Maybe that's why the young fellows themselves find it impossible to forget, and why one freshly released from the danger as Ted Williams just has been, feel in honor bound to speak for those who haven't."[17]

Williams was never that guarded in what we had to say, and rarely cared who was listening as he ventured his opinions. What had he actually said? A story by John J. Casserly in the *Record-American* quoted Ted on June 29 as he sat on his bunk at the base. "Williams wanted to talk more about the war than about baseball," Casserly wrote, and said "he is happy to be leaving Korea because he feels the U.S. is not trying to win the war." Specifically, Williams was quoted as saying, "Many Americans have forgotten this war. The United States of America ought to be ashamed of itself the way this thing is going on out here. You ask any guy in the squadron. With 150 million people, the U.S. drafts about 24,000 men a month. In the bunny hutch next door, there is a guy with six kids. And he can't get out of here because there is no one to take his place. Do you think he ought to be in Korea? Do you think we are trying? We've had the atom bomb for the whole three years of the war. Guys are getting killed every day in the line. Do you think we are trying? We've sat on the 38th Parallel for a year and a half and more. Still we sit there. And still more guys die. Do you think we are trying? We're not trying one-tenth of what we could. Don't you ever believe it, buddy, that we're trying."

It was, Ted added, "a forgotten war to all but the wives and kids, the mothers and maybe the girls of guys over here."[18] Williams explained that he'd not asked to leave Korea but that his ears had bothered him considerably since his very first few missions. "He said his ears hemorrhaged and burned after each mission," Casserly further reported.

The day before Cunningham's piece, Arthur Daley of the *New York Times* wrote a whole piece about Ted returning. "Captain Williams apparently hasn't changed a bit," Daley wrote. "Unwittingly or not, he always gets involved in a controversy of some sort. The later is that he both will and will not be discharged from the service in time to rejoin the Red Sox for the last month of the season. He also will be able to pick up where he left off without training and will require at least six months for the unlimbering of his baseball muscles.

"On top of all that he was quoted in one interview as saying with surprising bitterness that the United States was attempting to win the war in Korea 'without even trying.' Perhaps he will deny the accuracy of that quotation. At any rate it does serve to indicate a new maturity and a depth of perception he lacked in the past. Thumping Theodore lived baseball twenty-four hours a day and left the global thinking to others."[19]

"I was angry when I said that stuff the other day," Ted told reporters in a press conference when he first landed in the continental United States.[20] "I popped off a few weeks ago about conditions there, but I was in a mood. As for the flying and of the Korea War, I never met such a great bunch of fellows with such a willingness to do a job. When I left the fellows were griping for more missions."[21]

COMING HOME

Word that Williams would be coming home peppered the papers for weeks. In fact, it started months before it ever became a reality. "Writer Says Williams May Get Out," read the headline in the *Pacific Stars and Stripes*. An AP report from April 19, 1953 reported that Ted had written Bill Churchman, his instructor at Willow Grove, and Joe Cashman of the *Boston Record* quoted Churchman as telling him, "Ted wrote me that his ears clogged up in the fast descent when his plane was hit, took a nose dive and caught on fire in Korea and that his hearing has been impaired since. I'm inclined to think it's only a temporary condition, but it may be that he's hiding his ailment from his superiors. He's that kind of a great and game guy. I could read between the lines of his letter and could see that he was champing at the bit on that hospital ship. He wants action always and always wants to be top man at whatever he's doing. And believe me, he's a top man in the air just as he was a top man in baseball." Churchman added, "But if there's anything wrong with his hearing which can't be cured and it's discovered, his career as a Marine will soon be at an end and he'll be able to return to baseball this season."[22] The press had noted his pneumonia, but this was the first story about the ear condition.

By early June, well aware of the ongoing truce talks, Ted wrote his business manager, Fred Corcoran, that he hoped to be able to return Stateside in time to "give baseball a whirl before the season ends. Then, if I can hit .300, I'd like to keep playing for at least two more years."[23] Jack Barry noted in the *Globe* that Williams was due for discharge in early September but that he had compiled a "fine flying record and would be eligible for a quicker discharge." The letter Ted wrote Corcoran was written while Ted was on the tarmac on CAP alert. "I am writing this from my plane," he had written. "It's my letter a month to you. We are on the alert, but I want to get it off to you." Corcoran said that Ted had never thought he'd been able to play in '53, but now had begun to consider the possibility of play before the season was out. If he couldn't hack it at hitting, Corcoran said, Williams would concentrate on his 25% interest in the Southern Tackle Company of Miami, a recent investment. The company had done a million dollars' worth of business in 1952.[24]

A little over two weeks later, the word was that Williams was done. The *Boston Herald* of June 27, 1953 reported "No More Combat for Williams," explaining that a Marine spokesman in Korea said that he "probably will fly no more combat missions." An earlier report from the Personnel Department of the Marine Corps in Washington had said that he would not be kept in the Corps after September 1. Later that day, an AP report from 1st Marine Air Wing headquarters said that "Marine flight surgeons have ordered baseball star Ted Williams to the United States for treatment of an ear and nose ailment." He would be sent to a hospital in the United States. By using some accumulated leave, it was possible that Ted would be discharged earlier than the September date.

This announcement kicked off a daily status report that tracked Ted across the Pacific and across the country. The June 28 *Washington Post* explained that he had suffered a blockage "in his eustachian tube, between the nose and ears, after a sudden descent of his plane during combat. It has affected his hearing and his sense of balance, making it impossible for him to continue as a jet fighter, at least temporarily." The *Post* noted that Williams had been grounded on June 10 and under medical observation since that time, and that just the previous week Williams had been awarded three Air Medals for his duty. The paper anticipated his arrival any day at a West Coast Navy hospital.

If it is correct that he was grounded the day of his abort, that would prompt further speculation.

The *New York Times* noted on June 29 that Ted had packed his flight gear and prepared to head home, to "undergo radium treatments at a Navy hospital." Where Boston manager Lou Boudreau had guessed a couple of days earlier that "it would not take him long to get in shape," Williams himself said, "There's no use kidding myself. It would take a lot of sweat and a lot of time to get back in condition. I don't know if the Red Sox would want an old man like me... I'm almost 35 and I haven't played ball in a long time. I haven't even had a bat in my hand, except once

Ted Williams in Hawaii on his way back to the United States. July 8, 1953.
Courtesy of The Sporting News/Zuma Press.

when I was hitting flies to some of the boys, and I haven't done any throwing." Except for the occasional krondyking, one assumes. "The first thing I'm going to do is go fishing someplace. No more planes, no more rank, just fishing. Baseball? I just don't know." He said he wanted to see his daughter, who'd learned to swim while he was away. "I've never seen such a country for catching cold," he lamented, noting as well his narrow escape from death in the February crash-landing. "It was an act of God that the plane didn't blow up when it caught on fire. I'd hate to go through those minutes again."[25]

A photo ran in the June 29 *Globe* on page 1, showing Ted packing a trunk to come home.

A Marine spokesman said that Williams would head for Oak Knoll Hospital near San Francisco and that from that point on, "It's up to the doctors."[26]

A dispatch on July 1 informed readers that Williams landed in Japan, and was at the Marine Supply Squadron at Itami. The following day, a spokesman reported Ted was in southern Japan for a "rest and relaxation leave," visiting Kyoto while waiting for a flight back. He managed to elude the press for at least a few days. An INS story was headed "Ted Disappears in Japan." The lead ran, "Marine authorities were sure Captain Ted Williams was 'somewhere in Japan' today but that was as close as they could pin-point the whereabouts of the lanky baseball star. Williams arrived at Itami airbase in central Japan from Korea late last night and has not been seen since." The base Public Information Officer, perhaps somewhat disingenuously, said, "It's the strangest thing. I've been looking everywhere but he just isn't around. No one has seen him in the officers' club or bar." Ted had somehow managed to head off to Kyoto, rather than hang around the base. [27]

On July 7, he arrived at Barbers Point Naval Air Station in Honolulu. A report from Washington on the same day indicated that he could become a civilian within 10 to 14 days if the ear trouble might require long-term treatment. His case, it was noted, was now out of the hands of the Marine Corps and was one which would be settled by the United States Navy Bureau of Medicine and Surgery.

Col. Ray Crist of the USMC Public Information Office indicated that Ted could request and be granted transfer to a hospital near his home or, if the prognosis was indefinite (meaning the length of treatment indeterminate), he could ask to be separated from the service. "This is merely a routine request and it is granted automatically," Crist explained. Only if it were found that his condition could be cleared up within a short period of time would he be held in the Corps until his scheduled separation in October. One way or the other, he wouldn't be returned to combat duty in Korea.

From Honolulu, Ted flew to Moffett Field, San Francisco on a trans-Pacific DC-4. There was a full hour press conference on his arrival, before he went to USMC HQ in San Francisco to have his orders endorsed to Oak Knoll Naval Hospital. He praised his fellow pilots in combat: "I never saw so much eagerness and enthusiasm in going on a hop as among Marine pilots. You would think they were going after ice cream and soda." Ted might have been enjoying a little extra ice cream himself; he was 210 pounds now, 10 pounds overweight. He said he hadn't lifted a bat for a year and "firmly ruled out any possibility that he would return to baseball this season."[28] He did characterize his overall health as "pretty good" and explained that it was only at high altitudes that he experienced difficulties with his ears. Williams reminded reporters that major leaguer Lloyd Merriman was still serving with the Marines as a fighter pilot.

"My ear trouble began as soon as I got to Korea," he said, "I came down with colds and then pneumonia and the ear trouble developed. We have to fly high. It was one continual session in the infirmary. I guess my hearing is impaired and that may improve things as far as those left field bleachers are concerned." Ted was remembering his war with the leather-lunged antagonists in Fenway's left-field seats.

It was only much later that he confided in Johnny Pesky a tale about a time his congestion may have nearly killed him. "He nearly cracked up after blacking out at 17,000 feet without oxygen. He fell 15,000 feet before regaining consciousness and pulled out at tree-top level. He said it scared the giblets out of him."[29]

He was back home now, back from the war zone. Ted's arrival in California prompted a lot of activity. A squadron of MPs were present, "assigned, obviously, so they could see Williams rather than for the necessity of keeping order." Several hundred sailors found excuses to be in the area. Ted had arrived with 30 other Korean veterans. Aviation mechanic Ramon Rodriques said, "Captain Williams was a good companion. I came all the way from Tokyo with him." Ted was the last to leave the plane. "It seems wonderful to get home again," Ted said. "I only regret that more of the men couldn't come with me... Never in my life have I met such a great bunch of men." Then Ted acknowledged that he never truly quite meshed with the other Marines as well as he might have: "I only wish I fitted in better into their ways and feelings."[30]

He said he'd followed baseball via radio and *The Sporting News* while in Korea, and that there was a great deal of interest in the game, even more than there had been in World War II. As to the one time he'd held a bat, that was in large part due to a lack of equipment, he said. Noting that Merriman was on the same base, Ted explained that one time the commanding officer "decided that we two should show the boys a few things one afternoon a week if we had all our duties completed. But we found there were only 12 balls on the station and the field was rough. It was decided that it would be better for as many men as possible to throw them around rather than stuff them all up in one afternoon with us hitting. So that was the only time I had a bat in my hands."[31]

During his press conference, he took a phone call from the *Boston Herald*'s Arthur Sampson. Sampson had phoned at an inopportune time, as the Moffett operator explained. "Captain Ted Williams has just landed. He's surrounded by about a hundred reporters. He's been speaking over several radio stations. He's had to go on television. I don't think he can answer the phone right now." Sampson asked her to tell him that "an old man chewing an old cigar wanted to welcome him home." Ted yelled to the reporters, "You fellows will have to wait a minute. There's a guy on the phone I've got to bawl out." He then complained to Sampson, "Where were all those letters you promised to write to Korea? As soon as The Kid leaves the country you forget all about him." Sampson explained that he had indeed been a faithful correspondent, at which point Williams changed the subject: "How are the Red Sox doing with the Yankees this afternoon?"[32]

Sampson said the Sox were beating the New Yorkers, but that he himself was in Boston resting up for a trip to the All-Star Game in Cincinnati. Ted replied, "If I can make it, I'd like to see that All-Star game. Do you think you could get me a ticket? Who's hot this year anyway, Rosen, Berra, Mantle, I suppose. Any new guys around who can hit?"

As if Ted Williams would need someone to get him a ticket to the All-Star Game!

Sampson asked him if he was coming back to play ball in 1953. "How do I know?" he answered. "I'm not in a position to make any such decision. I'm still in the Marine Corps... My plans are simple. They're made for me." He added, "I don't know when I'll be released. I don't know whether I can hit a ball or catch one. I don't even know whether Yawkey, Cronin and Boudreau want me around. They're building a new team with kids. They may not want an old man around. I'm 35."

Williams and Sampson bantered back and forth a bit, Sampson telling Williams to stop asking questions of him and start answering some of the ones posed to him; after all, Sampson reminded him more than once, Sampson was the one paying for the call. "All right," Ted shot back. "Take down the following notes. The Kid is back home. He had 39 combat missions overseas. He's going to try to get to that hospital in Oakland sometime before the afternoon is over. He's happy to see the Red Sox doing so well. He's like to see the All-Star game. He'd like to play baseball again if he can. If he can't, he'll go fishing or something. And that's all there is to it so far as I know as of this moment. When I find out where I'm going I'll call you up and let you know. Maybe I'll see you in Cincinnati next Tuesday. Who knows? And now that I've kept those guys waiting 30 minutes, I'll get back to my interviewers. I wouldn't mind, but I haven't had any lunch."[33]

Ted's medical checkout was brief. "Once I got there, they said the hell with it, and mustered me out."[34]

Boston Red Sox outfielder Ted Williams arrives from Korea at Moffett Field in Sunnyvale, CA on July 9, 1953.
Photo by The Sporting News/ZUMA Press.

NOTES

1) Boston Globe, *June 27, 1953.*

2) *Interview with Bill Clem, December 23, 2002.*

3) *Ibidem.*

4) *Interview with James Fox, February 8, 2003.*

5) *Interview with Milton Rugg, December 18, 2002.*

6) *Ibidem.*

7) *Interview with James Walley, December 7, 2002.*

8) *Interview with Dale Purcell, December 12, 2002.*

9) *Ibidem.*

10) Boston Evening American, *January 7, 1958.*

11) *Interview with Tom Ross, October 1, 2002.*

12) *Interview with Jerry Coleman, April 5, 1997.*

13) Memphis Commercial Appeal, *March 21, 1965.*

14) *Steven R. Bullock*, Playing for Their Nation, *Lincoln & London: University of Nebraska Press, 2004, pp. 97, 98. DiMaggio argued that he "didn't enlist to play baseball" but whether he meant it or it was a remark made for public consumption is hard to discern. In any event, he played a lot of baseball in the service, and even slow-pitch softball.*

15) *Interview with Woody Woodbury, October 1, 2002.*

16) *Bill Cunningham*, Boston Herald, *July 3, 1953.*

17) *Bill Cunningham*, Boston Herald, *July 4, 1953.*

18) *John J. Casserly, "Lashes Attitude on Korea War,"* Boston Record-American, *June 29, 1953.*

19) New York Times, *July 2, 1953. Daley, interestingly, volunteered a comment on another facet of the Williams persona – his profanity. He wrote, "In his Red Sox uniform he liked to pose as a tough guy. On occasions he'd even be unnecessarily profane, almost as if he were afraid his good looks made him appear a sissy and he had to prove to the other kids that he was as much a down-to-earth roughneck as they were. At least that's the impression he always gave this observer. Yet he's the same fellow who secretly visited Boston hospitals and talked baseball to sick or crippled kids for hour after hour, charming them along the road back to health with his tenderness and sincerity. A psychiatrist would have trouble in unraveling Williams' tangled complexes."*

20) Boston Globe, *July 10, 1953.*

21) *Jack McDonald*, The Sporting News, *July 15, 1953.*

22) Pacific Stars and Stripes, *April 19, 1953.*

23) Boston Globe, *June 10, 1953.*

24) *Ibidem.*

25) New York Times, *June 29, 1953.*

26) New York Times, *June 30, 1953.*

27) *INS news report, July 2, 1953.*

28) New York Times, *July 10, 1953.*

29) *Cataneo, David, "Ted Williams Remembers",* Boston Herald, *May 26, 1997.*

30) Boston Globe, *July 10, 1953.*

31) *Ibidem.*

32) Boston Herald, *July 10, 1953.*

33) *Ibidem.*

34) *Freeze, Di, "Remembering the "Splendid Splinter",* Centennial Aviation and Business Journal, *August 2002.*

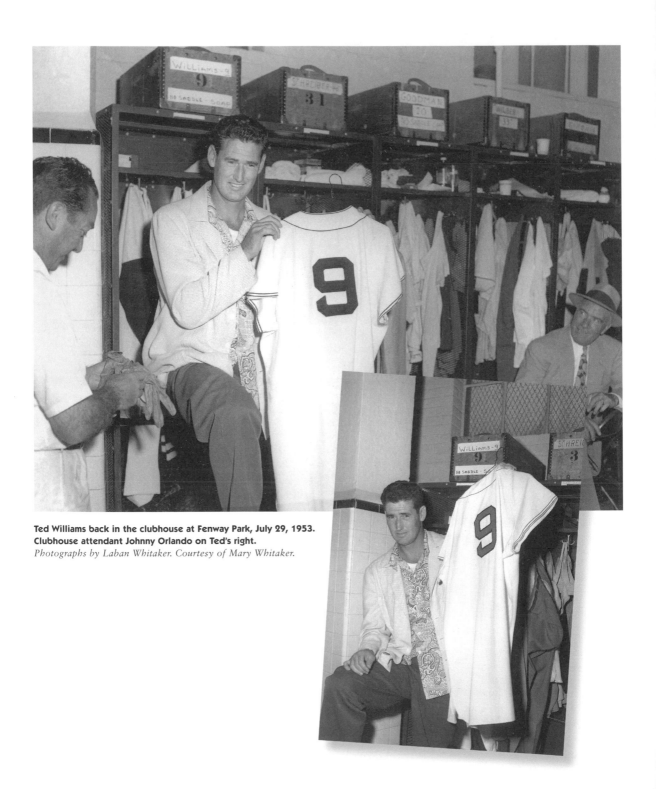

Ted Williams back in the clubhouse at Fenway Park, July 29, 1953.
Clubhouse attendant Johnny Orlando on Ted's right.
Photographs by Laban Whitaker. Courtesy of Mary Whitaker.

CHAPTER 17 – ALL-STAR GAME AND BACK TO BASEBALL

The All-Star Game was held on July 14, 1953 at Crosley Field in Cincinnati. Ted's mention of the game made the national AP wire, and was no doubt brought to the attention of the Commissioner and the league presidents. An invitation wasn't long in coming. Commissioner Ford Frick invited him and his business manager, Fred Corcoran.

Ted talked to Red Sox GM Joe Cronin on July 10, and Cronin said Ted was already asking about the new pitchers in the American League. He laughed off the idea that the Red Sox wouldn't want an "old man" like Teddy Ballgame back in uniform. "Absolutely we want him back. What a shot in the arm he would be for this club," manager Lou Boudreau interjected. A number of players joined the chorus, and trainer Jack Fadden said, "His locker is waiting for him just like he left it. No one's used it since he left. Will we welcome him home? Why, man, we'll tear down the clubhouse doors."[1]

An AP report a couple of days later informed readers that Ted Williams had checked into Bethesda Naval Hospital on July 13 for the medical checkup that would determine his future tenure with the Marine Corps. Williams checked in, but that same evening took a train to Cincinnati for the All-Star Game. Upon his return, he expected a week to ten days of tests so that a medical board could determine his future.

In Washington, before leaving for Ohio, Ted talked with Bill Ahlberg of the *Washington Post*. Ahlberg reports that Ted told him, "There's always a chance that these doctors after the examinations could look at me and say, 'You're no good to us any more.'" The February crash, Ahlberg passed on, "had nothing to do with his ailment. He says he was troubled before he had the accident. 'I think I've always had the ear trouble, it was just brought out by the flying.'"

Of the crash, Ted said, "I got a sprained ankle out of it from pushing on the brakes. I didn't even have any brakes and I must have pushed down pretty hard. It was rough."

Ahlberg mentioned that Williams was "surprised he was brought back to the States. He thought he would be given some kind of a staff job until his tour was up. He was disturbed slightly by all the fuss that has been made over him and was wondering why a couple of other pretty good ball players in Korea never got any mention. 'Why, you never see anything about Merriman being in Korea,' he said. 'Or Coleman either. I bet you guys don't even know that Lloyd had a crash himself and almost was killed.'"

Ted grumbled, "Everywhere I go, it's a press conference."[2]

AT THE GAME

Tom Yawkey had a car waiting for Ted when his train pulled in, and Williams had breakfast with the Red Sox owner, Corcoran, and GM Joe Cronin. *The Herald* portrayed a scene that reads as though it foreshadowed Williams' 1999 All-Star Game appearance: "The players and the reporters on the field surrounded him as soon as he put in an appearance. Stengel, who usually is surrounded by reporters on his bench during batting practice suddenly found himself sitting alone. 'That guy Williams must have arrived,' he winked as he scanned the barren bench. 'I haven't been left so absolutely alone since he went into the service.' As soon as some of the fans noticed who was causing the excitement, they, too, rushed on to the field in quest of autographs."[3]

Williams had been give a treatment at Bethesda the day before, and then given a three-day pass before his next treatment was due. Tom Yawkey offered a few words on the question of whether Williams would be playing again for the Red Sox that year. "I'm tickled to death that Ted is back. Whether he plays baseball again or not is not the big issue with me. He has had some pretty narrow escapes. I'm thankful that he is back, and so should everybody else who knows him. I'm willing to let fate and time answer the other questions. The big thing is that he's back with us and is still alive."[4]

An unnamed *Washington Post* reporter covering the All-Star Game wrote that Ted arrived at Crosley Field one hour before the game began, "wearing a tweed sports jacket and a loud shirt open at the collar and a grin that spread from ear to ear. He was recognized immediately."

Dizzy Trout said hello to him and asked Ted, "Are you going to play today?" "I will if you will," Ted joked back. It was Trout who had surrendered the home run to Ted in his last at-bat before he rejoined the Marine Corps in 1952.

National League President Warren Giles pumped Ted's hand and told him, "Glad you could make it, and glad you can't play."

He signed autographs, but never stopped grinning the whole time. He was glad to be back. He got a laugh at one point by mistakenly referring to the dugout as the "cockpit."

Arthur Sampson's article in the *Boston Herald* was headlined, "Williams Given Greatest Ovation." Ted Williams, he wrote, "has dominated several All-Star Games with his bat. Today he dominated the 20th annual game of this mid-season series without his bat... [He] didn't get a chance to bat but he created far more excitement than anything that took place during the competition between the All-Star players of the two major leagues.

"The returning war hero received an ovation that lasted for several minutes, and he threw out the first pitch – a strike into the glove of Roy Campanella."[5]

Williams was given special treatment. He did not return to the stands to sit in the Commissioner's box, but was given dispensation to sit on the American League bench as "an honorary member of the team." Ted brought a camera and took about 50 photographs from the dugout during the game, and "got a big kick out of bantering with his former teammates and many of his cherished rivals on the diamond." Unfortunately, most of Ted's photographs – like those he himself took in Korea – were all destroyed by a hurricane that washed through his house on the Keys later in the 1950s.

After the game, Ted said he regretted breaking up batting practice by entering the field. "I thought I could sneak in there," he told a reporter. "Ted," the reporter replied, "You couldn't sneak through a graveyard."

Ted was a "star among stars" who "was only a spectator but he obviously stole the show," wrote Arthur Daley. It was a "hero's welcome," wrote *The Sporting News*, which also reported Yankee Yogi Berra's job offer. "In Japan," Yogi said. "You can be our interpreter for our barnstorming squad." "No, thanks," Ted answered. "I'm back in this country to stay – I hope."[6]

It almost seemed like an afterthought that Ted mentioned at one point, "When I get my next three-day leave next week, I hope to be able to go home to Miami to see my family."[7]

How did this all go over back at K-3? As noted earlier, Bill Clem expresses at least one view. "I flew 86 missions over there. We came over on the same plane, and he came back... he was home by the time of the All-Star Game. We were all mad at him. It was a big deal. He was the big hero being at the All-Star Game and here we're still over there fighting the damn war, and he's home. That didn't sit too good." Clem did not say this with any bitterness, or expressing any anger. In fact, he said throughout his interviews that he liked Ted. No doubt there was a bit of understandable envy and irritation, though.[8]

It was on July 23 that the word was given: Ted Williams was to be released from duty immediately on discharge from the hospital, set for August 1. Marine Corps headquarters announced that it was policy to release reserve officers returning from overseas duty if they have less than three months to serve in their tours. "Tell the Boston fans to get their lungs warmed up," Ted said. "It looks like I'll be back." Even the ever-present razzing he expected to get from the fans who loved to taunt him wasn't going to faze Williams now. He wanted to get back in the game.

Karl Olson was also returning to the Red Sox. He appeared in five games in 1951, but then had been taken into the Army. Ted said that he and Olson were in the same boat; they'd both have to see if they still had what it took. Both did. Olson hit a ninth-inning double for the Sox on August 23, the game-winning hit in a 5-4 win over the Senators.

On July 27, 1953 the Armistice was signed, ending hostilities in Korea. It was on the 27th that VMF-311 flew its final mission of the Korean War.

Perhaps now that the Armistice had finally been signed, Ted's release date was pushed up a few days. The very day after the Armistice, on July 28, the Marine Corps "ordered" Capt. Ted Williams back to Fenway Park. Col. Kenneth B. Chappell issued Ted his deactivation papers in a small 9:30 a.m. ceremony at the Naval Gun Factory in Washington, and after Ted praised the Corps and the "wonderful bunch" of fellows he met in Korea, Chappell in turn praised Williams as an "inspiration to thousands and thousands of young men." Then, with a wink, Chappell pronounced, "These papers order you back to your home in Fenway Park."[9]

Ted had been given a complete bill of health, except that he could no longer pilot jet aircraft. Part of his problem was one of allergies, he said, adding that the doctors decided not to proceed with the radium treatment, since he wasn't going to be flying and because it might produce adverse effects.

Various newspapers expected him to take the train to Boston and appear that evening in the game at Fenway Park, perhaps to start working out with the team the following day. It was all happening a little too quickly, though; Ted learned of his impending discharge from a news report. He was staying at the Hotel Statler in Washington, not in a Marine Corps facility. Ted planned to drive north with an "old school friend" named Tom Johnson who "just happened to be around." He guessed he'd probably show up sometime after the game was underway.

He emphasized to the *Washington Post*'s Jack Walsh, "One thing I can't go for is any 'hero' stuff. I know I'm no hero. All right, I flew 39 missions – I know too many others who flew 100 and more. It's funny. I got a letter from a pal of mine in North Carolina. He flew 100 missions. Seems he got home and tried to get a better job. Didn't have any luck, though. There he is back doing just what he had been doing before he went to Korea. Nobody cares what he did over there. Just because I happened to be in baseball, it seems to be big news. Well, I'm not kidding myself and I'm not going to kid anyone else."[10]

That expression of sentiment is consistent with everything Ted ever said in the years that followed – there were plenty of others who were the real heroes.

After his discharge, Ted returned to Bethesda Naval Hospital – as a civilian – to visit Lt. Col. Walter Bartosh, who had been hurt in a May 24 helicopter crack-up in Korea and arrived at Bethesda just the day before.

Williams could well have shown up in his Marine Corps uniform at the All-Star Game; he was still in the service at the time. White Sox GM Frank Lane told a friend at the time, "Put yourself in his place. He was fresh back from Korea, where they had been fighting a rugged war and where he had seen considerable action. Not only that, he had a real close call while flying a jet in combat. He would have been a handsome figure of a man in his Marine uniform, with ribbons on his chest. But he came out to Crosley Field in civilian clothes – sport coat, sport short open at the throat – just as he has always dressed. I couldn't help thinking... how much I admired him for coming that way. None of that hero stuff for him."[11]

Capt. Ted Williams, USMCR, receives a final salute from a sentry as he leaves the Naval Gun Factory, Washington DC, after receiving the papers which place him on in active duty. July 28, 1953.
Photograph by PFC M. Sesera.
Courtesy of National Archives and Records Administration.

Massachusetts Governor Christian Herter issued a statement anticipating Williams' return to work in Boston. "We hope you hit .400," he concluded. Little did he know that Ted would do just that.

Expecting to see Ted, the largest crowd of the year crammed into Fenway that evening, some 35,385. Williams, though, had stopped overnight in Scarsdale, New York to go over some business at Fred Corcoran's office there.

On the 29th, Ted turned up and signed his contract for what remained of the '53 season. He out-foxed the fans by entering the park via Fenway's front door, rather than using the players' parking lot. His first words to Tom Yawkey and Joe Cronin were, "I'm happy to be back," he said, "and I'm lucky to be back. It will be great when we get the rest of those guys back from Korea."[12] It didn't take long to sign on with the Sox for the rest of the season. "The terms are a military secret," joked Cronin. Within four minutes, the League office and the Commissioner's office had both approved the contract.

Early bird fans saw Ted in his #9 uniform take some fielding practice very early on, but he eschewed batting practice until after the game. After the daytime crowd had dispersed, Williams took the field for a little late batting practice and hit a few – including one into the bullpen and another into the right-field stands. He drew a blister, and so brought the session to a halt. He said he felt like a rookie all over again, "just as young as I did when I came here 12 or 13 years ago."

A sportswriter asked Ted if he'd missed the press while he was overseas. "Terrifically," he frowned. A few minutes later, he "snarled a mock complaint to a radio man, 'You've had that microphone under my chin since I got here. See you later!'"[13]

Getting ready to get back into action wasn't easy. It would take some time. Food for Marine pilots was good in Korea; Ted said he was ten pounds heavier than when he'd left for the service and he was having a hard time taking it off. "My hands keep getting sore and I can't hit batting practice for more than ten minutes at a time." There was a lot of talk at the time about batting helmets; asked if he'd ever worn one, he said, "I never felt the need to. I always figured I needed a helmet more in left field than at the plate." Despite that reference to some of Fenway's fans, Ted said he wanted to say with baseball as long as he could be useful and that he wanted to finish out his career with the Red Sox. "I'm glad that I was never traded to the Yankees."[14]

"I'm stiff," Ted said. "I haven't swung a bat in nearly two years and I don't want to get in there and hurt the club because I'm not ready." Harold Kaese explained that the only time he had swung a bat was once in Korea when he and Lloyd Merriman had hit some fly balls to Marine Corps flyers. "I was sore for two weeks," Ted had said.[15]

Paul Schreiber was ready. Schreiber was a Red Sox coach who was Williams' favorite batting practice pitcher. Between World War II and Korea, he'd thrown more home run balls to Ted Williams than any other pitcher – a total estimated at around 1,000 homers. Schreiber said, "Williams is always serious when hitting in practice, which may explain the excellent use he has made of his talent. His timing is so exceptional that he can often meet the ball squarely even though fooled. His hands and wrists are so strong that he can reach out and pull a fastball on the outside to right field. He has unusual body control, which enables him to get hips and shoulders into the game's most flexible swing." [16]

Ted took a bit of time coming back, easing in with a few pinch-hitting appearances. He took batting practice wearing golf gloves – and thereby pioneered the use of batting gloves, which today is more common that not. On August 9, he hit his first home run, before a hometown crowd, and received an ovation that Lou Boudreau called "the greatest he ever heard given a ball player." It was on a 3-1 count, off Mike Garcia, struck in a pinch-hitting role in the bottom of the seventh inning. Number 325 of his major league career. "It felt good. It felt real good," Ted acknowledged, though he still didn't want to play regularly until he got up to strength. He'd only been back twelve days. "This one was nice, but it didn't win the game." It was quite a drive, though, over the Red Sox bullpen in right.[17]

Harry Jones, writing for the *Cleveland Plain Dealer*, suggested that Cleveland's 9-3 victory was almost forgotten by the Boston crowd in its delirium. For many of the 26,966, it was (he wrote) "the baseball thrill of a lifetime." Williams had been flying jets in Korea not that many weeks earlier, but now he "hit a jet-propelled missile more than 400 feet in his second pinch-hitting assignment since his return and the roar that followed was of atomic proportions." Ted himself was a "loose-jointed figure, one of the game's truly great performers, loping around the bases while the crowd, standing and waving madly, cheered with intensity that may never again be equaled... The instant he walked up the steps to the dugout, swinging two bats, the fans leaped to their feet and began applauding, shouting, roaring. The noise was deafening, and it continued as Williams walked toward the plate and stood there, watching Garcia.

"Presently, Williams stepped into the batter's box and a hush fell over the audience. He let the first pitch go by and it was a ball. The second pitch was also low for ball two. Then the third pitch and the third ball, high and inside. Now the fans booed. They didn't want to see Williams walked, they wanted to see him hit and they implored Garcia to get the ball over the plate. So he did. The next offering was right down the middle, Williams took it and the count went to 3-1." Jones must have been thinking of "Casey at the Bat" as he wrote his column.

"With the crowd silent again, Mike slowly wound up and delivered. Williams, fidgety as always, watched the pitch carefully and then swung. The crack of the bat was unmistakable. It was a home run, high over the Boston bullpen and into the right field bleachers. The din that followed must have been heard in Seoul and all points between here and there. Williams trotted around the bases, was greeted by all members of the Red Sox, who had left the dugout and were standing on the field, and still the fans roared.

"They roared for at least two minutes after his historic blast, perhaps in the expectation that he would oblige with an encore. And that was the ballgame. Nothing else mattered – not the Cleveland victory, though long-awaited, nor the Red Sox defeat. Williams' home run was only one of four hit in this game, but the other three by comparison were mere pop flies."[18]

A separate story reported that "Williams showered quickly and left the park before sports writers could talk with him."

It wasn't until a few days later, though, on August 14, that Ted would say, "Today for the first time, I feel I've got it again." On the 16th, he cracked the starting lineup for the first time, and hit both a double and a home run.

Maureen Cronin has always said that Ted Williams excelled on land (at baseball), in the air (as a Marine Corps pilot), and at sea (as a world-class fisherman now recognized in three fishing halls of fame). She might well have mentioned Ted's nearly unparalleled role as a fundraiser fighting cancer in children, with his 50 years of work for the Jimmy Fund.

A triumphal "Welcome Home" dinner was scheduled in Ted's honor, a $100-a-plate dinner to benefit the Jimmy Fund. Though Ted had made appearances to help Dr. Sidney Farber raise money for his Children's Cancer Research Foundation as early as 1947, the Jimmy Fund had been the official charity of the Boston Braves baseball team since 1948. Earlier in 1953, though, just days before the season opened, the Braves picked up stakes and moved to Milwaukee. When Williams had been invited back to the Marine Corps, Boston had been a two-team city. The Braves had preceded the Red Sox in Boston by a quarter-century. Now they were gone, and Lou Perini and the Braves had passed the Jimmy Fund baton to Tom Yawkey and the Red Sox. With Williams' homecoming, Ted became the leading face of the fundraising effort for the fifty years.

The August 17 banquet netted $150,000 for the Jimmy Fund, a tremendous sum by the standards of the day. The dinner at Boston's Hotel Statler dinner was so successful in part because of the $50,000 check presented to Ted by Edward M. "Ted" Kennedy on behalf of the Joseph P. Kennedy, Jr. Foundation. Another ingredient in the success was Ted's condition for consenting to the dinner – no one was to get in free to the benefit – and he insisted on paying $100 for his own dinner, too.

The *New York Times*' Arthur Daley wrote, anticipating Ted's return: "The Boston sportswriters, forced into daily contact with him, feuded with him constantly. His loathing for them was monumental."[19] Any brief honeymoon with Boston's baseball writers upon his return was only that. Speaking of honeymoons, no information has been garnered regarding Williams taking out time to be with his wife and daughter upon his return from the service.

Williams was welcomed around the league, though. His first game in Cleveland was, coincidentally, on his birthday, as the Red Sox played a 1:30 p.m. doubleheader against the Indians. The program sold by the Indians at Municipal Stadium noted that Williams "will make his first appearance in Cleveland since being discharged by the Marines. The Boston slugger has been a very popular performer here and is expected to receive a rousing welcome."[20]

Even more interestingly, the Indians score card ran a full page ad with a photograph of Ted, headlined "Welcome Back, Ted... but please don't kill us." The caption on the photo reads: "The Cleveland Baseball club and all baseball fans in this area are very happy to welcome back to the Stadium Boston's heavy-hitting outfielder, Ted Williams, who has just returned from active flying duty in Korea, with the U. S. Marines. Although we are certain that there will be many occasions in the future when we will wish that Williams were in some remote outpost of the world like Pago-Pago, Borneo or the South Pole, instead of stepping into the batter's box, nevertheless, we wish him well and hope he continues to be one of baseball's shining stars."[21]

Page from Cleveland Indians game program September 1953, welcoming Ted Williams back from the Marines.
Collection of Bill Nowlin.

Ted had a spectacular season, hitting up a storm in limited action. He had 91 at-bats in 37 games, and walked 19 times. He had 37 hits, but a full 13 of those were home runs. Extend that ratio over his career and he would have wound up with 932 homers. By season's end, Ted had hit .400 again – his final average was .407, with an on-base percentage of .509 and a slugging percentage of .901. Deprived of most of the 1952 and 1953 seasons, Williams took advantage of the limited action he did have, hitting .400 in 1952 and .407 in 1953. On September 27, the final day of the season, the Red Sox played the New York Yankees at Yankee Stadium. Jerry Coleman had re-joined the Yankees (he appeared in eight games) and Ted Williams was with the Red Sox. In the team dressing rooms that day, Grumman Aircraft presented both Marine pilots "handsome, wooden scale models of the Panther. The inscription on the base of Williams' Panther read: 'The trail you blazed in Korea has reflected brilliantly on the entire sports world. Your combat record in the Panther jet is a source of pride to all of us. We salute an outstanding American – The Grumman Family.'"[22]

"I find it difficult to explain how I did so well after being away so long," Williams said. "Maybe it was because we were in the real hot weather of the summer and you know how I like it. The pitchers may have been a little tired and I was fresh physically."[23]

Later in 1953, Ted added another championship to his year's accomplishments: he took individual honors in the International Sailfish Tournament at West Palm Beach, Florida. [24]

One war was over. Another one was underway: on January 24, 1954, Ted's wife Doris sued for separation support, charging that he beat, used obscene language, and abused her.[25]

1954 was not at all a happy year. On the first day of spring training, Ted fell trying to catch a fly ball and broke his collarbone. He was operated on several days later, on March 9, and was discharged from the hospital a week after that. In a *Saturday Evening Post* article, Williams wrote that he was "getting near the age when ball players begin to go downhill," that he would be 36 in October (he was still maintaining the fiction that his birthday was in October, not during the baseball season in August), and that this would be his final year.[26]

When he was able to play, he turned in a creditable season.

Including 1954, though, Williams was to play seven more years of major league baseball. He would go on to win two more batting championships, in 1957 and 1958, and to win election to the National Baseball Hall of Fame. It was never easy. He was beset with injuries, colds, a pinched nerve, and other physical ills. After Korea, he added 197 home runs to his totals and 575 more runs batted in. The Boston Red Sox, though, never challenged for the pennant again, until seven years after Williams retired in 1960. With substandard players surrounding him in the lineups, Ted never knocked in as many as 100 runs again, despite never failing to knock in 100 in the years before Korea (the sole exception was the 97 RBIs in 1950, the year he broke his elbow in the All-Star Game).

NOTES

1) *Cronin and Boudreau quotations both come from the* Boston Herald, *July 11, 1953.*

2) *Bill Ahlberg, "Ted Williams Would Like to Hit One Now," Washington Post, July 14, 1953.*

3) Boston Herald, *July 15, 1953.*

4) *Ibidem.*

5) Boston Herald, *July 15, 1953.*

6) The Sporting News, *July 22, 1953.*

7) Boston Herald, *July 15, 1953.*

8) *Interview with Bill Clem, December 23, 2002.*

9) New York Times, *July 29, 1953.*
   Actually, Ted showed up 15 minutes late for the ceremony, but no one seems to have held it against him.

10) Washington Post, *July 28, 1953.*

11) Christian Science Monitor, *July 29, 1953.*

12) Boston Record-American, *July 30, 1953.*

13) *Ibidem.* The Sporting News *of August 5, 1953 has an amusing cartoon by Darvas, showing a smiling Ted Williams unable to hear the boos of fans.*

14) *Gene Ward,* New York Mirror, *August 12, 1953.*

15) Boston Globe, *July 28, 1953.*

16) *Ibidem.*

17) The Sporting News, *August 19, 1953.*

18) *Harry Jones,* Cleveland Plain Dealer, *August 10, 1953.*

19) New York Times, *July 2, 1953.*

20) Indian News, *Vol. 7, No. 5, September 1953.*

21) *Ibidem.*

22) Plane News, *October 8, 1953.*

23) *Unattributed news column in National Baseball Hall of Fame archives.*

24) *News report December 11, 1953.*

25) *UPI report in* New York Times, *January 24, 1954.*

26) *Ted Williams as told to Joe Reichler and Joe Trimble,*
   "This Is My Last Year in Baseball", Saturday Evening Post, *April 7, 1954.*

Ted Williams and Dave Tolle at Seoul, May, 1953.
Courtesy of Dave Tolle.

CHAPTER 18 – WILLIAMS AND HIS FELLOW MARINES

Ted Williams the ballplayer was widely admired by his fellow players – teammates and opponents alike. It wasn't just admiration for his skill as a hitter. Most of those who played the game genuinely liked him, even if he did tend to be aloof off the field. He was typically generous with his time, and sometimes his money, when it came to helping others in the game – players, coaches, and umpires.

Ted Williams the Marine seems to have engendered a wider variety of feeling – ranging from positive to very negative – even within his own squadron. Given his fame, it's not surprising, either, that there are stories attributed to Williams which never happened.

As a man who has sometimes taken on legendary status, there are many stories about him – the time he crash-landed his plane in a creek bed, the time he chewed out an M.P., and so forth – which are told with certainty by otherwise-credible people. Yet when one tries to get more details or verify the account, it often doesn't pan out. Not only that, from time to time a given event is cited – even with considerable detail – that simply could not have occurred.

For instance, the 3 February 1953 raid on Ungok. The 5th Marine Regiment, under Col. Lew Walt, was determined to take two hills named Ungok and Kumgok in the code-named Operation Clambake. Lee Ballenger, a very respected author who has contributed greatly to our understanding of Marine combat in Korea, relied on a Marine tank commander named Ken Miller and offered the following convincing bit of history:

Pilots slated to conduct air strikes were briefed on the plan of maneuver and afforded the opportunity to walk the MLR where they noted actual targets from the ground. Attending this briefing was Capt. Ted Williams, professional baseball player turned Marine aviator. He later wrote, 'The raid was a big one. We were told there could be as many as 10,000 Chinese encamped behind their lines. As always, they'd be camouflaged damn well. Those bastards could hide in a bath tub. This meant we'd be dropping "daisy cutters," a very potent antipersonnel bomb.' At the briefing, one of the tank commanders, S/Sgt. Ken Miller, recalls Captain Williams remarked that the commander would be advised to lower the radio antenna on his tank if he didn't want it severed by a low-flying Corsair.

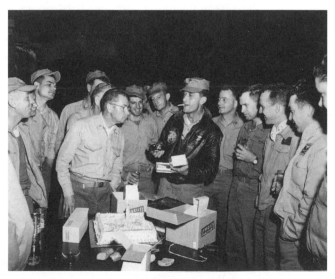

Marines celebrate on base. Ted is likely in the darkroom.
Courtesy of Russ Kelly.

The Williams quotation comes from an interview done with Henry Berry, which appears on page 263 in Berry's book *Hey Mac, Where Ya Been?* Ken Miller's account came from a first-person interview with the late Miller, by Lee Ballenger.

This could not have happened, at least in that time and place. First of all, Williams didn't fly Corsairs in Korea; he exclusively flew jets, one model or other of the F9F Panther. Secondly, and more conclusively, Williams' endorsement papers demonstrate that he only arrived in Korea from Japan on the very day of the raid on Ungok, formally reporting on 3 February at 1445 hours. The raid commenced at first light. Capt. Williams could not have participated in a tour of the Main Line of Resistance and a briefing conducted there the day before the raid.

The quotation from Williams seems to have been jumbled, too, in the way Berry presents it. Williams goes on to tell the story of how his plane was hit on this raid and how he was saved by Lieutenant Larry Hawkins. Ted was clearly telling Berry about the 16 February mission, but the way Berry presents it (not having seen the pre-edited transcript of his interview, it is hard to conjecture why this might have occurred), Ted indicates that his crash-landing happened after his stay on the hospital ship. We know that was not the case.

Another anecdote was found on a web site message board which gathered messages about the Marines in Korea. On March 24, 2002, Tommy Prater posted to the site. Prater had served with the MAG-33 Military Police. He wrote:

"I arrived at K-3 on July 29 1953 and was in the MP`s there until Sept of 54. They called me 'Tennessee' (when they weren't mad at me. LOL)

"My only claim to 'fame' was that Capt. Ted Williams chewed me out one night when he was on O.D. for having my hands in my pockets while on main gate duty.

"One night in Dec of 53, I and a KMC sergeant were on the midnight to 4 am main gate duty when we received a visit from the O.D. and his driver. I was standing in the darkness about 20 feet from the Guard Shack with my hands in my pockets, gloves and all, surveying the paddy that lay between us and the village of Pohang, because I thought I had heard a noise in the paddy. Sgt Cho, the KMC sergeant, was inside the guardshack. The O.D. and his driver came coasting up to us with lights out and motor off from inside the base. The O.D. was a long, tall captain, a marine pilot who had been grounded because of a medical problem and was pissed off because he had been put on O.D. during his grounding and chewed me out for a full 2 min for being away from my post and for having my hands in my pockets, although it was 1:45 am and was 6 below zero. When the captain stepped inside the guard shack to make a phone call, I asked the driver, who was actually in my squad, what the Captain`s name was. He said, 'The captain`s name is Ted Williams.' (Another one of my heroes) And oh, by the way, to cap this story off, I have since learned that Ted Williams' immediate superior officer was a Major by the name of John Glenn. I arrived at K-3 in Pohang Do on July 29,1953, 2 days after the armistice was signed and was in the MPs there until Nov of 54."[1]

Clearly, this never could have happened; contacted by this author, Prater agrees. The MP only arrived in Korea a month after Ted Williams was back in Boston working out with the Boston Red Sox. The day Prater arrived at K-3 was the day Williams arrived at Fenway and signed his contract; he had been formally discharged from the Marine Corps the day before. Prater's driver had erred. It may be worth clarifying that John Glenn was never Williams' superior officer; though he held a higher rank, they were both fellow pilots in VMF-311.

Those were two great stories – it's disappointing not to be able to cite them as fact. That the legend of the man would inspire such stories is itself noteworthy, but also a reminder that not every story one encounters is reliable. In the course of researching this book, at least a dozen instances turned up where Marines on the site recalled situations which could not be verified. In all fairness, it's been 50 years. A number of the stories are simple confusion of Williams with Marine pilot Jerry Coleman.

Ken Miller's story might have been one of those.

Then there was the story of how Ted crashed his plane a second time, in a creek bed right near K-3. Touched on earlier, that's a story we'll come back to in a later chapter.

How did Ted Williams get along with his fellow Marines on the base? It depends who you talk to. Some loved him. Some detested him. He tended to go his own way and keep to himself, and that didn't set well with some. Let's simply hear from a number of Marines and one can get an idea of the range of opinion. Whatever the diverse feelings about Ted are, pretty much everyone agrees that his arrival at K-3 was no big media event. Some heard that he was coming, maybe a day or two before he arrived, but Ted's actual appearance was not like the Second Coming. These were Marines at war, very active and centered men occupied with the business of combat. There might have been a bit of a ripple caused by Williams' integration into base life, but a number of people interviewed don't recall any anticipation and don't even recall the arrival of the four-time American League batting champion on their base. They more or less replied that it just happened that one day Williams was there. Likewise, when he left, it was a quiet, unheralded departure. One day, he simply was no longer there.

General Leo LeBlanc was a lieutenant in VMF-115 at the time, and one who flew in the 16 February mission. LeBlanc talked about Ted, saying, "There was just a few people that could talk to him. He was sort of a private guy. Trying to get near him, he wasn't all that approachable... The kids... the guys who were fixing his airplanes. They would have a beer bust or something and they'd invite him, and the next thing you know they'd have a softball and out they'd go. Merriman always did it, but Ted Williams to my knowledge, never did it. He was pretty good after he got out, though." LeBlanc agrees that Ted was a bit stand-offish: "He was loud. I didn't like him that much. Well... he wasn't boastful... but he was really loud. He was not my kind of guy."[2]

Leonard Waibel, line chief for 311, cited Ted's reluctance to play ball, too. "We tried to get him to play baseball, but he wouldn't do it. He would hit a few balls, and he'd throw the balls but he would not play baseball with us. He said he didn't want to be around all us crazy Marines, that we might hurt him. There might have been some sort of contract he had."[3]

For every person who characterized Williams as stand-offish, though, another had a different experience. Roger McCully, a crew chief (plane captain) at K-3, asked whether he'd describe Ted as stand-offish, answered, "No, no. When I talked to him... I talked to him several times... we used to talk fishing a lot. He used to go up to New Brunswick fishing. He didn't think himself special at all. He wasn't stand-offish at all. He was very, very friendly."[4]

Of course, McCully wasn't brass, and that might have colored Ted's approach. Ted sometimes mixed better with people he didn't really have to associate with as equals. With the brass, he liked some of them, but had little time for others. It all depended on his assessment of their motivations. Understandably, some higher-up who wanted to have dinner with Ted Williams – just to say he had – never earned Ted's respect.

And some of the regulars maybe got on Ted's nerves a bit, too.

Mike Canan (listed on VMF-311 squadron records as Christopher M. Canan) was a fellow pilot like LeBlanc, though Major Canan had a bit of rank on Williams. Canan explained, "He used to hum the Marine Corps Hymn every time I came in his face. He thought I was too gung ho, and I wanted him to do more."

[Wasn't that a little of rude of him, to hum that tune to you that way?] "Yeah, I kind of thought... but it was in jest. I know that he didn't like me that much, and that was his way of saying, 'You're gung ho. You go your way and I'll go mine.'"

[Would he give you an exaggerated salute, too, or something?] "Yeah, right. He was quite a character. I really feel sorry for Ted, and particularly now." Told that in later life, Ted always said how proud he was to have been a Marine, Mike said, "Well, that's nice. I'm glad to hear that. I had a different opinion of him."

Canan elaborated a bit more: "He was a loner. He never came to the club with us at all. I could understand his feelings, but it kind of irritated some people. It irritated me, and the people who were trying to do the job that was supposed to be done. He was kind of lackadaisical about it; he was kind of loose – he wasn't serious. He gave me the impression that he didn't care.

"He never did talk about himself, his stories. He'd maybe joke around with a group of people in the ready room, make a joke or something, or he would have some comment if somebody had said something. I never did know him to come to the club at all.

"The last time I saw Ted was in Washington DC and he was the manager of the baseball team. I went down to the dugout to say 'hi' to him, and he was rather cool. He never did like me too much."[5]

Even if Ted kept quiet, his demeanor may have conveyed a lack of respect. It may have gotten him in trouble, and may have soured his relationship with Barney McShane, his last C.O. in Korea.

Banshee Bob Johnson was a pilot with VMJ-1, which was based across the field at K-3. He expressed the way a lot of them appraised Williams. "Most of us understood that Ted was sort of a pissed-off guy there. Unhappy. It was just too bad. If he'd just said, 'Well, here I am. I'm stuck with it. Let's have fun doing it,' he'd have been a hell of a lot better. There's no doubt he had all the attributes and all the capability of an outstanding pilot." Johnson admits this was an impression, based on scuttle-butt. "I had no personal contact with him. As a result, all I can say is that any word that filtered over to us had probably been laundered six or seven times. I would guess that with anybody that reaches his stature in the world, there are going to be a million stories."[6]

Sometimes the size of the base did present obstacles. And, though Ted was very friendly with men like Ed Buchser in 115, sometimes the very fact of being in a different squadron may have been responsible for a bit of distance. George Banks was a lieutenant in VMF-115. He said, "I knew Ted Williams to say hello to. K-3 was a big base but his squadron, VMF-311 and mine, VMF-115, were quartered together, side by side, and shared the same mess and clubs. The only time I would be in his company was if we sat at the same table at mess. Odd, as I look back, as we were identical sort of people doing the identical mission, pilots from the two squadrons never mingled!

"Only other place I would see him was on the volleyball court where, needless to say, he was the best.

"But, he was not a friendly person – not unfriendly either – just kept to himself. Did not drink and so would never be in the club where we might 'let our hair down.'"[7]

"I was in Korea at K-3 from November 52 to October 53," Myron Hyatt wrote. "I was a corporal and I was a trumpet player in the band. I also had to take turns playing bugle calls. Two other guys and I were in a souvenir shop outside of the base in Itami, Japan once and we saw Ted Williams in there. One of the guys asked him if he could take a picture of him, and he said OK. He put his arm around the Japanese lady who was waiting on him, and this guy took a picture. The sad story to this is when we got outside the door, this guy who took the picture found out that he forgot to remove the lens cover. Boy, was he mad!"[8]

Darwin Glaese was the VMF-311 pilot who picked up Ted at K-13 after his wheels-up landing, and brought him back to K-3. He did have the opportunity go hunting some with Williams. "I went pheasant hunting with him, and also duck hunting. Super hunter." But Glaese recognized that Ted's circle of friends was a small one. "I would classify him sort of as a loner. He would make friends with a few people, and if he didn't like you, forget about it. He wouldn't even talk to you. He might say 'Hello' but not really have a conversation. I don't think I ever saw him in the Officers Club." [9]

Aviation electrician Edward Angst would see Williams once in a while, and understood that he kept to himself. "He was friendly enough. If they had a squadron party, he would usually come for a little while, but he didn't stay too long. John Glenn, he was more talkative, though. [Ted had one or two people] he was pretty friendly with. Other than that, he wasn't really all that friendly with most of the pilots, either. Except in the line of duty, we were never around them. They had their areas and we had ours." [10]

Williams probably discouraged too much contact through his body language. Celebrities learn this early on. Bob Flanagan, a plane captain with VMF-311, said that Williams often walked with a purposeful expression. "He had his eyes down at about a 45-degree angle, but locked. It was like, 'Jesus, I don't want to get bothered. Let me alone. Don't be doing anything.' And I must say that I was an 18 year old, rather in awe." [11]

Seabee Pat Morris was part of a team that worked extending K-3's runway. He was 19 at the time and says, "I recall seeing Ted Williams once at K-3. He was with some other Marine officers leaving what I remember was the officers dining hut. I worked on the electrical power line crew doing pole line work on the base so we were all over the base and saw and talked to a lot of other people there. Since Ted was a famous person, there were quite a few stories circulating about him. I always figured the stories were not always fair to him. There were a lot of Marine pilots there but I am sure no other pilot had everyone watching him and making judgments as did Ted.

"One of the stories that was circulated was that he would very often find problems with his aircraft and return to the base before reaching the target area with his load of bombs. It was claimed that he returned so often that the Air Force controllers in the tower would make bets with each other about whether he would make it to the target area before returning. The other side of the story is that the K-3 Marines were flying the older Panther jets and they probably did have quite a few problems with them. One of the stories we heard was that the jets that the Marines got at K-3 were the ones that were no longer safe to take off and land on carriers.

"One of the Marines that was there at that time contacted me a year or so ago. He said that Ted Williams was faulted for not doing the 'walk around' inspection of his plane before taking off.

"A Seabee mechanic that worked in our small Seabee machine shop there told me a couple of years ago that Ted Williams had asked him to repair a camera for him. It seems Ted had borrowed the camera and had dropped it in his cockpit, doing some damage to it.

"Then there is the softball story. This is the story that I heard the most about. A little different slant depending on who was telling the story. Just in front of our Seabee living area was a recreation softball field where different Marine units and the Seabees would field teams. It seems that a reporter was there doing a story about Ted Williams. Ted was asked to go to the ball field for some pictures of him playing ball with other military people. The story goes that my boss, Roy Harris from Fresno, California was the only pitcher that would volunteer to pitch to the great Ted Williams. Roy was a good fast ball pitcher and Ted hit a few of his pitches. As soon as they got their pictures, Ted was out of there. The first and last time he was at the ball field." [12]

Bob Janson, like Pat Morris, was also a Construction Electricians Mate 3rd Class. He remembers that during the spring of 1953, the Seabees and Marines at K-3 decided to have a softball game in an area clear enough to use as a ball field. "The Seabees came up with a team of anyone who could swing a bat, but the Marines fielded a team that consisted of a few that were out of our class, one of which was Ted Williams and the other was, I think, Jerry Coleman of the NY Yankees. John Glenn was also there at the time but I don't remember him playing. The game lasted about 7 innings or so and was a pleasurable pastime for all, with liquid refreshments on the sidelines for all. The Seabees got soundly defeated by about 21-3 or so, with most of the runs accounted for by Ted and his 4 home runs.

"There was some talk of removing him from the team because of some claimed unfair advantage – all in fun! The outfielders also got tired of chasing the ball almost out to the airstrip.

"Any talk with Ted was just general chit-chat, mostly about baseball, of course, but he was just one of the boys and very friendly to all of us."

Maybe Janson was thinking of Lloyd Merriman; Coleman was on another base. He was sure it was Coleman, and noted that "a lot of the pilots seemed to migrate back and forth from their home air-strips for visits or whatever, just as Glenn did. Maybe Coleman was visiting K-3 at the time and that may have been the reason that Williams consented to play a little pickup game with Coleman, maybe continuing the Boston/NY rivalry. I wasn't involved in the setting up of the game, so I'm not sure why he played this one.

"Ted seemed to be very serious about the actual 'play' of the game, but he was friendly enough and cracked a few smiles when not at the plate. He did some joking around with those nearby, but he didn't partake in any of the refreshments, that I saw.

"The only other time I remember seeing Ted, was when I was standing guard duty at one of the gates on the 'Marine' side of the airstrip. It was freezing cold and as I was writing up the vehicle number of the Jeep and number of occupants, Ted, who was sitting next to the driver, said something to the effect, 'was the .45-cal pistol I carried the only heater I had, or was there one in the guard shack?' This was said, jokingly, not sarcastically. I think I replied, 'Seabees don't need any external heat,' or something like that."[13]

Did Williams actually play in this game? Almost every pilot in the two jet squadrons agrees that Ted never played in a game. Roy Harris, the Seabees pitcher, says it was Lloyd Merriman. Roy was interviewed later the same day as Janson, and he said, "I don't think Ted was playing. It was Lloyd Merriman. Ted Williams didn't play over there with us. He kind of stayed by himself. Ted Williams was there, but I didn't pitch against him, but I did against Lloyd Merriman. We were playing softball. He was a good hitter. I played fast pitch here in town.

"I very seldom saw him [Ted]. He kind of stuck more to himself. We didn't see much of him in the activities as far as that was concerned. I never heard why, but everybody said he was kind of a loner. That's what they told us there, and we just took it as that. It's always nice, though, to know that there were some celebrities around. We'd see him come in, fly in after a mission. One time he had a couple of holes in the airplane, probably from ground fire."[14]

Jim Dolan, a former Navy commander, was hired as a tech rep by the Westinghouse aviation gas turbine division, and then sent to MCAS El Toro. After a couple of months at El Toro, he was sent to Atsugi, Japan, but primarily he worked with the 1st Marine Air Wing at K-3. "I was there for 18 months, covering the J-34 engines F2H-P at K-3 and the F3D night fighters at K-8 Korea. Ted Williams, I used to eat with him many times in the officers mess. He'd sit across the table. He was just another guy there. People would talk to him. I was never interested in baseball. I don't think many people talked much baseball. You're over there – flyboys were talking about flying. That's more important than baseball, because your ass is involved. We'd just sit at the table and just have a very pleasant chat. I never did get in any particular bull sessions with him. I think at that time he was thinking of getting back. He had some real ear problems. Of course, you can imagine what he gave up – in fact, all those guys gave up a lot.

"He was quiet. If he'd been telling stories, I would have remembered it. I would have been listening. I'd be chewing the fat with people I knew. I never really horned in on him. Outside of remembering his being a good guy, he was just one of the pilots but he had an ear infection, which up at high altitudes is a problem, and he went back to the States."[15]

Al Pommerenk retired as a Brigadier General. One of the rare three-war men in the Marine Corps, he served in World War II, Korea, and Vietnam.

"I was in the wing. I was the target priority officer. That was one of my jobs. The reconnaissance planes would go up and take pictures of different targets. Then what we'd do, we'd review those photos. Being there long enough, you knew the whole damn North Korea. Then we'd send them down to the operations officer in the squadrons – the latter part of the afternoon so the flight officer could go ahead and make up the schedule. The operations officer or the flight scheduler, he would assign the flight schedule for the squadron. That was their business to take care of. All we were doing was designating targets."

[What was his impression of Ted around the base?] "Everybody had different ideas and thoughts, you know. He was controversial. Very much so. I'd rather keep some of the stuff just to myself. I wasn't a close personal friend. When you've got people together, some people say this and some people say that. I don't think it's fair to the individual just for me to pop out and say this or that."[16]

Was Ted really "controversial"? "Well, no. He wasn't controversial in the squadron," says former Major James G. Fox "We all liked him and we called him 'Bush.' He wasn't an O Club hanger-outer. He said he was tying his fishing lures and developing his film. Things like that. Always squeezing the ball. He walked around with a glove in his hand sometimes and tossed a ball into it. The squeezing and everything, I always figured he was keeping himself in training for his profession. As a professional Marine and a professional aviator, I did things all the time that related to that. That was my profession."[17]

Rylen Rudy was another 311 pilot. As we have seen, he harbors strong opinions about Ted Williams. He didn't pull any punches. "Let me tell you this. I think he was the biggest asshole the world has ever known. I'm not the only one with that opinion by any means. What I saw of the bastard – I was in the same squadron with him – one, I thought he was a yellow sonovabitch. You couldn't get his ass in an airplane to make him go. The rest of us flew – not every day, but we flew missions as often as they came up. He was in the squadron about seven months and they got him in the air 37 times. Most of us spent six months in the squadron. We did right at 100 missions apiece, and then we went on to do other things.

"They'd get out and play sandlot and all that stuff and all that and he was never bothered to join them. He didn't really ever join in anything. He'd go over to the O Club and have a few drinks. I don't know what he did with his time, because he sure the hell wasn't flying."[18]

Another Texan was "Tex" Montague, and he was considered one of the eccentrics in the squadron. He was always out running in the morning, whatever the weather, and he shaved from a cold water tap. His impressions were simple. "I liked Ted real well. I got along real well with him. I thought he was a great guy."[19]

Jim Fox, asked about Rylen Rudy's remarks, said, "Ted was kind of his own man. There's two ways of looking at that." [Was there any scuttlebutt that Ted was dodging missions?] "I don't remember that. I don't even know how one would dodge a mission out there."[20]

Another pilot, with VMF-115, was Carrol Burch. His impressions of Williams were, frankly, "kind of mixed. I talked to him a lot. He was unhappy to be there. He was missing making a lot of money. His wife missed him, and she was important. I said to him, 'Well, my wife's important, too, and she misses me' – but I listened to him for hours. Hours. And he got out early. He's the only man I ever knew that could get out on an earache. He got early out with an earache."

Burch hadn't known that Williams was so sick that he twice was sent out to hospital ships. "I never knew that there was anything wrong with him. The main thing wrong with him – he didn't want to be there. I was regular. But he elected to join the Marine Corps, too.

"We had a bulletin board that was used for people that had a story in the paper about them – maybe their hometown paper – and they had clippings. There was a lot of newspaper clippings on this bulletin board that individuals had put up there. Then Ted Williams got there and it was absolutely covered up with Ted Williams stories. I don't know who put them up. I really don't know but they covered all the others up. There wasn't anything else but those. The main thing I had with him was over 15 cent drinks at the bar. He was very disgruntled, very unhappy that he was there. He didn't want to be there and he tried very hard to get out. I didn't drink a whole lot, either, but we did have drinks together. We'd get a few drinks and that would be it.[21]

The Far East Sikorsky Aircraft Field Rep was Harry Asbury. He worked with some of the helicopters based at K-3. Ted bitched to him over drinks, but maybe that was part of his personality. "Ted Williams dropped in one night at VMO-6 and landed at our airstrip. He had a few drinks in Chief Lew's tent and I was only in there for a few minutes. All he talked about was the screwing he got by the Marine Corps by calling him back to duty for Korea. He was talking to the wrong crowd of pilots. Over 50% of the VMO-6 pilots were reserves that had been called back. I remember one that was the station manager for TWA in St Louis that came back, but he never complained as much as Williams.

"I saw Williams down on Sugarloaf Key, Florida, in the mid sixties when he would stay at the Sugarloaf Lodge to go bone fishing. Talking to the fishing guides, he was still a bitcher."[22]

How was Ted Williams as a hutmate? "He was great! We were very friendly and we never had any conflicts of any kind. He used to get a little irritated with the situation in his... when I'd try to pump him on how he was doing... about the emotional aspects of leaving baseball and what have you at the time. Just in friendly conversation. He was very understanding and I would simply explain that it was his duty to come, but it was just a very untimely call. He wasn't happy at all. He was a very off-the-cuff guy. He used to give the fans the routine, too.

"We were flying about ten weeks or so and then going over to Japan. We'd really shower up over there and get sort of cleaned out, especially during that winter of '53 from '52. It was good to get over there and get kind of thawed out. We didn't shower too much at K-3 when it was real cold.

"There were gals and little kids that we had running around the camp there that would do laundry and that sort of stuff. I don't remember the details. I just remember we got our laundry done in some system like that."

Ted was married at the time and he had a young daughter of 5 or 6 years old. Did he ever talk much about missing his family or anything? "No, not much about his wife. I had the impression that maybe he was estranged from his wife, but I don't know. I thought there was some problem there, but I don't remember the details.

"He used to get mail, but he didn't get any unusual amount. If it had been something that would have gotten my attention, I would remember it, but it was just mail call."[23]

Jim Stehle was a Marine Corps pilot in the night squadron, VMF(N)-513. He traveled with Ted to Japan. "I went from Korea with him, from Korea to Japan on R&R. Oh God, must have been eight or ten times!"

[What did you do on R&R? Different people did different things.]

"You can draw your own conclusions from that. [Laughs.] I'll tell you one thing. Ted and I'd be walking down the street and these little kids would gather around and go, 'Ohhh! Ted Weel-eyums!' They'd recognize him. The Japanese newspapers kept up with him. He usually signed baseballs or scorecards, envelopes... letters they were supposed to mail... .He was pretty good. He didn't turn too many of them down. I never went to any Japanese baseball games. To my knowledge, he didn't go, either."

[But you'd go out for dinner and stuff?]

"Yeah."

[I don't know about the geisha girls...]

"We won't talk about that. [Laughs.] Afterwards, he told me, 'Come on down to Islamorada and I'll show you around' and I did. I used to go down there maybe once a month. He ain't no fun to fish with! If you're not excellent, you're a dummy. Once was enough. He was very moody. You'd go down there sometimes and he'd be fighting and this and that. I'd get up and go home."[24]

Let's end with two more views of Ted Williams. Ed Sample was a pilot in VMF-311. He flew 100 missions in Korea, and ultimately served 24 years in the Marine Corps during which time he became commanding officer of HMX, Marine Helicopter Squadron 1, based at Quantico. In that capacity, he served as personal pilot for the existing President of the United States and served both Presidents Johnson and Nixon. He arrived at K-3 in November 1952, and had thus been there a few months before Ted arrived.

"I thought he did his job real well. He was extremely antagonized by the press. He couldn't go to the outdoor john without photographers being all over him. He could not get away from them. I never thought of him as being controversial. I was a second lieutenant and he was a captain in 311.

"He was not highly thought of by some of his senior officers and some of his peers, but he and I got along very well and I thought he was a great guy.

"Being a second john at the time, I never did understand why. He had a little arrogance about him, but that was to be expected, the wages he'd been making and the status in life he had obtained. I imagine that was the reason. He and I got along very well.

"I never gathered any suggestion that he wasn't pulling his own weight as a pilot."[25]

Sample and Williams flew on four missions together, the first one being the 16 February mission. Sample says, "He was very fortunate to survive that" but, not atypically, adds, "I don't recall seeing him after, or whether or not we discussed it." It remains astonishing to the researcher that baseball star Ted Williams crash-landed an airplane, yet hardly anyone remembers talking with Ted about it afterward. Sample did not know about Ted's hospital ship stays, either. Again, one would think that everyone in the squadron would be extremely aware of the comings and goings of the great Ted Williams – but there seemed very little excitement about his arrival and some pilots seem not to have noticed his departure. We do have to remember that these men were working hard, and their work placed them in harm's way. They risked their lives. This was a war, and these pilots were oft-times very individual, capable, and forceful men in their own right.

And Ted didn't really socialize. Sample said, "The only social function I ever had with him was in the officer's club. He was like just another pilot. He didn't hold himself out to be any better than me. He called me 'Kid.' I was 21 at the time."

What about Rylen Rudy? "Yeah, I remember Rudy. He's in Austin, Texas. I didn't know that Rylen Rudy didn't care for him. Rylen Rudy had a big, big ego problem, although he and I are good friends."

[Ted rubbed a few people the wrong way. Ted had his own path he was following. He really didn't care all that much what other people thought.]

"I think I may have been even more so that way than Ted Williams was, had I been in his position."

[One of the reasons he was so great might have been because of his belief in himself.]

"That's right. If you talk to a member of Ted's family, I can commend his conduct in Korea. I thought the world of him."[26]

Al Pommerenk has the last word:

"I think he was a wonderful man. A wonderful ballplayer, but he was a moody individual. We all... in war time a lot of things happen."

[Thirty-nine missions is a healthy number.]

"That's all right. I'm still alive and I flew a hell of a lot more than that. But I never held that against him at all. My tour of duty down there was entirely different from his. He was land-based. They had certain targets. I was out on the carrier. It was the most exciting years of my life."

[Not talking about Ted Williams in particular, was that something that pilots often experienced? They'd do maybe a couple dozen missions and just something would happen and they just had to stop?]

"Yeah. Some guys just cracked. Oh yeah, I've seen that happen. It happened out on our carrier with two pilots. They might say nothing about it, just come back in the ready room and they just look at you and they reach up and pull the wing off and say, 'This is it. I've had it. I can't do it anymore.' I don't hold it against him, and away he goes. Some of them become ground officers. Some of them get out and make their fortune on the outside.

"Everybody had their own ways of doing things."[27]

NOTES

1) *Tommy Prater post to Korean War Project website at www.koreanwar.org, March 24, 2003.*

2) *Interview with Gen. Leo LeBlanc, December 27 and 31, 2002.*

3) *Interview with Leonard Waibel, December 19, 2002.*

4) *Interview with Roger McCully, December 5, 2002.*

5) *Interview with Mike Canan, December 31, 2002.*

6) *Interview with Bob Johnson, May 31, 2003.*

7) *Communication from George Banks, January 9, 2003.*

8) *Communication from Myron Hyatt, May 4, 2004. Hyatt explained that Ted was not romancing the lady; she was just someone waiting on him in the shop. Hyatt played both basketball and softball in the base leagues, but never knew either Williams or Lloyd Merriman to play on the base.*

9) *Interview with Darwin Glaese, December 17, 2002.*

10) *Interview with Edward Angst, December 27, 2002.*

11) *Interview with Bob Flanagan, June 2, 2003.*

12) *Interview with Pat Morris, December 31, 2002. Again, one must treat recollections with skepticism. The F9F-5 Panther jets were top of the line, not older planes "no longer safe to take off and land on carriers."*

13) *Communication from Bob Janson, January 3, 2003.*

14) *Interview with Roy Harris, January 3, 2003.*

15) *Interview with Jim Dolan, February 3, 2003.*

16) *Interview with Al Pommerenk, February 7, 2003.*

17) *Interview with James Fox, February 8, 2003.*

18) *Interview with Rylen Rudy, February 4, 2003.*

19) *Interview with Paul B. "Tex" Montague, February 11, 2003.*

20) *Interview with James Fox, February 8, 2003.*

21) *Interview with Carrol Burch, February 6, 2003.*

22) *Interview with Harry Asbury, January 6, 2003.*

23) *Interview with Joseph Mitchell, February 3, 2003.*

24) *Interview with James Stehle, February 1, 2003. There is a bit of hyperbole here, in that there is no way any pilot serving four months in Korea went on R&R eight or more times.*

25) *Interview with Ed Sample, February 5, 2003.*

26) *Ibidem.*

27) *Interview with Al Pommerenk, February 7, 2003.*

Ted on the flight line.
Photo courtesy of Frank Cushing.

CHAPTER 19 – HOW GOOD A PILOT WAS TED WILLIAMS?

*"I would guess that with anybody that reaches his stature in the world,
there are going to be a million stories."*
Banshee Bob Johnson

"He stood out because he didn't stand out."
Col. Ben Robertshaw, Commanding Officer

Whatever others thought about him, Captain T. S. Williams never kept it a secret: he didn't want to be serving in Korea in the middle of a war at age 34. Yet he was assigned to the elite squadron in the Marine Corps, VMF-311, the first squadron to fly jets in combat. He was with some of the very best pilots the Marines had. He'd been an instructor during World War II. He'd been recalled for Korea and he re-trained on jets. He must have been a pretty decent pilot. Or was he? As we have seen, he had his detractors and several of them questioned whether he really wanted to fly. If your heart isn't in it, could you really be a good pilot? Some of those who passed judgment were accomplished aviators themselves. And some were critical of Williams.

It is remarkable how there is such diversity, and depth, of opinion even within pilots of the two squadrons. It seems that these pilots, despite being thrown together and working hard together, each had their own realities, went their own ways.

The toughest judges are likely to be the pilots with whom he served.

One could ask: does it matter how good he was rated? He served. He sacrificed, he served, he flew 39 missions, and he came home. Nonetheless, let's further consider how he was viewed by some of his fellow pilots.

Art Moran, commanding officer of 311, always felt that Williams hadn't been trained as well as he should have been. Recalling the outburst that a Marine Corps general had delivered to him over the phone when he had launched Ted the morning after his crash-landing, Moran said, "The general grounded him when he got back from that second try. Ted got a hell of a cold that kept for about a week or so. But as far as I am concerned, he would have been a hell of a good pilot if the Marine Corps had trained him properly.

"I'll give you one example. He was flying wing, on the flight leader, on a flight of four one day. That flight leader was very experienced, he was a captain but he had a good background and flown a lot of airplanes and all that. And they had to make a penetration of a GCA [ground control approach, radar approach] for landing, the weather was that bad. Anyway, Mack, the flight leader, said, 'Take it over, Ted.' This was before they went into the clouds. Ted said, 'I'd rather not.' He said, 'Aw, come on, Ted, you can do it. I won't let you get in trouble.' But Ted passed it up. So that's an indication of how the other guys thought of him. At that time he didn't have a whole lot of weather time." Moran meant that the others trusted Ted as a pilot, even if he was himself reluctant to assume a leadership role in bad weather.[1]

Ted felt that instrument flying was one of his weak points, and he didn't like flying in poor weather. Just a couple of years after he'd returned, he told Joan Flynn Dreyspool of *Sports Illustrated*, "I wasn't too well trained in instrument flying and I was forever worried about running into instrument weather which I didn't know too much about. It's been proven the only way to become an instrument flyer is through practice and experience."[2]

Squadron C. O. Ben Robertshaw underscored Ted's concern with weather and instruments. "He was concerned primarily about flying instruments. He approached his commanding officer and they both approached me about his adequacy. I demonstrated to him with other records that he had as much training as anybody else, and that satisfied him."[3]

A number of pilots made negative comments about Williams and his flying, and a number of others on the base passed on some of what they had heard. In the last chapter, we saw that Rylen Rudy had nothing good to say about him.

"I think one of the greatest things that came up was Art Moran, who was the C.O. of the outfit, when the Discovery Channel used to have the different airplanes listed, and they came up with the Panther. They had Art Moran on there, since he'd been the squadron commander of 311 and the whole bit. One of the comments they made was, 'You had Ted Williams in the squadron. How was he?' You could see the wheels going around in Art Moran's head, trying to figure out, 'How can I be diplomatic and still say he wasn't worth a shit?' So he finally came up with the comment, 'Well, Ted came to us not very well trained and we didn't have time to do much for him.'

"Whatever he had, he was not – in my opinion – an asset to the squadron."[4]

Rudy did admit there was an element of the personal in here.

[He probably knew you didn't like him, anyhow. He probably picked that up.]

"I never showed it over there particularly. Hell, he was a captain and I was a lieutenant. I wasn't about to sit there and tell him he was an asshole to his face. I might have to fly with him tomorrow. It was unlikely – as seldom as he flew.

"And he never got to lead. Hell, he wasn't up to the leading status. He was strictly a wingman the whole time he was over there. I don't think they had to ask him. I think they found out real quick like that he didn't have the ability to lead. Several of us that were second and first lieutenants, well, it didn't take very long to pick out who's got the leadership qualities. Of course, we had an over-abundance of majors in the squadron, so as a lieutenant and even as a captain, you didn't get to be a division leader very often. But a section leader, a number three man, you got to be that if you had some ability. I got to fly number three towards the end of my tour over there. I never did get to the front position. I wasn't anywhere close to being enough rank. We had all these retired guys from World War II.

"I wasn't about to go on R&R with him, but I imagine he screwed everything he could get his hands on. I wouldn't have had anything to do with him anyway.

"He had ear trouble bad enough that he couldn't fly, but when they finally got tired of screwing around with him, he got to fly home. He flew home. I always thought that was ironic as hell. His ears weren't good enough to fly missions, but he could sure as hell fly in an airplane coming home. He didn't have any ear trouble at all coming home. I think his ear trouble was a big yellow stripe down the middle.

"As far as I know he flew 37 missions in 7 months, and that's the only times they could get him in the air. And that doesn't mean that he did anything. After the third mission, you didn't get him very close to the ground."[5]

That's a pretty strong indictment. Did Moran really feel the way Rudy suggested? The author had earlier interviewed Moran in person, at his home in Laguna Niguel, California, and did not get that impression at all. He spoke at length about Ted and seemed pleased to do so. As indicated above, Moran did not simply praise Williams. His words reflect his sense that Ted could have been better. He'd made the point that "he would have been a hell of a good pilot if the Marine Corps had trained him properly." He seemed to be candid in his appraisal, and then added, "You shouldn't go putting that out, or they'd cut off my retirement." There was no indication at any point in the interview that Moran felt Williams was sub-standard, but that he felt Williams could have been "a hell of a good pilot" had he been better trained.[6]

Though he was the most vocal about Ted personally, Rudy was not the only person with critical comments about Williams as a pilot. Mike Canan expressed some criticism as well: "They had a hell of a time getting him up in the air sometimes. He always came back, too. He aborted on a lot of them."

[Some people said that Ted was pretty particular about the condition of the aircraft. Maybe more so than some people?]

"Yeah, I guess I was too easy with them, but I think he really was meticulous."

[Of course, your life's on the line – and so is that of your fellow pilots – so you can hardly blame anyone...]

"Oh, heavens, no! We're all made up differently, that's all."

[John Glenn said that Ted was quite a good pilot.]

"Well, I don't expect John to say anything differently, you know.

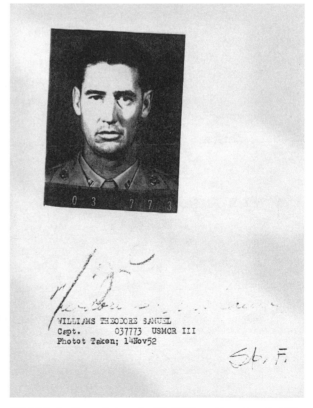

Official Marine Corps photograph of Ted Williams, November 14, 1952.
Courtesy of United States Marine Corps.

"He [Ted] just didn't have the enthusiasm of flying, as far as I could see. He would just do what he was told to do, and he didn't like it sometimes, what he was told to do. That's why he didn't like me. We had missions to go, and I would say… he was insubordinate, more or less, but that doesn't work too much in squadrons about things like that."[7]

It is worth noting that only two aborts by Williams are reported in the squadron's official command diary, by no means an unusual number. To say Ted aborted "a lot of them" is unsubstantiated by squadron records. It is quite conceivable, however, that Williams sometimes was excused from missions for one reason or another before the flight actually commenced. In that case, for instance due to a defective or unsafe aircraft, he would not have taken off and no abort would be recorded.

That Williams flew 39 missions, and not 100, and was in Korea for five months both seem unforgiving of his illnesses, and also of what he did accomplish. Col. Jack McGuckin explained a bit, "It really was not unusual to only be there four or five months. I was there a little longer on my first tour because when I got out of the squadron, they put me as provost marshal. I was in charge of all of the Marine Corps training of all the squadrons and everything. I guess they thought I must be doing

Ted at air base in Seoul with Captain Jim Cook, May 1953.
Courtesy Jim Cook.

too good a job, because they held me there for a while. But I was only there seven months. That was about a normal tour for a pilot. If you were flying the Corsairs, you could get 100 missions, but flying the jets you didn't get 100 missions. And not very many hours, because a two-hour flight and you're out of gas."[8]

Larry Hawkins had heard the criticism regarding the number of missions. "There was some contention. When we were flying 100, he was just barely making it over 30, so there was some resentment by some of the people, who were probably suffering some of the same physical... or were reservists called in the same way, and here was one guy who was getting away with a little more because of physical things. It was just about the same time we have an Ex. O. or a C.O. – it wasn't in our squadron – who said 'I'm not going to fly anymore' and he got himself grounded, and just quit. He wasn't going to carry on any more as an aviator."[9]

Ted truly was suffering. Hawkins noted, "When he started hitting 35 missions, that sinus problem of his was killing him. Most of us ruptured an eardrum. I woke up in the morning sometimes bleeding. You'd have a blood spot on the pillow. You know the pressurization systems on our F9's – we had two positions, one was full pressurization – which was about half of what you would get on an airliner today, or less – and then the other one was a combat switch. If you left it in the combat area, that meant that you were literally above 18,000 feet. If you're at 35,000 feet, you're actually flying along at 20,000 feet in the cockpit. There was a differential. If you start leaving down from that altitude, it's just like going down deep in the water. You go down below 15 or 20 feet and your ears start hurting like heck. You might not have broken an eardrum, but sometimes you didn't know you broke a capillary."[10]

Did Ted actually bug off missions? Ed Buchser was asked if he ever heard that some accused Ted of not pulling his own weight. He'd never heard such a suggestion, but even if there had been some truth in it, he said, the very question made Buchser a little angry. "What do they mean 'pulling his own weight'? The war was over! Oh yeah, yeah, it wasn't quite over, but...

"If he was bugging off missions, I'm for Ted. There was so much bullshit, and some missions were just 'make-up' missions, really. I heard an Air Force guy say his first mission in Vietman was a coal mine. Now what the hell are you going to do with coal? Burn it? He said, 'I guess that's what we'll do. Just go up there and burn it.' I don't blame Ted."[11]

Was Williams meticulous to a fault, turning down planes and therefore not joining as many missions as he should have?

M. T. Schuerman, 311 pilot, retired as a major. He flew dive bombers in WWII, but was recalled as a reservist for Korea, like Ted. He first got to know Ted at Cherry Point, but preceded him to Korea by several months. He was wrong on a number of points, saying that Ted got hit on about his 20th mission and that no matter how hard they tried, they could never get him back in a plane again! He said that at K-3 they flew F9F-2s whereas at Cherry Point, they had F9F-5s. So the ones in Korea were a little slower. Since they'd trained on the faster 5s, it took a little refresher to get familiar with the F9F-2s. He was the one who gave Ted refresher on the F-2s, and he said that it took most pilots a couple of hours to become comfortable with the 2s but with Ted it took a day and a half because he insisted on checking every little thing about the plane. He also said Ted always made things difficult for the plane captains, too, for the same reason. Checking over every little thing.[12] Schuerman may have experienced this when Williams first arrived at K-3, but squadron records show that the F-2s were very soon replaced by F-5s. It was an F-5 that Williams flew on 16 February, his third mission, and F-2s were rarely flown thereafter.

The members of his ground crew that we could locate for this book didn't express such negativity, though. Roger McCully, plane captain, had nothing but good things to say about Ted. Was Ted exceptionally meticulous? "He checked it over very well before he got into it. He looked it over a little closer than most, yeah." Was this in line with the way he checked his fishing gear whenever he was fishing, or was it perhaps that he was hesitant to fly? "No, no, he wasn't afraid to go."[13]

One Marine heard the opposite, that Williams didn't check a thing. Terry Stewart, an electronics tech in the Comm Section of Headquarters Squadron at MAG-33, spent 13 months at K-3 but never saw Ted. The base was large enough, and people were busy enough that there was not nearly as much interaction as one might expect. Stewart heard some scuttlebutt, though. "The word was his ground crew were not too fond of him. Something about he never would do his pre-flight inspections, but would just take the clipboard and sign it. Then when something went wrong he would blame the ground crew. He was also reported to have had a lot of 'emergency landings' – going off the end of the runway, etc. Something about hydraulic failures and such. We supposedly had the shortest runway in Korea at the time and it was not really uncommon for an F9 to go off the end of the runway."[14]

Granted, McCully was Ted's plane captain, while Stewart was only reporting what he'd heard, but we have here again illustration of the varying stories which have attached themselves to Ted Williams, the pilot in the public eye.

Leonard Waibel, line chief, took some time and gave a balanced assessment.

"He lost his temper with me a couple of times, Ted did. I didn't ever get to call him 'Ted.' I always called him 'Captain,' naturally. He lost his temper with me a couple of times. Not bad. Sometimes he'd get a little upset. This one time, he came in after a flight and he rode the brakes and he said the brakes weren't any good. I happened to say, 'Well, if you wouldn't ride them, they wouldn't be the way they are. Come here, I'll show you why they're no good.' He had the brakes red hot. He didn't like that, when I told him that. He just said, 'That isn't the reason why.' Of course, I never argued back with the guy.

"I did help him a lot. He couldn't start a darn airplane right. He'd always flood it. In those days, our jet engines would tend to flood real easy and we'd get a lot of fluid in the tailpipe. I had a little trick. I would get up alongside of him in the cockpit and I had a little trick how to start it. Sometimes it would look like the airplane was going to explode! But it would start.

"He was always cordial with me. You know what the poopy suit is? The pilots had to wear these rubberized suits when they went on missions, because if they went in the water, it was so cold that they wouldn't survive. They were really tight around the neck, and they were rubber. Oh, I remember onc time, he ripped that thing off! I had to laugh. He couldn't get it off fast enough, and he just ripped it. He was upset with it.

"He could fly that airplane, though. I recall one time he got blasted. I went up there and saw that plane. It was full of holes. He was lucky to get that baby on the ground. He got hit by anti-aircraft. I know those airplanes. I was around F9s there. He got hit. He could have got some secondary, but you don't get secondary in the stabilizer. He had them in the elevator, too. He had it all over. He was lucky to get back."[15]

There had been suggestions that Williams was a little reckless with equipment and also crash-landed one of his planes in a creek bed right near K-3. The command diaries have to report lost and damaged aircraft, and account for same. There is no indication at all that anything like this ever happened during any of the months that Ted Williams served in Korea, February through June inclusive 1953.

On Ted's last mission, he had to abort because the fire warning light would not go off. This hardly seems Ted's fault, and in any event it was not that uncommon an experience, Waibel explained. He also added another bit of information; even though Ted may have accidentally screwed up, it seems that he was by no means alone. "We had fire warning lights in that aircraft, yes, but sometimes it didn't work. It was just little electrodes that were around the engine and if it got hot to a certain temperature, it would put a light in the cockpit showing there was something wrong. Sometimes it was just a short circuit.

Capt. Ted Williams at K-3, 1953. Living quarters seen in background.
Photo by E. Buchser.

"I can remember once he salvaged all the bombs right on the deck before he took off. They were waiting to take off. He was carrying daisy cutters, 250-pound bombs. We used a lot of those, and it has a long wire on it and they have to drop so far before the impeller on the front – the little propeller – arms it. He isn't the only one who ever did that. They used to sit out there and they're fooling around with all the instruments and it's still dark, lots of times, and they'd hit the wrong switch and salvage the bombs. The ordnance men would have to go out there and lift them back up; that's all we had to do. He was no different than the rest of them."[16]

Waibel confirmed that sometimes there was a colonel or a general that simply wanted to hang around Ted Williams, or have him fly wing for them. It was partly for bragging rights, but no one is going to fly into combat with a wingman on whom they couldn't rely. "He had lots of company. I saw a lot of them that wanted to have him fly on their wing. I remember Glenn. I remember Cushman, and I remember Jerome. I guess so they could have that at happy hour. The wing man is very important. I don't know the tactics of flying, but a lot of them seemed to want him as wingman, and like I said, we had a lot of visiting high-ranking officers that flew when he was there.

"I would oversee all takeoffs. I would sit there in my Jeep and make sure they all got off. We'd have to get the aircraft ready. We'd start them all. We'd get everything ready. The ordnance would get them all loaded. I would give the operations officer the aircraft that were ready to fly, and he would assign them. I wouldn't assign them. I would just take it in there and I would watch him while he's putting it on the board.

"The biggest event we had was when Koreans came in with P51s. That was like a circus. I never saw such landings. They would bounce off the side of the runway. I don't think they had more than five hours in those airplanes."

Waibel said that he hardly ever left the base. There was a village nearby "where we used to get the shrimp from. I think I went to town one time." He does not recall any unusual number of reporters dogging Ted.

"There was a Marine Corps photographer. Of course, they didn't come out on the flight line. I guess they weren't allowed to. I didn't see him all the time. I would see him in the ready room. I would see him when I'd wake him. And then I would see him on the flight line. That's the end of it. I wouldn't see him after that.

"I always wanted to send a card to Ted Williams. I knew he lived in Florida but I never had his address.

"We did talk about fishing once. I was no buddy of his, but I had a relationship with him. I liked him, and he treated me great. He was just one of the squadron I was in. The officers knew him a lot better than the enlisted. The officers knew him a lot better than the enlisted, because the only ones that really spoke to him were the plane captains and myself, among the enlisted. We were the only ones that had any contact with him. They'd help him in, you know, and strap him in.

"We'd have the cart to start him. We had little electrical carts and you'd hook those up. You'd have to get up to so many rpm and then you'd hit the starter. If he couldn't get started, they'd turn around and I'd make sure they got started. Now remember, these are jet engines that are the first ones we got. They were crude to people nowadays. But you'd hit the flame igniter to start it, and then turn. Sometimes you'd miss – if you didn't get the sequence right, it'll flood it and the igniters won't operate and you'd get a pool of diesel fuel back there. If you know how to do it – which wasn't really legal – you could start it. It looked like a bomb going off, but it would start. Flames! Like a flame-thrower. But it would start.

"He was a good pilot, though. Sometimes I could tell he was irritated. When he did that, I used to... I didn't see him every time, but I made sure when he came in, that we got him out of the cockpit as fast as we could – get him unbuckled and everything... because I liked the guy. I liked him. Like I said, I never saw him that he ever badgered an enlisted man, or talked mean to them or anything."[17]

Another plane captain was Bob Flanagan. He remembered one time in particular.

"Did someone tell you about the helmet incident? This was after he'd begun flying again. They went out and all of them jumped in their aircraft – I remember this real well. The parachute riggers – those were the people that took care of the personal equipment. My bunkmate. The parachute riggers were responsible for the oxygen system, and the oxygen masks that the pilots wore along with the parachutes. In any event, on this particular event, they came out and started engines. Three of them taxi-ed out and away they go, and Williams is in the airplane – the canopy is back and he's slapping his hands on the side. The plane captain goes up the step and comes down. Somebody went running up for the parachute rigger and the radio people. They came down there. In the meantime, the other three had taken off. And Williams shut the airplane down. He was madder than a wet cat. He walked up to the parachute shop and took off his helmet and they checked it out.

"On the helmets, you have a boom mic attachment that goes into the oxygen hose that's located in the aircraft. You had an oxygen mask mic. One or the other of them has to be plugged in there. And evidently when he hooked up, he plugged his boom mic into the microphone connection on his oxygen hose. When he was making his radio check, naturally they loosely hook their oxygen mask on. They flew with their oxygen mask on the entire flight. The boom mic was there for use if you did not have an oxygen mask on. You're supposed to pull the one plug out and put the other one in. In any event, he had his boom mic into the radio and he was trying to talk into his oxygen mask mic. He swore to bejesus that the radio was kaput because he could hear everyone but he couldn't talk to anyone. He dicked up."

It was suggested to Flanagan that Ted probably was not the only guy who ever made that mistake. He agreed; it was only Williams' frustrated reaction that was maybe excessive.

"Un unh. But he was extremely disturbed about it and he just shut the airplane down and got out of it. He didn't give them a chance to come down and straighten it out. He went stomping on back."

Flanagan summarized what he'd heard from other pilots on the line: "In speaking to the other pilots, I think skill-wise, he was not a bad pilot. And skill-wise, I didn't hear them mention anything about him being extremely good, either."[18]

Col. Robertshaw (later a general) was a highly respected pilot, and Ted's C.O. for a portion of the time he was in Korea. His take on Ted was complimentary, and should be accorded some real weight. "I often flew on missions with him. He stood out because he didn't stand out. He was an acceptable pilot, just like anybody else. He wasn't deficient, and he did his share. Of course, that forced landing that he had certainly established him as skillful and brave.

"His nature wasn't much in terms of being a showoff or somebody who wanted to out-do other people. He did his share and that's what he wanted to do, but he wanted to be sure that he was capable of doing it."[19] General Robertshaw repeated the characterization – "he stood out because he didn't stand out." Other ranking officers, interviewed later, found that an apt description, if a surprising one for a man so often the center of controversy.

Jack Bolt was the only Marine ace of the Korean War, and only one of seven Americans to become an ace in both Korea and the Second World War. He was the only Marine Corps (or Navy) pilot to become an ace in the two wars; he won three Distinguished Flying Crosses and the Navy Cross.

Bolt flew with sister squadron VMF-115. He'd enlisted two weeks before Pearl Harbor, and served twenty years. Retiring as a lieutenant colonel, Bolt then went on to practice law in Florida. Practically the first thing he said, when asked about Ted Williams was that Ted was a "great complainer. Bitching all the time." He went hunting with Ted and Ed Buchser four or five times, and considered himself a member in good standing of the Pohang Rod and Gun Club. But how was Ted as a pilot? "Ted was in a different squadron, but his reputation was he flew his missions and flew them creditably. Did what's sufficient to be a hero. He was a decent pilot. There were joint missions we were on, but he never stood out. John Glenn got shot up so much, everybody kind of knew him already!

Magnet Ass! Glenn is the bravest man I've ever known. He's fabulous.

"Nobody ever accused him [Williams] of shirking his missions. He was just reclusive. He didn't mix. People who were around him didn't really know him very well." Bolt went hunting with Ted off-base, a fellow member of the Pohang Rod and Gun Club. He says he never heard anyone say anything negative about Ted, but acknowledged that he "wasn't known for any unusual proficiency." In effect, Bolt underscored Robertshaw's assessment.[20]

VMF-311 pilot Tex Montague added, "I thought he was a good pilot. I'd say he was above average as far as pilots were concerned. He was good. Good solid pilot. He sure knew what he was doing, all right."[21] Major Jim Fox, also a pilot in 311, asked if it would be fair to call Ted an average pilot, said, "Most people thought he was a natural, which means he was a lot better than just the average. Some of us have to learn how to fly and some of us just kinda feel it. Ted was one of the feelers, I think. Everybody worked at it, though. It saved your life if you did."[22]

Bill Armagost, another 311 pilot, is deceased but his wife Elizabeth remembered, "Bill really liked Ted. He said Ted was a hell of a pilot. Bill said he was a good guy. Ted just wanted to do his job. What he disliked was the damn press bugging him! He wanted to do his job; he just wanted the press to leave him alone."[23]

Carrol Burch, VMF-115 pilot, harked back to the 16 February flight, which was one of an intense number of missions scheduled over several days. Talking about Ted, in context, Burch said, "He did fly some good missions. In one particular case, we went up on the Yalu, up on the river. There was a complex of bridges. I think there was seven – I forget how many bridges there were, either four or seven – and 278 guns. Anti-aircraft guns. We went up there 11 days in a row. It was too far to go from K-3 and so we staged out of a field that was closer, an Air Force base. It might have been K-13. It was a massive effort. I think we lost seven pilots the first day. We went after the guns the first day. After we took care of the guns, we got the bridges.

"After we got the bridges, the traffic backed up for miles. Trains and everything. I know the first day my load went right on a gun position. There were five guns in a gun position and my load went right on that and it blew that one off. After you dropped your bombs, you went down on the water and stayed as low as you could until you got out to the ocean.

"I think we lost seven the first day. We kept going. The last day I hit a train and it blew up. The guy behind me said he passed debris from that train at 7,000 feet! So it had either ammunition or gasoline on it.

"Those 11 days or whatever it was that we went up there every day. That was probably the roughest missions that we went on.

"Ted Williams got hit on one of those days." Though there is no question that the February 16 mission was a large one, none of the seven pilots lost were from either 115 or 311. Squadron records lead one to believe that Burch was referring to a mission in January 1953, some weeks before Ted had arrived in Korea and begun flying with 311. Burch recalls John Glenn as well.

"John Glenn, now there was an eager beaver. We had about eight of us and we were bridge busters. We would guarantee that we would take out any bridge that they wanted us to, with four airplanes. John Glenn was one of them. Jack Bolt was another. I was one of them."[24]

None of the seven pilots lost were from K-3.

One pilot who joined the squadron near the end of Ted's tenure was Bob Peine; a veteran of the Rabaul campaign in World War II, Peine joined the squadron three weeks to the day before Williams left. He flew with Ted on Williams' very last complete mission. He was introduced to Ted by Lee Scott, who also hailed from the state of Washington. Scott was one of Ted's hutmates. Clearly, he didn't get to know Ted Williams well, but he did develop an impression and what he picked up in scuttlebutt was also reflective of Williams' four months of service with 311. "He liked his privacy," Peine recalled.

"And at the time, I think he was going through some difficulties with his family. I'll tell you what, the guy was a great aviator from what I learned. His eyesight was exceptional. When he was flying... gunnery training in the States, he was superior, absolutely superior, in a class by himself. He didn't feel as kindly toward regular Marines, though, as he did towards reserves. It didn't take him long to differentiate which you were – whether you were a regular or a reserve. He was given to asking a very simple question: are you a reserve or regular?

"I think he had a lot to complain about. I think his family was in sort of disarray. He'd been taken away from a pretty good job as a ballplayer. I think he probably felt that it wasn't too important... I don't know this to be the case, but I think he might have felt that Korea was not the top of the list of importance in the world.

"He had some serious medical problems. I always look at my association with him as a very plus factor. I know that he was very outspoken, very straightforward. But you knew where you stood with the guy all the time. I think he wanted to be left alone because he'd had so much adulation... you could understand why the guy was the personality that he was.

"I retired as a light colonel. And regret that I didn't make it to bird. I don't know what it was, how it happened. That's the way the old ball bounces. My exposure to Ted was very limited. He kind of fought the system a little bit. But that was his prerogative. Other people did that, too. I wasn't one of them, but..."[25]

Barney McShane was the last C.O. under whom Ted served, in charge of the squadron when Williams was discharged and sent Stateside. He was not impressed at all with Ted Williams as a pilot. We will return to McShane in much more depth in the next chapter. Referring to Williams' ear problems, he said, "That's the basis of what we sent him home on. It was serious enough, and documented enough, to do that. But he was never a slacker, not wanting to fly. The real problem, really, was to get people to fly with him."

It was a little difficult to draw words out, because McShane is a gentleman and did not want to speak ill of Ted Williams after his passing. The exchange was interesting.

[Why was it hard to get people to fly with him? Wasn't he an adequate pilot?]

"Well... barely."

[Barely OK? Did people worry about their safety?]

"Yes."

[It wasn't just his personality?]

"Oh, no."

[I did notice that he never led a mission.]

"Oh, no. *[said with emphasis]*. He'd drop his bombs too low and bust up his airplane and all that kind of stuff."[26]

Joe Mitchell, VMF-311 pilot and Operations Officer (and one of Ted's hutmates) said, "I always considered myself a friend. We weren't bosom buddies. He used to chide me a lot. I was the Operations Officer of the squadron. The flight officer and scheduling officer. He used to chide me and say, 'Geez, you regular officers are going to kill me! Don't schedule me with Glenn! Don't schedule me with yourself!' He felt we were too gung-ho. He didn't appreciate when we were up there flying with the real thing... he didn't appreciate when we wanted to go down and answer these ground guys' call for more ammunition. When we got through dropping bombs in a close air support mission, they'd say, 'Can you strafe that ridge line over there?' Using our 20MM cannons. We'd say, 'Yeah, talks on 20 mike mike' – boom – and we'd give it to them. Ted would kind of ease off a little bit. He wouldn't drive in like we would.

"He wasn't afraid. Just caution. And also it was something new to him. You could see these guys were shooting at you.

"I think he was competent. I think he could have been a better pilot with a little more experience [like] we had. We tried to make him feel comfortable so he didn't feel like he wasn't performing. I think a lot of it was just getting used to doing what he was doing, which wasn't his normal day's work for him."[27]

John Beck, VMF-115 pilot, was one of the few pilots that report seeing Ted Williams ready to leave Korea. Asked, in terms of technical abilities, how Ted was as a pilot, Beck answered firmly, "Oh, good pilot! His reactions were quick. From baseball, his reactions were out of sight. Good pilot. Never heard anybody complain about him." Beck illustrates here once more the different circles in which those stationed on the base inhabited. Whether justified or not, there certainly were people who did not think well of Williams. But Beck apparently never heard the critics. This was not uncommon.

Beck remembers Ted as ready to go home. He remembers seeing him outside Operations on the day Williams left K-3. "He was just standing against the building and he was fidgeting around waiting for the transport to come over and get him. I talked with him a little bit. He was glad to get out of there. Glad to get out of there."[28]

Whatever the feelings of his fellow pilots, Marines on the ground appreciated the close air support provided them by the Marine Air Wing. Here is a letter sent the author of this book by one of the "grunts on the ground":

"The last name is Putnam, James H. I served in the 1st Marine Division, 7th Marine Regiment, Weapons Co., 2nd Battalion and was attached to both Dog and Fox companies at different times. I was a section leader for the 1st Section of Heavy Machine Guns and served in Korea from 9/52 thru 10/53.

"I have many memories of air support we received from Marine, Navy, and, occasionally, Air Force pilots. We called for air cover quite frequently. It seems to me the bulk of our cover was provided by piston engine aircraft, primarily Corsairs and AD-7s; however, Marine jets were also involved. I would estimate that probably 60 to 70% of our cover were provided by the former and jets 30 to 50%. At least that's the way it seemed to me.

"They, of course, were an absolute Godsend to we grunts on the ground. Their mere appearance immediately silenced Chinese/NK artillery and kept that off our back as well as providing us with the ability to reinforce, withdraw, and maneuver with a minimum of risk. As you know, the Chinese had a vast superiority in manpower and ground support helped level the playing field.

"I recall many, many instances of jet support, which was primarily dropping napalm on Chinese positions. They could obliterate a whole hill in a flash. The jet aircraft that I saw were primarily used for this purpose as well as destroying enemy artillery, mortar, and troop assembly positions behind their lines.

"The Corsairs and ADs were much more effective against front line troops and bunkers because they were much slower and could get much lower than the jets. The latter were just too fast to be as effective as the Corsairs.

"We were trying to hold our outpost positions, The Hook in Oct./Nov. 52, Vegas, Reno and Carson in March of 53, and the Berlins and Boulder City in July of 53, and could not have done so without air cover. We were taking so much incoming that it was suicide to get out of your "hole" and the appearance of an air strike and consummation of same would immediately shut down the incoming and knock out many of their positions.

"As soon as the sun went down, the incoming would get heavy, i.e., no air cover at night, and would continue all night long. I hoped and prayed that they could develop some way that we could have air cover at night. Didn't happen at least while I was there. Consequently, 99% of the fighting took place at night. The only enemy ground action that occurred during daylight hours was conducted only in bad weather when the air support was grounded.

"My last night on line, which occurred the night of 25/26th July, 53, we were on Outpost Boulder City. The Chinese assault began shortly after dark, which was about 2100 or 2200 hrs. We had the remnants of 2 inf. Co's on the Hill, Fox Co. 7th. Marines and, I believe, Charlie Co. 1st. Marines, and were hit with about two battalions to a regiment of Chinese. They got into our trenches about midnight and the fight ebbed and flowed, sometimes hand to hand, all night long. We lost about 1/3 of the hill but at daybreak were still holding on by our fingernails. As soon as first light, the Navy/Marine air was on station and the Chinese began withdrawing. We took a lot of casualties that night, however we held the hill and surely could not have done so without air on station the first thing in the morning. This is just one of many instances when air cover saved our bacon.

"There were also some humorous instances. I was watching an air strike shortly after arriving in country in September '52. The strike was occurring on a Chinese hill immediately to my front (can't remember its name) and the aircraft were diving from behind us. We were standing in the trench watching the strike and the planes were firing their 20MM/40MM (can't remember which) as they dove. The kid next to me had his helmet off when he got conked by a spent shell casing from the diving plane. It knocked him silly for a few minutes as well as giving him a nice laceration on the top of his head. A tough way to get a Purple Heart!!

"Bill, hope the foregoing can give you some idea of how important air cover was to us and our staying alive in Korea. I often wondered if one of those pilots was Ted Williams and very likely it was.

"I was born and raised in Michigan and have always been a Detroit Tigers fan. I had the opportunity to see Ted play a couple of times before I went into the service and watched him kill my Tigers on more than one occasion. I was also aware that he had been a Marine pilot during WWII and had been recalled during the Korean Action. I also knew that he was flying in Korea at the time I was there but didn't know he was flying combat missions. I assumed that because of his fame they would have him in some cushy job; however, knowing Williams' disposition, should have known better.

"Most of the kids in my section were baseball fans and we often wondered, while watching air strikes if one of the pilots could have been Ted. We often would say we could tell the difference between married and single pilots because the married ones always made a much more shallow dive than the single ones. The latter (it seemed) would stay in their dive until they were practically scraping the Chinese hill. I'm sure Ted was one of the latter."[29]

Tom Hulihan concurs. Hulihan was a staff sergeant who served with the U. S. Army's 3rd Infantry Division in Korea in 1952 and 1953. He remembers those days clearly, saying, "Every time a plane flew over, I would say to the guys, 'There goes Ted Williams.' They'd ask me, 'Is he the only guy that flies those jet planes?'

Hulihan explained more about his own background and what Williams meant to him:

"I went into the Army as a Red Sox fan. I started rooting for the Red Sox in '48 and '49 because they'd go down to the last game. Don't forget, I was living in New York State, so I was really a minority. Everyone else was rooting for the Yankees and they always won, so I figured I'd pick the underdog.

"I had an opportunity to go to Fenway Park one time before I went to Korea, to see Ted play, and when I got there, the game got rained out. I said to myself, 'I'll never get to see him play.'

"I was a kid that got drafted off the street corner into the Army. I was living in Troy, New York. I went to basic training and at the end of basic training, they stood up and told me I was a trained killer. I didn't really feel like one. I got to Korea. I met my company commander and he said, 'War is my game, and I love it.' I said to myself, 'I'm never going to see Troy again alive.' So I needed some kind of inspiration to keep going. I wasn't an Audie Murphy. I was in a situation where I was just trying to stay alive, and I needed an inspiration – and I mean, it was my inspiration – the fact that Ted Williams and I were in this thing together. He was there, and I was there, and every time I saw a plane go overhead, I was inspired. He was there and I was there. It was just like a common bond that we had.

"We were right up on the front lines. We were around Heartbreak Ridge. They [Marine Corps close air support pilots] would come low. You could feel the heat of the napalm on your face, they were dropping them that close. They'd come down and dive and you'd swear they were going to dive into the ground, and they would at the last second pull out and drop that napalm. It was amazing to watch them."[30]

And Hulihan took comfort that one of those jets was flown by Ted Williams, bringing firepower that was needed to hold back the enemy. It was a real morale-booster for this infantryman, one he still savors more than half a century after the fact.

Another infantryman was PFC Charles W. Harvey of Item Company, 3rd Batallion, 7th Marines, Ist Marine Division. He told about a time when he believed that Williams flew overhead. "I don't have much of a story to tell," he began, "but it was a real morale booster. I was with I-3-7 Marines on a 50 MG in front of Tae Dak Song on June '53. We were on a knoll with a 50, maybe 150 feet above the paddies. We were shelled daily, mortars and 76s. I don't know how many casualties we had in our unit, as we were by ourselves and didn't have any visitors. We were isolated. Things were static at the time. The unit sent patrols out and so did he enemy, at night. Close air support meant a lot to us.

"Somewhere along that time, the word was passed that Ted Williams would be flying over our sector at a certain time, like, say, 1500, Ted Williams was supposed to fly over our sector. I'm sure it was only seconds, the time he was flying over us. It was three or four jets. I couldn't look in the cockpit, I'm just going by what they told us. I remember his tipping the wing, in acknowledgement. What I am feeling is, he's saying hello to me. It's probably not true, but that's what I wanted to believe.

When you're on the line, and things aren't going well, anything like that – you want to grab at anything – it just meant so much! It really lifted our spirits."[31]

It is hard to minimize the feeling expressed by Harvey. The mere fact that Ted Williams was serving in Korea truly did mean a lot to so many other servicemen. Whether or not Williams got along with everyone in his unit, refused to play baseball on the base, kept to himself and was maybe even a little standoffish – none of that mattered to hundreds and maybe thousands of men serving in Korea, men who never met him but who nonetheless were touched and inspired by his presence.

Television host Ed McMahon served as a Marine fighter pilot, too. McMahon's service number was just 13 numbers off from Ted Williams, but they were on parallel tracks and never met during World War II. While Ted was at Chapel Hill, Ed was training in Athens, Georgia.

McMahon explained: "I knew about him; he didn't know about me. It would get in the paper that he was doing dive bombing training. When he was in, say, dive bombing training, I was in dive bombing training. I was able to follow his career in the newspaper and we paralleled each other. We paralleled each other but we never met. When the war was over, he went about his business and I went about my business. Then we were both called back for the Korean War. Our numbers were 13 numbers apart. So when he was called back, I knew I'd be called back."

Like Williams, McMahon served as a fighter pilot instructor in World War II. McMahon taught carrier landings and served as a test pilot. He had not flown at all during the years in between. Both McMahon and Williams were sent to Korea. McMahon was assigned to work as an artillery spotter.

"I was an artillery spotter flying light aircraft over the front lines, directing artillery fire. He was in fighter jets. We were there about the same time. I was there from about January or February 1953 until the end of the war. I was stationed at… it wasn't a base, it was a small field, a dirt strip right behind the front lines. We were attached to the First Marine Division. It was a light aircraft, a Cessna 172. We'd be 1,000 feet, 2,000 feet. We'd do whatever our assignment was. That's not my favorite activity. You don't want to do that work over the front lines!"

Though primarily directing artillery fire, it is reasonable to assume that some of the information McMahon relayed may well also have been used by VMF-311 and VMF-115 in their close air support.

McMahon readily agreed that having Ted Williams flying fighter planes in Korea meant a lot to the other men serving there. Was it a bit of a boost in the morale department? "Absolutely. He was a hero in baseball. He was a hero in his flying. We were all kind of heroes, but we read about him. He was world-famous, but he was doing the same sort of work that we were doing. Flying. In Korea, fighting the war."

Captain McMahon finally met Captain Williams right at the end. "The last night I spent in Tokyo, he also spent that night in Tokyo. We hooked up together and tore up the town a little bit. We just happened to meet, I think it may have been at the bar in the Imperial Hotel. That was a favorite hangout of Marine pilots. Two Marine pilots. I introduced myself, told him what a fan I was, told him about our numbers being so close together. We hit it off and we became pals. We just had a good time. We were relaxing. It was an R&R night. It was a nighttime thing and it had to do with food and a few drinks. Nothing serious, but a few drinks. Just kind of hanging out. He didn't play on his fame. It wasn't a big deal, no 'I'm Ted Williams!' Very nice guy… very pleasant."[32]

NOTES

1)   Interview with Art Moran, May 8, 1997.

2)   Sports Illustrated, August 1, 1955.

3)   Interview with Gen. L. B. Robertshaw, November 16, 2002.

4)   Interview with Rylen Rudy, February 4, 2003.

5)   Ibidem.

6)   Interview with Art Moran, May 8, 1997.

7)   Interview with Mike Canan, December 31, 2002.

8)   Interview with Jack McGuckin, February 11, 2003.

(9)   Interview with Larry Hawkins, December 21, 2002.

10) Ibidem.

11) Interview with Ed Buchser, November 26, 2002.

12) Interview with M. T. Schuerman, December 10, 2002.

13) Interview with Roger McCully, December 5, 2002.

14) Communication from Terry Stewart, January 6, 2003.

15) Interview with Leonard Waibel, December 19, 2002.

16) Ibidem.

17) Ibidem.

18) Interview with Bob Flanagan, June 2, 2003.

19) Interview with Gen. L. B. Robertshaw, November 16, 2002.

20) Interview with Jack Bolt, January 9, 2003.

21) Interview with Paul B. "Tex" Montague, February 11, 2003.

22) Interview with James Fox, February 8, 2003.

23) Interview with Elizabeth Armagost, December 23, 2002.

24) Interview with Carrol Burch, February 6, 2003.

25) Interview with Robert Peine, June 27, 2004.

26) Interview with Barney McShane, December 30, 2003.

27) Interview with Joseph Mitchell, February 3, 2003.

28) Interview with John D. Beck, December 13, 2002.

29) Communication from Jim Putnam, January 1, 2003.

30) Interview with Tom Hulihan July 19, 2004.
    Later, after Korea, Tom did get to see Ted play, but never met him in person until two Bosox Club trips at the very end
    of the 20th century, when Tom and other club members enjoyed lunch with Ted in Inverness, Florida.

31) Interview with Charles Harvey done January 4, 2003.

32) Interview with Ed McMahon done May 6, 2005.

CHAPTER 20 – A COURT-MARTIAL FOR TED WILLIAMS?

One of the most shocking things encountered in researching this book was the notion that Ted Williams' commanding officer had recommended him for a general court-martial. This first surfaced as a result of an e-mail from John Toler. I reached out to Toler about something he had written, and he e-mailed back: "I did a story about Ted Williams for our newspaper (Fauquier Times-Democrat, Warrenton, VA) shortly after he died. As you might expect, most of what I gathered from the normal sources was really positive info. That is, until I spoke with a widow of a VMF-311 pilot here in Warrenton who had some quite negative comments about Ted that she got from some of his contemporaries. So, instead of a tribute, it was more of a 'balanced' story. Then I heard from a few more people who really liked Ted, and they gave me more positive stuff. I think Ted was a rugged individualist, and did well to serve. He was one of my heroes when I was growing up." (1)

Information supplied by Toler pointed in the direction of Colonel Leonard Orr. Orr had written about Ted Williams, in his self-published book *The Life and Adventures of a Missouri Farm Boy* by Colonel Leonard L. Orr:

There was a lot of friendly competition in sports. Bronson [Naval Air Base, near Pensacola] had either three or four pro baseball players when I was there. All were cadets. One would not play any sport for fear of getting an injury that might restrict his earning power in the future. The others were just cadets and played any sport their counterpart cadets did. Unfortunately, I can only remember the spoiled baby's name, Ted Williams, and there will be more about them all on down the road. Williams was the only VIP I saw in World War II who exhibited every attribute of a spoiled brat. But that is the way you learn about real people. The later events concerning this batch of pro athletes really affected my maturity of thinking, particularly about devotion to duty under various circumstances, and will be discussed later...

Ted next to fully-loaded jet.
Photograph by Curt Giese.

I previously mentioned Hall of Fame baseball player Ted Williams. Captain Williams was recalled for Korea the same time I was and had been running parallel to my training for combat except he was sent through jet training and consequently was at K3 flying jets. One week I got some guff from Air Force pilots about fuel management by a Marine aviator. I did not know what they were talking about. Then the Pacific Stars and Stripes *came out with a picture of Captain Williams in it and it stated that he had an aircraft emergency etc. I did not know the details except I heard repeatedly it was fuel mismanagement. The emergency had happened on about his twentieth mission. Four years later, his former Commanding Officer told me that he had recommended a General Court Martial. The charges I would presume after he told me the specific acts would have been "Undermining Morale." The Commandant of the Marine Corps stopped the action by ordering him back to the states and I presume releasing him from active duty.*

About 1958-1959, the Marine Corps was going to cooperate with the city of Kansas City and have a big baseball celebration. I was being briefed by a Lieutenant Colonel far senior to me about how this fine Future Baseball Hall of Famer AND Marine Aviator was willing to help in any reasonable way. I was just seething and just erupted. "There will be no Aviation Marines there!!!" I do not even remember being so curt or disrespectful to someone so senior. However that was the end of that plan!

BUT of all people who should have "hated his guts" perhaps even more than his squadron mates in K3 were two of his running mates. They were the cadets at Bronson and they too had been recalled in 1952. One was Jerry Coleman (I think) who was then with the Yankees. Coleman was at K6 and was a good pilot and flew his missions. One day he had engine failure on takeoff and flipped. He was about to choke on his chin strap when a crash crewman cut it. He flew the next day! Quite a contrast to the spoiled brat, and that is using the very nicest term I can think of now! I marvel at the idea that the press has let all of this be swept under the rug for fifty years. I am sure some of them know. I know a lot of Marines who know about him who would be willing to sink his good ship of public relations. I wrote the only letter I have ever written to the Commandant of the Marine Corps in 1996 when the Commandant gave Williams some recognition. I just asked him to look at Williams' personal record before any more recognitions![2]

Personal vituperation is one thing, but this sounds like a very serious charge. Was it really true that Ted's C.O. had recommended a court martial, and only the intercession of the Commandant of the Marine Corps stopped the action? That would be a major revelation, if true. This required further investigation.

Colonel Orr was contacted on November 16, 2002, and reaffirmed the story in an interview:

"I ran across him as a cadet at Bronson Field in Pensacola. As a cadet, we had four pro ballplayers. Three of them played whatever they were told. One of them wouldn't play a damn thing because he was afraid that he might get hurt, and that was Mr. Williams. The other three, they played whatever the rest of us were playing. Coleman was one of them. [Here Orr is likely referring to ballplayer and Marine Joe Coleman, not Jerry Coleman.] I can't tell you the names of the other two now. The one who should hate his guts most of all, because he got the praise of this poor bastard... it might have been a pitcher... it might have been Coleman... .This guy had engine failure at K-6 in Korea and flipped on takeoff. The airplane of course landed on top. He was choking to death and the guy cut his chin strap and got him out of there, and he flew the next day. Quite a contrast.

"Williams and I went overseas about the same time. I don't recall seeing him at all during the Korean fracas. I got a lot of B.S. from the Air Force guys because he was up one time and declared an emergency and all he had was stupid management of his own fuel. Any amateur would know that but the Air Force was giving me a hard time – you know, poking fun – because I was a Marine, a fellow Marine. Just B.S., back and forth. Nothing serious. They were laughing and making fun of him because he declared an emergency, and it was just mismanaged fuel.

"At that time, he had about 20 missions and I had about 60 missions. But we came overseas about the same time.

"Barney McShane, he was a commanding officer. He was Williams' commanding officer and he recommended him for a general court martial. I do not know the issue. I do know that he drove a couple of his roommates until they went to the commanding officer and said, 'You get that sonovabitch out of our room or we're going to kill him, and we mean it.' They weren't kidding. He just got on their nerves so bad. Every day he was giving them a hard time because they were still flying, and they were both married. You know, trying to drive a guy to distraction. He succeeded, except that he didn't succeed quite the way he intended. Anyway, McShane is still pretty bitter. The Commandant of the Marine Corps, instead of a court martial – with all the bad publicity both for Williams and the Marine Corps – brought him home to the United States and discharged him. That's a way to get rid of it."[3]

Orr admitted an intense dislike. "I disliked him so much I wouldn't have anything to do with him. I guess he made my list when he wouldn't do anything the rest of the cadets were required to do at Bronson Field. I think that was the end as far as Williams and I were concerned. I didn't want anything to do with a goldbrick. I was a little disappointed and shocked that John Glenn was saying how great he was as a pilot. I know he's said that, but I don't know what pilot he was talking about."[4]

Col. Orr suggested contacting one of his commanding officers, Paul Noel. First, though, it seemed like a good idea to ask Barney McShane himself. Reached at his home by telephone, he would neither confirm nor deny the account, out of respect for the recently-deceased Ted Williams. "Well, you know he's dead. So I don't like to talk about him now. The official record contains all my feelings about the gentleman... it's all part of the official record, but now that's he dead, I had made up my mind that I was not going to comment about him at all any more."[5] If McShane were prepared to praise Williams, one suspects he'd not hesitate to do so.

The day after speaking with McShane, Noel was contacted. His comments were in line with Orr. He started with a bit of humor: "I think this was rather serious. I'll tell you what. At the time that it occurred – the rumors – a lot of folks were laughing. They were saying they would bet that any sportswriter from the Boston area, their paper would pay enough to get that story that the reporter could buy their retirement house on it! There's a lot of newspaper people who would have been glad to stick it to him." Noel then continued:

"But I will not tell you anything that's a rumor. You're going to have to get it from Barney McShane or somebody who was... I would say in the senior channel from Barney McShane. All I can tell you is that way back in those days, the Marine Corps at the very top made a certain decision. These guys – Barney McShane, and I didn't know that Robertshaw was Barney McShane's boss, but that's the way it goes. And then Robertshaw had a boss that was a general – I don't remember who it was at that time – and then from that general it would have gone up into Hawaii or Washington. The whole thing was structured, and there had to be a lot of people chop off on 'this is the way we're going to handle it.'

"Actually, the decision would be, 'What would be best for the Marine Corps?' Would the Marine Corps in the eyes of the public look particularly bad if they did something bad to Ted Williams? Or did something to Ted Williams that the public would see as being bad. Would the kids like you be absolutely torn apart? Would the youth rebel and not listen to the Marine Corps because they put it to Ted Williams?

"Either you're following the rules, or you're not following the rules. The decision was made to... I think the word 'cover-up' probably was used, or whatever it was.

"My understanding was that there was a dual trail of paper. They always say, 'Follow the paper.' My understanding was that in this case, there was a dual administrative chain of paper – one was classified and one was for the public.

"The problem is that Barney McShane made two reports. One was THE report, which was classified, and my understanding was that it ended up in the Commandant's safe, and not available to anybody. The other trail, and I'm sure that Barney must have choked down the bile when he had to write it, was the one that went public.

"I took the position a long time ago that if Barney McShane can swallow it and not say a word, I'm not going to say a word about anything I heard. My hearsay is strictly through buddies, who claimed to be on the inside in actually handling the case.

"If Robertshaw's got nothing to say, and Barney McShane's got nothing to say, they're still living up the Code and that's alright by me. All I can tell you is if you go after something with this Freedom of Information Act, you've got to remember that there's two trails and they may throw a bone to you. I'm sure that in Ted Williams' jacket, his Marine Corps record – wherever it might be – there's a piece of paper that shows he got sick and it shows that he got brought home because he got sick and poor guy and yak yak yak. Some place there's another trail."[6]

This seemed pretty conclusive, and pretty damning. Three senior officers all either stating, or seeming to affirm by declining to deny, that Ted Williams was nearly court-martialed but spared because of his stature as a prominent public figure.

But was it really true?

There was no hint at all in an interview with Gen. Robertshaw, who had spoken positively about Ted Williams and spent time with him after Williams's service was complete. Robertshaw had known Ted Williams since 1945. "I met him during World War II in Hawaii. He was in a replacement status and had to undergo carrier training before he went any further. I was in operations then, AirFMFPac – that's Aircraft Fleet Marine Force Pacific. I met him through the training of a replacement pilot, which he became. In Hawaii, we played volleyball almost every day after work, and he participated in that often, along with Ted Lyons. I just worked with him on rare occasions there. The next time I met him was in Korea." Let's also remember that Robertshaw had said kind things about Williams. To repeat: "I often flew on missions with him. He stood out because he didn't stand out. He was an acceptable pilot, just like anybody else. He wasn't deficient, and he did his share. Of course, that forced landing that he had certainly established him as skillful and brave. His nature wasn't much in terms of being a showoff or somebody who wanted to out-do other people. He did his share and that's what he wanted to do."[7]

Robertshaw had flown on the 16 February mission with Williams. In all, they flew together on six missions. Only a dozen pilots flew more missions with Ted. On most of the missions Robertshaw flew with Ted, he was in a leadership or observer status. Had he been uncomfortable with Williams' performance, he simply could have declined comment in the interview. Instead, his remarks seemed measured and judicious, and not indicative of an effort to cover up.

Still, the possibility had been broached, and the suggestion that not even a Freedom of Information Act request could uncover the true story. A number of other pilots and personnel stationed at K-3 were asked whether they had ever heard of things being so bad that a court-martial might have been discussed.

Major James Walley, third in the command structure under McShane, said, "Ted Williams was a very strong-willed individual and I could understand how he could get cross-wise with people. As far as I know, most of the pilots got along with him. I know I did. I don't think Ted was much of a drinker or anything. Some of the people we had were pretty good party folks."[8]

Lou Weatherford, who was a Marine private who had guard duty at the ordnance ammo dump on the base, had heard something. "As I recall, and you must understand that at my junior rank I didn't have a great deal of knowledge, but as I remember McShane – and I remember I ran into him sometime later on... oh hell I don't know, I may have been a second lieutenant by then... but he was a very... a very stern leader. To say the least. Sort of an unforgiving kind of fellow." Weatherford said that Williams was "a damn good pilot" but was not surprised at the idea that there might have been some tangle and that there might have been a decision taken to simply transfer Ted out, thereby defusing the situation. "He was very... you've got to understand that this was probably a lot of envy, among other things. He was not admired, I don't think, by the majority. I think the pilots and the people in general. I guess he was kind of a... even in later life, he was kind of a stand-offish sort of fellow. You know. Kind of a lone eagle. I don't think I ever heard anyone who did not speak highly of his ability. It's just him personally." Weatherford retired as a captain in 1972.[9]

Recalling the helmet/boom mic incident, Weatherford added:

"We didn't hear a damn thing about what goes on in officer's country, but it may have had something to do with that helmet incident, where he said he had a bad radio and shut the engine down, got out of the airplane and stomped on back. It was his mistake. He shouldn't have shut the engine down; he should have let people come out there and check his hookup. That very well may be why McShane had a chip knocked off his shoulder.

"You've got to remember, too, that McShane had a whole hell of a lot of other pilots in that squadron. At any given time, most of the pilots were reserve recallees. I'm sure that each and every one of them were aces in their fields, to some extent, just not as notable.

"How would you like to be the commanding officer of a starburst like that [Ted Williams]? And you've got all of these news weenies around. Anything that you say to him, you as his commander are probably under the magnifying glass as much as he. No censorship. And who knows what might be said?" [10]

That said, Williams may have ruffled feathers by being too outspoken. The provost marshal Ed Buchser, VMF-115 pilot and one of Ted's closest friends at K-3, told of a time Ted nearly hung himself: "I thought Ted was going to get court-martialed one night at dinner! The Colonel – Robertshaw – he asked me, 'Buck, do you think Ted could come and have dinner with us tonight?' And I said, 'Well, I'll ask him.' Usually nobody ate at that table except the skipper, the exec, the doctors and like that. So we did and as we were talking, well, old Ted – Theodore Samuel – he said, 'Well, Goddamnit, Colonel, what's this bullshit about we can't fly north of the Yalu River, but the MiGs come down south all the time and we can't go up there?' There were a lot of incongruities. It was actually our State Department. This was the beginning of how it got so fucked-up in Vietnam. He was talking to Colonel Robertshaw. They were arguing. Now, Robertshaw's very quiet, very capable, and he just held his temper. Finally Ted just shut up. Ted was not dumb, for Chrissake. I was just afraid that Robertshaw would really get at him."[11]

We noted in chapter 7 that Col. Jack McGuckin appreciated how Ted Williams had not sought softer duty when recalled. "He went for the toughest test of all," McGuckin has written. "He checked out in jets and went to Korea. When I met him there, I wondered why he had to prove anything. He was the best at what he did in baseball, and I suppose his pride refused to let him settle for anything less, even in a war." [12]

Jon Mendes, another 311 pilot, flew five missions with Ted. He also knew McShane, and said, "McShane was a really good man. For a regular, he was OK. You don't realize, but at the end of the war we had 32 reserve officers and two regulars in the squadron. We were all reserve officers.

We were the leading squadron in the whole goddamn Marine Corps in the Korean War – we were flying F9's. But we were all reserve officers. Barney McShane and Mike Canan, who was a major junior to me [were regulars] – and the rest of us were all reserves. I am so proud of the fact that we came out of civilian life and did our job. We didn't think anything about it. That's the way it was.

"Barney didn't like Ted. He thought he was a s-h-i-t. When I spoke to Barney about Ted, several years ago, my impression was that he said, 'Ted was always bitching all the time. Giving me a headache. He was bitching about things.' I don't remember it."[13]

Asked in a later exchange to characterize Lt. Col. McShane's relationship with Ted Williams, Mendes wrote, "he told me a few years ago that Ted was nothing but trouble for him... an attitude problem. I got along fine with Ted as an acquaintance not as a friend. In jest he said to me once that I had a problem. I was a Reserve officer with the attitude of a regular. I considered this a compliment although I'm not sure it was intended that way."[14]

Joe Mitchell described his hutmate Ted Williams: "I knew he was in pain with his ears. That happened just before I left the squadron. There was some discussion in the squadron – just talking to people out there – about Barney's dissatisfaction that Ted wouldn't get in the air. Something like that. I think if he had a gripe, he just didn't think that Ted was maybe responding to the need of everybody participating."[15]

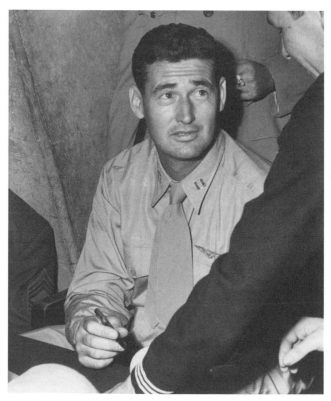

Ted on arrival in United States.
Courtesy of The Sporting News/ZUMA Press.

The target priority officer for the 1st Marine Air Wing, Al Pommerenk, had heard that Ted begged off flying. "I think the biggest thing that I heard is the fact that he just came back from one hop and said, 'That's it. I'm not going to fly any more.' That's the only thing that I can say – and I don't want to hold it against him. I don't know all the details or anything about it."[16]

Pilot Bill Clem was not surprised by the notion, and he'd known Ted since Roosevelt Roads. As noted in chapter 16, Clem claimed that Ted rejected flying an F9F-2: "He wasn't afraid or anything, but it was an inferior aircraft. So they had to assign someone else to it. They took the mission. The next day, the C.O. transferred him to the group, out of the squadron. MAG-33." Was Williams close to a court-martial? "He was close. I don't know if you knew that. I've never seen that in print. That's the truth. But it was awful quiet. I think the Marine Corps covered it up, because they didn't want that to happen. So then they made up this deal about his being sick. They sent him out to a hospital ship and then they sent him home. He did have some ear problems. A lot of people had ear problems."[17]

But could this be correct? As suggested earlier, the chronology doesn't seem to fit. According to the squadron command diaries, F9F-2s were flown only rarely after February. One flew in a mission on 16 March, one flew on 27 March and one flew on 14 April. Not a single F9F-2 flew even once in the months of May or June. If Ted were transferred the "next day" after refusing to fly an F-2, one would first have to ask why it would have been suggested he fly one. If only three F-2s had flown in the preceding four months, and none at all since mid-April, then why in mid-June would Ted Williams be asked to fly one?

Jon Mendes had mentioned that Mike Canan was, other than McShane, the only other regular in the squadron. Canan commented on the question of a court-martial. "I know that McShane was a little put out with him. I think they wanted to write him up for a court-martial, but the higher-ups didn't want to. That's exactly why he left so soon, I think – they wanted to get him out of there." Above, we have seen Canan say, "I could understand his feelings, but it kind of irritated some people. It irritated me, and the people who were trying to do the job that was supposed to be done. He was kind of lackadaisical about it; he was kind of loose – he wasn't serious. He gave me the impression that he didn't care."[18]

McShane was new to the squadron, having only joined it on June 1. Ted's last mission was just nine days later. There must have been an instant dislike, because that's not much time for any work that might need to be done on a relationship.

Milton Rugg arrived five days after Williams had departed. He was the squadron Education Officer. As we learned in Chapter 16, Rugg's understanding was that Ted "came back from a mission and he put an airplane in a creek bed and I guess they figured he'd flown enough, and they sent him home."[19]

So here is another story – that Ted had landed a plane in a creek bed, not that he'd refused to fly an F9F-2. Jon Mendes led the last mission Ted was on, and he hadn't heard that one. Specifically as to Ted landing his plane in a creek bed: "I know nothing about it." He also said he never heard about any rumors of a court-martial.[20] Since Mendes led the last mission Ted was assigned to – the 10 June mission Ted had to abort – one might think he also would have heard if Williams had (a) refused an aircraft, (b) landed a plane in a creek bed, or (c) been guilty of serious fuel mismanagement. That there could be at least three specific allegations associated with one event – Ted Williams being ordered to leave the base for medical treatment – is at least indicative of the impression that Ted Williams used to attract stories and legends the way a lighted lamp attracts moths.

Paul Janssen, another pilot in the squadron, discounted the idea of the creek bed landing: "You don't land F9s in creek beds. Not and walk away from them. I never heard anything like that. If you went in short, you went into a field." After all, you'd be a lot safer landing on a flat surface.[21]

Another source said that Ted had crashed another plane just outside K-3, and made his way back to the base. According to this telling, by the time Ted had reached the gate to the base, the Koreans living in the area had already stripped the plane for salvage and parts had already turned up in the village outside the base. This sounds like a good story, but maybe no more than a good story. Two planes were lost after a close air support mission on 6 May, when pilots Carruthers and Bailes lost their planes while trying to land. Captain Carruthers had to ditch his plane in the ocean, and was rescued one hour later. Captain Bailes' plane crashed on land, and the wreckage and his scattered remains were found the following day. Other than those two losses, there is no indication of any damage done to any of the squadron's aircraft in the months of April, May, or June, according to the daily logs which are supposed to report loss or damage to aircraft. It seems rather unlikely that Williams would have damaged a plane so badly that parts were showing up in the village outside the base, yet no damage to any aircraft was ever recorded in the unit maintenance report.

However, Hank Kirby, a hospital corpsman on the *USS Consolation*, volunteered, "As the story was related to me he was ordered to fly a mission off his carrier, complained of stuffiness and hearing problems, but was ordered to go anyway. Upon return he had a rough landing with some damage to the aircraft. As he was nearing the end of his call-up period, his CO ordered him to the hospital ship, AH-15, and very shortly was sent to Japan and back to the states for release. As rumor had it, this was ordered done rapidly to make it more difficult to bring charges.

"It's my suspicion that because of his heavy landing and damaging the aircraft, that he was going to be court-martialed, and that the commanding officer, knowing that he had a very short time left in his callup as a Marine Reserve, [figured] he would get him back to Hawaii and separated. They generally didn't follow officers after they were separated, and give them any reprimands or trials. I think this was the case, but it's only a strong suspicion. I have no facts to back it up."[22] Ted Williams was always land-based, though, and never flew off carriers in Korea, so it's likely that Major Kirby mixed up more than one case here, or else the story he'd been related had become distorted in the telling. Ted's stay on the *Consolation* was also quite a bit earlier in the spring. Kirby had noted that Ted was genuinely ill at that time: "Even an amateur such as I could detect that there was something wrong. The characteristic stuffiness and red eyes, talking as though you're stuffed up, were evident."[23]

Rylen Rudy, not surprisingly, given his passionate dislike of Ted Williams, was asked if he had heard that McShane might have recommended a court-martial for Williams, said, "I didn't know that, but I don't doubt it at all. You know, even as a ballplayer he was an asshole. You've got to respect the guy's ability, as a ballplayer. You had to respect it. Of course, as a Marine aviator, he didn't get to go any place in World War II. After World War II was over, he did like a lot of guys. Hell, if he stayed in the reserves, he not only got to fly airplanes but he made about $3000.00 a year. That's good easy money and it's fun because you got to fly airplanes. That was his choice. When it all hit the fan, you know, then he comes out there and at that time they're probably paying a captain about five or six thousand dollars, which was a hell of a lot less than he was paying in taxes. I can understand why he was not overly happy, but he made his choices. Lloyd Merriman and the guys that came out there that were in the same basic boat – now, they didn't make the kind of money that he did, but at the same time, they came out there, put a smile on their face, did their job and came home."[24]

John Glenn, on the other hand, had said, "I certainly welcomed the opportunity to fly with him, because I thought he would be a good pilot. Whether he was a good baseball player or not doesn't ..what you're interested in out there was what sort of a pilot he is, obviously....He did a great job and he was a good pilot. He wasn't out there moaning all the time or trying to duck flights, or anything like that. He was out there to do the job and he did it. He did a helluva good job."[25] Glenn had joined VMF-311 on 15 February, just twelve days after Ted Williams.

How does Rudy reconcile Glenn's praise of Williams, not only in these comments, but at least as effusively in other places, including his own books? Rudy was asked, "Wasn't John Glenn always very complimentary about Ted Williams?" Yes, he was, Rudy agreed. "Glenn always has been. I am not a politician. I guarantee it. And I consider Williams the biggest asshole I ever met."[26]

How does one reconcile the whole issue addressed in this chapter?

Maybe one doesn't.

Three superior officers mentioned the issue, but for two of them (Orr and Noel) it was by rumor, or something they had heard. McShane had only been in 311 for 9 days, during which time Ted flew just two missions, both on 10 June. Lt. Col. McShane was not a stranger, though. He'd been with MAG-33 since 21 April, and had flown three prior missions with Ted Williams. Others who served in MAG-33 included Robertshaw, Walley, Glaese, and Bartosh, all of whom seemed to have worked well with Williams.

Of course, Ted's reputation would have come to McShane's attention. As a "stern, unforgiving" C.O. wanting to be sure he maintained control of his squadron at a time when the war was clearly winding down (the armistice was signed less than 60 days after he arrived), he would have paid attention to what scuttlebutt he heard. Ted's griping, perhaps intensified as his ear problem lingered, would undoubtedly have rubbed such a man the wrong way. Refusing flights became a problem around this time, with Marine Corps reservists. "They refused a lot of flights. I do know this. At the end of the war, they said that the war was going to end at noon tomorrow or something, and it was a hell of a thing to get any reservists up – and I don't blame them. The last, you couldn't get any reservist up on any mission and I flew four missions that day."[27]

It's too bad that Barney McShane wouldn't be more specific. Well, why not give him another call a year later and see if he was more willing to speak, given now that Ted's death was not as recent? He was. Thirteen months had passed. Respecting his desire to not speak ill of those who were no longer around to defend themselves, McShane was read a prepared statement, and then asked to correct anything that might be wrong or misleading.

The dialogue went as follows, asking specifically about Ted Williams:

[I have to do a write up on him in particular, and I don't want to project a false image one way or another. Let me say something that I wrote out here, and tell me if you think that I would be inaccurate to write something like this.]

OK

[This is what I wrote: "Williams was always a loud and controversial character. Some liked him. He rubbed others the wrong way. Two Marines I spoke with told me that they knew Ted's commanding officer, Barney McShane, recommended him for a general court-martial, because Williams was disturbing the morale of the outfit. McShane declined to comment. Several other pilots told me they wouldn't have been surprised, however. My surmise is that had the Marine Corps followed McShane's recommendation, it might have been considered too embarrassing for the Marine Corps and their VIP pilot, Ted Williams. The war was clearly almost over. To those above McShane, it may have seemed preferable simply to see Williams brought home and discharged honorably, to more or less save face all the way around." If I say something like that, am I being misleading in some fashion?]

Well, it never got to the point of recommending him for a general court-martial.

[It's just something that was contemplated... ?]

No. We grounded him. And we decided that the best thing to do was to send him home on a medical. He had some ear problems from swimming out in the salt water all the time. And so we sent him back on a medical. We didn't need his goddamn flight pay, or his pay or anything, and he didn't need it. There just wasn't anything to be gained by bad-mouthing him.

[I had heard that he just griped a lot about the equipment. I never heard anybody say that he actually declined a mission. Well, one person said he thought he had.]

No, I don't think he ever declined. The problem was, we couldn't get anybody to fly with him! It just got to the point where he wasn't adding anything to the squadron. As a matter of fact, at one time all the pilots came to me and said if I didn't get rid of him, they were going to put in for a mass transfer out of the squadron. He just wasn't very well accepted by the other pilots at all.

[I've talked to a number of other pilots, and I don't know if they're just being diplomatic but they say nice things about him. Certainly, John Glenn says nice things about him...]

Well, he was a hell of a good baseball player! Sure.

[I do understand he wouldn't play ball with anybody in Korea. He did in World War II. He did a lot of exhibition baseball. He just kind of kept to himself, I guess, in Korea.]

Yeah.

[He did spend a lot of time on hospital ships, on the *Haven* and the *Consolation* both, at one time or another.]

I don't remember.

[So I guess he did have some kind of ear problem, I guess.]

That's the basis of what we sent him home on. It was serious enough, and documented enough, to do that. But he was never a slacker, not wanting to fly. The real problem, really, was to get people to fly with him.

[Why? He was supposed to be an adequate pilot.]

Well... barely.

[Barely, OK? Did people worry about their safety?]

Yes.

[It wasn't just his personality.]

Oh, no.

[I did notice that he never led a mission.]

Oh, no. [said with emphasis].28

Talking with Col. McShane, then, several points are worth understanding. No, as McShane tells it, Ted Williams was never recommended for a court-martial, and it wasn't contemplated. Williams did not decline a mission. And "he was never a slacker, not wanting to fly." That was reassuring.

What McShane did say, though, was perhaps damning enough. He says that the other pilots in the squadron did not want to fly with him, and that they worried about their safety when they did so. Further, McShane made the discontent seem universal, when he said that "at one time all the pilots came to me and said if I didn't get rid of him, they were going to put in for a mass transfer out of the squadron."

How likely was that? ALL the pilots? Aside from McShane and Williams, there were 40 pilots in the squadron as of June 1. In the many interviews for this book, there were any number of criticisms leveled at Williams. Some likely well-founded, and some demonstrably unsupportable. The idea that pilots were worried about flying with him was not mentioned.

Ted's earlier commanding officers hadn't apparently had problems with Williams, or if they had, they'd kept them in perspective and worked with him. Art Moran and Ben Robertshaw, for instance, were both generally positive in their comments.

Who else was in 311 at the time Lt. Col. McShane arrived? John Glenn was, and he has nothing but highly complimentary things to say about Ted Williams. John Glenn is the man who said, "Ted only batted .406 for the Red Sox. He batted a thousand for the Marine Corps and the United States."[29]

Many of the Marines in 311 have died in the intervening 50-plus years. Others proved impossible to locate. Interviews were done with every pilot who could be located, some 22 in all. None of them mentioned approaching McShane and threatening a mass transfer, though some indicated awareness that there was tension between Ted and McShane.

There is no doubt that Ted Williams was an opinionated individual. He never had any serious problems with authority per se (as mentioned, he was never once ejected from a major league ballgame), but his irreverent humming of the Marine Corps hymn to Mike Canan, his tendency to bitch all the time, his keeping to himself as much as he did – all this might have contributed to disquiet his new commanding officer.

So many stories – the creek bed, etc. – just don't seem to be supportable. Yet McShane might well have heard such stories. It may have simply seemed like too much to him, and he may have just want-ed to remove the sour note, one that he wasn't as prepared to want to deal with. His own superiors in MAG-33 and the 1st Marine Air Wing may have felt, "Listen, Williams has put in his time. The war's ending. The squadron is at full strength now. He's really not needed as a pilot any more. He could become more disaffected and become a morale problem that we don't really need, either. He's suffering a recurring ear problem. Let's just send him home, rather than inflame a brewing personal-ity conflict, and spare the Corps (and the squadron) what could be unnecessary and easily avoidable potential for disruption. Let's avoid any black eye, and save face for everyone. Let's go on about our business, and let him get back to his."

If that was the reality, and that was the thinking, that would have been wise counsel on the part of those who helped make the decision. Williams may never have known of the discussions that McShane must have had, and that would have all been for the better, too. Ted Williams was left with a good feeling for his time in the Marine Corps, and most of the Marines who served with him were spared feeling ill of Ted Williams. History has to record the possibility of this blemish on his military career. Perhaps the Commandant has another file locked away in a safe somewhere. If so, it must be joined by thousands of other compromises and accommodations reached over the years. Today, the Marine Corps is proud of having Ted Williams' service and Ted Williams was proud of having served in the Marine Corps. History really is happier this way.

Postscript

In what may be considered by some to be a bit of irony, Captain Theodore S. Williams was presented his three Air Medals by Lt. Col. McShane on 12 June 1953. Later in the year, General Lemuel C. Shepherd, Jr., Commandant of the United States Marine Corps, forwarded Williams the certificates for the Air Medal and Gold Stars in lieu of a second and third Air Medal. His letter said that the medals had been presented "for meritorious achievements in aerial flights during operations against enemy aggressor forces in Korea." Gen. Shepherd added, "Be assured of my deep appreciation of your devotion to duty and gallant action which were in keeping with the highest traditions of the United States Marine Corps."

The actual award of the medals had originally been over the signature of Major General V. E. Megee. The letter accompanying the Gold Star in lieu of the third Air Medal read "For meritorious acts while participating in aerial flight against the enemy while attached in the 1st Marine Aircraft Wing in KOREA for 26 April 1953 to 17 May 1953. Captain WILLIAMS successfully completed his twenty-first through thirtieth missions against the enemy where enemy fire was either expected or received. His courageous actions and devotion to duty throughout were in keeping with the highest traditions of the United States Naval Service." Virtually identical language accompanied the other Gold Star.

No doubt this was standard language for such awards and not necessarily indicative of particular individual accomplishment. Language that was Williams-specific, however, was that contained in the Officer Fitness Report that was completed periodically throughout his service. During World War II, the only report that could be retrieved from Marine Corps files covered the period from April 1, 1945 through June 5, 1945, during which time Williams was stationed at the Naval Auxiliary Air Station, Bronson Field, Pensacola, working as a Flight Instructor. He was rated either "Good" (defined as average) or "Very Good" (defined as above average) in every category observed, except one. Amusingly, the one where he was rated only "Fair" was "Military bearing and neatness (dignity of demeanor; neat and smart appearance)." Sounds a bit like Ted Williams, the man known to avoid neckties whenever possible.

Commander H. E. Carlson's report recommended Williams for commission in the regular Marine Corps. When the war was over, though, Williams apparently preferred to return to baseball.

Williams' fitness reports in Korea are interesting, though. The first report was completed by Lt. Col. Jack R. Moore, Commanding Officer at Willow Grove. It covered the period 2 May 52 to 28 May 52, beginning with the day Ted reported for duty. "Officer's choice for next assignment" was "Fighter Pilot." He was given the equivalent of "Very Good" across the board, with two exceptions. In the area of public relations, he was only given the equivalent of a "Good," his lowest grade. He was given the highest marks under "Improving Effectiveness," where it was said he "actively seeks out opportunities to improve his effectiveness."

For the two months at Cherry Point, with Major John H. McEniry, Jr. evaluating, the lowest mark Williams earned was "Excellent" and he received a number of "Outstanding" ratings – in Endurance, Cooperation, and Loyalty. Maj. McEniry wrote, "Successfully completed Flight Refresher Training syllabus and jet checkout in an outstanding manner. This officer's attitude toward his recall to active duty and flying is that to be desired by all Reserve officers. Recommended for promotion when due." The major checked off the highest rate "particularly desire to have" when asked what his attitude would be toward having the officer under his command during war.

The Officer Fitness Report for the next two months at Cherry Point was completed by Lt. Col. Hoyle S. Barr. Williams indicated his first choice of duty was to serve overseas, his second choice was to serve at El Toro, and his third choice was to serve in the Miami area. Barr wrote, "Recommend officer's first choice." Williams was rated Above Average, Excellent, and Outstanding. The brief narrative read, "Captain Williams had made rapid strides in both his work and flying since reporting to this organization and is considered a fine young officer. His personality and appearance create a distinctly favorable impression." Young? Perhaps he had not realized his subject's age.

Lt. Col. Bernard McShane presents Capt. Ted Williams with the Air Medal and two Gold Stars in lieu of the second and third Air Medal. McShane is commanding officer of VMF-311. June 24, 1953.

Defense Department photograph by Cpl. Gerald Harrington.
Courtesy of National Archives and Records Administration.

Barr again completed the report. He again rated Ted highly, though a bit lower. His overall rating dropped from "Excellent" to "Above Average." Still believing Ted to be young, he wrote, "Captain Williams is a young officer of fine potentialities and is an excellent pilot and should do well in a combat assignment. His personality and appearance create a favorable impression."

For the period "8Dec52 to 28Jan53", Major Alton McCully, the Officer in Charge Third Airlift January 1953 Aviation Replacement Draft, based at Marine Corps Air Station El Toro, signed off on the papers but noted that he had not observed Williams.

Williams arrived in Korea and the first Officer Fitness Report was completed by Lt. Col. Francis K. Coss, Commanding Officer, VMF-311. Williams was a jet pilot with additional duties as an Ordnance Officer and (following in his father's footsteps?) Photographic Officer. Coss's overall rating was "Excellent." In most categories, Ted was rated "Excellent," though he was Outstanding in two areas and Above Average in three. Coss's narrative covered Ted's first combat missions, as the period ended 28 February 1953. The report read: "This officer has completed his initial combat indoctrination within this squadron in an excellent manner. He is eager to learn and makes a determined effort to perform his duties in a satisfactory manner. He is recommended for a regular commission but does not desire a regular commission. He is recommended for promotion when due. This duty was performed in a combatant unit in Korea during which time he actively participated in flying combat missions."

Lt. Col. Coss's next report covered the period 1 March 1953 to 20 April 1953. Again, the overall rating was Excellent. Ted had improved, apparently. All grades were Excellent or Outstanding. No grades were as low as "Above Average" – much less the three lower grades. Coss wrote, "This officer has completed his transition to combat flying in a highly commendable manner. He is aggressive, cheerful and cooprcrative. He does not desire a regular commission but is recommended for a regular commission. He is recommended for promotion when due. These duties were performed within a combatant unit in Korea during which time he actively participated in flying combat missions."

TED WILLIAMS: "ABOLISH THE MARINE CORPS"?

VMF-311 pilot John Verdi recalls some spirited jousting between Art Moran and Ted Williams which may give us some insight. Someone who didn't understand Ted as well, or lacked a leavening sense of humor, might have taken Ted's remarks in a much more serious light.

"I walked to the Club, picked up a can of beer, and went on into the Mess. I looked about the noisy room, spotted a table of 311 types, swiped a chair from another table, and joined them.

"Art Moran and Ted Williams were engaged in an exchange of words on the subject of the Marine Corps...

"'You know, Ted,' observed Art, 'You're a lot safer out here driving these airplanes than you were in Fenway Park dodging all those pop-bottles.'

"Williams grew a little more livid.

"'I'll fix all of you muckers. I'm going to campaign for the abolition of the Corps, by God! I'm going to write magazine articles. You'll all be absorbed by the Army, and then you be RIF'ed! All you Reggies will have to earn an honest living. Yes, sir! Wait 'til I get back home. I'll fix you bastards!'

"Art launched another thrust: 'Ted,' he said – somehow combining malice with concern – 'You're an old man. You're all washed up in baseball, I'll tell you what: There's not much demand for thirty-four-year-old Captains, but if you'll put in for a Regular Commission, I'll put a favorable endorsement on your application.'

"At this, even Williams' outraged roar was drowned by the chorus of laughter."

John M. Verdi
First Hundred: A Memoir of The Korean War, *1952-1953, privately printed, 1989, p. 149*

Verdi noted Ted's comment in *My Turn At Bat*: "I was no hero. There were maybe seventy-five pilots in our two squadrons and 99 percent of them did a better job than I did."

Ted Williams, My Turn At Bat, *p. 182*

The next report was signed by Lt. Col. Arthur M. Moran on 31 May 1953. Moran had succeeded Coss as Commanding Officer of VMF-311. He rated Ted overall as "Excellent" and said he would "particularly desire to have" Williams under his command in combat. Moran, of course, did have Williams under his command and flew 12 combat missions with him. No one flew more; only Lovette flew as many. So Moran's was not a hypothetical comment, but rather one based in experience. The individual category ratings were mostly Excellent, with two Above Average, and two Outstanding. The narrative: "Capt. Williams flew twenty-five (25) combat missions during this period to bring his Korean total to thirty-seven (37). He has shown great improvement in his flying and with a few more missions and experience I feel he will be a very efficient and capable leader. He is to be commended for the manner in which he has made the transition from his position in baseball to that of one as a combat pilot in Korea. A very fine officer and pilot. Qualified for promotion."

The two reports by Coss and the one by Art Moran cover Williams' arrival in Korea and the first 37 of his 39 missions. On any of the three reports, the commanding officer could have said they would be "glad to have" him under their command in combat, or that they would be "willing to have" him. They chose instead to check off the highest possible rating, saying that they would "particularly desire to have" Williams under their command in combat. As we know, Barney McShane did not share their assessments. It seems clear that McShane would "prefer not to have" Williams under his command.

Given all of his fitness reports in training, and the excellent reports for his first 37 missions, six different commanding officers had given Williams rather high ratings. It also seems clear that McShane was the exception. Williams flew two missions under McShane. Any number of things could have happened to make McShane want to get rid of Williams. Whatever might have occurred, it seems to be outside the norm. The problem might have been Williams. The problem might have been McShane. The problem might have simply been the chemistry between them. We don't have the information to be able to draw conclusions. We could only speculate.

How did McShane's fitness report read? We may never know. Moran's was signed on 31 May, and Williams signed his acknowledgement of having read the report on 4 June. The next report in Williams' personnel file covers the period 2 July through 30 July, during

Verdi insists, in response, "If what he meant to relate was that he flew thirty-nine missions February to June, which was about half the average for everybody else, that much was true. But he could have stopped at ten – which was the first time he was out of commission medically. He could have stopped in the next decade; and the next. For over and above all the 'negative-motivators' was an aero-medical disqualifier: Otis Media, Acute. In the wonderful double-speak of the quacks, this is a condition in which sero-purulent fluid engorges the middle ear. What it feels like is: There is an Incubus inside your head, and the diabolical little bastard is trying to get out by drilling a hole in your ear-drum. How I know this is that I have had it. Pain? I hope to shit in your mess-kit! Worse, it can be disabling. Meaning: it can knock you over in flight, and the Board will be asking why you lost control of the airplane (there won't be enough left for AFIP to tell them).

"Why didn't 'they' ground him? Well, 'they' eventually did. But we need to understand exactly who 'they' were. The Flight Surgeon is one of 'them' – but the Flight Surgeon doesn't 'ground' anybody – if you don't believe it, ask Rocco Bianchi (he'll tell you the true tale of the U.N.'s only one-eyed carrier pilot). It's the Commanding Officer who 'grounds' you; and if the reason is medical, he usually accepts the Surgeon's recommendation. Usually – not always. So in Ted's case: As Rocco flew with one infected eye patched, so Ted flew with one infected ear. Three times it got bad enough to put him on the ground and into bed; three times he got back up and flew again....

"I couldn't have done it. And I never want to hear anybody bad-mouthing Ted for flying 'only' thirty-nine missions.

"Ted was under Art Moran's command for most of this time. Art likes to insist that he never differentiated between people. Okay – I won't contradict him (aloud, anyway); but it's quite obvious (was at the time) that Ted did represent a special problem. Had Art been somebody of the wrong kind, he could have: (a) grounded Ted and put out an unfavorable news release (quick way to get rid of him); or (b) looked the other way while Ted pushed himself to a fatal conclusion (another way to get rid of him).

which period he was en route home and separated from the service. That was a "Not observed" report filed by Col. K. B. Chappell, the officer in Washington who formally discharged Ted Williams. McShane had assumed command on 1 June. So where is the report covering the month of June, the final month that Ted served in the squadron?

> "The fact of the matter was – over and above Ted's pride and determination – that we were short of pilots of any kind, which meant we were even shorter of qualified and experienced pilots... so we needed Ted. And he was good..."
>
> *Verdi, op. cit., p. 152*
>
> Verdi then mentions flying on the 4 May mission. The mission was composed of Bill Clem, Williams, Verdi, and it was Jack Campbell's 100th mission. "Everybody did exactly what he was supposed to do. I was by then experienced enough to make an evaluation based on a single flight (more especially a combat sortie); and the man ahead of me [Williams] did it all – formation, air-ground tactics, bombing, flight discipline. We didn't yet have Stan-Eval in those days, but if we had had it, I would have written it up 4.0. I'm doing it now – thirty-five years post-facto.
>
> "So Ted's ninety-percentile self-rating was backwards. I rate him in the upper tenth; and I'm a qualified judge who has flown with a lot of people. Whenever I have to go to war again, I'll be pleased to have Ted in the same Ready Room – if he's available (!)..."
>
> *Ibidem*
>
> Verdi added the observation that Ted Williams received one medal not found in any official USMC ledgers – the Foxworth Medal. This highly-sought medal was awarded, he explained, "for going home with one hole in your ass."

The only document we find which embraces the month of June was one affixed inside Williams' flight log book. It covered the entire period of his posting in Korea, from February 2 to June 29, 1953 and stated "No accidents or flying regulation violations during this period." It was over the signature of B. McShane, LTCOL, USMC, COMMANDING.

Given the comments made by Paul Noel that the true official record might have been placed in the Commandant's safe, one does wonder if McShane's actual fitness report was simply removed. A closer look at Moran's report shows that someone has drawn a line through the closing date from 31 May 1953 to 1 July 1953, and noted "extended" next to it. Some initials were added to the alterations. The apparent intent was to close the gap in the file. Perhaps a copy does exist in another location. We will probably never know. And perhaps history is happier that way.

In the end, fellow Marine pilot and fellow major league ballplayer Jerry Coleman's take on Ted and his final separation from the Corps was probably the simplest one. Coleman truly admired Ted's service and was proud to speak of Ted as a Marine during the celebration of Ted's life, held in Boston a few weeks after Ted's passing. Jerry notes that Ted was in his mid-30s, a lot older than himself, and he summarizes, "He damned the Marine Corps. He was upset that they made him do things that really hurt him. He really gave the Marine Corps hell. He was sick and they finally said, 'Let's just get him out of here.'" (30)

As Ted himself once put it, "It finally occurred to them that a nearly-deaf, pneumonia-prone, 34-year old pilot with a bum elbow maybe wasn't combat material. They mustered me out of the Marines, and I headed home." (31)

12 August 1953, letter from the Commandant of the Marine Corps, accepting Williams' resignation:

> *"A review of your Marine Corps service reveals that your separation entitles you to an Honorable Discharge, the highest type discharge awarded, a certificate of which is enclosed herewith. The Commandant takes this occasion to express his appreciation of your service."*
>
> *In all, the "total net service completed" in the United States Marine Corps Reserve was 11 years, 2 months and 5 days.*

NOTES

1) *Communication from John Toler dated October 24, 2002.*

2) *Leonard L. Orr, The Life and Adventures of a Missouri Farm Boy, Gallatin, MO, Gallatin Publishing, 1997, pp. 21, 42, 43.*

3) *Interview with Leonard Orr, November 16, 2002.*

4) *Ibidem.*

5) *Interview with Barney McShane, November 24, 2002.*

6) *Interview with Paul Noel, November 25, 2002.*

7) *Interview with L. B. Robertshaw, November 16, 2002.*

8) *Interview with James Walley, December 7, 2002.*

9) *Interview with Lou Weatherford, December 12, 2002.*

10) *Ibidem.*

11) *Interview with Ed Buchser, November 26, 2002.*

12) *Jack McGuckin, Split Second From Hell, pp. 70, 71.*

13) *Interview with Jon Mendes, December 18, 2002.*

14) *Communication from Jon D. Mendes, June 19, 2003.*

15) *Interview with Joseph Mitchell, February 3, 2003.*

16) *Interview with Al Pommerenk, February 7, 2003.*

17) *Interview with Bill Clem, December 23, 2002.*

18) *Interview with Mike Canan, December 31, 2002.*

19) *Interview with Milton Rugg, December 18, 2002.*

20) *Interview with Jon Mendes, December 18, 2002.*

21) *Interview with Paul Janssen, December 23, 2002.*

22) *Interview with Hank Kirby, January 10, 2003.*

23) *Ibidem.*

24) *Interview with Rylen Rudy, February 4, 2003.*

25) *Interview with John Glenn, October 1, 1996.*

26) *Interview with Rylen Rudy, February 4, 2003.*

27) *Interview with Mike Canan, December 31, 2002.*

28) *Interview with Barney McShane, December 30, 2003.*

29) *Jim Prime and Bill Nowlin, Ted Williams: The Pursuit of Perfection, p. 84.*

30) *Interview with Jerry Coleman, June 8, 2004.*

31) *Ted Williams with David Pietrusza, Teddy Ballgame, p. 99.*

Ted Williams, U.S. Speaker of the House of Representatives Thomas P. "Tip" O'Neill, John Glenn. Wang Center, Boston, August 30, 1988, on occasion of Ted Williams' 70th birthday.
Photo courtesy of Phil Ayoub.

John Glenn, Ted Williams, and unknown in mess hall.
Photo courtesy of Skip Rothrock.

CHAPTER 21 – TED WILLIAMS AND JOHN GLENN

'Like it or not, he was in 311 in 1953, and he had to make what he could of it. What he could have made of it was what certain others made of it – like the guys who turned in their wings (after they got overseas and decided they didn't like being shot at.) Or the USMC who aborted three of his only six missions, and then petitioned the Medical Department to issue him a grounding-chit for arthritis of his middle finger (where would you suppose that finger had been?).'

John Verdi [1]

Whatever else, Ted Williams flew 39 combat missions – a very respectable number. He did not try to dodge missions; McShane makes that clear. He was an unhappy camper, and they didn't need him any more. Given his evident and persistent ear problem, his superiors reached the quite reasonable conclusion to return him home. Reading the comments of a Barney McShane still leaves one feeling disappointed. Most of us want heroes in life. Was Ted Williams less of a hero because there were a number of fellow Marines who had their criticisms, and sometimes quite strong ones?

It's probably a safe bet that John Glenn, too, had moments he's not proud of. No doubt he has his detractors as well. But there aren't too many Americans with as heroic an image as Senator Glenn – a decorated combat pilot, one of the very first astronauts, a United States Senator, and a man who returned to space at age 77 in continuing service to his country. John Glenn served in VMF-311 alongside Ted Williams for most of the time Ted was in Korea. And Williams won John Glenn's respect, just as he won the respect of most of the Marines in their squadron. In later years, Glenn and Williams became closer still, and with John and his wife Annie visiting Ted at his Florida home a couple of times each year right up until Ted's passing. And Ted Williams was there at Cape Canaveral when Glenn took that last flight into space.

On learning that Ted Williams had died, Glenn told the *St. Petersburg Times*, "He may have gone to greater heights in baseball, but there were greater things than baseball. That was our country, and when Ted got that call, he answered it. That's to his everlasting credit."

In his autobiography, Glenn remembered Ted and the squadron at K-3.

> "The pilots of VMF-311 were a great bunch. One of them was the Boston Red Sox star Ted Williams. I had just joined the squadron and was sitting in the pilots' ready room one day when he walked in and came over and introduced himself....We lived in opposite ends of the same Quonset hut....There was certainly nothing 'bush' about him as a Marine combat pilot; he gave flying the same perfectionist's attention he gave to his hitting." [2]

Glenn was sometimes criticized for being too aggressive, for diving too low on some of his bombing missions. Among his squadron mates, he earned the nickname "Magnet Ass" because of the anti-aircraft fire he attracted with his low-level runs. Glenn was hit by anti-aircraft fire on fully 12 occasions. In the process, he downed five MiGs and also won himself the Distinguished Flying Cross five times. *Redbook* magazine said he flew a total of 149 missions in World War II and Korea, and that in addition to earning the five DFCs and 18 clusters, he "amused himself in odd moments by flying up close to his squadron planes and tickling their wing tips."[3] The magazine added, "Baseball player Ted Williams, who flew several missions with him in Korea, described his daring as 'absolutely crazy.'"

Glenn had a few stories to tell about Ted. In his memoirs, he wrote, "Ted was flying as my wingman one day on a run over the Haeju peninsula. He was pulling out of his run when he radioed that he'd been hit. I flew around his plane looking for damage as we headed to the rendezvous. I saw a hole in the bottom of his tip tank but no hole in top. I couldn't figure it out. We got back to the base, where the crew removed the tank and found a rock inside, apparently thrown up by the secondary... Ted and I flew together a lot... Ted flew about half his missions as my wingman. He was a fine pilot and I liked to fly with him."

There was one time, though, when Major Glenn worried that Williams had blundered badly. "One day Ted and I had flown back from the north without finding any targets, and when I crossed the lines I swung around and headed into North Korea and fired my rockets at a small bridge that had already been hit.

"Ted followed me around and made the same run I did, but his rockets didn't go off. He pulled up and made a level turn until he was headed back toward our lines. I saw him push over into a shallow dive, but just as I started to call to tell him not to fire, the rockets were on their way.

"I had a terrible sickening feeling as I watched those rockets hit and explode. Some of our troops had recently taken casualties from friendly fire. Our group commander had put out orders saying that the next time it happened the flight leader was going to be held responsible and court-martialed. I double-checked the impact point against the landmarks I could see and compared it with my flight chart. It looked as if Ted's rockets had hit behind our lines. My first concern was whether any of our troops had been hurt, but I could also see myself sitting at a court-martial table.

"We flew back to K-3, and Ted and I went to the operations shack to tell them what had happened. There on the wall was a bigger chart than I had in the plane, and it showed that the lines had shifted more than half a mile south. Ted had fired into an enemy troop pocket. He said he knew it all along, but I kidded him anyway about almost getting me court-martialed.

"I never took off on another mission without closely checking the ops office chart against my flight chart. I made that part of the squadron briefing from then on."[4]

On more than one occasion, Glenn repeated words to the effect that "Ted flew about half his missions as my wingman." Glenn was being generous. To have flown half his 39 missions as Glenn's wingman would have been extraordinary. A review of the VMF-311 command diaries show that no pilot flew more than twelve missions with Ted. That distinction is held by two men: Capt. Lenhrew Lovette and Lt. Col. Art Moran. Capt. Joseph Carruthers flew eleven. John Glenn flew eight missions with Ted.

Ranked By Quantity (7 or more):

Lovette 12

Moran 12

Carruthers 11

Clem 9

Armagost 8

Glenn 8

Miller 8

Skinner 8

Street 8

Warren 8

Keck 7

The John Glenn/Ted Williams missions were:

22 April

25 April

27 April

30 April

9 May – this was a mission that Ted had to abort

16 May

17 May

21 May

So, depending on how you look at it, 7 full missions or 8, if you count the one Ted had to abort. It did count as one of Ted's 39 missions.

On 26 April, both pilots flew, technically on different missions but coordinated in the same general activity.

It is nice that Glenn remembers having flown more with Ted than he actually did, and it represents a real compliment. It just wasn't the case. The story of these two Marines who both served in VMF-311 is worth telling in more detail. This will also give us the opportunity to present Sen. Glenn's comments on Ted Williams at more length. Unless otherwise noted, Glenn's remarks come from an interview conducted by this author on October 1, 1996.

When John Glenn boarded *Discovery* to return to space late in 1998, Ted Williams boarded a helicopter to travel to the Kennedy Space Center at Cape Canaveral to witness the historic launch. These two heroes of our time are both former Marine pilots and they have enjoyed a friendship going back nearly 50 years. "John Glenn is my idol in life right now," Williams told Dave Anderson of the *New York Times* shortly before the launch.[5]

They first got to know each other during the frigid Korean winter at a desolate air base at Pohang during the Korean War. Both aviators flew combat missions together and both narrowly escaped death. Ted's plane was hit by groundfire on at least two occasions and Glenn's was hit a full dozen times.

The experience they shared created a bond which has lasted over the years, despite one being a Democrat and one a Republican.

Ted remembers when he first really got to know John Glenn. When he first entered the squad room, one of the very first people he met was a pilot from Ohio named Glenn.

"When I first got there, I didn't know anybody so I went to the pilots' room just to get acquainted. I looked over to the other end of the room and I saw two Marine majors there. I didn't know who they were, but they looked good to me. One was John Glenn." Williams had actually arrived a number of days before Glenn.

"I think I first met him at Cherry Point going through jet refresher," recalls Glenn. "I didn't know him well there. When we got to Korea, though, I was assigned as operations officer of the squadron out there, VMF-311. Ted was assigned as my wing man and flew with me. That didn't mean that every single mission you went out on, you flew with exactly the same person, but it mean that if you're both on the schedule going to go up a certain day, those two people would go up together. I guess probably half the missions that Ted flew in Korea he flew as my wing man. You get to know that guy pretty well."

Glenn flew 63 missions in Korea and, as we know, Williams flew 39. "The squadron was VMF-311 and he was flying all sorts of air to ground missions, some of them were interdiction missions, which means you were way up country doing work on roads and bombers or trucks -- things you found out along the road up there. Or we were doing close support work, and we did a lot of close support work right out in front of the First Marine Division, and the Army divisions, too. When we got out there, the situation was not as fluid as it had been and so the lines were pretty well drawn. And so we worked in very close to our own troops and our own Marines along that front line area; in fact, you worked in close enough that you almost hated to drop for fear you'd do something wrong and get our own people. We really worked in tight. So that's the kind of stuff Ted did all during all of his combat missions.

"Those were missions involving bombing, strafing, rocket firing and napalm drops on enemy targets," explained Glenn. "You fly as a two-person element. We call it a section. That means two planes, and then your next flight formation is four planes. You put those two sections into a division as it's called, and then build on up to a squadron from there. Your two people stick together and if you're going into combat, why, they fly together and if there's air to air combat, then you watch out for each other and you fly back and forth together. We were doing a lot of close air support work and things like that, with napalms and bombs on the ground and rockets and so on. And if somebody got hit then you stuck with him, you stuck with that guy, and you made every effort to get him back. It was that type of situation. We were under intense anti-aircraft fire on almost every mission. By the time we got out there which was in late '52 and then into '53 it was a rare mission you went on when you didn't see anti-aircraft fire."

These were true combat missions. Glenn talks about one such mission with Ted Williams: "On one mission we were assigned an area where we thought they had ammunition stored. Well, one of the best things that ever happened on a mission like that was if you got a good hit and got right into the bunkers, their ammunition would start going off. That's what you call a secondary explosion. The first explosion was from the bomb. The secondary explosion was when all their stuff on the ground started going off.

"I went in on this run and got a good hit and it was blowing up on the ground. Ted was coming right in behind me and he pulled out of his run right behind me and he yelled on the radio he'd been hit, he'd been hit. Under the right wing tip was a good-sized hole. He still had the airplane under control and there wasn't any problem so we flew on back and landed. What had happened was he'd had a rock blown up from the ground on a secondary and hit him in the tip tank. We always kidded him about the Williams anti-aircraft fire."

So the enemy was throwing rocks at Ted Williams now? "I don't know how you spell it [but I understood that] krondyke was the Korean word for rock, and sometimes if you wanted to get somebody's attention at night and you're coming back from the club or something, you picked up a handful of gravel or something and threw it at a Quonset hut. [With those metal roofs] you could imagine what a racket that makes inside. And this was known as Krondyking. Ted became known as the 'Krondyke Kid' after he got hit by that rock.

"We did a lot of flying. Some of the more memorable missions, we were doing road reconnaissance. You'd take off real early in the morning, before dawn, before there was any first light even and you flew up at altitude. You'd be way up north, oh maybe 150 miles or so up behind enemy lines, and then you'd let down, just at first light when you could see enough that you could come down and skip along on the roads flying at real low level. One plane would fly down there and the other plane would fly along about a thousand feet along behind and direct the first plane on the ground to make a right over the next ridge or so on to keep him on the road and you'd shoot up any trucks and things like that. I remember some of those, a couple of those flights with Ted in which he and I flew together. I'd fly down low for 10 minutes or so and hit whatever targets I could and then we'd switch off and he'd fly low, and you'd switch off back and forth and work your way back down to the front and come on home."

Glenn knew who Ted Williams was before he met him. "I knew about Ted Williams. I used to follow baseball when I was a kid all the time. I was well aware of Ted Williams, of course, and his records in baseball. Who knows what those records might have been if he hadn't had two hitches in the Marine Corps?" Williams almost had his career cut short after 10 seasons in the majors. He still would have been the last man to hit .400. He still would have had his two Triple Crowns, a feat only Rogers Hornsby has ever matched. Ted only barely missed having three. He still would have had an exceptional career, but he would have wound up with just 324 home runs had he been killed in Korea.

Though he wasn't on the February 16 mission, Glenn remembered the day clearly. In 1998, Glenn told the *New York Times*, "When the F9 got hit and caught on fire, the tail would blow off almost every time. So the standard orders were that if you had a fire in the back of the plane, you were to eject immediately."[6]

A couple of years earlier, Glenn had described the events in detail to this author (see Chapter 11 above), and had ended his recollection: "He knew he was on fire and didn't want to get out, and he was just lucky. He brought the thing around and couldn't get the gear down and bellied it in and it slid up the runway and he jumped out of the cockpit and ran off and stood there watched it melt down. He was just lucky the thing didn't blow."[7]

Glenn, asked to evaluate Ted overall, concluded, as we have noted: "He did a great job and he was a good pilot. He wasn't out there moaning all the time or trying to duck flights, or anything like that. He was out there to do the job and he did it. He did a helluva good job."[8]

It was never widely known that Williams and Glenn served in the same squadron until 1988, when an evening at Boston's Wang Center celebrating Ted Williams' 70th birthday was scheduled as a fundraiser for Boston's Jimmy Fund. Joe DiMaggio, Tip O'Neill, and a number of other celebrities were introduced from the stage. Ted invited Senator Glenn. "Ted... when he had his birthday party up there in the theatre with David Hartman back several years ago. I think that was on his 70th, wasn't it? He invited me to come up for that and I was up there with the DiMaggios and the Doerrs and all the rest of the group, and we had a great time.

"David Hartman set this up as though it were a camping scene, a fishing camp or something like that on stage. And each person would come out in turn and David would interview each of us sitting there in a chair, and then we'd go over there and like sit around the bar on the other end of the stage. And we all told Ted Williams stories. And at the end of the evening Ted came out and he went through one by one and told his version of these same stories. It was a riot; we had a lot of fun.

"I've seen him several times throughout the years. I was down about a year ago. I knew about him having a stroke and that almost got him. About a year ago I was down in Florida, so we drove up there and took a day and spent the day with him. We just had a great time. My wife and my daughter were with me, and we stayed for lunch and talked."[9] The Glenns enjoyed the 1995 visit to Ted's home so much, they began to come once or twice each year.

"The Marine Corps meant so much to Ted," said Glenn. "I remember going to visit him a year ago and he was sitting in his chair wearing a sweatshirt with a huge USMC emblem on it and a matching hat. He was an excellent pilot, a courageous pilot, and he wasn't one to hold back," Glenn said. "He was always pressing the attack."[10]

That the two had known each other was not a secret, revealed at the Wang Center for the first time. In fact, a few months after Glenn's February 20, 1962 flight in orbit, Williams had mentioned Glenn in a front page article in the *Boston Sunday Globe* on June 17, 1962. Writing in a column about knowing when to retire, Ted referred to "the fantastic, history-making flight of Col. John Glenn" as being a triumph for "us 'old-timers'" (both Williams and Glenn being in their 40s at the time). Williams wrote, "There has been so much written about John's flight, and rightfully so, that there's nothing I can add except as a personal note. John and I are old buddies from the Korean war. We flew together. As a matter of fact, we both got shot down, but not together – you can carry 'togetherness' a little too far. I know this may sound corny coming out at this time, but during the Korean war I got to know John quite well. This was a man destined for something great; it was an intuitive feeling that I had. John always had exceptional self-control and was one of the calmest men I have ever met, no matter how perilous the situation."[11]

Perhaps in contrast, and perhaps because they served in different units in Korea, whenever Jerry Coleman and Ted Williams got together in recent years, they talked more about baseball than Korea. Shaun O'Neill wrote in the *North County Times*, that "especially as Williams began making regular visits back to San Diego, they rarely talked about their military experiences. Baseball was a much more joyful subject. 'It's not something you really want to relive,' Coleman said."[12]

Glenn was impressed with Williams's dedication. "I'm sure he could have been [an astronaut] if he'd put his mind to it," said Glenn, the first American in orbit, at Fenway Park July 22, 2002.

NOTES

1) *John Verdi*, Hundred Missions, *op. cit., p. 152.*

2) *John Glenn*, John Glenn: A Memoir,
   NY: Bantam Books, 1999, pp. 130-137.

3) Redbook, *January 1965.*

4) *John Glenn*, John Glenn: A Memoir, *op. cit., pp. 130-137.*

5) New York Times, *October 29, 1998.*

6) *Ibidem.*

7) *Interview with John Glenn, October 1, 1996.*

(8) *Ibidem.*

9) *Ibidem.*

10) *Lt. Christopher C. Wilson,*
    "Ted Williams embodied meaning of sacrifice,"
    Marine Corps Heritage Foundation, *July 29, 2002.*

11) *"When to Quit?"* Boston Globe, *June 17, 1962.*

12) *Shaun O'Neill,*
    "Williams, Coleman shared more than baseball,"
    North County Times, *July 6, 2002.*

ANOTHER SIDE OF TED

"Ted and I once spent a week together in Japan on R&R – rest and recreation – a week of stand-down from flying. Even in 1953, the Japanese were avid baseball fans and many were very familiar with Ted and his records. The Japanese media had noted Ted's R&R visit to Japan, so he was recognized quite often. As tall as he was, in the land of the Japanese it's hard not to be recognized.

"In Kyoto, a small group of children had gathered, as we stopped to look at something or other. They were looking at Ted and chattering to each other, not really sure whether he really was who they thought he was. They spoke no English and we spoke no Japanese. Finally, one brave little kid stepped out, took a hitting stance, swung an imaginary bat and pointed questioningly to Ted. Ted laughed and nodded, yes, he was who they thought he was.

"The boy hitter swung again but this time Ted scowled at him. He went over to where the boy was standing, put him in a batting position and proceeded to correct his form! He made this little kid stand with his feet farther apart, more bend at the waist, head more lined up with an imaginary pitcher, and arms farther back to start the swing.

"Leaving the boy in that stance, Ted stepped back several paces, took a pitching position, and threw an imaginary baseball at the boy, who swung with all his might. Ted ducked, let out a whooshing, whopping big yell, swung around 180 degrees as though that non-existent baseball was headed for the centerfield bleachers.

"The kids were jumping up and down. No one was more surprised than the batter. I'm sure he was an instant hero. Ted got more of a kick out of that than the kids did. As to spoken language, not a word was said in either direction, but it was not necessary."

John Glenn
remarks at the celebration of Ted Williams' life
held at Fenway Park, July 22, 2002

After leaving the Marines, Ted was always glad to meet servicemen visiting the ballpark.
Late 1950s photograph courtesy of The Sports Museum.

CHAPTER 22 – POST-WAR FLAP

Ted's feelings about his service in the Marine Corps went through a few ups and downs after discharge. He had never been happy about being recalled, and he never made a secret of that at the time. Of course, he was grateful to have survived the experience. In time, he realized what an important part of his life his service had been. As he realized how deeply many people admired him for having risked his life in combat at the call of his country, he understandably began to take more pride in his Marine Corps days. Had he only served in World War II and not in Korea, he might well have hit another 40 home runs. He might have hit the 2,000 RBI mark. He probably would have made the 3,000 Hit Club. He might have won another batting title. His stature as a ballplayer could hardly be higher, though, than it already is, and he likely came to understand that his status as a man, as an American, was deeply enriched by his combat experience. Limping back from a mission, crash-landing his aircraft, and then going up for another 36 missions made Ted Williams into a legend and not just a great baseball player.

He was welcomed back at the All-Star Game, and welcomed back to Boston as well. As noted, the welcome home evening of August 17 was turned into a fundraiser for the Jimmy Fund. Nearly fifty years later, now-United States Senator Ted Kennedy wrote, "For half a century, the Jimmy Fund has been making an extraordinary difference for children with cancer, and throughout that period, Ted Williams has been among its strongest advocates and most faithful supporters. In my book, he's a champion on the diamond, and a champion for children with cancer too.

"I still remember the excitement and the awe of meeting Ted at the 1953 Statler dinner honoring the Jimmy Fund and welcoming Ted's return to the Red Sox from his service in the Korean War."[1]

One of Ted's remarks that evening in 1953 included a reference to what he'd just come through: "All the bullets and all the bombs that explode all over the world won't leave the impact, when all is said and done, of a dollar bill dropped in the Jimmy Fund pot by a warm heart and a willing hand... You should be proud and happy to know that your contribution will someday help some kid to a better life."

John B. Hynes, the mayor of Boston, awarded Ted Williams the Korean Service Medal on behalf of the City of Boston. The only other non-resident awarded this medal was General Douglas MacArthur.

As we have noted, Ted did well on the baseball field as well. After the season, Ted enjoyed getting back to his fishing and, maybe, his family – though his marriage ended in divorce the following year.

Some of the resentment at being recalled still remained, and it resurfaced even a few years later, in 1957. Just before the baseball season opened, there was Ted Williams again, back in the headlines. The *Boston Herald* headline of April 2 read "Williams Scores Taft, Marines." Arthur Sampson, writing the story, began with the lead: "Ted Williams, the explosive Red Sox star who is no novice at 'popping off' about matters not concerned with baseball, was in 'hot water' again today." Sampson explained how Williams had been in the New Orleans airport and was approached informally by Crozet Duplantier, the executive sports editor of the *New Orleans States* newspaper. Duplantier was a former Marine himself, and had been introduced to Ted by *Boston Globe* sportswriter Hy Hurwitz, another ex-Marine. Duplantier was asking Ted about the unfairness of having had to serve twice. The subject obviously hit Ted the wrong way at the wrong time. Ted popped off.

He said he "had no use" for the Marines. "I'll tell you about the Marines," he said. "They got the government to appropriate a lot of money. They said they had all the pilots they needed but needed planes for them. Actually they had no pilots, so when they got the money, they had to recruit 11,000 guys, including guys like me. Most of us hadn't flown a plane for many years, but they wanted to make a good show. That's why they got a big name like myself. I got a raw deal from the Marines and I've said before I've got no use for them."

Williams continued, "What makes me mad about the government is these phony politicians." He told reporters what he meant by that: "I always thought Taft was a good guy because of the stand he took on labor. But let me tell you about him. I found out that he was a phony, too. I have a very good friend high up in the government and without my knowing it, he went to Taft to try to stop my recall by the Marines. He asked Taft why the Marines wanted a guy like me. He said Taft told him, 'I can't do a thing. I know he [Williams] has a proper grievance but I can't do a thing for him. Anybody else I could help but I can't touch him... He's too big.'" 2

Duplantier said that Williams spat on the ground when Taft's name was mentioned. Ted quickly tried to distance himself from his comments, saying that whatever comments he might have made were not for public consumption. He thought he was just chewing the fat, not being interviewed. Red Sox GM Joe Cronin said it was his understanding that, "It was just one Marine talking to another." Williams said later, "I will never talk to a drinking writer again." Peter Finney wrote in the July 6, 2002 *New Orleans Times-Picayune* that Duplantier was picked up for DWI just a week later.

Of course, one wonders whether Ted's friend truly did approach Taft without Ted's knowledge. Of his quoted remarks, Ted's denial of the remarks on Taft and the Marines read more like a confirmation. About reports that he'd also condemned Truman and the U. S. Government, he angrily charged, "That's a damn lie. If I did say it, I don't remember it. But if I'd said it, I'd remember. I remember everything else."3

The whole story echoed Ted's blast of "gutless draft boards, gutless politicians and gutless baseball writers" a year earlier, in a case involving Johnny Podres and his draft board. "Why don't you fellows do something about things like the Podres case?" he had shouted in March 1956. Podres had won two games for the victorious Brooklyn Dodgers during the 1955 World Series, becoming a national figure in the process. "Here's this kid who was deferred three years ago for a bad back and then what happens? He wins a couple of games, gets famous and some two-bit draft board puts the arm on him. It's a damn shame and something should be done. Why didn't they put the finger on him two years ago, when he couldn't win for losing?"4

"If Podres had lost those World Series games, he would probably still be with the Dodgers," Ted told reporters.5 Ted kept up his attack: "They're going to take 20 percent of the kid's money-earning time, and for what? Are we at war? No! Do they need him? No! It's just a big act by the government and some politicians. You get into college and you hide behind a book until Hell wouldn't have you. Couple of hours a week of rifle drill or something and the college kid never gets touched. Guys who work for big corporations, too. What a lot of malarkey. The president of the corporation goes to the draft board, pleads his man is indispensable and whambo, the guy is deferred. Nobody is indispensable... The athlete gets famous and he's gone right away. They get their best years snatched away from them because gutless draft boards and politicians get a few letters and panic." 6

Two weeks later, Ted was talking about taxes, complaining that business executives have ways of avoiding taxes that are not available to ballplayers. "If a player gets a big salary, he just gives 50% or more of it to the government. His career is comparatively short and he never has much left to save. But business executives have planes, cabin cruisers, and automobiles – and who pays for them? The company."[7]

The day after the Duplantier story broke, Williams (through the Red Sox) issued a written "apology to anybody who might be offended by remarks alleged to me by a drinking reporter." He didn't deny the remarks other than those about Truman and the U.S. Government. At the very same time, Ted gave the flap a new twist by indeed criticizing the government for its pursuit of boxer (and veteran) Joe Louis over income tax troubles. "Look at the terrible treatment Joe Louis is getting," he railed. "Here's a guy who has been a credit to his race and his country and look at the treatment he's getting. I think it's a shame the way he's being hounded for the payment of his back income taxes. He'll never be able to pay all that money he owes the government. He's stuck for life. The interest keeps climbing every day and there isn't a damn thing he can do about it. Why doesn't the government make some sort of settlement with him? Or better yet, wipe out the entire debt? If some big shot, phony politician was in the same predicament, they'd allow him to settle it by paying two cents on the dollar. But here's a guy who has done so much for his country, who has given them three years of the best part of his life and now he's stuck. Sure he made a mistake and spent all his money. Does that mean he has to pay for it the rest of his life?"[8]

The firestorm lasted for days, even drawing comment from former President Harry S. Truman, who diplomatically said of Ted Williams, "He's a great ballplayer. I like to watch him."

Bob Considine, a major syndicated writer of the day, said that "to rap the Marine Corps which he served so valiantly is to spit on graves from Tripoli to the Yalu, which one feels he didn't mean to do."

A later column by Bill Cunningham explained that one of these reasons Ted blew was probably in frustration at the team being kept waiting for six hours at the New Orleans airport due to a driving rainstorm – nearly a tornado. When Duplantier asked Ted to say something nice about the Marines to help local enlistments, Ted boiled over. Duplantier might well have been surprised. Harold Kaese of the *Boston Globe* noted that in the post office in Sarasota just a couple of weeks earlier, he'd picked up a Marine Corps pamphlet with Ted's picture on it under the slogan "I was a Marine."[9]

Mike Gillooly saw the whole affair as "a sorry situation of Ted's own making." Williams had "maneuvered himself into a position where he can't clear his throat, hiccough or even burp without making headlines... He is being painted as the great hater, a man whose heart pumps nothing but venom through his veins. This is a false portrait. Ask a thousand kids to whom Ted has gone out of his way to be kind. Ask the Jimmy Fund executives about the tremendous amount of good Ted has done for the sick children." Gillooly noted that Ted didn't perform those good works for publicity. The main problem with Williams was that he "simply is a guy without a bit of deceit in his frame... If he'd had the foresight to always precede his remarks with the words 'this is off the record,' most of the conflagrations never would have been public. But that wasn't his style."[10]

Ted did issue an apology to the Marine Corps, though everyone assumed it was penned by the Red Sox PR department. "I have too many friends, and have spent too much time, in the Marine Corps to not know that the organization is tops." *Boston Record* cartoonist Bob Coyne showed Ted and a champagne bottle blowing its cork, popping off. "He can spit at ex-Presidents, tell the Marines off, blast draft boards, spit at everybody – and yet – THE FANS STILL LOVE THE GUY!!"

Hy Hurwitz, the former Marine sportswriter who had introduced Williams and Duplantier, said that Ted teed off saying he still resented being called back. "I wouldn't have resented it if they had recalled everyone in the same category as myself," Williams said, "But they didn't. They picked on me because I was a ball player and widely known. I was at the height of my earning power. I had already served three years. My career was short enough without having it interrupted twice." Hurwitz says that Ted spat once or twice, but it was "more or less in general disgust" than directed toward Truman or anyone in particular. Ted had said that he'd turned down opportunities to meet both Eisenhower and Truman. "I don't like politicians," he said.

A Marine Corps spokesman said that Williams was a private citizen and could say whatever he wanted to, adding, "We made no commitment to Williams or any other individual that we would not use him as we see fit."[11]

On the 4th of April, Mrs. Ann Cella of the Orange County Society for Crippled Children mentioned that Ted had been very gracious in a visit to two five-year-old amputees, adding that he "had put really himself out to make friends with the kids." The day after that, Williams sent a telegram to the Commandant of the Marine Corps, saying, "My four years spent in the Corps are the proudest of my life. I would never say anything nor suffer anything to be said which would detract one iota from the Corps and the wonderful men who compose it. Even though I am no longer a member of the Corps I will always be a Marine at heart."[12]

We can conclude that, when first recalled, Ted played it better than in 1942 – yet while Williams said all the right things in 1952, he was seething inside. Understandably so, said most of the other men in his squadron, if only because he was losing so much more than them in a career everyone understood was coming to a close. As we have seen, he felt so strongly that within his squadron, he'd even spouted off about campaigning to abolish the Corps. We also saw that many of his mates saw Ted's mouthing off in context, and excused him for it.

That Williams still harbored such strong passion on the subject four years after discharge, and that the Marine Corps felt compelled to distance themselves from the idea that he might have been promised he'd not be recalled, both tend to validate the notion that there might have been something unusual about the recall itself. One picks up no sense of allusion to something unusual about the discharge.

It does seem that once he got it off his chest this time in 1957, nothing of this nature surfaced again. From that time forward, Ted Williams always expressed how proud he was to have been a Marine.

One of Ted's personal friends, Steve Brown, acknowledged that Ted hated being recalled and that he had indeed said some things against the Marines. "Yes, he did. Ted was so disgruntled and he was so upset. And he regretted that. He regretted those things and he tried to make up for them at the last. That weighed heavier than anything Ted was doing at the last. He beat himself up [for having made those comments]." Brown concluded that, at the end, "Ted was absolutely in love with the Marines. He said, 'I'll always be a baseball player because the fans keep me there, but I will always be a Marine because my heart keeps me there.'"[13]

NOTES

1) *Letter from Edward M. Kennedy, September 11, 1998.*

2) Boston Herald, *April 2, 1957.*

3) *Ibidem.*

4) Boston Globe, *March 14, 1956.*

5) *Ed Linn*, Hitter, *op. cit., p. 282.*

6) *Ibidem.*

7) Boston Globe, *March 30, 1956.*

8) Boston Herald, *April 3, 1957.*

9) Boston Globe, *April 2, 1957.*

10) Mike Gillooly, *"A Sorry Situation of Ted's Own Making,"* Boston Record, *April 3, 1957.*

11) Associated Press *report, April 1, 1957.*

12) Boston Globe, *April 5, 1957.*

13) *Interview with Steve Brown, July 19, 2004.*

Capt. T. S. Williams, USMCR.
Courtesy of the May Williams Collection.

CHAPTER 23 – PROUD TO BE A MARINE

"Every one you walk away from is a good one."
Jon D. Mendes, on war[1]

"Ted used to be pretty argumentative and one time we were going back and forth, and finally I said, 'Ted, I'm going to pull rank on you this time.' [Gorman was a Navy veteran of higher rank.] Ted told me, "Lou, no one out-ranks a Marine fighter pilot!"
former Red Sox general manager Lou Gorman[2]

Late in life, Ted was interviewed by Jeff Idelson of the National Baseball Hall of Fame and he was asked briefly about his time in the service. This was the exchange:

HOF: You had two tours of duty in the service, World War II and Korea. In Korea you flew 39 missions and twice could have conceivably lost your life while airborne. How did you deal with the fear of mortality?

TW: Scared to death, holding on. I sat in the cockpit and I said, "If there's anybody up there that can help me, now's the time to do it." I did say that.

HOF: You loved the Marines.

TW: The Marines were allotted more planes because they had to keep up with a certain percentage that strengthened the Navy. During the war, they had let the Marines drop a lot, and finally it was time to try to rebuild the Marines. So I was called up and the next thing I knew I was back in reserves and I requested jets. A friend of mine had been in Korea. An old Marine buddy, one of my great friends, Bill Churchman. So I requested jets and I wasn't guaranteed a thing, but that's what I was trying to get. So sure enough, I got jets.

I have to say this: how lucky I've been in life, I know how lucky I've been in life, more than anybody will ever know. I've lived a kind of precarious life style, precarious in sports, flying, and baseball. And oh boy. I know how lucky I've been. The two things I'm proudest of in my life, is that I became a Marine pilot and that I became a member of the Baseball's Hall of Fame. I worked hard [at flying]. I wasn't prepared to go into it. Then I had to work hard as hard as hell to try to keep going, to try and keep up. I did have reasonable flying abilities. I had cars and I had been running up and down the highways. I had done a lot of shooting. I think that's as great an accomplishment as anything I'd done in my life. The other thing, of course, is that I had a great baseball career.[3]

> **Teddy was in the military long before the Korean Conflict, he was a Soldier in Christ as a Corps Cadet in the SALVATION ARMY in San Diego, Ca. So was I AND I have my certificate of 6 years to prove it! Yea, May, Teddy, and I were in battle together with Satan and when she was ill, May still refought her Wars with me.**
>
> *Communication from Ted's cousin Manuel Herrera, February 16, 2000*

> **Ted Williams said his three favorite songs were "The Star Spangled Banner", "The Marine Corps Hymn," and "Take Me Out to the Ballgame."**

The sentiment that is key, of course, is that of how proud Ted was to have been a Marine. Ted told Lou Gorman one time, "If I didn't have baseball to go back to, I'd have stayed in the Marine Corps. I loved the Marine Corps."[4]

Lt. Gen. Tom Miller, talking of Ted Williams, Jerry Coleman, and John Glenn, said, "All I can say, they were great people to have in the squadron and most people highly respected them. In the squadron I was in, most of the pilots were reserve pilots, you would have thought that there would have been a little bit more animosity because of the fact that they were so famous and they might be getting privileges that others wouldn't. But both Jerry and Ted went out of their way to be sure that they were not treated in a special way, and I know in our own squadron everybody thought that Jerry was one of the finest guys in the squadron. I think the same thing was involved in 311. I know John. John is very sincere. I don't think he felt any more close to anyone out there than to Ted Williams."[5]

John Glenn offered his evaluation of his fellow Marine aviator: "I'll tell you. Ted isn't one who sits around and moans about what might have been. And there's nobody, I swear, there's nobody that served in the Marine Corps that isn't any more proud of having been a Marine than Ted Williams."

[And he's a model of modesty, too. He's quoted as saying there were 75 men in the two squadrons and 99% of them did a better job than he did.]

Glenn continued, "I disagree with his assessment. He did a great job and he was a good pilot. He wasn't out there moaning all the time or trying to duck flights, or anything like that. He was out there to do the job and he did it. He did a helluva good job."[6]

Another U. S. Senator shared a background in the Marine Corps with Glenn and Williams. An unattributed news clipping found in Hall of Fame files tells of the time Williams was introduced to another politician:

"Baseball legend Ted Williams was a dyed-in-the-wool Republican who had little time for Democrats. But he made an exception for Sen. Zell Miller (D-Ga.).

In 1995, Miller, then governor of Georgia, was introduced to Williams by New York Yankees star Mickey Mantle, who had a lake home near Atlanta.

"When Mick introduced me as the governor of Georgia, Williams thrust his hand forward with a bark, 'Are you a Democrat or Republican?' When I answered Democrat, he dropped my hand as if I had some contagious disease and growled, 'Well, I'm a Republican,' and turned abruptly," Miller recalled Monday.

Intimidated by Williams' reaction, Miller blurted, "I was in the Marines."

Williams, a former Marine combat pilot, said, "Well, you're all right then!"

Taking Williams at his word to keep in touch, Miller called him two years later to ask for a "blurb" for a book he had written about the Marine Corps.

Williams not only agreed to the request, but invited Miller to dinner at his home in Florida. Afterwards, he asked, "Now what was it you wanted me to say about that book?"

Without waiting for an answer, Williams said, "How about a grand slam?"

"I knew the book was a bloop single at best, and I bet he did too," Miller recalled Monday. "But the brotherhood of the Corps is strong. You'll never be able to tell me that Ted Williams was not a nice guy."[7]

President George H. W. Bush, a true Republican, was a lifelong admirer of Ted Williams. In 1991, on the 50th anniversary of Williams' unsurpassed .406 season, President Bush invited Ted to the White House to receive the Medal of Freedom – the nation's highest civilian honor. The www.medaloffreedom.com website explains the Medal, and provides the language which accompanied its award to Ted Williams.

The Presidential Medal of Freedom is the highest civilian award in the United States. It was established by President Harry Truman in 1945 to honor service during WWII. President John F. Kennedy revived the medal and began the tradition of awarding the medal annually, on or near July 4. The award is awarded to several people annually. Unlike many other US awards, the Presidential Medal of Freedom can be awarded to non-US citizens.

The Presidential Medal of Freedom recognizes individuals who have made "an especially meritorious contribution to the security or national interests of the United States, or to world peace, or to cultural or other significant public or private endeavors."

THEODORE SAMUEL WILLIAMS

Awarded by

President George Bush

November 18, 1991

Theodore Samuel Williams – Ted Williams, the "Splendid Splinter"—is perhaps the greatest hitter of all time. Williams made it look easy. He won six batting titles, blasted 521 home runs, and half a century ago amazed America by becoming the last man to bat over .400. He also gallantly served his country in two wars and retired from baseball as only a hero could—with a home run in his final at bat. A conservationist, avid fisherman, and baseball Hall of Famer, Ted Williams is a living legend.

The plight of fellow Marines often reached Williams in unexpected ways. A UPI story of April 25, 1965 bore what looked to be a fairly innocuous headline: "Ted Williams Aids Ex-Marine", but the story was not at all a typical one.

"Former Boston Red Sox star Ted Williams has gone to bat for a fellow ex-Marine who helped save his life in Korea but is now in prison.

"According to attorney Ted Salveter, Williams has asked the Sears & Roebuck chain store to provide a job for Coy D. Hammers, 30, if Hammers obtains a parole from his 5-year term. His hearing is scheduled early next week. Williams sells his sporting and fishing equipment through Sears.

"Salveter said Hammers once saved Williams' life in Korea. Williams' jet plane was burning from a crash landing when Hammers, a member of a rescue unit, pulled the former baseball star from the aircraft.

"Greene (Springfield) County sheriff Mickey Owen, another ex-baseball star and teammate at one time of the Red Sox slugger, verified that Williams was interested in the case.

"Hammers, a veteran of the Marine Corps for 13 years, was given an honorable discharge in 1963. He recently was sentenced to prison after pleading guilty to a burglary charge here."

The *Boston Globe* ran the story, on the same day:

"When a guy helps to pull you out of a burning plane, you owe him a debt.

"Ted Williams thinks so. And that is the reason that the former Red Sox slugger is going all-out for Coy D. Hammers...

"The rescue crew was ready, Hammers among them. They pulled Williams out of the wreckage, and Williams later said, 'God was with me.'

"So was Hammers and his squad.

"Hammers was discharged from the Marines in 1963. Things got bad for him and he was picked up and convicted on a burglary charge.

"After 13 years as a good Marine, Hammers was in trouble.

"Last election time Greene County elected a new sheriff, fellow named Mickey Owen. Mickey is a former Red Sox catcher, a former National League star noted for his explosive temper on the ball field as well as his exceptional ability.

"Owen naturally enough came into contact with Hammers. He learned of Hammers' part in saving Ted's life. No, Ted hadn't forgotten.

"How can you? You owe a guy a debt.

"Ted Salveter, an attorney in Springfield, Mo., is the one who let out the story. Williams wouldn't. He doesn't like publicity that deals with favors.

"Williams won't like this publicity either. But that is immaterial. He wants to give a brave guy a fresh start.

"He'll know the answer next week."[8]

Attempts to follow up on this story proved impossible. As of mid-2004, Owen was in a nursing home and unable to reason. The current sheriff of Greene County tried to research the case but was unable to trace it. Attorney Salveter was contacted but has no records, nor did he recall the disposition of the case. There is no Coy Hammers with a listed telephone number in the United States.

After his World War II service, Williams was often called upon to honor veterans and active duty servicemen. He often did, right up to the end of his life. In some cases, these were functions and in others they were simply personal visits to individual servicemen.

On July 15, 2000, Ted flew to Dayton, Ohio to surprise an old friend. Joe Foss was a WWII Marine Corps ace and a Medal of Honor recipient. They had met when Ted was a cadet in training at Chapel Hill and Joe had come to speak to the class. Joe, whose postwar positions included Governor of South Dakota and first commissioner of the American Football League, was the emcee for the annual induction at the National Aviation Hall of Fame. Year 2000 inductees included astronauts Buzz Aldrin and Eugene Cernan. It had been announced that Tom Brokaw, NASA administrator Dan Goldin, and Ted Williams would each greet the assembled crowd via videotape. As the large screen bore the words "An Audio Message from Ted Williams," Ted's voice filled the hall. While all watched the screen, Ted was wheeled through the room and right up next to Foss before Foss spotted him. Foss jumped to his feet in surprise and Ted received a standing ovation.

Ted told the crowd, "Gee, I feel pretty dumb up here. All these world record guys and special guys. I'm just an old ballplayer. Anybody who tells me this old gag about nobody has anybody to look up to, well, what about Joe Foss? What about John Glenn and those guys?" Ted added, "I'm the only guy in here they could cheer one minute and the next minute say, 'You big bum!'" As he left, Buzz Aldrin was the first to run up and shake Ted's hand.[9]

Ted's interest was not just in the famous, though. Army soldier Thomas Paul Chmura was seriously injured in the Battle of Luzon in the Philippines on February 2, 1945. He'd been machine-gunned on his left side, from the ankle through the left knee and left hip. After treatment in a couple of facilities, he ended up at Murphy General Hospital in Waltham, Massachusetts. After seventeen operations to remove bone chips, he was discharged in late 1947, though many more visits were necessary over the years to come.

While still in the hospital those two years, though, Chmura's grandson Mike Zhe wrote, "Nothing lifted his spirit like a visit from a fellow veteran."

One veteran who visited frequently was Theodore Samuel Williams. It was a story not chronicled in the Boston papers, but after Williams' death, Zhe wrote about his visits for New Hampshire's *Portsmouth Herald*.

"Nothing stood out more during those long years than the regular visits of the man who'd become known as the Splendid Splinter. Williams was a favorite at Murphy in those days. As someone who had already served one tour of duty as a Marine Corps pilot in World War II (he would serve another during the Korean War), he wasn't just a Red Sox slugger. He was one of them.

"It was an age where country came first, and Ted Williams was one of the highest-profile examples of that selfless attitude.

"When his first tour was over, he regularly stopped by the hospital, where he would spend hours at the foot of the veterans' beds telling stories. He would take the able ones down to Fenway Park for ball games and show up with words of encouragement before they went in for their surgeries.

"Some days he'd bring baseball tickets. Or balls signed by the team. Some days, knowing the restrictive policies of the hospital, he'd show up with a forbidden bottle and a stack of small paper cups that he'd tuck it away in the bathroom so the vets could enjoy small swigs of normalcy."[10]

Chmura died in 1976. His widow Sophie emphasized that Ted wasn't a particular friend of her husband, "Everybody that was there was either in a cast from the neck through the hip or the leg up through the thigh. Ted Williams did not favor any one person. When he came through, he spoke to them all, because he was a veteran, too. He made it a little easier... a lot easier for them, because he listened."[11]

Williams did keep in touch with other Marines, even relatively soon after the war. Earl Traut recalls:

"I did meet him one time at Opa Locka, at the Naval Air Station. He came up from Islamorada. We had a luncheon for him. There was a group of the reserve pilots there that he knew and we all had lunch with him there. That would have been towards the end of 1959.

I retired in '68. I put in 24 years. Lieutenant Colonel. I had some good assignments. I was commanding officer of a helicopter squadron in Vietnam for about three months." [12]

"Slugger Best Medicine for Ailing Ex-Marine"

Ted always responded when Marines invoked the Corps. A 1958 news account tells of a 1956 visit to Red Sox Spring training in Sarasota, when ex-Marine Ed Bambera's wife Ann brought her ailing husband to try to meet Ted Williams. Ed had multiple sclerosis. When Ted heard there was an ex-Marine outside the clubhouse, he came out and greeted the Bamberas. It turned out that Bambera had first seen Ted at Cherry Point during World War II, but it was only to admire Ted from a distance while stationed there. Bambera ended up serving in China. He began to realize as early as 1946 that there was deterioration in his eyes, and then his legs.

Williams met the Bamberas and became friendly with them. They traveled to Boston to watch the Red Sox play, both in 1956 and 1957, and were looking forward to spring training 1958 when reported Mike Gillooly spoke with them. Neither could say enough about Ted, it seemed. Once he'd heard the "password: 'Ex-Marine,'" Ted went all out, even helping secure specially-made shoes for the M.S. victim. "Nobody could imagine the life I get every time when Ted stops to say hello every time he sees me. He's the best prescription I have has since I've been sick."

Ann echoed Ed's comment: "Ted Williams has done more for Ed than all the doctors he has seen," said Ann. More than all the medicine he could possibly take. Ted has been a vitalizing tonic." Ed added, "They say that sickness is eased by a happy frame of mind. Well, Ted and the Red Sox have created just that for me... He's always asking about my health. Always asking if there isn't something else he can do for me."[13]

In Williams' final years, the Marine Corps bestowed an honor on Ted Williams. Theodore Samuel Williams was promoted to a Colonel in the Marine Corps in February 1996, in a proclamation read at the Ted Williams Museum by General Randy West. From that date forward, many of those closest to Ted addressed him as "Colonel," a compliment he clearly enjoyed.

General West explained the promotion in an e-mail:

"Since he wasn't on active duty, he could not be made a Lt Colonel or Colonel at the recommendation of the President and with the confirmation of the Senate, but the paper signed by the Commandant was an officially staffed package that is not often approved.

"There may never be another like him... he had an ability to reach plateaus of service and performance that is well beyond the average reach!

"The Marines hold Ted Williams in particularly high regard... for what he did in baseball of course, but, even more so for his patriotism... and for all he did for his Country and his Corps. We were very proud that he agreed to play on our team!"[14]

One of Ted's closest friends in later years was Maj. Gen. Larry S. Taylor. "What did he like to talk about?" Gen. Taylor asked rhetorically.

"Marines and aviation. He would ask tough, highly technical, questions. He would ask me the wing-loading of the Harrier 'jump-jet.' The wing-loading is the measure of stress on the wing in foot-pounds per square inch. I'm supposed to know this? My guess is most Harrier pilots don't know this. When I checked out in the 747, he was fascinated by the power, measured in pounds of thrust that the engines put out. His F9 Panther in Korea put out about 5,000 lbs thrust; each of the 4 engines on a 747 put out over 10 times that... he insisted on telling other people that, even though they had no clue of what he was talking about.

"I guess one of the reasons we got along was because I was a professional in aviation who was a baseball fanatic, and he was a professional in baseball who was an aviation fanatic... ..that, and the fact that I outranked him! Seriously, although we were from different generations and had never served together, when I would 'pull rank' (jokingly) into our frequent debates, I always had the impression that he accepted his 'juniority.' By the way, he was very proud of the fact that, around '96, the Commandant of the Marine Corps 'promoted' him from Captain to Colonel.

"Another reason we may have gotten along is because he knew I didn't want anything from him, which had the opposite effect, in that he was always giving me stuff. The first gift is still my favorite. I was visiting in the summer of '94, and he was spending his usual morning in the office signing stuff, while we B.S.'d about whatever. The phone rang for him, and while he was on the phone, I walked over to admire a picture on the wall... it was an autographed limited edition print... him in Korea in his flight suit, helmet in the crook of his elbow, with his F9 Panther superimposed in the front. He hung up and said, 'You like that? It's yours.' I protested (but only a little). It was too big to fit in my bag, so he said they'd send it to me. A week or so later a packing cylinder arrives with a note from him: 'Thought you'd like this one better.' It's the same print, except this one is personalized 'To General Taylor, your friend, Ted Williams.' I stare at it all the time.

"That reminds me of another story; twice I arranged for the Commandant to call him on his birthday. I was not there either time, but I got the story from [Ted's son] John-Henry or Buzz [Hamon]. The first time, I knew the Commandant had graduated from Exeter Academy in New Hampshire around '60, before he went to Annapolis. I figured any kid who went to school in New England about that time had to be a Ted Williams fan. We kept it a surprise, and when the phone rang and John-Henry answered, he told me, he said, 'Dad, it's the Commandant.' Ted said, 'Who?' John Henry said, 'It's the Commandant, Gen. Krulak' – and, according to John-Henry, Ted tried to stand up (!), in his own living room, out of respect for the man on the phone. The second time, by-then Commandant Gen. Jim Jones (now Supreme Allied Commander Europe), called him all the way from France!"[15]

After Ted Williams died, a memorial celebration was held in Boston's Fenway Park, with over 20,000 in attendance. Ted's fellow ballplayer and fellow Marine Corps aviator Jerry Coleman was among those who paid tribute to Ted. The *New York Post*'s Kevin Kernan recalled a conversation he'd had with Ted Williams about Jerry Coleman.

"About 10 years ago, Williams told me Coleman was the better pilot. 'Best damn pilot I ever saw,' Williams said in his gruff but lovable style.

"Coleman does not stand for such praise. 'Nobody is the "best damn flier,"' he said. 'We just appreciated the fact we were there together. To me, that's the highlight of my career. And Ted loved it, too. Being a Marine pilot, that was special.

"'There were a lot of great pilots,' Coleman added with a laugh, 'but none of them could hit the curveball like Ted.'"[16]

If there had been disagreements in the relationship between Ted Williams and the United States Marine Corps, they had long since been reconciled. The image of Ted struggling to stand up in his living room because he was taking a phone call from the Commandant of the Marine Corps bespeaks a tremendous respect for both the officer and the Corps.

Once a year, the Ted Williams Museum hosts a Legends Weekend when it inducts new members into the Hitters Hall of Fame, and recognizes other accomplishments in baseball. Ted always enjoyed greeting old friends, and the opportunity to meet and honor some of the new players in the game. The program always begins with the entry of a Marine Corps color guard and the playing of the National Anthem. Ted Williams always stood visibly straighter, pride in his bearing, as the Marines presented the colors and as the Anthem was performed.

There can be no question that Ted Williams was one of the very greatest hitters ever to play baseball. There can also be no question that his extended service to his country defined him in ways that set him apart from other ballplayers.

> *"The two things I'm proudest of in my life, is that I became a Marine pilot and that I became a member of the Baseball's Hall of Fame."*
>
> Ted Williams

NOTES

1) *Interview with Jon Mendes, December 18, 2002.*

2) *Interview with Lou Gorman, March 7, 2005.*

3) *Jeff Idelson, "A Visit With Hall of Famer Ted Williams,"*
   2000 Yearbook, National Baseball Hall of Fame and Museum, *pp. 22, 23.*

4) *Interview with Lou Gorman, November 26, 2005.*

5) *Interview with Tom Miller, February 7, 2003.*

6) *Interview with John Glenn, October 1, 1996.*

7) *"Marine Ties Prevailed," unattributed newspaper article.*

8) UPI *story, April 25, 1965.*

9) *"On Deck" newsletter from the Ted Williams Museum, issue #1, 2000.*

10) *Mike Zhe, "Grandmothers story of veteran's comfort strikes splendid chord,"* Portsmouth Herald, *July 6, 2002.*

11) *Interview with Sophie Chmura, February 24, 2003.*

12) *Interview with Earl Traut, September 23, 2004.*

13) *Mike Gillooly, "Slugger Best Medicine for Ailing Ex-Marine,"* Boston American, *January 23, 1958*

14) *Communication from Gen. Randy West, June 1, 2004.*

15) *Communication from Gen. Larry S. Taylor, September 13, 2004.*

16) *"True Heroics Came in Pilot's Uniform",* New York Post, *July 6, 2002.*

SOURCES

Thanks to a number of Marines who read the manuscript either in full or in part, and spared me from committing a few errors here and there. I am particularly grateful for the careful reading by Bill Churchman, Larry Hawkins, and Larry Taylor.

Interviews
PILOTS

VMF-311 – Ted's squadron in Korea

Lt. Col. Barney McShane, November 24, 2002 and December 30, 2003

Lt. Col. Arthur M. Moran, May 8, 1997

Maj. Christopher M. "Mike" Canan, December 31, 2002

Maj. James G. Fox, February 8, 2003

Maj. Darwin Glaese, December 17, 2002

Maj. John H. Glenn, Jr., October 1, 1996

Maj. Marvin Hollenbeck, February 3, 2003

Maj. Jonathan D. Mendes, November 13, 2002 and June 19, 2003

Maj. Jack W. Milt, June 28, 2004

Maj. Joseph A. Mitchell, February 3, 2003

Maj. Robert Peine, June 27, 2004

Maj. James W. Walley, December 7, 2002

Capt. Marshall S. Austin, May 8, 1997

Capt. Williams P. Brown, February 8, 2003

Capt. Jack W. Campbell, Jr., November 27, 2002

Capt. William B. Clem, December 23, 2002

Capt. Paul B. Montague, February 11, 2003

Capt. Mervyn T. Schuerman, December 10, 2002

1st Lt. Lawrence R. Hawkins, June 2, 1997 and December 21, 2002

1st Lt. Paul G. Janssen, December 23, 2002

1st Lt. Rylen B. Rudy, February 4, 2003

2nd Lt. Edward J. Sample, February 5, 2003

VMF-115

Lt. Col. John D. Beck, December 13, 2002

Maj. John W. Bolt, January 9, 2003

Maj. Ed Buchser, September 26, 2002 and November 26, 2002

Maj. Thomas J. Ross, October 1, 2002

Capt. Carroll B. Burch, February 6, 2003

Capt. Harvey L. Jensen, December 13, 2002

Capt. Thomas R. Kelly, April 6, 2004

Capt. Walter N. Roark, Jr., December 21, 2002

Capt. George Winewriter, November 28, 2002

2nd Lt. Jesse "F" Baird, March 29, 2003

2nd Lt. Charles E. Baker, December 28, 2002 and February 2, 2003

2nd Lt. George S. Banks, Jr.,, January 9, 2003

2nd Lt. L. J. LeBlanc, Jr., December 27 & 31, 2002

1st Lt. Lloyd Merriman, November 16, 2002

1st Lt. Robert D. "Woody" Woodbury, Jr., October 1, 2002

OTHER MARINES FROM VMF-311

Sgt. Edward Angst, December 27, 2002 (aviation electrician)

Cpl. Bob Flanagan, June 2, 2003 (plane captain)

S/Sgt. Jerry Goldberg, November 27, 2002 (radio shop)

S/Sgt. Chuck Ingle, December 21, 2002 (mechanic)

Cpl. Roger McCully, December 5, 2002 (crew chief)

Cpl. Ned Offner, December 27, 2002 (oxygen, pressurization)

Cpl. Elmer Plaetzer, December 27, 2002 (metal shop mechanic)

Cpl. Harlan Peacock, March 27, 2004 (head, hydraulics section)

1st Lt. Milton Rugg, December 18, 2002 (education officer)

S/Sgt. Bill Sullivan, December 28, 2002 (radio/radar shop)

Sgt. Leonard Waibel, December 19, 2002 (line chief)

Sgt. George Warnken, April 30, 2004 (ordnance)

Cpl. Lou Weatherford, December 12, 2002 (plane captain)

Cpl. Earl E. Weller, November 19, 2005 (plane captain)

Sgt. Jerry Willsie, December 27, 2002 (mechanic)

OTHER MARINES also at K-3

M/Sgt. Lou Capozzoli, chief correspondent 1st Marine Air Wing, May 31, 2002

James J. Dolan, tech rep with 1st MAW, February 3, 2003

Jack Gross, Marine combat correspondent, 1st MAW, May 31, 2003

Wilford House, Seabee, January 9, 1950

Capt. Bob Johnson, pilot VMJ-1, May 31, 2003

Don Muller, crew chief, K-3, August 8, 2004

Sgt. Ernest Needham, maintenance tech, December 12, 2002

Al Pommerenk, 1st Marine Air Wing target priority officer, February 7, 2003

Capt. Dale Purcell, VMJ-1, November 5 and December 12, 2002

Maj. Robert Sabot, VMJ-1, December 13, 2002

Col. Louis B. Robertshaw, Commanding Officer MAG-33, November 16, 2002

Capt. Jim Stehle, 1st MAW, February 1, 2003

Terry Stewart, K-3 electronics tech, January 6, 2003

1st Lt. Earl Traut, test pilot, Marine Air Squadron 33, September 23, 2004

Cpl. Jim Tyler, metalsmith, VMF-115, August 5, 2004

Ranks provided indicate rank during the period that Ted Williams was in Korea. Several of these officers rose to significantly higher ranks in later years.

Other interviews

Elizabeth Armagost, December 23, 2002

Harry Asbury, February 6, 2003

Dr. John Bartlett, Navy Corpsman, February 10, 2003

Rita Beatty, Navy Nurse, March 20, 2003

Harold Breece, August 7, 2004

Steve Brown, July 19, 2004

Virginia Brown, Navy Nurse, December 20, 2002

Margie Carter, Navy Nurse, December 21, 2002

Sophie Chmura, February 24, 2003

Bill Churchman, USMC, April 27, 1997

Capt. Jerry Coleman, USMC, April 5, 1997 and June 8, 2004

Lt. John Dager, USAF, December 20, 2002

M/Sgt. William Danyo, USMC, March 28, 2003

Fred Dickerson, USN, December 7, 2005

Lt. Jim Dodge, USN, August 7, 2006

Walt Dropo, August 15, 2001

Hank Evanish, USMC, October 21, 2003

Lou Finger, Naval aviation cadet roommate at Amherst, August 7, 2004

Lou Gorman, USN, March 7, 2005

Sgt. Richard Gross, USAF, December 17, 2002

Roy Harris, USN Seabees CEL, January 3, 2003

PFC Charles Harvey, January 4, 2003

Bill Heflin, January 9, 2003

Jan Herman, Chief Historian at the Navy Bureau of Medicine and Surgery, December 17, 2002

S/Sgt. Tom Hulihan, US Army, July 19, 2004

Myron Hyatt, USMC, May 04, 2004

Bob Janson, USN Seabees CEL, January 3, 2003

Bob Kennedy, USMC, January 1, 2004

Maj. Hank Kirby, hospital corpsman, January 10, 2003

S/Sgt. Charley Lye, USMC, January 5, 2003

Wade MacDonald, USN, September 22, 2004

Roy Makepeace, December 15, 2002

Ron Masanz, USN, September 20, 2004

Frank Maznicki, Naval aviator, December 18, 2002

Pat McGlothin, Naval aviator, February 7, 2003

Jack McGuckin, VMF-224, February 11, 2003

Capt. Ed McMahon, USMC, May 6, 2005

Tom Miller, MAG-12, February 7, 2003

Pat Morris, USN Seabees CEL, December 31, 2002

Larry Niswenden, US Army, January 2, 2003

Capt. Paul Noel, November 25, 2002

Capt. Leonard Orr, November 16, 2002

Johnny Pesky, USN, November 16, 1998 and May 11, 1999

Len Poth, USN pilot, June 2, 2003

PFC Palmer Porter, USAF, March 29, 2004

Tommy Prater, USMC, December 31, 2002

Mrs. Raymond Schlage, December 28, 2002

Lt. Col. Harold Schlendering, USMC, February 1, 2003

Bob Scowcroft, USMC, December 20, 2002

Raymond Sisk, USMC, December 18, 2002

Virginia Stickney, May 31, 2004

Capt. Jim Stygles, USMC, VMF-117, April 6, 2004

S/Sgt. Frank Sullivan, US Army, November 26, 2004

Gen. Larry S. Taylor, USMC, September 13, 2004

Virginia Tipps, US Army Nurse, August 12, 2005

David Tolle, USMC, April 24, 2001

Bill Wagner, Naval aviator, February 7, 2003

Hollis Walsh, USAF, December 27, 2002

Ray Webster, USMC, April 7, 2003

CAPTAIN THEODORE S. WILLIAMS, 037773, USMCR

Air Medal 14 Feb-11 Apr 1953 Korea

Gold Star in lieu of 2d Air Medal 12 Apr-25 Apr 1953 Korea

Gold Star in lieu of 3d Air Medal 26 Apr-17 May 1953 Korea

Navy Unit Commendation 1952-1953 1st MAW Korea

American Campaign Medal 1944-45 & 45-46 United States

Asiatic-Pacific Campaign Medal 1945 Asiatic-Pacific Area

Victory Medal 1944-1946 World War II

National Defense Service Medal 1952-1953 United States and Korea

Korea Service Medal 1953 Korean Area with 2 bronze stars 3rd Korean Winter

Korea, Summer-Fall, 1953

United Nations Service Medal 1953 Korean Area

Korean Presidential Unit 1951-1953 1st MAW Citation Korea

Compiled by Decorations and Medals Branch 27 August 1959

CHRONOLOGY

1918

August 30 – Marine aviator and baseball star Theodore (Ted) Samuel Williams was born at San Diego, California. Ted's father Samuel Stuart Williams had served in the United States Cavalry during the Philippine insurrection. His mother served in the Salvation Army.

1941

September 28 – Ted Williams, entering final day of 1941 season, is batting .399. He goes 6-for-8 and raises his average to .406.

December 7 – Pearl Harbor, Hawaii, attacked by a Japanese air strike, prompting an American declaration of war against Japan.

1942

January 3 – Ted Williams phones Eddie Collins to let him know that he had been re-classified from III-A to I-A and was due to report for a physical on January 8.

January 8 – Ted Williams passed physical examination in Minneapolis.

January 15 – President F. D. Roosevelt gives major league baseball the "green light" to play baseball during wartime.

February 16 – Ted's younger brother Danny Williams enlists in the U. S. Army.

February 27 – Ted Williams deferred from the draft, re-classified III-A as sole support of his mother May Williams. Some stir up controversy over the deferment of a prominent athlete.

March 4- Williams visits Great Lakes Naval Training Center.

April 12 – a crowd including a sizable contingent of servicemen cheer Williams at Fenway Park before an exhibition game with the Boston Braves.

April 29 – Williams meets Whitey Fuller, who will recruit him into the Navy's V-5 program.

May 6 – Williams visits Naval air facility at Squantum, Massachusetts w. Fuller and Red Sox executive Ed Doherty.

May 17 – Williams officially requests reclassification to I-A status.

May 22 – Ted Williams enlists in the United States Navy Reserve at 150 Causeway Street, Boston.

July 13 – Williams and Johnny Pesky are among 250 Naval aviation cadets who start classroom work at Boston's Mechanic Arts High School.

August 7 – Williams officially becomes a United States Navy Reserve Aviation Cadet, NATB Pensacola.

November 17 – Williams, Pesky, and others begin training as Naval Aviation Cadets at Amherst and Turners Falls, Massachusetts. Training is officially described as CPT, a three-month course in Pipers.

December 1 – Williams receives his civilian pilot training wings.

1943

March 17 – hernia operation at Chelsea Naval Hospital.

April 10 – September 15 Pre-flight school, Chapel Hill, University of North Carolina.

July 12 – Ted Williams, Babe Ruth, and other ballplayers participate in a benefit game held at Fenway Park.

July 28 – Ted Williams, Babe Ruth, and other ballplayers participate in a benefit game held at Yankee Stadium.

September 12 – November 5 – course N2S 1943 (primary flight school) at Bunker Hill Naval Air Station, Peru, Indiana.

December 6 – Williams ordered to Pensacola for advanced flight training.

December 13 – Williams begins advanced flight training at Pensacola – 14 months from 1943-44 SNV-SNJ-Instr.

1944

May 2 – Theodore Samuel Williams was appointed a Second Lieutenant in the U. S. Marine Corps Reserve, over the signature of H. F. MacComsey, Captain, U. S. Navy. The appointment and rank took effect as of 1 May. He was "appointed a Naval Aviator (Heavier-than-Air) and detailed to duty involving actual flying in and control of aircraft, effective from and including 2 May 44."

May 20 1944 – June 6 1945 – Staff, NATB Pensacola. Aviation Detachment, Marine Barracks. NA and NA Instructor.

June 6 – D-Day. Allied invasion of Europe begins.

1945

June 2 – posting to NAS Jacksonville announced.

June 7 – August 9 under instruction, MFOTU – NAS Jacksonville.

June 12 – 18 – "delay."

June 18 – August 9 – Temporary duty involving flying under instruction in VF type air. MFOTU-NAS-Jacksonville special service school Fighter (VMF) "F4U."

August 6 – atomic bomb dropped on Hiroshima, Japan. Second A-bomb dropped on Nagasaki on August 9.

August 15 – Japanese government agrees to surrender, while Ted Williams is in San Francisco prepared to head to the Pacific.

August 19 – September 2 "delay" in Williams' transportation to the Pacific.

September 2 – formal articles of surrender signed aboard USS Missouri.

September 3 – November 25 Williams serves with Comd 1055, HQ-B, 3 MAW, SoPac.

September 5 – left United States via government aircraft to Air, Fleet Marine Forces, Pacific (Hawaii).

September 6 to 18 awaiting orders.

September 19 – October 8 temporary duty to Fleet Marine Force, Pacific.

September 26 – first game of 1945 "All-Star Game" of US Navy at Furlong Field, Hawaii.

October 9 – November 18 awaiting orders.

November 19 – detached to Marine Air West Coast (HqSq, PersSp, MCAD, Miramar, San Diego, Calif), though still based in Hawaii. Williams turns in flight uniform and equipment.

November 25 – embarked and sailed from Pearl Harbor, T.H., via USS Texas.

December 4 – returned to United States, disembarking San Diego on December 5.

During World War II, he was last stationed in Hawaii from July to November, 1945. Upon returning to the United States, he served on the West Coast until 28 January 1946, when he was released to inactive duty.

1946

January 12 – "detached to home awaiting relief from active duty" (discharged at Camp Miramar, CA.).

January 25 – signed 1946 contract with Boston Red Sox.

January 26 – May 1, 1952 – Relieved from active duty. Status: Inactive AvnU 11thMCRD San Diego Calif.

February 25 – arrived for spring training with Boston Red Sox.

1947

July 28 – The President of the United States appoints Theodore S. Williams (037773) as First Lieutenant (Temporary) in the Marine Corps Reserve of the United States. Signing for the President are John L. Sullivan, Secretary of the Navy, and Captain G. T. Green, USMC.

1949

June 30 – In Boston, before Major Sherman W. Parry, Ted Williams signs Acceptance and Oath of Office, accepting appointment as a First Lieutenant (Permanent) in the U. S. Marine Corps Reserve.

1950

August 9, 1950 – May, 1, 1952 Inactive. Officially part of AvnU 1st MCRD Boston Mass.

1951

January 1 – Ted Williams appointed Captain, United States Marine Corps Reserve.

1952

January 9 – Ted Williams officially recalled by US Marines, while fishing in the Florida Keys.

April 2 – Ted Williams and Jerry Coleman both pass physical before a Marine Corps medical board at Yukon, Florida (near NAS Jacksonville.) Found physically fit for return to active duty. Neither had flown a plane for six years.

April 12 – Easter Sunday. First game of the year in Boston. The Red Sox host the Boston Braves at Fenway for first annual pre-season "City Series" game. Ted hits two home runs and knocks in 5 runs.

April 15 – Opening Day. Ted triples off the Senators' Bob Porterfield in eighth inning of the game in Washington, but pulls a muscle in the calf of his left leg sliding into third base. It's a muscle that's been bothering him for several days. With the triple, Ted kept alive his "never-hitless-in-an-opener" streak.

April 16 – Ted pinch-hits for Ted Lepcio in the 7th, but strikes out.

April 18 – Ted lines out in the 5th, pinch-hitting for Ike Delock.

April 20 – Ted singles for Lepcio, pinch-hitting in the 7th.

April 21 – Grounds out for Gumpert in an 8th inning pinch-hit role.

April 30 – Ted Williams Day – Ted's first start since pulling leg muscle (pinch-hit some) Ted Williams Day declared by Boston Mayor John B. Hynes. Ted said he'd be honored but didn't really like the idea. "I don't want fans chipping in money and buying me things," Ted told Life. "I don't want to be obligated to anybody." The plan was to give Ted's daughter Bobby-Jo a doll carriage and a two-wheel bicycle, with Ted receiving an aviator's watch. The committee got a little carried away, though, and Ted ends with a Cadillac and a number of other gifts, essentially the kind of hoopla he'd been hoping to avoid. In what might well have been his last at-bat in major league baseball, Williams hits a 2-run HR last time up, to break a 3-3 tie with the Tigers and win the game for the Red Sox, 5-3.

Life *magazine reported the Ted invited "people he likes" to a party after the game. Included, the magazine said, were bellhops, garage men and the like. "No big shots, just guys who stuck by me," Ted told Life. [May 12, 1952].*

May 2 drives with two friends from Boston and reports to Willow Grove PA to begin 8-week refresher course. Upon completion of the course, he is due to go back into active service at Cherry Point NC.

May 29 – June 8 on leave.

June 9 – 12 – Travel and Awaiting Assignment.

June 13 – July 28 Attack Refresher Course & TV-2 Jet Check-out. Unit: VMAT-20, MTG-20, AirFMFLant, Cherry Point NC.

June 25 – qualified as expert on the .38 caliber pistol.

July 29 – December 7 Squadron Pilot, VMF-223, MAG-14, 2dMAW, Cherry Point.

August 28 – Ted at Cherry Point, "due to go to Korea next week" (but then things changed).

September 25 – departs Cherry Point for Roosevelt Roads via Guantanamo Bay.

October 26 – departs Roosevelt Roads back to Cherry Point. More training at Cherry Point through December 6.

November 14 – At Cherry Point, Capt. Ted Williams received orders to report to Marine Corps Air Station El Toro by January 2, 1953 to await transfer overseas.

December 8 – January 28, 1953 – Pilot, January Replacement Draft.

Three weeks off for Christmas; heads for Miramar immediately after Christmas.

1 9 5 3

January 1 – "assigned ready reserve category, effective 1Jan53."

January 3, – Ted was in El Toro, and was ordered with 38 others to travel to Camp Pendleton via government surface transportation, for "temporary additional duty in connection with Cold Weather Training at Camp Pickel Meadows for the period 14 January to 24 January 1953."

January 14 – Ted and other officers reported for duty at the Marine Barracks, Camp Pendleton.

January 15 – the detail was ordered to report for Cold Weather Training, through January 23. Report back to duty at El Toro on January 24.

January 26- orders were given for a roster of 35 men, such that "on or about 28 January 1953" the detail will "stand detached" from its present station and duties, and proceed via government aircraft "to such place beyond the seas as the 1st Marine Aircraft Wing may be located."

January 28, 0800 – the men reported for duty and to be transported beyond the seas.

January 29 – the detail arrived in Honolulu, and stayed overnight at Barber's Point Naval Air Station, due to travel on 30 January on trip 424.

February 1 – trip 424 arrived at Fleet Logistic Air Wing Terminal at NAS Atsugi, Japan at 1945 hours.

February 2 – nearly 24 hours later, at 1900 hours, the detail departed Atsugi and arrived in Korea.

February 3 – Ted Williams officially joins unit VMF-311, per unit records. Pilot VMF(Jet), VMF-311, MAG-33, 1stMAW, FMF.

February 4 – AP report from Seoul – Ted to begin one-week training course. AP reports that he will begin combat missions "after a familiarization and orientation program."

February 14 – First familiarization flight MISSION #1.

February 15 – first true combat mission MISSION #2.

February 16 – crash-lands plane at K-6 Suwon Air Force base MISSION #3.

February 17 – MISSION #4.

*March 12 or 14 – Ted arrives on board hospital ship
(conflicting reports, but it seems the 12th is the more reliable date).*

March 24 – Ted reportedly aboard hospital ship recovering from pneumonia.

*March 26 – New York sportswriter Frank Graham provided an eyewitness account of Ted Williams'
February 16 crash landing in Korea, and that Williams had told Joe Giaimo, "I expect to be killed,
of course. Why shouldn't I feel that way? So many are being killed."*

April 1 – Ted returns to flight status after being hospitalized 22 days.

April 4 – first mission after long layoff MISSION #5.

April 6 – MISSION #6.

April 7 – MISSION #7.

April 8 – MISSION #8.

April 11 – MISSION #9.

April 12 – MISSION #10.

April 13 – MISSION #11.

April 14 – Ted reportedly begins rest leave.

*April 16 – telegram from Ted from Toyonaka, Korea addressed to Lou Boudreau wishes Sox well on
Opening Day (Sox win 18-6).*

*April 17 – letter from Ted to Bill Churchman made public.
Says he is on hospital ship recovering and that a rapid descent also plugged up his ears.
"Bothered by deafness." If permanent, might have to come back early.*

April 18 – Hy Hurwitz report says Ted in Japan on R&R.

April 21 – MISSION #12.

April 22 – MISSION #13 and MISSION #14.

April 23 – MISSION #15 and MISSION #16.

April 24 – MISSION #17 and MISSION #18.

April 25 – MISSION #19.

April 26 – MISSION #20.

April 27 – Ted's plane hit on MISSION #21 (left tip tank hit).

April 29 – MISSION #22.

AT WAR

April 30 – MISSION #23.

May 2 – MISSION #24.

May 4 – MISSION #25 and MISSION #26.

May 5 – MISSION #27.

May 6 – MISSION #28.

May 9 – MISSION #29.

May 16 – MISSION #30.

May 17 – MISSION #31.

May 18 – MISSION #32.

May 19 – MISSION #33.

May 20 – MISSION #34.

May 21 – MISSION #35.

May 23 – MISSION #36 and MISSION #37.

May 24 – MISSION #38.

June 10 – Ted's last combat mission. MISSION #39 Ted forced to abort "almost immediately" on what would have been mission #40 (and earned him his fourth Air Medal, if he hadn't been killed!) Ted grounded.

June 12 – Lt. Williams awarded three Air Medals.

June 27 – Ted ordered back to US by Marine flight surgeons for treatment of an ear and nose ailment.

July 2 – Ted arrives at Itami air base in southern Honshu for a rest and relaxation leave on his way from Korea to the US. Ted visits Kyoto. Officially enroute July 2 – July 9.

July 7 – Ted departs via plane from Atsugi air base in Japan and arrives at Barbers Point Naval Air Station, Honolulu, T.H. on way back to United States (Hawaii was not a state in 1953).

July 9 – Ted arrives in San Francisco at Moffett Naval Air Station and heads to Oak Knoll Naval Hospital in Oakland.

July 10 – Ted "sk" at USNH Oakland (sick).

July 12 – Leaves San Francisco for Bethesda, and from there to attend the All-Star Game. "Travis Air Force Base officers said he doubted he'd be part of any special ceremonies."

July 13 – Reports to Bethesda, then travels to Cincinnati for All-Star Game.

July 14 – 18 – on leave.

*July 14 – Ted throws out first pitch at All-Star Game in Cincinnati,
a guest of Commissioner Ford Frick.*

July 19 – 27 sk USNH Bethesda MD Unit: CasDet MB USNAW USNH Bethesda MD.

July 22 – Ted applies for release from active duty, in accordance with policy.

July 24 – Ted got leave from Bethesda, checked in Washington DC hotel.

*July 27 – Armistice signed on Korea. Williams writes letter to
Secretary of the Navy requesting resignation.*

*July 28 – Ted granted release (effective August 12) from Marine Corps at Marine Barracks at the
Naval gun factory in Washington DC. "Ordered" by Marine Col. Chappell to report to Fenway Park.
Immediately after being released, he heads back to Bethesda Naval Hospital to visit Walt Bartosh,
a wounded Marine who had arrived the day before. Plans to drive to Boston.*

*July 29 – season's largest crowd at Fenway (35,385) hoping Ted would make an appearance.
He arrives later than expected but does not appear (there had been no plan he would.)*

*July 30 – Ted signs contract for 1953 and 1954, 26 hours after final discharge. Hits 2 "home runs"
in batting practice.*

July 31 – August 12 Inactive.

August 13 – Resignation of Commission.

*August 16 – In his first start since returning to baseball from the Korean War,
Williams hits a double and a home run.*

September 27 – Williams ends season in New York. In 91 at-bats, he hit 13 homers and batted .407.

1996

February – appointed Colonel United States Marine Corps.

INDEX

* = Marine pilots who served with Ted in Korea

TED WILLIAMS

August 30, 1918 – July 5, 2002

For those who want to learn more about the roots of this great ballplayer and Marine pilot, read **THE KID: Ted Williams in San Diego**. This companion book, a collaborative effort of nine authors, explores Ted's early years up to the start of his career in major league baseball.

Ted was lucky, he often said, to have grown up in San Diego where a kid can play baseball year-round. At the same time he recognized that had he been seen as Hispanic (his maternal grandparents were both Mexican), he would have suffered from the prejudices of the day. A high school hero, Ted Williams came from a remarkable family – his mother a Salvation Army worker and his father a photographer, and uncles who were cowboys, longshoremen, cement truck drivers, mariachi musicians, and ballplayers on Mexican-American teams.

Based on extensive interviews with dozens of family members and others who knew *The Kid* as a kid, this volume presents the most extensive look at the background of a major league ballplayer ever published.

$24.95 at fine bookstores everywhere, or postpaid from **www.rounderbooks.com**

Rounder Records Corp.
One Rounder Way
Burlington, MA 01803
1-800-ROUNDER (768-6337)